Toyota Hi-Ace and Hi-Lux Owners Workshop

Acknowledgements

Our thanks are due to the Toyota Motor Sales Company Limited (USA) and Toyota (GB) Limited for their assistance with technical information and certain illustrations. Toyota (GB) Limited also loaned the Toyota Hi-Lux Pick-up used as our project vehicle. Thanks are also due to Castrol Limited who provided lubrication data and the Champion Sparking Plug Company who provided the colour illustrations showing the various spark plug conditions. The bodywork repair photographs used in this manual were provided by Lloyds Industries Limited who supply 'Turtle Wax', 'Dupli-color Holts' and other Holts range products.

Lastly, thanks are due to all those people at Sparkford who helped in the production of this manual. Particularly Brian Horsfall, Les Brazier, Lee Saunders and David Neilson.

About this manual

Its aim

The aim of this book is to help you get the best value from your vehicle. It can do so in two ways. First it can help you decide what work must be done (even should you choose to get it done by a garage), the routine maintenance and the diagnosis and course of action when random faults occur. However, it is hoped that you will also use the second and fuller purpose by tackling the work yourself. This can give you the satisfaction of doing the job personally. On the simpler jobs it may even be quicker than booking the car into a garage and going there twice, to leave and collect it. Perhaps most important, much money can be saved by avoiding the costs a garage must charge to cover their labour and overheads.

Haynes Owner's Workshop Manuals are the only manuals, available to the public, which are actually written from practical experience. We obtain an example of the vehicle to be covered by the manual. Then, in our own workshops, the major components of that vehicle are stripped and rebuilt by the author and a mechanic: at the same time all sequences are photographed. By doing this work ourselves, we encounter the same problems as you will and having overcome these problems, we can provide you with practical solutions.

The book has drawings and descriptions to show the function of the various components so that their layout can be understood. Then the tasks are described and photographed in a step by step sequence so that even a novice can cope with complicated work. Such a person is the very one to buy a vehicle needing repair yet be unable to afford garage costs.

The jobs are described assuming only normal tools are available, and not special tools. But a reasonable outfit of tools will be a worthwhile investment, many special workshop tools produced by the makers merely speed the work, and in these cases guidance is given as to how to do the job without them. On a very few occasions the special tool is essential to prevent damage to components, then its use is described. Though it might be possible to borrow the tool, such work may have to be entrusted to the official agent.

Using the manual

The manual is divided into thirteen Chapters - each covering a logical sub-division of the vehicle. The individual Chapters are divided into Sections, and the Sections into numbered paragraphs.

Procedures, once described in the text, are not normally repeated. If it is necessary to refer to another Chapter the reference will be given in Chapter number, section number and, if necessary, paragraph number.

There are two types of illustration: (1) Figures which are numbered according to Chapter and sequence of occurrence in that Chapter; (2) Photographs which have a reference number on their caption. All photographs apply to the Chapter in which they occur so that the reference figure pinpoints the pertinent Section and paragraph number.

When the left or right side of the vehicle is mentioned it is as if looking forward from the rear of the vehicle.

Great effort has been made to ensure that this book is complete and up-to-date. However, the vehicle manufacturers continually modify their cars, even in retrospect without giving notice.

Whilst every care is taken to ensure that the information in this manual is correct no liability can be accepted by the authors or publishers for loss, damage or injury caused by any errors in, or omissions from, the information given.

Contents

Introduction to the Toyota Hi-Lux and Hi-Ace

Hi-Ace

The Hi-Ace is available in several body types. Until 1976 they are powered by the 1587cc ohv type engine. After 1976 the 1968cc ohc engine is used (see Chapter 13, Supplement). The van, personnel carrier and camper versions are of integral unitary construction but the truck versions are based on a separate chassis.

Due to the forward control design, servicing and repair will be rather unusual and slightly more difficult for the home mechanic compared with more conventional layouts but any disadvantage must be weighed against the virtue of the extra load space available.

The driving cab is designed to hold three people and the vehicle is very well equipped in its standard form.

Hi-Lux

The Hi-Lux pick-up is a ruggedly constructed vehicle having a separate chassis and all-steel welded body. The vehicle is equipped with one of four engine types depending upon the date of production and the market in which it is destined to operate.

The standard of equipment is very high and few options are available (or indeed needed) except for automatic transmission and air conditioning on the larger engined versions.

The Hi-Lux is easy to maintain and very accessible and is completely conventional in design.

Buying spare parts and vehicle identification numbers

Buying spare parts

Spare parts are available from many sources, for example Toyota garages, other garages and accessory shops, and motor factors. Our advice regarding spare part sources is as follows:

Officially appointed Toyota garages - This is the best source of parts which are peculiar to your vehicle and are otherwise not generally available (eg; complete cylinder heads, internal gearbox components, badges, interior trim etc). It is also the only place at which you should buy parts if your vehicle is still under warranty: non-Toyota components may invalidate the warranty. To be sure of obtaining the correct parts it will always be necessary to give the storeman your vehicle's engine and chassis number, and if possible, to take the 'old' part along for positive identification. Remember that many parts are available on a factory exchange scheme - any parts returned should always be clean! It obviously makes good sense to go straight to the specialists on your vehicle for this type of part for they are best equipped to supply you.

Other garages and accessory shops - These are often very good places to buy materials and components needed for the maintenance of your vehicle (eg; spark plugs, bulbs, fanbelts, oils and greases, touch-up paint, filler paste, etc). They also sell general accessories, usually have convenient opening hours, charge lower prices and can often be found not far from home.

Motor factors - Good factors will stock all of the more important components which wear out relatively quickly (eg; cylinders/pipes/hoses/seals/shoes and pads etc). Motor factors will often provide new or reconditioned components on a part exchange basis - this can save a considerable amount of money.

Vehicle identification numbers

The engine number is stamped on a machined face on the side of the engine cylinder block (photo).

The vehicle serial number plate is screwed to the side of the engine compartment. On North American vehicles, the serial number is repeated on the top surface of the instrument panel just inside the windscreen (photo).

The chassis specification plate is rivetted to the inner side panel of the driving compartment (photo).

On North American vehicles, additional labels or stickers are affixed giving emission control and other details for tune-up and adjustment.

Location of engine number

Vehicle serial number plate

Chassis specification plate

Toyota Hi-Lux (North American specification). Inset. Hi-Ace pick-up (UK specification)

Use of English

As this book has been written in England, it uses the appropriate English component names, phrases, and spelling. Some of these differ from those used in America. Normally, these cause no difficulty, but to make sure, a glossary is printed below. In ordering spare parts remember the parts list will probably use these words:

Glossary

English	American	English	American
Aerial	Antenna	Layshaft (of gearbox)	Counter shaft
Accelerator	Gas pedal	Leading shoe (of brake)	Primary shoe
Alternator	Generator (AC)	Locks	Latches
Anti-roll bar	Stabiliser or sway bar	Motorway	Freeway, turnpike etc.
Battery	Energizer	Number plate	Licence plate
Bodywork	Sheet metal	Paraffin	Kerosene
Bonnet (engine cover)	Hood	Petrol	Gasoline
Boot lid	Trunk lid	Petrol tank	Gas tank
Boot (luggage compartment)	Trunk	'Pinking'	'Pinging'
Bottom gear	1st gear	Propeller shaft	Driveshaft
Bulkhead	Firewall	Quarter light	Quarter window
Camfollower or tappet	Valve lifter or tappet	Retread	Recap
Carburettor	Carburetor	Reverse	Back-up
Catch	Latch	Rocker cover	Valve cover
Choke/venturi	Barrel	Roof rack	Car-top carrier
Circlip	Snap ring	Saloon	Sedan
Clearance	Lash	Seized	Frozen
Crownwheel	Ring gear (of differential)	Side indicator lights	Side marker lights
Disc (brake)	Rotor/disk	Side light	Parking light
Drop arm	Pitman arm	Silencer	Muffler
Drop head coupe	Convertible	Spanner	Wrench
Dynamo	Generator (DC)	Sill panel (beneath doors)	Rocker panel
Earth (electrical)	Ground	Split cotter (for valve spring cap)	Lock (for valve spring retainer)
Engineer's blue	Prussion blue	Split pin	Cotter pin
Estate car	Station wagon	Steering arm	Spindle arm
Exhaust manifold	Header	Sump	Oil pan
Fast back (Coupe)	Hard top	Tab washer	Tang; lock
Fault finding/diagnosis	Trouble shooting	Tailgate	Liftgate
Float chamber	Float bowl	Tappet	Valve lifter
Free-play	Lash	Thrust bearing	Throw-out bearing
Freewheel	Coast	Top gear	High
Gudgeon pin	Piston pin or wrist pin	Trackrod (of steering)	Tie-rod (or connecting rod)
Gearchange	Shift	Trailing shoe (of brake)	Secondary shoe
Gearbox	Transmission	Transmission	Whole drive line
Halfshaft	Axle-shaft	Tyre	Tire
Handbrake	Parking brake	Van	Panel wagon/van
Hood	Soft top	Vice	Vise
Hot spot	Heat riser	Wheel nut	Lug nut
Indicator	Turn signal	Windscreen	Windshield
Interior light	Dome lamp	Wing/mudguard	Fender

Miscellaneous points

An "Oil seal" is fitted to components lubricated by grease!

A "Damper" is a "Shock absorber", it damps out bouncing, and absorbs shocks of bump impact. Both names are correct, and both are used haphazardly.

Note that British drum brakes are different from the Bendix type that is common in America, so different descriptive names result. The shoe end furthest from the hydraulic wheel cylinder is on a pivot; interconnection between the shoes as on Bendix brakes is most uncommon. Therefore the phrase "Primary" or "Secondary" shoe does not apply. A shoe is said to be Leading or Trailing. A "Leading" shoe is one on which a point on the drum, as it rotates forward, reaches the shoe at the end worked by the hydraulic cylinder before the anchor end. The opposite is a trailing shoe, and this one has no self servo from the wrapping effect of the rotating drum.

General dimensions, weights and capacities

Dimensions and weights

	Hi-Lux Standard	Hi-Lux Long wheelbase
Wheelbase:		
Up to 1971	99.8in (2535mm)	—
1972 on	101.6in (2580mm)	109.8in (2790mm)
Front track:		
Up to 1971	50.8in (1290mm)	—
1972 on	51.6in (1310mm)	—
Rear track	50.8in (1290mm)	—
Overall length:		
Up to 1971	165.9in (4191mm)	—
1972 on	168.7in (4285mm)	184.6in (4690mm)
Overall width:		
Up to 1971	63.2in (1605mm)	—
1972 on	62.2in (1580mm)	—
Overall height	61.8in (1570mm)	—
Ground clearance (depending upon tyre size and type)	7.1 to 7.5in (180.3 to 190.5mm)	
Kerb weight:		
Up to 1971*	2435 lbs (1105kg)	—
1972 on with manual gearbox	2430 lbs (1102kg)	2500 lbs (1134kg)
1972 on with manual gearbox (California)	2445 lbs (1109kg)	2515 lbs (1141kg)
1972 on with 5-speed manual gearbox	2480 lbs (1125kg)	2550 lbs (1156kg)
1972 on with 5-speed manual gearbox (California)	2495 lbs (1132kg)	2565 lbs (1163kg)
1972 on with automatic transmission	2450 lbs (1111kg)	2520 lbs (1143kg)
1972 on with automatic transmission (California)	2465 lbs (1118kg)	2535 lbs (1150kg)

* Consult vehicle chassis plate

	To 1976	1977 on	
	Hi-Ace Pick-up *	Hi-Ace Pick-up	Hi-Ace Panel
Wheelbase	90.2in (2290mm)	90.6in (2300mm)	92.5in (2350mm)
Front track	53.3in (1355mm)	56.3in (1430mm)	56.3in (1430mm)
Rear track	53.3in (1355mm)	53.5in. (1360mm)	53.5in. (1360 mm)
Overall length	171.3in (4350mm)	169.1in (4290mm)	169.7in (4310mm)
Overall width	66.3in (1685mm)	66.5in (1690mm)	66.5in (1690mm)
Overall height	74.6in (1895mm)	77.0in (1955mm)	75.2in (1910mm)
Ground clearance	7.1in (180mm)	7.1in (180mm)	7.1in (180mm)
Kerb weight	2610 lbs (1185kg)	2690lb (1220kg)	2855lb (1295mm)

There are slight variations in dimensions for other bodystyles - consult current vehicle specification.

Capacities

	Hi-Lux	Hi-Ace
Fuel tank:		
Early	11.4 Imp. gal (52 litres/13.7 US gal)	Van models. 11.4 Imp. gal (52 litres/13.7 US gal)
Later standard	10.1 Imp. gal (46 litres/12.2 US gal)	Other models. 9.9 Imp. gal (43 litres/11.5 US gal)
Later LWB	13.3 Imp. gal (61 litres/16 US gal)	—
Engine oil including new filter:		
8 R-C	7½ Imp. pts (4.3 litres/4.5 US qts)	—
18 R-C	9 Imp. pts (5.1 litres/5.3 US qts)	—
20 R	8 Imp. pts (4.5 litres/4.8 US qts)	—
12 R	7¼ Imp. pts (4.2 litres/4.4 US qts)	7¼ Imp. pts (4.2 litres/4.4 US qts)
Gearbox:		
Type (up to 1971)	1.7 Imp. qts (1.9 litres/2 US qts)	1.6 Imp. qts (1.8 litres/1.9 US qts)
Type (L 40)	1.7 Imp. qts (1.9 litres/2 US qts)	—
Type (L 42)	1.7 Imp. qts (1.9 litres/2 US qts)	1.7 Imp. qts (1.9 litres/2 US qts)
Type (W 50)	2.3 Imp. qts (2.6 litres/2.7 US qts)	—
Rear axle	1.4 Imp. qts (1.6 litres/1.7 US qts)	1.4 Imp. qts (1.6 litres/1.7 US qts)
Automatic transmission	5.6 Imp. qts (6.4 litres/6.8 US qts)	—
Steering box		
Warm oil sector	0.5 Imp. pt (0.28 litre/0.29 US qt)	0.31 Imp. qt (0.35 litre/0.37 US qt)
Recirculating ball	0.3 Imp. qt (0.32 litre/0.3 US qt)	1.0 Imp. pt (0.6 litre/0.7 US qt)
Cooling system:		
8 R-C/18 R-C engine	13¼ Imp. pts (7.5 litres/9 US qts)	—
20 R engine	14 Imp. pts (8 litres/8.5 US qts)	—
12 R engine	12½ Imp. pts (7 litres/7¼ US qts)	12½ Imp. pts (7 litres/7¼ US qts)

Recommended lubricants

Component										Lubricant
1 Engine	...	...	...	...	...	...	...	...	...	Castrol GTX
2 Gearbox										
Manual	...	...	...	...	...	...	...	...	...	Castrol Hypoy
Automatic	...	...	...	...	...	...	...	...	...	Castrol TQF
3 Rear axle	...	...	...	...	...	...	...	...	...	Castrol Hypoy
4 Wheel bearings	...	...	...	...	...	...	...	...	...	Castrol LM Grease
5 Brake and clutch systems	...	...	...	...	...	...	...	...	...	Castrol Girling Universal Brake and Clutch Fluid
Steering box	...	...	...	...	...	...	...	...	...	Castrol Hypoy
Steering balljoints and bushings			...	...	...	...	...	...	...	Castrol MS3

The above are general recommendations only. Different climatic conditions require different lubricants. Consult your Toyota dealer or Driver's Handbook if in doubt.

Routine maintenance

Maintenance is essential for ensuring safety and desirable for the purpose of getting the best in terms of performance and economy from the vehicle. Over the years the need for periodic lubrication - oiling, greasing and so on - has been drastically reduced if not totally eliminated. This has unfortunately tended to lead some owners to think that because no such action is required the items either no longer exist or will last for ever. This is a serious delusion. It follows therefore that the largest initial element of maintenance is visual examination. This may lead to repairs or renewals.

Every 250 miles (400km/or weekly)

Engine
Check oil level and top-up if necessary (photo).
Check coolant level and top-up if necessary.
Check battery electrolyte level and top-up if necessary.

Brakes and clutch
Check master cylinder reservoir fluid level (photos).

Steering and suspension
Check tyre pressures.
Check tyres visually for wear or damage.

Lights, wipers and horns
Check operation of all lights, front and rear.
Check operation of windscreen wipers and horns.
Check and top up windscreen washer reservoir fluid.

After first 1,000 miles (1,600km) - new vehicle

Engine
Check valve clearances.

Filling the engine with oil

Inspecting brake master cylinder reservoir fluid level

Checking clutch master cylinder reservoir fluid level

Sump drain plug

Gearbox filler/level plug

Gearbox extension housing (type L42) filler/level plug

Rear axle filler/level plug

Gearbox drain plug

Check torque of cylinder head bolts.
Check drivebelt tension.
Check idling speed.
Check dwell angle.
Check ignition timing.
Renew engine oil.

Chassis and body

Check tightness and torque wrench settings (where applicable) of all nuts and bolts.

Every 6,000 miles (9,600km)

Engine

Renew engine oil and filter (photo).

Brakes

Check travel of pedal and parking brake lever.
Check front disc pads for wear.
Inspect condition of all brake lines and hoses.

Transmission

Check gearbox oil level and top-up (photos).
Check automatic transmission fluid level and top-up.
Check rear axle oil level and top-up (photos).

Steering and suspension

Move position of road wheels to even out tyre wear.

Every 12,000 miles (19,000km)

Engine

Check and adjust valve clearances.
Inspect condition of drivebelts.
Check torque of cylinder head bolts.
Renew engine oil and filter.
Inspect condition of cooling system hoses.
Check condition of exhaust system.
Renew spark plugs.
Renew distributor contact points.
Inspect condition and check operation of all exhaust emission control systems and components.

Blow out air filter element and check operation of automatic temperature controlled air cleaner (where fitted).

Brakes

Check rear brake linings for wear.
Check front brake linings for wear.

Steering

Check all linkage and balljoints for wear.
Check steering box oil level.
Check front wheel alignment (toe-in).

Every 24,000 miles (38,000km)

Engine

Renew drivebelts.
Renew coolant.
Renew fuel filter.
Renew air filter element.
Renew fuel filler cap gasket.
Renew contact breaker points.
Renew PCV (crankcase vent) valve.

Transmission

Renew rear axle oil.
Renew manual gearbox oil (photo).
Renew automatic transmission fluid.

Steering

Clean and repack front hub bearings.
Lubricate steering balljoints.
Lubricate front suspension arm pivot bushes.
Lubricate steering centre arm bracket.

Every 50,000 miles (80,000km)

Brakes

Renew all rubber seals and hydraulic fluid.

Fuel system

Renew carbon canister element (fuel evaporative control).

Jacking and towing

Hi-Lux

The jack and tools are located behind the seats within the driving compartment (photo).

For wheel changing, jack-up the front wheel under the chassis frame as shown, or in the case of a rear wheel, under the rear axle.

When carrying out repairs, the front of the vehicle should be jacked-up under the front crossmember and the chassis sideframe then supported on stands. The rear of the vehicle can be raised by placing a jack under the rear axle casing and then supporting the bodyframe on axle stands.

When being towed, use the towing hook under the front of the vehicle.

When towing another vehicle, attach the tow-rope to one of the (rear) rear spring shackles.

The spare wheel is suspended under the rear of the body. To remove it, insert the rod supplied in the tool kit, fit the handle to the rod and then wind down the wheel which is supported on a chain (photos).

When towing a vehicle equipped with automatic transmission, it is recommended that the propeller shaft is removed, otherwise the transmission may be damaged due to lack of lubrication. If this is not practicable do not tow it more than 30mph (48km/h) nor for a distance exceeding 50 miles (80km).

Hi-Ace

The details as given for Hi-Lux will apply except that the method of attaching the spare wheel is slightly modified.

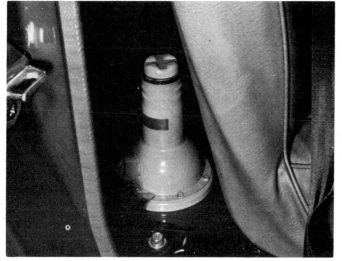

Jack and tool storage position

Front jacking point

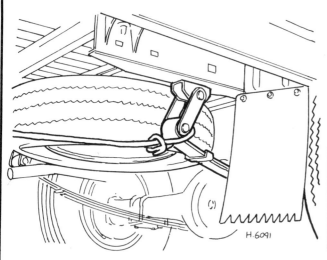

H.6091

Rear tow-rope attachment

Lowering the spare wheel (Hi-Lux)

Spare wheel lowered (Hi-Ace)

Rear jacking point

Tools and working facilities

Note: All nuts and bolts and threads are metric throughout.

Introduction

A selection of good tools is a fundamental requirement for anyone contemplating the maintenance and repair of a motor vehicle. For the owner who does not possess any, their purchase will prove a considerable expense, offsetting some of the savings made by doing-it-yourself. However, provided that the tools purchased are of good quality, they will last for many years and prove an extremely worthwhile investment.

To help the average owner to decide which tools are needed to carry out the various tasks detailed in this manual, we have compiled three lists of tools under the following headings: Maintenance and minor repair, Repair and overhaul, and Special. The newcomer to practical mechanics should start off with the 'Maintenance and minor repair' tool kit and confine himself to the simpler jobs around the vehicle. Then, as his confidence and experience grows, he can undertake more difficult tasks, buying extra tools as, and when, they are needed. In this way, a 'Maintenance and minor repair' tool kit can be built-up into a 'Repair and overhaul' tool kit over a considerable period of time without any major cash outlays. The experienced do-it-yourselfer will have a tool kit good enough for most repair and overhaul procedures and will add tools from the 'Special' category when he feels the expense is justified by the amount of use these tools will be put to.

It is obviously not possible to cover the subject of tools fully here. For those who wish to learn more about tools and their use there is a book entitled 'How to Choose and Use Car Tools' available from the publishers of this manual.

Maintenance and minor repair tool kit

The tools given in this list should be considered as a minimum requirement if routine maintenance, servicing and minor repair operations are to be undertaken. We recommend the purchase of combination spanners (ring one end, open-ended the other); although more expensive than open-ended ones, they do give the advantages of both types of spanner.

Combination spanners - 10, 11, 13, 14, 17 mm
Adjustable spanner - 9 inch
Engine sump/gearbox/rear axle drain plug key (where applicable)
Spark plug spanner (with rubber insert)
Spark plug gap adjustment tool
Set of feeler gauges
Brake adjuster spanner (where applicable)
Brake bleed nipple spanner
Screwdriver - 4 in. long x ¼ in. dia. (plain)
Screwdriver - 4 in. long x ¼ in. dia. (crosshead)
Combination pliers - 6 inch
Hacksaw, junior
Tyre pump
Tyre pressure gauge
Grease gun (where applicable)
Oil can
Fine emery cloth (1 sheet)
Wire brush (small)
Funnel (medium size)

Repair and overhaul tool kit

These tools are virtually essential for anyone undertaking any major repairs to a motor vehicle, and are additional to those given in the basic list. Included in this list is a comprehensive set of sockets. Although these are expensive they will be found invaluable as they are so versatile - particularly if various drives are included in the set. We recommend the ½ square-drive type, as this can be used with most proprietary torque wrenches. If you cannot afford a socket set, even bought piecemeal, then inexpensive tubular box spanners are a useful alternative.

The tools in this list will occasionally need to be supplemented by tools from the Special list.

Sockets (or box spanners) to cover range 6 to 27 mm
Reversible ratchet drive (for use with sockets)
Extension piece, 10 inch (for use with sockets)
Universal joint (for use with sockets)
Torque wrench (for use with sockets)
'Mole' wrench - 8 inch
Ball pein hammer
Soft-faced hammer, plastic or rubber
Screwdriver - 6 in. long x 5/16 in. dia. (plain)
Screwdriver - 2 in. long x 5/16 in. square (plain)
Screwdriver - 1½ in. long x ¼ in. dia. (crosshead)
Screwdriver - 3 in. long x 1/8 in. dia. (electricians)
Pliers - electricians side cutters
Pliers - needle nosed
Pliers - circlip (internal and external)
Cold chisel - ½ inch
Scriber (this can be made by grinding the end of a broken hacksaw blade)
Scraper (this can be made by flattening and sharpening one end of a piece of copper pipe)
Centre punch
Pin punch
Hacksaw
Valve grinding tool
Steel rule/straightedge
Allen keys
Selection of files
Wire brush (large)
Axle stands
Jack (strong scissor or hydraulic type)

Special tools

The tools in this list are those which are not used regularly, are expensive to buy, or which need to be used in accordance with their manufacturers instructions. Unless relatively difficult mechanical jobs are undertaken frequently, it will not be economic to buy many of these tools. Where this is the case, you could consider clubbing together with friends (or a motorists club) to make a joint purchase, or borrowing the tools against a deposit from a local garage or tool hire specialist.

The following list contains only those tools and instruments freely available to the public, and not those special tools produced by the vehicle manufacturer specifically for its dealer network. You will find occasional references to these manufacturers special tools in the text of this manual. Generally, an alternative method of doing the job without the vehicle manufacturers special tool is given. However, sometimes, there is no alternative to using them. Where this is the case and the relevant tool cannot be bought or borrowed you will have to entrust the work to a franchised garage.

Valve spring compressor
Piston ring compressor
Ball joint separator
Universal hub/bearing puller
Impact screwdriver
Micrometer and/or vernier gauge
Carburettor flow balancing device (where applicable)
Dial gauge
Stroboscopic timing light
Dwell angle meter/tachometer
Universal electrical multi-meter
Cylinder compression gauge
Lifting tackle
Trolley jack
Light with extension lead

Buying tools

For practically all tools, a tool factor is the best source since he will have a very comprehensive range compared with the average garage or accessory shop. Having said that, accessory shops often offer excellent quality tools at discount prices, so it pays to shop around.

Remember, you don't have to buy the most expensive items on the shelf, but it is always advisable to steer clear of the very cheap tools. There are plenty of good tools around, at reasonable prices, so ask the proprietor or manager of the shop for advice before making a purchase.

Care and maintenance of tools

Having purchased a reasonable tool kit, it is necessary to keep the tools in a clean and serviceable condition. After use, always wipe off any dirt, grease and metal particles using a clean, dry cloth, before putting the tools away. Never leave them lying around after they have been used. A simple tool rack on the garage or workshop wall, for items such as screwdrivers and pliers is a good idea. Store all normal spanners and sockets in a metal box. Any measuring instruments, gauges, meters, etc., must be carefully stored where they cannot be damaged or become rusty.

Take a little care when the tools are used. Hammer heads inevitably become marked and screwdrivers lose the keen edge on their blades from time-to-time. A little timely attention with emery cloth or a file will soon restore items like this to a good serviceable finish.

Working facilities

Not to be forgotten when discussing tools, is the workshop itself. If anything more than routine maintenance is to be carried out, some form of suitable working area becomes essential.

It is appreciated that many an owner mechanic is forced by circumstance to remove an engine or similar item, without the benefit of a garage or workshop. Having done this, any repairs should always be done under the cover of a roof.

Wherever possible, any dismantling should be done on a clean flat workbench or table at a suitable working height.

Any workbench needs a vice: one with a jaw opening of 4 in. (100 mm) is suitable for most jobs. As mentioned previously, some clean dry storage space is also required for tools, as well as the lubricants, cleaning fluids, touch-up paints and so on which soon become necessary.

Another item which may be required, and which has a much more general usage, is an electric drill with a chuck capacity of at least 5/16 in. (8 mm). This, together with a good range of twist drills, is virtually essential for fitting accessories such as wing mirrors and reversing lights.

Last, but not least, always keep a supply of old newspapers and clean, lint-free rags available, and try to keep any working area as clean as possible.

Spanner jaw gap comparison table

Jaw gap (in.)	Spanner size
0.250	¼ in. AF
0.275	7 mm AF
0.312	5/16 in. AF
0.315	8 mm AF
0.340	11/32 in. AF
0.354	9 mm AF
0.375	3/8 in. AF
0.393	10 mm AF
0.433	11 mm AF
0.437	7/16 in. AF
0.472	12 mm AF
0.500	½ in. AF
0.512	13 mm AF
0.551	14 mm AF
0.562	9/16 in. AF
0.590	15 mm AF
0.625	5/8 in. AF
0.629	16 mm AF
0.669	17 mm AF
0.687	11/16 in. AF
0.708	18 mm AF
0.748	19 mm AF
0.750	¾ in. AF
0.812	13/16 in. AF
0.866	22 mm AF
0.875	7/8 in. AF
0.937	15/16 in. AF
0.944	24 mm AF
1.000	1 in. AF
1.023	26 mm AF
1.062	1 1/16 in. AF/27 mm AF
1.125	1 1/8 in. AF
1.181	30 mm AF
1.250	1¼ in. AF
1.259	32 mm AF
1.312	1 5/16 in. AF
1.417	36 mm AF
1.437	1 7/16 in. AF
1.500	1½ in. AF
1.574	40 mm AF
1.614	41 mm AF
1.625	1 5/8 in. AF
1.687	1 11/16 in. AF
1.811	46 mm AF
1.812	1 13/16 in. AF
1.875	1 7/8 in. AF
1.968	50 mm AF
2.000	2 in. AF
2.165	55 mm AF
2.362	60 mm AF

A Haltrac hoist and gantry in use during a typical engine removal sequence

Chapter 1 Engine

Contents

Specifications

Note: Where an 'X' appears in a column, the relevant specifications will be found in a column to the left. N/A = not applicable.

Engine type and application
North America:
Hi-Lux pick-up 1969 to 1971 8R-C ... ... 4 in-line overhead camshaft (ohc)
Hi-Lux pick-up 1972 to 1974 18R-C ... ... 4 in-line overhead camshaft (ohc)
Hi—Lux pick-up 1975 on 20R ... ... 4 in-line overhead camshaft (ohc)
Territories except North America:
Hi-Ace all models to 1976 12R ... ... 4 in-line overhead valve (ohv)
Hi-Lux pick-up to 1976 12R ... ... 4 in-line overhead valve (ohv)
Hi-Ace all models 1977 on 18R ... ... 4 in-line overhead camshaft (ohc)
Hi-Lux pick-up 1977 on ... ... 4 in-line overhead camshaft (ohc)

Engine type Engine general	8R-C	18R-C	20R	12R
Bore and stroke	... 3.39 x 3.15 in (86.0 x 80.0 mm)	3.48 x 3.15 in (88.5 x 80.0 mm)	3.48 x 3.50 in (88.5 x 89.0 mm)	3.17 x 3.07 in (80.5 x 78.0 mm)
Total piston displacement ...	... 113.4 cu in (1857 cc)	120.0 cu in (1968 cc)	133.6 cu in (2189 cc)	96.8 cu in (1587 cc)
Compression ratio	... 9.0 : 1	8.5 : 1	8.4 : 1	8.5 : 1
Maximum BHP	... 108 @ 5500 rev/min	97 @ 5500 rev/min	96 @ 4800 rev/min *	90 @ 5400 rev/min
Maximum torque	... 117lb/ft (16.2kg/m) @ 3800 rev/min	106 lb/ft (14.6 kg/m) @ 3800 rev/min	120 lb/ft (16.6 kg/m) @ 2800 rev/min	98 lb/ft (13.5 kg/m) @ 3000 rev/min
Firing order ... ... * *90 Bhp - California*	... 1 - 3 - 4 - 2	1 - 3 - 4 - 2	X	X
Cylinder head				
Material	... Cast-iron	X	Aluminium	Cast-iron
Maximum permissible warpage	... 0.002 in (0.05 mm)	X	0.006 in (0.15 mm)	0.002 in (0.05 mm)
Cylinder block				
Material	... Cast-iron	X	X	X
Maximum permissible warpage	... 0.002 in (0.05 mm)	X	X	X
Bore	... 3.386 to 3.388 in (8.00 to 86.05 mm)	3.484 to 3.486 in (88.5 to 88.55 mm)	3.4842 to 3.4854 (88.5 to 88.53 mm)	3.170 to 3.171 in (80.50 to 80.55 mm)
Maximum permissible cylinder bore wear	... 0.008 in (0.2 mm)	X	X	X
Maximum permissible bore difference between cylinders ...	... 0.002 in (0.05 mm)	X	X	X
Maximum permissible taper or out of round	... 0.0008 in (0.02 mm)	X	X	X
Pistons and rings				
Standard diameter	... 3.3846 to 3.3866 in (85.97 to 86.02 mm)	3.481 to 3.484 in (88.44 to 88.49 mm)	3.4827 to 3.4839 in (88.46 to 88.49 mm)	3.167 to 3.169 in (80.45 to 80.50 mm)
Oversize - 0.25	... 3.3941 to 3.3961 in (86.21 to 86.26 mm)	3.492 to 3.494 in 88.69 to 88.74 mm)	N/A N/A	
Oversize - 0.50	... 3.4039 to 3.4059 in (86.46 to 86.51 mm)	3.502 to 3.504 in (88.94 to 88.99 mm)	3.5024 to 3.5035 in 88.96 to 88.99 mm)	Oversize 0.25
Oversize 0.75	... 3.4138 to 3.4158 in (86.71 to 86.76 mm)	3.511 to 3.513 in 88.19 to 89.24 mm)	N/A N/A	0.50 0.75
Oversize 1.00	... 3.4236 to 3.4256 in (86.96 to 87.01 mm)	3.521 to 3.523 in (89.44 to 89.49 mm)	3.5220 to 3.5232 in (89.46 to 89.49 mm)	1.00 1.25 and 1.50
Gudgeon pin diameter	... 0.8663 to 0.8669 in (22.004 to 22.019 mm)	X	X	0.7876 to 0.7880 in (20.004 to 20.016 mm)
Gudgeon pin bore in piston ...	... 0.8661 to 0.8667 in (22.00 to 22.015 mm)	X	X	X
Piston ring end-gap	... 0.004 to 0.012 in (0.1 to 0.3 mm)	X	0.004 to 0.012 in (0.1 to 0.3 mm)	X
Piston ring to groove clearance:				
Compression rings ...	... 0.0012 to 0.0028 in (0.03 to 0.07 mm)	X	0.008 in (0.2 mm)	0.0012 to 0.0028 in (0.030 to 0.070 mm)
Oil control ring	... 0.008 to 0.0028 in (0.02 to 0.07 mm)	Zero (spring type)	X	0.0010 to 0.0028 in (0.025 to 0.070 mm)
Piston to cylinder wall clearance	... 0.0020 to 0.0028 in (0.05 to 0.07 mm)	X	0.0012 to 0.0020 in (0.03 to 0.05 mm)	0.0004 to 0.0020 in (0.01 to 0.05 mm)
Connecting rods				
Length (between centres) ...	... 5.441 to 5.445 in (138.20 to 138.30 mm)	X	X	Information not available
Big-end bore	... 2.2047 to 2.2057 in (56.0 to 56.024 mm)	X	X	Information not available
Standard endfloat	... 0.0043 to 0.0097 in (0.110 to 0.246 mm)	0.006 to 0.010 in 0.16 to 0.26 mm)	X	0.003 to 0.010 in (0.08 to 0.24 mm)
Maximum endfloat	... 0.012 in (0.3 mm)	X	X	X
Small end bush internal diameter (after reaming)	... 0.8666 to 0.8672 in (22.012 to 22.027 mm)	X	X	X
Gudgeon pin to small end bush running clearance	... 0.0002 to 0.0004 in (0.005 to 0.011 mm)	X	X	X
Maximum permissible gudgeon pin to small end bush clearance ...	... 0.0006 in (0.015 mm)	0.0008 in (0.02 mm)	0.0006 in (0.015 mm)	X
Big-end bearing running clearance:				
Standard	... 0.0008 to 0.0020 in (0.02 to 0.05 mm)	0.0010 to 0.0021 in (0.025 to 0.055 mm)	X	0.0009 to 0.0019 in (0.024 to 0.48 mm)
Maximum permissible big-end bearing running clearance ...	... 0.003 in (0.08 mm)	X	X	X

Engine type	8R-C	18R-C	20R	12R
Crankshaft				
Number of main bearings 5	5	X	X	3
Endfloat	0.002 to 0.010 in (0.05 to 0.25 mm)	0.0008 to 0.008 in (0.02 to 0.20 mm)	X X	0.0016 to 0.051 in (0.04 to 0.13 mm)
Maximum permissible endfloat ...	0.12 in (0.3 mm)	X	X	0.008 in (0.2 mm)
Maximum out-of-round or taper for journals and crankpins	0.0004 in (0.01 mm)	X	X	10.0008 in (0.02 mm)
Crankshaft journal running clearance	0.0006 to 0.0016 in. (0.016 to 0.040 mm)	X X	0.0010 to 0.0022 in (0.025 to 0.055 mm)	X X
Maximum journal or crankpin running clearance	0.003 in (0.08 mm)	X	X	X
Crankpin journal finished diameter:				
Standard bearing	2.3613 to 2.3622 in (59.976 to 60.000 mm)	X X	X X	1.966 to 1.9685 in (49.976 to 50.000 mm)
Undersize - 0.25	2.3504 to 2.3508 in (59.701 to 59.711 mm)	X X	X X	1.9547 to 1.9594 in (49.75 to 49.77 mm)
Undersize - 0.50	2.3406 to 2.3410 in (59.451 to 59.461 mm)	X X	N/A N/A	1.9488 to 1.9496 in (45.50 to 49.52 mm)
Undersize - 0.75	2.3307 to 2.3311 in (59.201 to 59.211 mm)	X X	N/A N/A	1.9390 to 1.9398 in (49.25 to 49.27 mm)
Undersize - 1.00	2.3209 to 2.3213 in (58.951 to 58.961 mm)	X X	N/A N/A	1.9291 to 1.9299 in (49.00 to 49.02 mm)
Flywheel				
Maximum permissible run-out ...	0.008 in (0.2 mm)	X	X	X
Maximum regrind reduction in overall depth	0.04 in (1.0 mm)	X	Not recommended	0.04 in (1.0 mm)
Camshaft				
Standard endfloat	0.0017 to 0.0066 in (0.042 to 0.168 mm)	X X	0.0031 to 0.0071 in (0.08 to 0.18 mm)	0.002 to 0.005 in (0.05 to 0.13 mm)
Maximum permissible endfloat ...	0.010 in (0.25 mm)	X		0.008 in (0.2 mm)
Bearing running clearance ...	0.001 to 0.002 in (0.03 to 0.05 mm)	X X	0.0004 to 0.0020 in (0.01 to 0.05 mm)	0.0010 to 0,0026 in (0.025 to 0.066 mm)
Maximum bearing running clearance	0.004 in (0.1 mm)	X	X	X
Cam lift:				
Inlet	0.4 in (10.0 mm)	0.317 in (8.04 mm)	1.6783 to 1.6819 in (42.63 to 42.72 mm)	0.2506 to 0.2526 in (6.365 to 6.415mm)
Exhaust	U.4 in (10.0 mm)	0.319 in (8.10 mm)	1.6806 to 1.6841 in (42.69 to 42.78 mm)	0.4549 to 0.2569 in (6.475 to 6.525 mm)
Camshaft journal finished diameter:				
Standard bearing	1.3768 to 1.3778 in (34.972 to 34.996 mm)	X X	1.2984 to 1.2990 in (32.98 to 33.00 mm)	No. 1 1.8291 to 1.8297 in (46.459 to 46.475 mm)
Undersize - 0.125	1.3718 to 1.3722 in (34.843 to 34.853 mm)	X X	N/A N/A	No. 2 1.8193 to 1.8199 in (46.209 to 46.225 mm)
Maximum journal out of round or taper	0.0004 in (0.01 mm)	X	0.008 in (0.2 mm)	No 3 1.8094 to 1.8100 in (45.959 to 45.995 mm) Undersizes 0.125 - 0.250 - 0.500
Oil pump driveshaft				
Standard endfloat	0.002 to 0.005 in (0.06 to 0.13 mm)	X	Information not available	Information not available
Maximum permissible endfloat ...	0.012 in (0.3 mm)	X	Information not available	Information not available
Driveshaft bearing running clearance ...	0.0010 to 0.0026 in (0.025 to 0.066 mm)	X	Information not available	Information not available
Maximum permissible driveshaft running clearance	0.003 in (0.08 mm)	X	Information not available	Information not available

Engine type	8R-C	18R-C	20R	12R
Valves				
Head diameter:				
Inlet	1.687 to 1.699 in (42.85 to 43.15 mm)	1.608 to 1.620 in (40.85 to 41.15 mm)	X X	1.569 to 1.581 in (39.85 to 40.15 mm)
Exhaust	1.333 to 1.345 in (33.85 to 34.15 mm)	1.411 to 1.423 in (35.85 to 36.15 mm)	X X	1.333 to 1.344 in (33.85 to 34.15 mm)
Overall length	4.476 in (113.7 mm)	4.457 in (113.2 mm)	In. 4.52 in (115 mm) Ex. 4.46 in (113.4 mm)	4291 in (109.0 mm)
Valve stem diameter:				
Inlet	0.3140 to 0.3144 in (7.975 to 7.985 mm)	X X	0.3138 to 0.3144 in (7.97 to 7.99 mm)	X X
Exhaust	0.3132 to 0.3140 in (7.955 to 7.975 mm)	X X	0.3136 to 0.3142 in (7.87 to 7.98 mm)	X X
Standard stem to guide clearance:				
Inlet	0.0010 to 0.0022 in (0.025 to 0.055 mm)	X X	0.0006 to 0.0024 in (0.02 to 0.06 mm)	0,0010 to 0.0024 in (0.025 to 0.060 mm)
Exhaust	0.0014 to 0.0030 in (0.035 to 0.075 mm)	X X	0.0012 to 0.0026 in (0.03 to 0.07 mm)	0.0014 to 0.0028 in (0.035 to 0.070 mm)
Maximum stem to guide clearance:				
Inlet	0.003 in (0.08 mm)	X	X	X
Exhaust	0.004 in (0.10 mm)	X	X	X
Valve head contact angle	45°	X	X	X
Valve clearance (cold):				
Inlet	0.007 in (0.18 mm)	X	N/A	N/A
Exhaust	0.013 in (0.33 mm)	X	N/A	N/A
Valve clearance (hot):				
Inlet	0.008 in (0.20 mm)	X	0.008 in (0.2 mm)	0.008 in (0.2 mm)
Exhaust	0.014 in (0.36 mm)	X	0.012 in (0.3 mm)	0.014 in (0.3 mm)
Valve guide overall length:				
Inlet	1.949 to 2.185 in (49.5 to 55.5 mm)	X X	X X	X X
Exhaust	2.303 to 2.343 in (58.5 to 59.5 mm)	X X	X X	X X
Valve guide inner diameter (after reaming)	0.315 to 0.316 in (8.01 to 8.03 mm)	X	X	X
Valve guide outer diameter:				
Standard	0.5521 to 0.5528 in (14.023 to 14.041 mm)	X X	X X	X X
Oversize - 0.05	0.5541 to 0.5548 in (14.073 to 14.091 mm)	X X	X X	X X
Valve guide projection	0.63 in (16.0 mm)	X	X	X
Valve spring free length:				
Inner	1.74 in (44.1 mm)	X	N/A	N/A
Outer	1.83 in (46.5 mm)	X	1.787 in (45.4 mm)	1.728 in (43.9 mm)
Valve rocker shaft outside diameter	0.7272 to 0.7277 in (18.470 to 18.483 mm)	0.7269 to 0.7277 in (18.464 to 18.483 mm)	1.6287 to 1.6295 in (15.97 to 15.99 mm)	0.7273 to 0.7278 in (18.474 to 18.487 mm)
Rocker arm bush running clearance	0.0012 to 0.0015 in (0.030 to 0.038 mm)	0.0007 to 0.0020 in (0.017 to 0.051 mm)	0.0004 to 0.0020 in (0.01 to 0.05 mm)	0.0008 to 0.0014 in (0.020 to 0.035 mm)
Maximum permissible running clearance	0.002 in (0.05 mm)	0.003 in (0.08 mm)	0.003 in (0.08 mm)	0.002 in (0.05 mm)
Timing chain tensioners				
Lower tensioner spring free length	2.70 in (67.4 mm)	X	N/A	N/A
Upper tensioner spring free length	3.08 in (77.0 mm)	X	N/A	N/A

Engine oil capacities

8R-C
  With filter   7½ Imp. pts (4.3 litres) 4.5 US qts
  Without filter   6½ Imp. pts (3.6 litres) 3.7 US qts
18R-C:
  With filter   9 Imp. pts (5.1 litres) 5.3 US qts
  Without filter   8 Imp. pts (4.5 litres) 4.8 US qts
20R:
  With filter   8 Imp. pts (4.5 litres) 4.8 US qts
  Without filter   6½ Imp. pts (3.7 litres) 3.9 US qts
12R:
  With filter   7¼ Imp. pts (4.2 litres) 4.4 US qts
  Without filter   6¼ Imp. pts (3.5 litres) 3.7 US qts

Torque wrench settings

	lb f ft	Nm
8R-C and 18 R-C engines		
Crankshaft main bearing cap bolts	75	102
Big-end bearing cap bolts	45	61
Camshaft bearing cap bolts	15	20
Crankshaft rear oil seal retainer bolts	15	20
Oil pump driveshaft thrust plate bolts	15	20
Camshaft sprocket to driveshaft bolt	70	95
Camshaft to sprocket bolt	16	22
Crankshaft pulley bolt	50	68
Sump bolts	5	7
Cylinder head bolts:		
Stage 1	30	41
Stage 2	60	83
Stage 3	87	118
Camshaft sprocket bolts	12	16
Rocker shaft pillar bolts	15	20
Rocker shaft oil pipe unions	15	20
Drive plate to torque converter bolts	32	44
Clutch bellhousing to cylinder block bolts:		
8R-C series	33	45
18R-C series	50	68
Timing cover bolts	15	20
Manifold bolts	35	48
Rocker cover bolts	7	10
Flywheel to crankshaft bolts	55	75
Driveplate to crankshaft	45	61
20R engine		
Camshaft bearing cap	15	20
Camshaft sprocket bolt	60	82
Thermostatic valve bolts	15	20
Inlet manifold bolts	15	20
EGR valve	11	15
Exhaust manifold bolts	35	48
Cylinder head/rocker bolts:		
Stage 1	25	34
Stage 2	40	54
Stage 3	64	87
Front chain cover bolt	11	15
Distributor drivegear retaining bolt	65	88
Rocker cover bolts	11	15
Exhaust pipe flange nuts	32	44
Timing cover bolts	11	15
Crankshaft pulley bolt	94	128
Sump bolts	9	12
Big-end bearing bolts	40	54
Main bearing bolts	80	109
Flywheel bolts	68	92
Bellhousing to cylinder block	50	68
Driveplate to torque converter bolts	32	44
Driveplate to crankshaft	60	82
12R engine		
Big-end bearing bolts	35	48
Main bearing bolts	80	109
Camshaft thrust plate bolts	11	15
Timing cover bolts	11	15
Crankshaft pulley bolt	35	48
Sump bolts	9	12
Cylinder head bolts:		
Stage 1	30	41
Stage 2	60	82
Stage 3	85	116
Rocker pillar bolts	18	25
Manifold bolts	30	41
Flywheel bolts	47	64
Oil pump to crankcase	11	15
Bellhousing to cylinder block	33	45

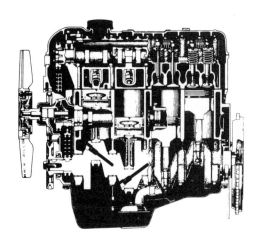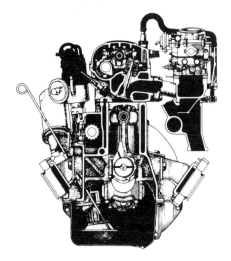

Fig. 1.1. Sectional views of 8R-C and 18R-C type engine

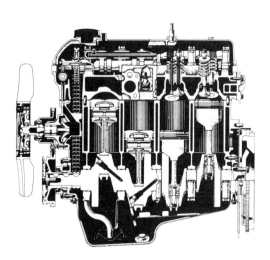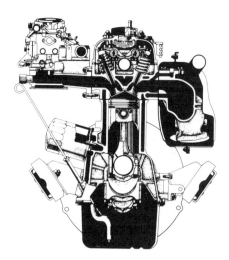

Fig. 1.2. Sectional views of the 20R type engine

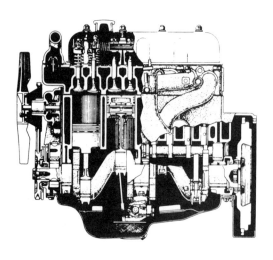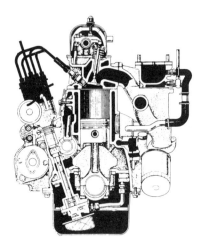

Fig. 1.3. Sectional views of the 12R type engine

1 General description

1 Four types of engine are covered by this Chapter. Hi-Lux models built up until 1971 and available in North America were fitted with an 8R-C engine and from 1972 until 1974 with an 18R-C engine. Both these engines are similar except for capacity, the 18R-C type having a larger bore.
2 From 1975, North American Hi-Lux models are fitted with a 20-R engine.
3 Hi-Ace vehicles and Hi-Lux models not destined for North America are equipped with a 12R engine.
4 All engines are of the 4-cylinder in-line type.
5 8R-C and 18R-C engines are of overhead camshaft (ohc) design with the valves operating from a single rocker shaft.
6 20R engines are also of overhead camshaft design, but the valves are operated from separate inlet and exhaust rocker shafts.
7 The 12R engine is of the overhead valve (ohv) type with push-rod operated valve gear. Timing gears are used in this engine, no chain being employed.

2 Major operations with the engine remaining in the vehicle

1 The following operations can be carried out with the engine still installed in the bodyframe:

   a) *Removal and installation of camshaft or rocker cover. On vehicles equipped with air conditioning, the flexible pipe clamp must be removed from the camshaft cover and the pipe pulled away sufficiently to provide clearance to withdraw the cover.* **On no account** *disconnect any of the air conditioning circuit pipes or unions.*
   b) *Removal and refitting of the camshaft and cylinder head.*
   c) *Removal and refitting of the timing chain and gears (Detach sump first, see paragraph 2).*
   d) *Removal and refitting of the engine front mountings and the transmission rear mounting.*

2 If a hoist is attached to the engine lifting hooks and its weight taken by the hoist, the engine mountings can be removed and the engine raised an inch or two. Disconnect the steering relay rod, drop arm and idler arm rods (Chapter 11) to permit the following operations to be carried out:

   a) *Removal and refitting of the sump (detach strengthener brackets first).*
   b) *Removal and refitting of the oil pump.*
   c) *Removal and refitting of the piston/connecting rod assemblies (through the top of the cylinder block).*
   d) *Renewal of crankshaft main bearings.*

3 Major operations only possible with the engine (or gearbox) removed

1 The following operations are only possible with the engine (or gearbox) removed:

   a) *Removal and installation of the flywheel or driveplate.*
   b) *Removal and installation of the crankshaft rear oil seal and retainer.*
   c) *Removal and installation of the flywheel (or driveplate - auto transmission).*

4 Method of engine removal

1 *On Hi-Lux models,* if a manually-operated transmission is fitted, remove the gearbox first as described in Chapter 6 and then lift out the engine. Alternatively, the engine and manual gearbox may be removed together and separated later.
2 If an automatic transmission is installed, the engine can be removed leaving the transmission in position in the vehicle.
3 Removal of the engine alone leaving the manual gearbox in position is not possible, as the engine cannot be pulled far enough forward to clear the primary shaft of the gearbox. Where a Hi-Lux vehicle is equipped with a 12R type engine, the upper clutch bellhousing bolts are inaccessible unless the gearbox is first lowered and so the gearbox or gearbox/engine may just as well be removed, as attempting, at this stage, to remove the engine on its own.
4 *On vehicles equipped with air conditioning:* the system must be discharged of refrigerant gas so that the compressor connecting pipes can be disconnected. This and the later recharging of the system are jobs for the service engineer. **It is extremely dangerous to disconnect any part of the system if it has not been discharged.**
5 To remove the engine from Hi-Ace vehicles, it can either be removed together with the gearbox or, if the gearbox is removed first, it can then be withdrawn on its own. Removing the engine alone, leaving the gearbox in the vehicle is not possible. The engine and gearbox are both removed downwards from beneath the vehicle.

5 Engine (Hi-Lux) - removal (manual gearbox previously withdrawn)

1 These operations are applicable when the manual gearbox has already been removed as described in Chapter 6.
2 Disconnect the lead from the battery negative terminal.
3 Drain the cooling system.
4 Drain the engine oil.
5 Mark the position of the bonnet hinge plates, remove the securing bolts and with the help of an assistant, lift the bonnet from the vehicle.
6 Disconnect the upper and lower radiator hoses, unbolt the radiator and remove it from the engine compartment. Note the battery negative lead connection under the radiator bolt. On some models, a radiator fan shroud is fitted. Remove this after the radiator (photos).
7 Remove the air cleaner from the carburettor.
8 Disconnect the fuel inlet pipe from the fuel pump.
9 Disconnect the heater hoses.
10 Disconnect the controls from the carburettor.
11 Disconnect the brake servo unit vacuum hose from the inlet manifold.
12 Disconnect the leads from the following components: Starter solenoid, alternator, oil pressure switch, water temperature transmitter, emission control unit and coil (HT and LT leads). (photos).

5.6a Battery negative lead connection to radiator bolt (Hi-Lux 12R)

5.6b Removing radiator fan cowl (Hi-Lux 12R)

5.12a Water temperature and TCS (emission control) switches (Hi-Lux 12R)

13 Disconnect the vacuum hoses from the emission control unit. It is important that these are carefully identified to ensure exact refitting in their original positions.
14 Working beneath the vehicle, disconnect the exhaust downpipe from the exhaust manifold (photo).
15 Using a suitable hoist and slings positioned securely round the engine, raise the hoist so that it just takes the weight of the engine. Unbolt the engine mountings from the crossmember. Hoist the engine out of the engine compartment (photos).

9 Using a suitable hoist and slings positioned securely round the engine, raise the hoist so that it just takes the weight of the engine. Unbolt the engine mountings from the front crossmember.
10 Place a jack under the transmission housing and then unbolt and remove the rear mounting support crossmember and the mounting.
11 Remove the jack from below the transmission which will allow it to drop a few inches. Hoist the combined engine/transmission up and out of the engine compartment at a steeply inclined angle.

6 Engine (Hi-Lux) - removal, complete with manual gearbox

1 To remove the engine complete with manual gearbox, first carry out the operations described in paragraphs 2 to 14 of the preceding Section.
2 Unbolt the clutch operating cylinder from the clutch bellhousing, also the hose support bracket and the cylinder up out of the way; there is no need to disconnect the hydraulic line.
3 Disconnect the exhaust pipe support bracket from the transmission housing.
4 Unbolt the handbrake cable equaliser and lower the equaliser complete with cables.
5 Disconnect the speedometer cable from the transmission housing.
6 Remove the floor-mounted gearshift lever (see Chapter 6) or disconnect the steering column type control rods from the levers on the gearbox.
7 Mark the edges of the rear propeller shaft and rear axle pinion flanges so that they can be refitted in exactly the same relative positions to maintain balance. Unbolt the flanges and push the propeller shaft slightly forward to separate them and then withdraw the shaft to the rear.
8 Where the propeller shaft is of the three section, centre bearing type, then the connecting flanges at the front of the propeller shaft should be separated in addition to the rear pinion flange and the complete propeller shaft removed after detaching the centre flexible bearing from the bodyframe.

7 Engine (Hi-Lux) - removal, leaving automatic transmission in position in vehicle

1 Repeat the operations described in paragraphs 2 to 5 and 7 to 14 of Section 5.
2 Disconnect and plug the fluid cooler lines from the radiator and then remove the radiator from the engine compartment.
3 Disconnect the throttle to transmission kick-down rod.
4 Support the transmission unit on a jack and remove the lower cover plate from the front face of the torque converter housing. Withdraw the starter motor.
5 Unscrew and remove the bolts which secure the driveplate and torque converter together. These can be removed one at a time if the crankshaft is rotated to bring each one into view. Mark the relative position of the driveplate to the torque converter.
6 Unscrew and remove the torque converter housing to engine securing bolts. At this stage, take steps to prevent the torque converter moving forward when the engine is withdrawn with consequent loss of fluid. The best way to do this is to bolt a short flat bar to one of the lower converter housing bolt holes so that it maintains pressure on the front face of the torque converter in a rearward direction.
7 Take the weight of the engine on a hoist and remove the two front mountings. Pull the engine forward to disengage it from the transmission and then hoist it up and out of the engine compartment.

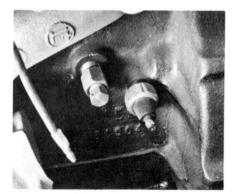
5.12b Oil pressure switch and cylinder block drain tap (Hi-Lux 12R)

5.12c Alternator connections (Hi-Lux 12R)

5.12d Starter motor connections (Hi-Lux 12R)

5.14 Exhaust downpipe disconnected (Hi-Lux 12R)

5.15a Right-hand engine mounting and engine earth connections from battery (Hi-Lux 12R)

5.15b Left-hand engine mounting (Hi-Lux 12R)

8 Engine (Hi-Lux) - removal complete with automatic transmission

1 Repeat operations 2 to 5 and 7 to 14 of Section 5 and 2 of Section 7.
2 Drain the transmission fluid.
3 Remove the propeller shaft (see Chapter 7).
4 Disconnect the speed selector linkage at the transmission.
5 Disconnect the exhaust pipe from the transmission bracket.
6 Disconnect the speedometer drive cable from the transmission.
7 Pull the fluid filler tube from the transmission, plug the open hole and retain the 'O' ring seal.
8 Disconnect the handbrake intermediate lever from the rear mounting crossmember.
9 Take the weight of the engine on a hoist. Remember that the combined weight of the engine and automatic transmission will require a heavy duty hoist and lifting tackle.
10 Unbolt and remove the front mountings and the rear crossmember. Detach the rear crossmember from the mounting brackets.
11 The engine/transmission will take on a steeply inclined attitude and it can be hoisted up and out of the engine compartment.

9 Engine (Hi-Ace) - removal (manual gearbox previously withdrawn)

1 These operations are applicable when the manual gearbox has already been removed as described in Chapter 6.
2 Disconnect the lead from the battery negative terminal.
3 Drain the cooling system.
4 Drain the engine oil. Raise the centre seat in the driving compartment.
5 Disconnect the radiator upper and lower hoses, and unbolt and remove the radiator, in order to prevent damage to it later. The radiator is withdrawn downward and the front of the vehicle must therefore be raised to provide sufficient space for this to be done, or the vehicle positioned over an inspection pit.
6 Remove the air cleaner from the carburettor.
7 Disconnect the fuel inlet pipe from the fuel pump and disconnect the heater hoses.
8 Disconnect the alternator and remove it upwards from the engine.
9 Disconnect the accelerator cable and the choke cable from the carburettor.
10 Disconnect the leads from the starter motor, oil pressure switch and water temperature transmitter.
11 Disconnect the LT and HT leads which run between the coil and the distributor.
12 Disconnect the exhaust pipe from the manifold.
13 The engine is now ready for removal and the engine can only be removed downwards from the bottom of the engine compartment. Unless a cantilever type engine crane can be positioned inside the driving cab in order to support the weight of the power unit, one of the following alternative methods must be used.

   a) *Raise the front of the vehicle sufficiently enough, and support securely, so that the engine can be held on a jack and the mountings disconnected. The jack can then be lowered and the engine removed from beneath the vehicle.*
   b) *Position the vehicle over an inspection pit and, with the help of three assistants, support the engine while the mountings are released and use the combined efforts of the assistants to lower the engine into the inspection pit.*

14 Having decided upon which method to use, disconnect the engine mountings and lower the engine from the engine compartment.

10 Engine (Hi-Ace) - removal complete with gearbox

1 Carry out the operations described in Section 9, paragraphs 2 to 12 inclusive.
2 Now refer to Chapter 6, Section 4 and carry out the operations described in paragraphs 2 to 12.
3 Again refer to the preceding Section and decide upon which method is to be used to first support and then lower the combined engine/gearbox from the vehicle.
4 Having decided upon which method to use, disconnect the front engine mountings and the mounting above and to the rear of the gearbox extension housing and lower the engine/gearbox from the bottom of the chassis frame.

11 Engine - separation from manual gearbox

1 Remove the starter motor. On Hi-Ace vehicles and Hi-Lux with 12R engines, remove the clutch bellhousing lower cover.
2 Unscrew and remove the bolts which connect the clutch bellhousing to the cylinder block.
3 Pull the gearbox from the engine in a straight line, supporting the gearbox so that its weight does not hang upon the gearbox input shaft, even momentarily, whilst it is still engaged with the clutch mechanism.

12 Engine - separation from automatic transmission

1 Unscrew and remove the oil cooler pipes from the transmission.
2 Remove the starter motor.
3 Remove the 'kick-down' rod.
4 Remove the two brackets which connect the sides of the transmission casing to the cylinder block.
5 Remove the torque converter lower cover plate, then remove the torque converter to drive plate securing bolts. The drive plate will have to be rotated to reach each of the bolts in turn. Mark the relative position of the drive plate to the torque converter using a spirit pen or a dab of quick drying paint so that they can be fitted in their original relative positions.
6 Unscrew and remove the bolts which secure the automatic transmission torque converter housing to the engine. Pull the automatic transmission unit from its connection with the engine, keeping it in a straight line and supporting its weight during the operation. There will probably be some loss of fluid from the torque converter during the separation procedure so be prepared to catch it in a suitable container, unless the torque converter is secured with the device described in Section 7, paragraph 6.

13 Engine dismantling - general

1 It is best to mount the engine on a dismantling stand but if one is not available, then stand the engine on a strong bench with a comfortable working height. Failing this, the engine will have to be stripped down on the floor.
2 During the dismantling process the greatest care should be taken to keep the exposed parts free from dirt. As an aid to achieving this, it is a sound scheme to thoroughly clean down the outside of the engine, removing all traces of oil and congealed dirt.
3 Use paraffin or a good water soluble grease solvent. The latter will make the job much easier, as, after the solvent has been applied and allowed to stand for a time, a vigorous jet of water will wash off the solvent and all the grease and filth. If the dirt is thick and deeply embedded, work the solvent into it with a wire brush.
4 Finally, wipe down the exterior of the engine with a rag and only then, when it is quite clean should the dismantling process begin. As the engine is stripped, clean each part in a bath of paraffin or petrol.
5 Never immerse parts with oilways in paraffin, ie; the crankshaft, but to clean, wipe down carefully with a petrol dampened rag. Oilways can be cleaned out with wire. If an air line is present all parts can be blown dry and the oilways blown through as an added precaution.
6 Re-use of old engine gaskets is false economy and can give rise to oil and water leaks, if nothing worse. To avoid the possibility of trouble after the engine has been reassembled always use new gaskets throughout.
7 Do not throw the old gaskets away as it sometimes happens that an immediate replacement cannot be found and the old gasket is then very useful as a template. Hang up the old gaskets as they are removed on a suitable hook or nail.
8 To strip the engine it is best to work from the top down. The sump provides a firm base on which the engine can be supported in an upright position. When the stage where the sump must be removed is reached, the engine can be turned on its side and all other work carried out with it in this position.
9 Wherever possible, replace nuts, bolts and washers fingertight from wherever they were removed. This helps avoid later loss and muddle. If they cannot be replaced then lay them out in such a fashion that it is clear from where they came.

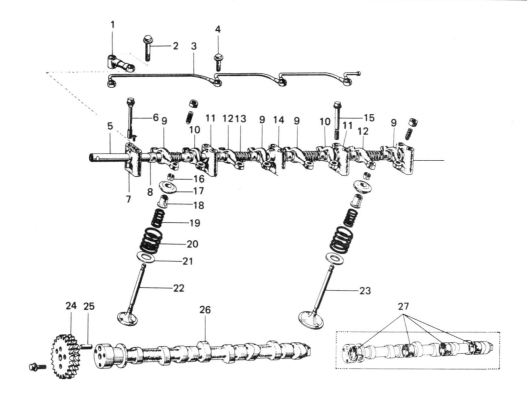

Fig. 1.6. Exploded view of rocker and valve gear and camshaft (8R-C/18R-C engine)

1	Oil pipe union	8	Bearing	15	Bolt
2	Thermostat housing cover	9	Rocker arm	16	Split collets
3	Oil pipe assembly	10	Rocker arm	17	Valve spring retainer
4	Union bolt	11	Rocker shaft support pillar	18	Valve stem oil seal
5	Rocker shaft	12	Rocker arm	19	Valve (inner) spring
6	Bolt	13	Spring	20	Valve (outer) spring
7	Rocker shaft support pillar	14	Rocker shaft support pillar	21	Plate

22	Exhaust valve
23	Inlet valve
24	Camshaft sprocket
25	Dowel pin
26	Camshaft
27	Camshaft shell bearings

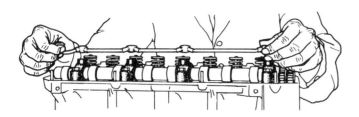

Fig. 1.4. Removing rocker oil feed pipe (8R-C/18R-C engine)

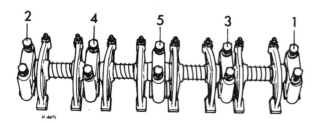

Fig. 1.5. Loosening sequence for rocker shaft support pillar bolts
(8R-C/18R-C engine)

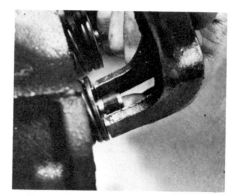

15.13 Compressing valve spring (Hi-Lux
8R-C/18R-C)

14 Engine ancillary components - removal

1 With the engine removed from the vehicle and separated from the gearbox, the ancillary components should now be removed before dismantling proper begins.

2 Unbolt the clutch pressure plate assembly from the flywheel and remove the clutch mechanism complete with driven plate, (manual gearbox).

3 Bend back the tabs of the locking plates which are located under the bolts which secure the flywheel (or drive plate - automatic transmission) to the crankshaft rear flange. Remove the bolts and lift off the flywheel or drive plates as the case may be.

4 Where the vehicle is equipped with air conditioning, remove the air compressor and idler pulley.

5 Remove the dipstick, the fuel pipes, and loosen the distributor clamp. Withdraw the distributor complete with cap and HT leads. Remove the spark plugs followed by the fuel pump (not 20R) and the oil filter/mounting assembly. If desired, the side cover (not 20R), oil pressure switch and engine mounting brackets may also be removed.

6 Remove the heater pipes, the crankcase ventilation hose, and then unbolt and remove the carburettor complete with heat insulator from the inlet manifold. Remove the manifold assembly, water pump bypass hose, drivebelt adjustment strap, alternator, and fan belt. The alternator mounting bracket and left-hand engine mounting bracket may be removed if desired.

7 From the front of the engine, remove the water pump and fan assembly.

8 From the top of the engine, remove the thermostat housing and the thermostat, also the rocker cover.

9 The engine has now been stripped of ancillary components and is ready for dismantling, as described in the following Sections. On 8R-C engines before March 1971, an air pump (crankshaft driven by vee-belt) is fitted as part of the emission control system: this should be removed from its mountings.

15.16a Valve stem oil seal (Hi-Lux 8R-C/ 18R-C)

15.16b Removing a valve (Hi-Lux 8R-C/ 18R-C)

15 Engine dismantling (Hi-Lux 8R-C and 18R-C)

Rocker gear

1 Unscrew and remove the union bolts and withdraw the oil feed pipe.

2 Unscrew the rocker shaft pillar bolts in the sequence shown in Fig. 1.5 to ensure that the pressure of the valve springs is relieved gently to prevent distortion of the shaft.

3 Remove the rocker shaft assembly from the cylinder head.

4 The rocker shaft does not normally require dismantling unless the heels of the rocker arms are scored or badly worn or one of the coil springs is broken.

5 If dismantling is essential, first remove the retaining screw which secures the rocker shaft front support pillar to the shaft. The rear pillar is retained to the shaft by means of the two securing bolts which engage in cut-outs in the shaft.

6 As each rocker arm, spring and pillar is withdrawn, keep them in strict sequence for refitting.

Camshaft

7 Unbolt the gearwheel from the end of the camshaft. A semi-circular plastic plug is provided for access to the bolts.

8 Use a hooked piece of wire to support the chain while the gearwheel is removed and to prevent the chain becoming disconnected from the drive sprocket. This is particularly important when the camshaft is being removed with the engine in position in the car and further dismantling is not anticipated.

9 Remove the four camshaft bearing caps, keeping them in strict sequence for correct refitting (they are usually numbered 1 to 4).

10 Remove the camshaft.

Cylinder head

11 *If the engine is still in the car,* drain the cooling system and disconnect all leads and hoses from the cylinder head, carburettor and spark plugs.

12 Unscrew the cylinder head bolts half a turn at a time in the sequence shown in Fig. 1.7.

13 Unscrew and remove the two bolts which secure the top end of the timing chain cover to the cylinder head.

14 Lift the cylinder head straight up to clear the locating dowels. If the cylinder head is stuck, do not attempt to prise it off by inserting a screwdriver or chisel in the gasket joint, as this will only damage the machined faces of the head and block. Tap the sides of the head using a hammer and hardwood block or, alternatively, screw in the spark plugs and turn the engine by means of the crankshaft pulley bolt so that compression (all valves closed) will assist in breaking the seal.

15 Each valve should be removed from the cylinder head using the following method:

16 Compress each spring, using a valve spring compressor, until the collets can be removed. Release the compressor slowly, remove it and then remove the retainer, double springs, oil seal from the valve stem and the washer. Finally withdraw the valve from its guide (photo).

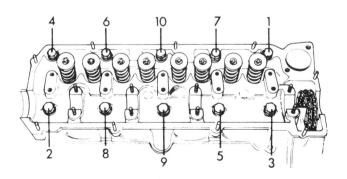

Fig. 1.7. Cylinder head bolt loosening sequence (8R-C/18R-C engine)

17 If, when the valve spring compressor is screwed down, the valve spring retaining cap refuses to free to expose the collets, do not continue to screw down on the compressor as there is a likelihood of bending the valve stem.

18 Gently tap the top of the tool directly over the cap with a light hammer. This will free the cap. To avoid the compressor jumping off the valve spring retaining cap when it is tapped, hold the compressor firmly in position with one hand.

19 Slide the rubber oil control seal off the end of each valve stem and then drop out each valve through the combustion chamber (photos).

20 It is essential that the valves are kept in their correct sequences unless they are so badly worn that they are to be renewed. If they are going to be kept and used again, place them in a sheet of card having holes numbered 1 to 8 corresponding to the relative positions the valves were in when fitted. Also keep the valve springs, washers etc in the correct order.

Sump and timing gear

21 *If the engine is in the car,* drain the engine oil and disconnect the battery negative lead. Remove the cylinder head as described previously in this Section. Remove the radiator.

22 Unbolt and remove the re-inforcement brackets from the rear of the sump.

23 Unscrew and remove the sump securing bolts and lift the sump from the crankcase. If the engine is in the car, the front mountings will have to be disconnected and the engine raised slightly, also the steering relay rod, drop arm and idler arm rods disconnected to provide more clearance for the sump.

24 Unscrew the crankshaft pulley bolt with the sump removed, by jamming the crankshaft with a piece of wood to prevent the engine turning as the bolt is loosened. If the pulley is being removed with the engine in position in the vehicle then, *if fitted with a manual gearbox,* engage a gear and apply the handbrake fully to prevent the crankshaft rotating. *With automatic transmission,* remove the starter and jam the

ring gear with a large screwdriver or cold chisel.

25 Remove the crankshaft pulley. It will usually pull straight out but if necessary, remove it by placing two tyre levers behind it or use a puller (there are two holes tapped in the pulley for this purpose).

26 Unbolt and remove the timing cover. Note that the upper bolt is entered from the rear.

27 Remove the camshaft drive chain. The oil pump driveshaft sprocket and the chain tensioners should be withdrawn.

28 Remove the crankshaft sprockets, and oil pump driveshaft sprocket, complete with chain as one assembly. Remove the chain damper.

29 Remove the oil pump driveshaft thrust plate and withdraw the driveshaft and engine front plate. Unbolt and remove the oil pump assembly from within the crankcase.

Piston/connecting rod assemblies

30 *If the engine is still in the vehicle,* first remove the cylinder head and sump as previously described, then turn the crankshaft so that the pistons are all part way down their bores. Using a bearing scraper, carefully remove as much as possible of the 'wear' ridge at the top of each cylinder bore. This operation is essential to prevent the piston rings breaking as the pistons are extracted through the top of the block.

31 With quick drying paint, mark each piston, connecting rod and big-end bearing cap. Number the components of each assembly 1 to 4 (from the front of the engine) and also the relative positions of the components to each other and to the crankcase, so that if the original assembly is to be refitted, it will be installed in its exact, previously located position.

32 Unbolt the big-end caps from the connecting rods and then push each piston/connecting rod assembly out through the top of the block. Take great care that the threads of the big-end studs do not score the cylinder bores during this operation. If the bearing shells are to be used again, identify them in respect of exact original location.

Piston rings and gudgeon pins

33 With the piston assemblies removed, the piston rings may be removed by opening each of them in turn, just enough to enable them to ride over

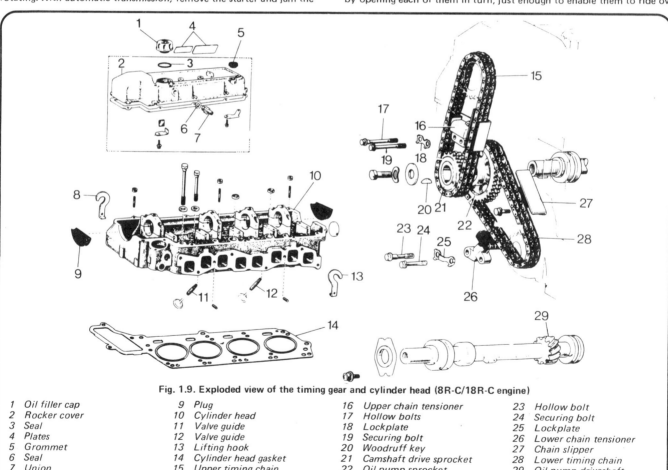

Fig. 1.9. Exploded view of the timing gear and cylinder head (8R-C/18R-C engine)

1 Oil filler cap	9 Plug	16 Upper chain tensioner	23 Hollow bolt
2 Rocker cover	10 Cylinder head	17 Hollow bolts	24 Securing bolt
3 Seal	11 Valve guide	18 Lockplate	25 Lockplate
4 Plates	12 Valve guide	19 Securing bolt	26 Lower chain tensioner
5 Grommet	13 Lifting hook	20 Woodruff key	27 Chain slipper
6 Seal	14 Cylinder head gasket	21 Camshaft drive sprocket	28 Lower timing chain
7 Union	15 Upper timing chain	22 Oil pump sprocket	29 Oil pump driveshaft
8 Lifting hook			

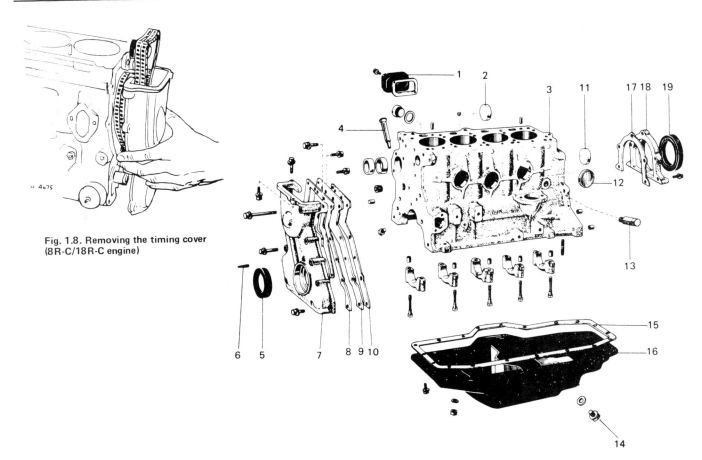

Fig. 1.8. Removing the timing cover
(8R-C/18R-C engine)

Fig. 1.10. Exploded view of cylinder block components (8R-C/18R-C engine)

1 Side cover	6 Timing index pointer	11 Core plug	16 Sump
2 Core plug	7 Timing chain cover	12 Core plug	17 Rear oil seal retainer gasket
3 Cylinder block	8 Gasket	13 Cylinder block drain plug	18 Engine rear oil seal retainer
4 Dipstick guide	9 Engine front plate	14 Sump drain plug	19 Crankshaft rear oil seal
5 Timing cover oil seal	10 Gasket	15 Sump gasket	

the lands of the piston body.

34 In order to prevent the lower rings dropping into an empty groove higher up the piston as they are removed, it is helpful to use two or three narrow strips of tin or old feeler blades inserted behind the ring at equidistant points and then to employ a twisting motion to slide the ring from the piston.

35 To remove a gudgeon pin, first extract the circlips (one at each end) and then immerse the piston in hot water at a temperature of approximately 140°F (60°C). After a few minutes, the gudgeon pin will be able to be pushed out of the piston and connecting rod with finger pressure only.

36 Mark each gudgeon pin as it is removed with the piston sequence number (use masking tape) so that it can be refitted in its original location.

Crankshaft and main bearings

37 Unbolt and remove the crankshaft rear oil seal retainer.

38 Mark each of the main bearing caps with quick-drying paint (numbered 1 to 5 from the front of the engine), making sure that the caps are also marked as to which way round they are to be refitted. Some caps are marked with a triangle, the apex of which points to the front of the engine and they are already numbered but check before removing them.

39 Unscrew the main bearing cap bolts and remove the caps complete with shell bearings. The centre main bearings shells incorporate thrust flanges.

40 Lift the crankshaft from the crankcase. If the bearing shells are to be used again, identify them in respect of exact original location.

16 Lubrication system, oil pump and filter (Hi-Lux 8R-C and 18R-C engines)

1 Pressure for the engine lubrication system is generated by a trochoid type oil pump located within the crankcase. The pump is driven by an extension of the distributor driveshaft which in turn is meshed with a short driveshaft driven by chain from the crankshaft sprocket. The pressurised oil is first passed through an externally mounted cartridge type disposable oil filter then to all the bearings and friction surfaces of the engine. Oil pressure also actuates the timing chain tensioners. Excess oil pressure is controlled by an integral relief valve within the oil pump.

2 The oil pump normally has a very long life but in the event of low oil pressure (not due to worn bearings or lack of oil) being observed, remove the pump for servicing. If the engine is in position in the vehicle, the sump will first have to be removed as described in Section 15, paragraph 18.

3 To service the pump, first remove it from the crankcase (three screws) by pulling it straight down.

4 Unscrew and remove the pressure relief valve.

5 Unbolt the oil strainer.

6 Separate the cover from the pump body (three screws).

7 Withdraw the oil pump shaft and driven rotor from the body.

8 Examine all components for wear and using feeler blades, carry out the following clearance tests.

9 Measure the clearance between the tips of the drive and driven rotors. This should be between 0.004 and 0.006 in (0.10 and 0.15 mm). If the clearance exceeds 0.008 in (0.2 mm) renew both rotors as a matched set.

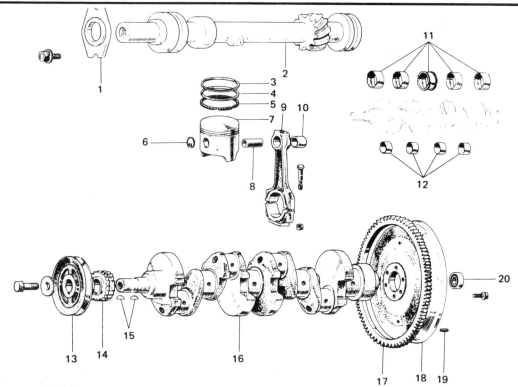

Fig. 1.11. Exploded view of crankshaft and oil pump driveshaft components (8R-C/18R-C engine)

1 Oil pump driveshaft thrust plate	6 Circlip	11 Main shell bearings	16 Crankshaft
2 Oil pump driveshaft	7 Piston	12 Connecting rod bearings shells	17 Starter ring gear
3 Top compression ring	8 Gudgeon pin	13 Crankshaft pulley	18 Flywheel
4 Second compression ring	9 Connecting rod	14 Crankshaft sprocket	19 Dowel pin
5 Oil control ring	10 Small end bush	15 Woodruff keys	20 Input shaft spigot bearing

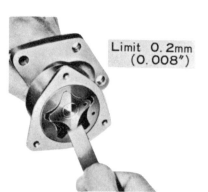

Fig. 1.12. Checking oil pump rotor tip clearance (8R-C/18R-C engine)

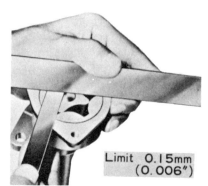

Fig. 1.13. Checking the end-clearance of the oil pump rotors (8R-C/18R-C engine)

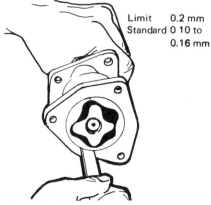

Fig. 1.14. Checking oil pump driven rotor to body clearance (8R-C/18R-C engine)

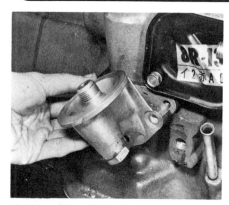

16.14 Removing oil filter base (Hi-Lux 8R-C/18R-C)

16.15 Installing oil filter cartridge (Hi-Lux 8R-C/18R-C)

17.3 Oil filler cap 'O' ring seal (Hi-Lux 8R-C/18R-C)

10 Using a straight-edge, check the clearance between the end faces of the rotors and the body flange. This should be between 0.001 and 0.003 in (0.03 and 0.07 mm). If the clearance exceeds 0.006 in (0.15 mm) the rotors should be renewed and possibly the pump body as well to achieve the correct tolerance.

11 Finally, measure the clearance between the outer rotor and the inside of the pump body. The clearance should be between 0.004 and 0.006 in (0.10 and 0.16 mm). If the clearance exceeds 0.008 in (0.2 mm), renew the pump body.

12 Check the free length of the pressure relief valve. If it exceeds 1.85 in (47.0 mm) renew it.

13 Reassembly and installation are reversals of removal and dismantling but ensure that the rotor punch marks will face downwards when the pump is installed. Always use a new gasket when fitting the pump to the crankcase.

14 The cartridge type oil filter incorporates a non-return valve to prevent oil draining from the filter when the engine is switched off. A bypass valve is built into the filter base which opens in the event of the filter clogging to ensure normal (though unfiltered) oil circulation (photo).

15 The filter cartridge can be removed using a chain wrench or special filter strap. Fit the filter using hand pressure only. Always use the new gasket supplied and smear its sealing face with grease before tightening (photo).

17 Crankcase ventilation system (Hi-Lux 8R-C and 18R-C engines)

1   As part of the emission control system (described in Chapter 3), a positive crankcase ventilation system (PCV) is fitted.

2   Every 12,000 miles (20,000 km) check the operation of the PCV valve. To do this, let the engine run at idling speed and first pinch and then release the hose just above the valve at the same time, listening for the sound of the valve seating. If it does not close or is sluggish in operation, remove it and wash it thoroughly in fuel. Other indications of a faulty PCV valve are evidence of oil in the air cleaner and rough idling.

3   Every 24,000 miles (38,000 km) renew the PCV valve and at all times make sure that the connecting hoses and clips are secure and in good condition, also the 'O'-ring seal of the oil filler cap (photo).

18 Engine dismantling (Hi-Lux 20R)

Cylinder head, rocker shafts and camshaft

1   *If the engine is in the vehicle,* disconnect the battery negative lead, all hoses, controls and leads from the rocker cover, cylinder head and carburettor. Disconnect the exhaust downpipe, drain the cooling system and remove the air cleaner and the distributor.

2   Unbolt and remove the rocker cover.

3   Remove the rubber semi-circular plug from the front edge of the cylinder head and remove the bolt which is exposed.

4   Withdraw the distributor drive gear but leave the cam sprocket and chain undisturbed.

5   Remove the chain cover bolt from directly in front of the cam sprocket. **This must be done before attempting to remove the cylinder head bolts.**

6   Unscrew the cylinder head bolts in the sequence shown in Fig. 1.23 to prevent warpage of the cylinder head.

7   Withdraw the rocker assembly which is secured by the cylinder head bolts (now removed). The rocker pillars are located on dowels and both ends of the assembly must be turned upwards simultaneously to prevent distortion.

8   Push the cam sprocket forward off its mounting flange and remove the cylinder head by lifting both ends simultaneously as this too is located on dowels.

9   If this work is being carried out while the engine is still in the vehicle, once the cylinder head is removed, it is recommended that the engine oil is drained and discarded as it will have become contaminated with coolant. Failure to observe this recommendation may result in corroded crankcase components.

10 Remove the EGR valve from the cylinder head.

11 Unbolt and remove the inlet manifold complete with carburettor.

12 Remove the thermostatic valve.

13 Unbolt and remove the exhaust manifold heat insulator.

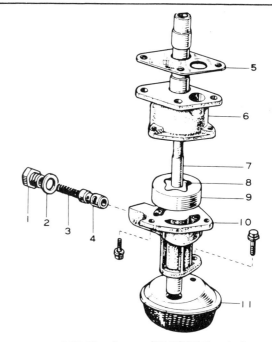

Fig. 1.15. The oil pump (8R-C/18R-C engine)

1 Pressure relief valve plug	6 Oil pump body
2 Gasket	7 Shaft
3 Spring	8 Inner rotor
4 Valve	9 Outer (driven) rotor
5 Gasket	10 Oil pump cover
	11 Filter

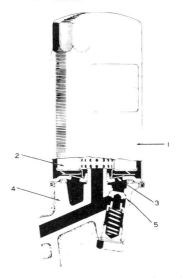
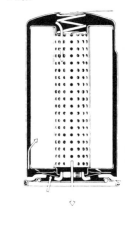

Fig. 1.16. The oil filter (8R-C/18R-C engine)

1 Filter casing	4 Oil filter base
2 Element	5 Bypass valve
3 Non-return valve	

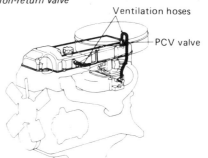

Fig. 1.17. Crankcase ventilation system (8R-C/18R-C engine)

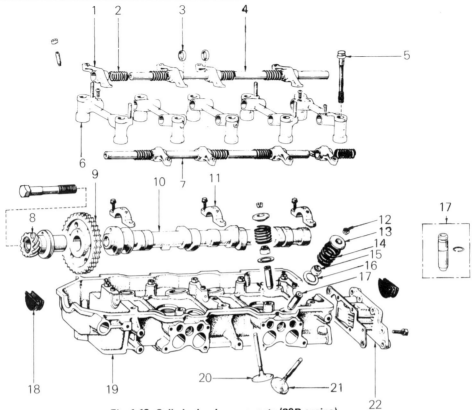

Fig. 1.18. Cylinder head components (20R engine)

1	Rocker arm	6	Rocker pillar	11	Camshaft bearing cap	17	Valve guide
2	Spring	7	Rocker shaft (exhaust side)	12	Split collets	18	Semi-circular plug
3	Spacer	8	Distributor drivegear	13	Valve spring retainer	19	Cylinder head
4	Rocker shaft	9	Cam sprocket	14	Valve spring	20	Inlet valve
5	Cylinder head bolt	10	Camshaft	15	Valve stem oil seal	21	Exhaust valve
				16	Seat	22	Rear cover (EGR cooler)

Fig. 1.19. Removing rocker cover (20R engine)

Fig. 1.20. Removing cam gear/sprocket bolt (20R engine)

Fig. 1.21. Removing distributor drive gear (20R engine)

Fig. 1.22. Removing chain cover bolt (20R engine)

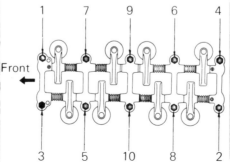

Fig. 1.23. Cylinder head bolt removal sequence diagram (20R engine)

Fig. 1.24. Removing the EGR valve (20R engine)

Fig. 1.25. Removing the thermostatic valve (20R engine)

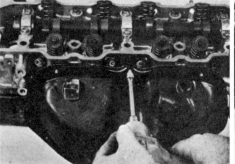

Fig. 1.26. Removing exhaust manifold heat insulator (20R engine)

Fig. 1.27. Removing exhaust manifold (20R engine)

Fig. 1.28. Measuring camshaft endfloat (20R engine)

Fig. 1.29. Removing a valve stem oil seal and spring seat (20R engine)

Fig. 1.31. Removing water pump bypass tube bolts (20R engine)

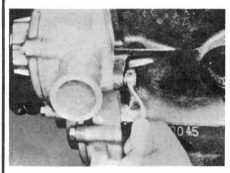

Fig. 1.32. Removing timing cover rear face bolt (20R engine)

Fig. 1.33. Removing timing cover front face bolt (20R engine)

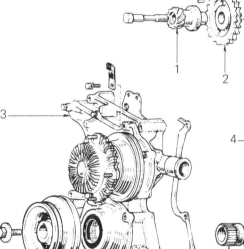

Fig. 1.30. Exploded view of the timing chain and gears (20R engine)

1	Distributor drive gear	6	Crankshaft pulley
2	Cam sprocket	7	Oil pump drive gear
3	Timing cover	8	Crankshaft sprocket
4	Chain guide	9	Chain tensioner
5	Chain guide	10	Timing chain

14 With the heat insulator removed, unbolt and withdraw the exhaust manifold.
15 Unscrew and remove the spark plugs.
16 At this stage, measure the camshaft endfloat, using a feeler blade. If it exceeds 0.0098 in (0.25 mm), the complete cylinder head assembly will have to be renewed.
17 Remove the camshaft bearing caps and lift out the camshaft.
18 Remove the valve from the cylinder head using a valve spring compressor. Extract the split collets and withdraw the valve spring retainers, the springs, valves, seals and seats.
19 Keep the valves in their original fitted sequence. A piece of card with holes numbered 1 to 8 punched in it is useful for this purpose.

Timing gears and chain

20 *If the engine is still in position in the vehicle,* then the cylinder head must first be removed as described in paragraphs 1 to 9 of this Section. Unbolt and remove the sump. Remove the radiator. Slacken and remove the drivebelts, the air pump and disconnect the alternator link from the timing chain cover.
21 Remove the crankshaft pulley bolt and draw off the pulley using a suitable extractor.
22 Remove the two bolts which secure the water bypass tube.
23 Remove the single bolt which is located at the rear of the timing cover on the left-hand side of the crankcase.
24 Unscrew and remove the timing cover bolts as indicated in Fig. 1.33. The bolts which are not arrowed secure the oil pump in position.
25 Remove the timing cover by tapping it off with a plastic faced mallet.
26 Remove the timing chain together with the camshaft sprocket.
27 If necessary, the crankshaft sprocket and oil pump drive can be withdrawn using a two-legged extractor.
28 Unbolt and remove the chain tensioner and guides.

Pistons and connecting rods

29 *If the engine is still in position in the vehicle,* remove the cylinder head and sump as previously described.

30 Carefully scrape away any wear ridge from around the tops of the cylinder bores. If this is not done, the piston rings or piston itself could be damaged during removal from the top of the cylinder block.
31 Unbolt and remove the oil pick-up tube/filter screen.
32 Repeat the operations described in Section 15, paragraphs 31 and 32.

Piston rings and gudgeon pins

33 Repeat the dismantling operations described in Section 15, paragraphs 33 to 36 inclusive.

Crankshaft and main bearings

34 Repeat the dismantling operation described in Section 15, paragraphs 37 to 40.

19 Lubrication system, oil pump and filter (Hi-Lux 20R engine)

1 Pressure for the engine lubrication system is generated by a gear type oil pump located on the front end of the crankshaft just behind the crankshaft pulley.
2 The pressurised oil is first passed through an externally mounted, cartridge type disposable oil filter, then to all the bearings and friction surfaces of the engine. Excess oil pressure is controlled by an integral relief valve within the pump. Oil pressure also actuates the timing chain tensioner.
3 The oil pump normally has a very long life but in the event of low oil pressure being observed (not due to worn bearings or low oil level), remove the oil pump for servicing.
4 Remove the sump and oil pick-up tube/strainer.
5 Remove the drivebelts from the crankshaft pulley and withdraw the pulley.
6 Unbolt and remove the oil pump. Pick out the sealing 'O'-ring.
7 Withdraw the pump drive gear from the front end of the crankshaft.
8 Unscrew and remove the relief valve components and then withdraw the inner and outer gears from the pump body.
9 Clean and inspect all components for damage.

Fig. 1.34. Removing oil pump drive gear (20R engine) Puller arrowed

Fig. 1.36. Removing oil pump bolts (20R engine)

Fig. 1.35. Cylinder block and crankcase components (20R engine)

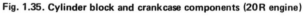
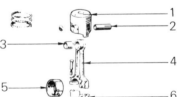

1 Piston
2 Gudgeon pin
3 Small end bush
4 Connecting rod
5 Big-end bearing shells
6 Big-end cap
7 Cylinder block
8 Rear oil seal retainer
9 Rear oil seal
10 Timing cover oil seal

11 Main bearing shell
12 Thrust washers
13 Crankshaft pulley
14 Oil pump drive gear
15 Crankshaft sprocket
16 Crankshaft
17 Clutch input shaft pilot bearing
18 Flywheel
19 Flywheel bolt

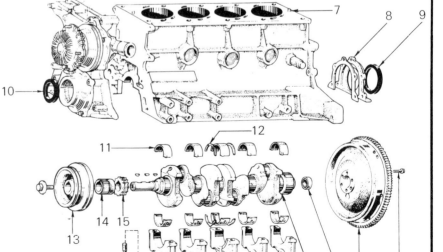

10 Using a feeler blade, check the clearance between the outer gear and the pump body. This should not exceed 0.008 in (0.2 mm) otherwise renew one or both components.

11 Now measure the tip to crescent clearance between the gears which should not exceed 0.012 in (0.3 mm), when all gears are in position within the pump body.

12 Using a straightedge and a feeler blade, measure the gear endfloat within the pump body. This should not exceed 0.0059 in (0.15 mm).

13 Renew the oil seal if there have been signs of oil seepage from this part of the engine. Drive out the defective seal with a piece of tubing and install the new one in the same way.

14 Reassembly is a reversal of dismantling but make sure that the punch marks are visible when the gears are installed.

15 When installing the oil pump, renew the 'O'-ring and apply jointing compound to the threads of the uppermost securing bolt.

20 Crankcase ventilation system (Hi-Lux 20R engine)

1 Refer to Section 17, but note the difference in layout of the system on this engine (Fig. 1.41).

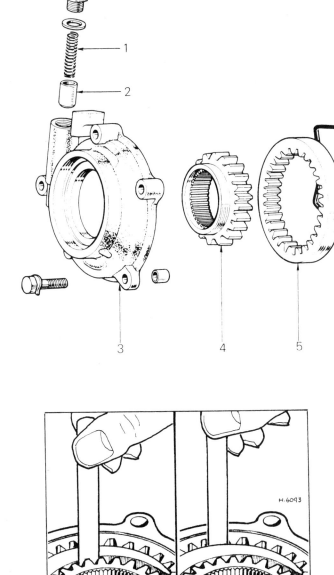

21 Engine dismantling (Hi-Lux and Hi-Ace 12R)

Rocker gear

1 Unbolt and remove the rocker cover.

2 Unscrew the rocker pillar securing bolts and nuts half a turn at a time, working on the end ones first, then the inner ones.

3 Remove the rocker assembly from the cylinder head.

4 If the rocker gear must be dismantled, extract the lock screws, shaft end clips and springs and withdraw the rocker arms and compression springs and support pillars, taking great care to keep them in their original sequence for reassembly.

5 Withdraw the push-rods, keeping them in order. One way to do this is to insert them into a piece of card which has been punched with holes numbering 1 to 8.

Cylinder head and tappets (cam followers)

6 If the engine is still in the vehicle, drain the cooling system, and then disconnect all hoses, leads and control wires from the cylinder head and carburettor.

7 Disconnect the exhaust downpipe from the manifold.

8 Unscrew and remove the cylinder head bolts working in a diagonally opposite sequence from the end ones inwards.

9 Remove the cylinder head and gasket. If the head is stuck, do not prise it by inserting a lever in the gasket joint, but strike it all round using a hammer and a block of hardwood as an insulator.

10 Unbolt and remove the tappet chamber cover and its gasket.

11 Withdraw the tappets and retain them in a tray with divisions numbered so that the tappets can be refitted in their original locations. Remove the valves as described in Section 15, paragraphs 15 to 20 inclusive.

Fig. 1.37. Exploded view of the oil pump (20R engine)

1 Spring
2 Relief valve
3 Pump
4 Inner gear
5 Outer gear
6 'O' ring
7 Crankshaft drive gear

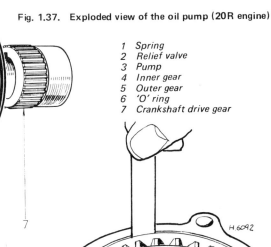

Fig. 1.38. Checking oil pump outer gear to body clearance (20R engine)

Fig. 1.39. Measuring tip to crescent clearance (20R oil pump)

Fig. 1.40. Measuring oil pump gear endfloat (20R engine)

34

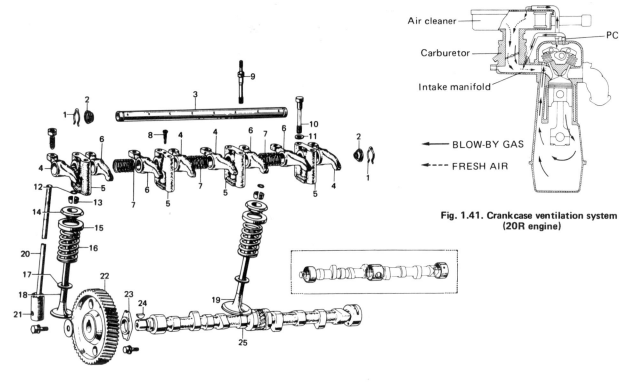

Fig. 1.41. Crankcase ventilation system
(20R engine)

Air cleaner
PCV valve
Carburetor
Intake manifold

← BLOW-BY GAS
←--- FRESH AIR

Fig. 1.42. Camshaft and valve gear (12R engine)

1	Spring clip	7	Spring	13	Split collets	19	Inlet valve
2	Coil spring	8	Locking screw	14	Valve spring retainer	20	Pushrod
3	Rocker shaft	9	Rocker cover bolt	15	Oil shield	21	Tappet (cam follower)
4	Rocker arm	10	Rocker pillar bolt	16	Valve spring	22	Timing gear
5	Rocker pillar	11	Washer	17	Washer	23	Thrust plate
6	Rocker arm	12	'O' ring	18	Exhaust valve	24	Woodruff key
						25	Camshaft

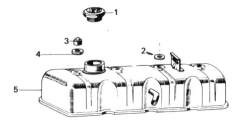

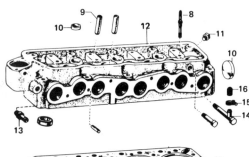
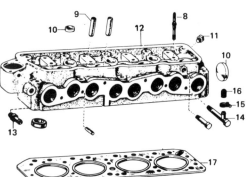

Fig. 1.43. Cylinder head components (12R engine)

1	Oil filler cap	10	Core plug
2	Washer	11	Plug
3	Nut	12	Cylinder head
4	Grommet	13	Water bypass union
5	Rocker cover	14	Heater hose union
6	Gasket	15	Hose clip
7	Cylinder head bolt	16	Plug
8	Rocker cover bolt	17	Gasket
9	Valve guide		

Oil pump and timing gear

12 If the engine is in the vehicle, disconnect the battery negative lead, drain the cooling system, remove the cylinder head, drain the engine oil and remove the sump. Remove the radiator.

13 Release the oil pipe unions and then unbolt the oil pump and remove it complete with pick-up filter.

14 Withdraw the crankshaft pulley and then unbolt and remove the timing cover and gasket.

15 At this stage, check the timing gear backlash. Ideally, a dial gauge should be used but a feeler blade can be used as an alternative, by inserting it between the teeth of the two gears. If the backlash exceeds 0.012 in (0.3 mm) renew the gears.

16 Turn the crankshaft until the first camshaft thrust plate bolt comes into view in the hole in the camshaft gear wheel. Unscrew and remove the bolt. Continue turning until the second bolt comes into view and then unscrew and remove it.

17 Pull the camshaft/gearwheel assembly forward taking great care not to damage the bearings as the lobes of the cam pass through them. Do not attempt to unscrew the camshaft gear wheel securing bolt while the gearwheel is meshed with the gear on the crankshaft. The teeth of the gear wheels will be damaged if this is done. Once the camshaft has been removed, it can be gripped securely in the jaws of a vice, adequately protected with pieces of aluminium sheet and the gearwheel bolt unscrewed.

18 If necessary, the timing gear oil nozzle and end plate and gasket can be removed.

Piston/connecting rod assemblies

19 Repeat the operations described in Section 15, paragraphs 30 to 32.

Piston rings and gudgeon pins

20 Repeat the operations described in Section 15, paragraphs 33 to 36 inclusive.

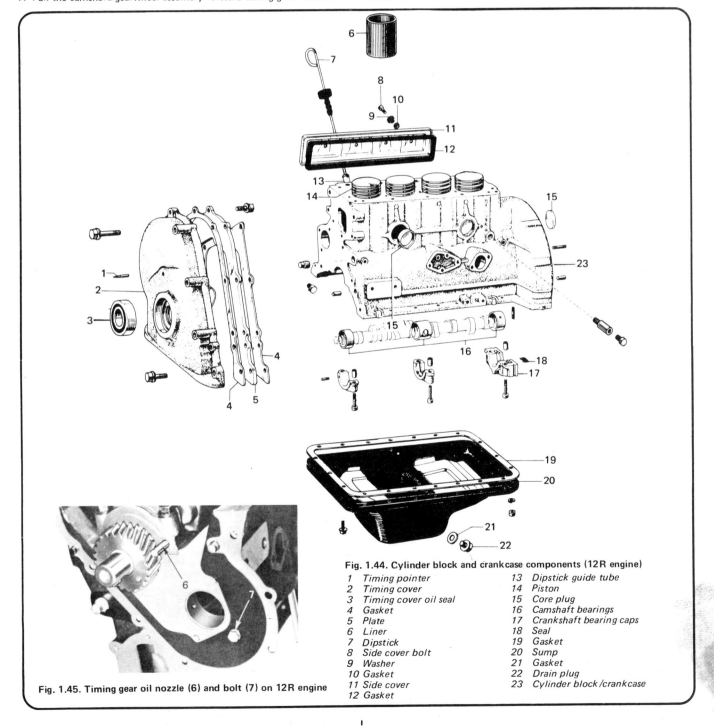

Fig. 1.45. Timing gear oil nozzle (6) and bolt (7) on 12R engine

Fig. 1.44. Cylinder block and crankcase components (12R engine)

1	Timing pointer	13	Dipstick guide tube
2	Timing cover	14	Piston
3	Timing cover oil seal	15	Core plug
4	Gasket	16	Camshaft bearings
5	Plate	17	Crankshaft bearing caps
6	Liner	18	Seal
7	Dipstick	19	Gasket
8	Side cover bolt	20	Sump
9	Washer	21	Gasket
10	Gasket	22	Drain plug
11	Side cover	23	Cylinder block/crankcase
12	Gasket		

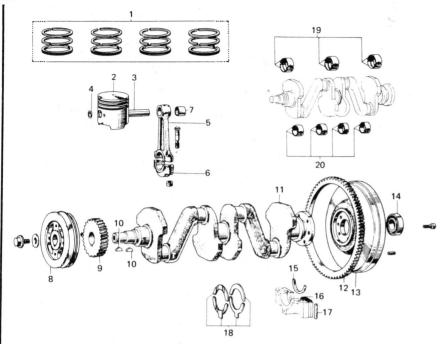

Fig. 1.46. Crankshaft and piston components
(12R engine)

1 Piston rings
2 Piston
3 Gudgeon pin
4 Circlip
5 Connecting rod
6 Big-end cap
7 Small end bush
8 Crankshaft pulley
9 Timing gear
10 Woodruff keys
11 Crankshaft
12 Starter ring gear
13 Flywheel
14 Input shaft bearing
15 Rear oil seal
16 Seal
17 Sealing strip
18 Thrust washers
19 Crankshaft main bearing shells
20 Big-end bearing shells

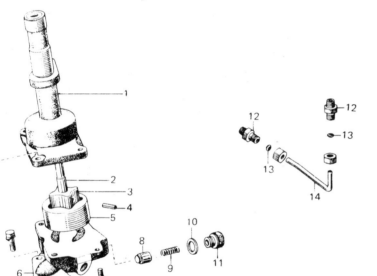

22.10 Oil filter drain plug and centre bolt
(Hi-Lux 12R)

Fig. 1.47. Exploded view of the oil pump
(12R engine)

1 Body
2 Shaft
3 Inner rotor
4 Pin
5 Outer rotor
6 Cover
7 Strainer
8 Pressure relief valve
9 Spring
10 Gasket
11 Plug
12 Unions
13 Olives
14 Oil connecting pipe

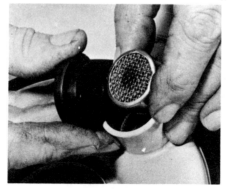

23.2a Crankcase vent filter in air cleaner
body (Hi-Lux 12R)

23.2b Removing crankcase vent valve
(Hi-Lux 12R)

Crankshaft and main bearings
21 The crankshaft main bearing caps should be numbered 1 to 3 from the front of the engine. If this is not the case, dot punch them before removal. Each cap has a directional arrow marked on it which points to the front of the engine.
22 Unscrew and remove the main bearing cap bolts and remove the caps complete with bearing shells. Note that semi-circular thrust washers are located either side of the centre bearing, and that the rear bearing cap incorporates the half section oil seal.
23 Lift the crankshaft from the crankcase and mark the exact location of all the bearing shells, if it is intended to refit them and not to renew them.

22 Lubrication system, oil pump and filter (Hi-Lux and Hi-Ace 12R engine)

1 The oil pump is of trochoid type, and it is driven from the lower extension of the distributor driveshaft which itself is driven from a gear on the camshaft.
2 The pressurised oil is first passed through an externally mounted oil filter and then to all the bearings and friction surfaces of the engine. Excess oil pressure is controlled by an integral relief valve within the pump.
3 The oil pump normally has a very long life, but in the event of low oil pressure being observed (not due to worn bearings or low oil level), remove the oil pump for servicing. Remove the pump as described in Section 15, paragraphs 12 and 13.
4 Unbolt and remove the pick-up strainer, then unbolt the two halves of the oil pump body.
5 Extract the driveshaft/rotor assembly and the driven rotor.
6 Unscrew the plug and extract the components of the relief valve.
7 Clean and examine all components for scoring or damage.
8 Measure the clearance between (i) the tips of the inner and outer rotors, (ii) the outer rotor and the pump body and (iii) the rotor endfloat, all as illustrated in Figs. 1.12, 1.13 and 1.14, except that the maximum clearances should be:

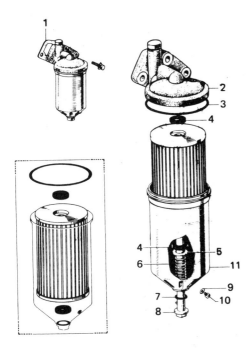

Fig. 1.48. Oil filter (12R engine)

1 Gasket
2 Filter base
3 'O' ring
4 Seal
5 Washer
6 Spring
7 'O' ring
8 Centre bolt
9 Washer
10 Plug
11 Filter bowl

Fig. 1.49. Method of extracting main bearing shell with crankshaft still in position

(i) Rotor tip clearance - 0.008 in (0.2 mm)
(ii) Outer rotor to body clearance - 0.008 in (0.2 mm)
(iii) Rotor endfloat - 0.006 in (0.15 mm)

9 Reassembly is a reversal of dismantling, but on completion it is recommended that the pump is primed with oil. To do this, immerse it in engine oil and turn the pump driveshaft until oil comes out of the discharge hole.
10 The oil filter is externally mounted. To renew the internal paper element, first remove the drain plug at the base of the filter bowl and let the oil drain into a container (photo).
11 Unscrew and remove the centre bolt, and withdraw the filter assembly.
12 Tip out the oil filter element and discard it. Wipe out the interior of the filter bowl and insert the new element.
13 Renew the centre bolt and filter base rubber seals using the new ones supplied, and then refit and tighten the centre bolt.

23 Crankcase ventilation system (Hi-Lux and Hi-Ace 12R engines)

1 This is an essential part of the emission control system as it directs oil and fuel fumes from the crankcase into the intake manifold where they are burned during the normal combustion cycle.
2 Maintenance comprises keeping the connecting hoses in good condition and occasionally cleaning the filter in the air cleaner casing to which the crankcase breather hose is connected (photo). If any doubt exists regarding the operation of the Positive Crankcase Ventilation Valve (PCV), start the engine and let it idle. Pinch the hose just above the PCV valve. If it can be heard to click it is operating correctly. If no noise is detected, remove the valve and clean it in solvent. If it still does not operate correctly, renew it (photo).

24 Examination and renovation - general

With the engine stripped down and all parts thoroughly cleaned, it is now time to examine everything for wear. The following items should be checked and where necessary renewed or renovated as described in the following Sections. The information applies to all engine types except where specifically annotated.

25 Crankshaft and main bearings - examination and renovation

1 Examine the crankpin and journal surfaces for signs of scoring or scratches. Check the ovality of the crankpins at several different positions using a micrometer. If more than 0.001 in (0.0254 mm) out of round, the crankshaft will have to be reground. Check the journals in the same manner.

2 If it is necessary to regrind the crankshaft and to fit new bearings, your Toyota dealer will decide how much to grind off and he will supply new oversize shell bearings to suit. Details of regrinding tolerances and bearings are given in the Specifications.

3 If the crankshaft is in good condition and requires no attention, it is always worthwhile renewing the bearing shells at the time of a major overhaul. Renew them with ones of the same size as the originals.

4 It is possible to renew the main bearing shells while the engine is still in the car. To do this, remove the sump and then detach one of the main bearing caps.

5 Renew the bearing shell in the cap.

6 Insert a flat-headed screw in the crankshaft journal oil hole and carefully turn the crankshaft. The head of the screw will push the second bearing shell from its seat. Install the new shell in a similar way, having first oiled it liberally.

7 The crankshaft endfloat should be checked now by temporarily installing all the main bearing caps and shells and tightening to the specified torque.

8 Push and pull the crankshaft in both longitudinal directions and measure the total endfloat with feeler blades or a dial gauge. The endfloat should be as shown in the Specifications according to engine type.

9 Where the endfloat is incorrect, renew the centre main bearing shells which incorporate the thrust washers (8R-C/18R-C engines). On 20R and 12R engines, semi-circular thrust washers are used (photo).

When carrying out the operations just described, make sure that the arrows on the main bearing caps point towards the front of the engine and that the caps and shells are located in their original sequence.

10 The clutch input shaft spigot bearing is located in the centre of the rear mounting flange of the crankshaft. Renew if worn, greasing its reverse side before fitting.

26 Connecting rods and bearings - examination and renovation

1 Big-end bearing failure is indicated by a knocking from within the crankcase and a slight drop in oil pressure.

2 Examine the big-end bearing surfaces for pitting and scoring. Renew the shells in accordance with the sizes specified in the Specifications. Where the crankshaft has been reground, the correct undersize big-end shell bearings will be supplied by the repairer (photo).

3 Install each connecting rod to its respective crankpin and, using a feeler blade, check the side-float. If this exceeds the tolerance specified in the Specifications, the connecting rod will have to be renewed.

4 Check each small-end bush for wear or scoring. Each gudgeon pin should be a push fit in its bush using thumb pressure only. If the bush is worn it will have to be pressed out and a new one fitted, ensuring that the oil holes of the bush and the connecting rod coincide. As the bush will have to be reamed after fitting, this is probably a job best left to your Toyota dealer.

27 Cylinder bores - examination and renovation

1 The cylinder bores must be examined for taper, ovality, scoring and scratches. Start by carefully examining the top of the cylinder bores. If they are at all worn a very slight ridge will be found on the thrust side.

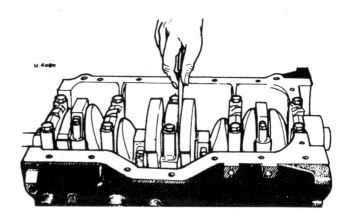
Fig. 1.50. Checking crankshaft endfloat

This marks the top of the piston ring travel. The owner will have a good indication of the bore wear prior to dismantling the engine, or removing the cylinder head. Excessive oil consumption accompanied by blue smoke from the exhaust is a sure sign of worn cylinder bores and piston rings.

2 Measure the bore diameter just under the ridge with a micrometer and compare it with the diameter at the bottom of the bore, which is not subject to wear. If the difference between the two measurements is more than 0.008 in (0.2 mm) then it will be necessary to fit special pistons and rings or to have the cylinder rebored and fit oversize pistons. If no micrometer is available remove the rings from a piston and place the piston in each bore in turn about halfway down the bore. If an 0.0012 in (0.03 mm) feeler gauge slid between the piston and cylinder wall requires less than a pull of between 2.2 and 5.5 lbs (1.0 and 2.5 kg) to withdraw it, using a spring balance, then remedial action must be taken. Oversize pistons are available as listed in the Specifications.

3 These are accurately machined to just below the indicated measurements so as to provide correct running clearances in bores taken out to the exact oversize dimensions.

4 If the bores are slightly worn, but not so badly worn as to justify reboring them, then special oil control rings and pistons can be fitted which will restore compression and stop the engine burning oil. Several different types are available and the manufacturer's instructions concerning their fitting must be followed closely.

5 If new pistons or rings are being fitted and the bores have not been reground, it is essential to slightly roughen the hard glaze on the sides of the bores with fine glass paper so the new piston rings will have a chance to bed in properly.

6 If the cylinder bores have been bored out beyond the limit so that the maximum oversize pistons available cannot be fitted, then sleeves can be supplied which after installation and boring will accept standard sized pistons. This again is a job for your Toyota dealer or motor engineering works.

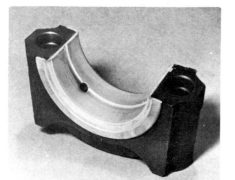
25.9 Centre main bearing shell incorporating thrust washers (Hi-Lux 8R-C/18R-C)

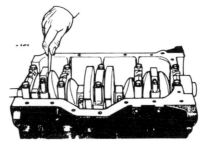
Fig. 1.51. Checking a connecting rod for side-float

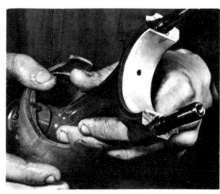
26.2 Big-end bearing shell and oil hole (8R-C/18R-C engine)

28 Pistons and piston rings - examination and renovation

1   If the original pistons are to be refitted, carefully remove the piston rings as described in Section 15, paragraphs 33 and 34.
2   Clean the grooves and rings free from carbon, taking care not to scratch the aluminium surfaces of the pistons.
3   If new rings are to be fitted, then order the top compression ring to be stepped to prevent it impinging on the 'wear ring' which will almost certainly have been formed at the top of the cylinder bore.
4   Before fitting the rings to the pistons, push each ring in turn down to the bottom of its normal travel (use an inverted piston to do this so that the ring is kept square in its bore) and then measure the piston ring end gap. This should be as shown in the Specifications. If the gap is incorrect, carefully grind the ends of the ring.
5   Now test each ring in its groove for side clearance using a feeler blade. If the clearance exceeds that specified, renew the piston as it will be the groove that is worn.
6   Where necessary a piston ring which is slightly tight in its groove may be rubbed down holding it perfectly squarely on an oilstone or a sheet of fine emery cloth laid on a piece of plate glass. Excessive tightness can only be rectified by having the grooves machined out.
7   The gudgeon pin should be a push fit into the piston when heated in water to a temperature of 140°F (60°C). If it appears slack, then both the piston and gudgeon pin should be renewed.

29 Camshaft and camshaft bearings - examination and renovation

8R-C and 18R-C engines
1   Check the camshaft journals for scoring or grooves and then measure each journal at several different points to detect any taper or out of round. If the difference between the measurements exceeds 0.0004 in (0.01 mm). the camshaft must be reground and oversize shell bearings fitted. This is a job for your Toyota dealer.
2   With the camshaft installed on the cylinder head complete with shell bearings and caps and the cap bolts tightened as specified, check the camshaft endfloat. This should be as shown in the Specifications, otherwise renew the bearing shell which incorporates the thrust flanges.
3   Firstly examine the camshaft lobes for scoring or wear. Using a micrometer, check the overall lengths of the inlet and exhaust valve cam lobes and compare them with those specified. If they are worn, renew the camshaft complete.

20R engines
4   Check the camshaft for wear, as described in the preceding paragraphs but where bearing running clearance or camshaft endfloat is found to be excessive, then the cylinder head will have to be renewed as the camshaft runs directly in bearings and caps which are in-line machined, no detachable bearing shells are fitted.

12R engines
5   Check the camshaft and bearings as described in paragraphs 1, 2 and 3, and compare the measurements with those listed in the Specifications.
6   If the endfloat is excessive, renew the camshaft thrust plate.
7   If the bearings are worn, have your Toyota dealer renew them as special tools are required to remove and install them and they must be in-line reamed after installation

30 Timing components - examination and renovation

1   Examine all the sprocket teeth for wear or 'hooked' appearance and renew if necessary.

8R-C, 18R-C and 20R engines
2   Wash the timing chains thoroughly in paraffin and examine for wear or stretch. If the chain is supported at both ends so that the rollers are vertical then a worn chain will take on a deeply bowed appearance while an unworn one will dip slightly at its centre point.
3   Check the chain tensioners and guides for wear and renew the slippers if they are cut or grooved.

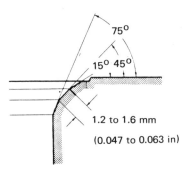

Fig. 1.52. Valve seat cutting sequence (20R engine)
Cutting sequence
1 – 15° cutter
2 – 75° cutter
3 – 45° cutter

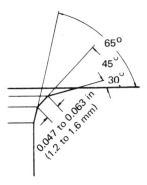

Fig. 1.53. Valve seat cutting diagram (8R-C, 18R-C, 12R engines)
Cutting sequence
1 – 30° cutter
2 – 65° cutter
3 – 45° cutter

31 Cylinder head and valves - examination, renovation and decarbonising

1   Examine the heads of the valves for pitting and burning, especially the heads of the exhaust valves. The valve seatings should be examined at the same time. If the pitting on valve and seat is very slight the marks can be removed by grinding the seats and valves together with coarse, and then fine, valve grinding paste.
2   Where bad pitting has occurred to the valve seats, it will be necessary to recut them and fit new valves. The valve seats are re-cut using specially angled cutters and in the sequence given in the relevant illustration. This will ensure that the burned material is removed and the seat is refinished to the correct angle. In practice, it is very seldom that the seats are so badly worn that they require renewal. Normally, it is the valve that is too badly worn to use again, and the owner can easily purchase a new set of valves and match them to the seats by grinding.
3   Valve grinding is carried out as follows: Smear a trace of coarse carborundum paste on the seat face and apply a suction grinder tool to the valve head. With a semi-rotary motion, grind the valve head to its seat, lifting the valve occasionally to redistribute the grinding paste. When a dull matt, even surface finish is produced on both the valve seat and the valve, wipe off the paste and repeat the process with fine carborundum paste, lifting and turning the valve to distribute the paste as before. A light spring placed under the valve head will greatly ease this operation. When a smooth unbroken ring of light grey matt finish is produced, on both valve and valve seat faces, the grinding operation is complete.

4   Scrape away all carbon from the valve head and the valve stem. Carefully clean away every trace of grinding compound, taking care to leave none in the ports or in the valve guides. Clean the valves and valve seats with a paraffin soaked rag then with a dry rag, and finally, if an air line is available, blow the valves, valve guides and valve ports clean.

5   Wear in the valve guides can best be checked by inserting a new valve and testing for rocking movement in all directions. The clearance between the guide and valve stem must not exceed that shown in the Specifications.

6   To renew a valve guide on *8R-C and 18R-C engines,* drive it out from the valve spring side into the combustion chamber of the cylinder head. Drive in the new guide by reversing the process but the guide must protrude by 0.63 in (16.0 mm) on the valve spring side of the head.

7   Finally, ream the new guide to provide a clearance between valve stem and guide of between 0.0010 and 0.0022 in (0.025 and 0.055 mm) for inlet valves and between 0.0014 and 0.0030 in (0.035 and 0.075 mm) for exhaust valves.

8   To renew a valve guide on *20R engines,* drive it out into the combustion chamber using a suitable drift: New guides are supplied complete with a circlip. Drive in the new guide from the camshaft bearing side of the cylinder head until the circlip contacts the head. Ream the guide using an 0.315 in (8.0 mm) diameter reamer.

9   To renew a valve guide on *12R engines,* drive out the old guide into the combustion chamber, and install the new one from the top face of the cylinder head until it projects as shown in Fig. 1.55.

10 Ream the guide to give an internal diameter of between 0.315 and 0.316 in (8.01 and 8.03 mm).

11 The valve springs should be compared with their specified free lengths. Renew the springs as a set if they differ from their specified new length or have been in operation for more than 24,000 miles (38,000 km). Always renew the valve stem oil seals.

12 With the cylinder head removed, use a blunt scraper to remove all trace of carbon and deposits from the combustion spaces and ports. Scrape the cylinder head free from scale or old pieces of gasket or jointing compound. Clean the cylinder head by washing it in paraffin, and take particular care to pull a piece of rag through the ports and cylinder head bolt holes. Any grit remaining in these recesses may well drop onto the gasket or cylinder block mating surface as the cylinder head is lowered in position and could lead to a gasket leak after reassembly is complete.

13 With the cylinder head clean, test for distortion if a history of coolant leakage has been apparent. Carry out this test using a straight edge and feeler gauges or a piece of plate glass. If the surface shows any warping in excess of 0.002 in (0.05 mm), then the cylinder head will have to be resurfaced which is a job for a specialist engineering company. The depth of the cylinder head must never be reduced by more than 0.008 in (0.2 mm) when resurfacing it.

14 Clean the piston and top of the cylinder bores. If the pistons are still in the block, then it is essential that great care is taken to ensure that no carbon gets into the cylinder bores, as this could scratch the cylinder walls or cause damage to the piston and rings. To ensure this does not happen, first turn the crankshaft so that two of the pistons are at the top of their bores. Stuff a rag into the other two bores or seal them off with paper and masking tape. The waterways should also be covered with small pieces of masking tape to prevent particles of

carbon entering the cooling system and damaging the water pump.

15 Press a little grease into the gap between the cylinder walls and the two **pist**ons which are to be worked on. With a blunt scraper carefully scrape away the carbon from the piston crown, taking great care not to scratch the aluminium. Also scrape away the carbon from the surrounding lip of the cylinder wall. When all carbon has been removed, scrape away the grease which will now be contaminated with carbon particles, taking care not to press any into the bores. To assist prevention of carbon build-up the piston crown can be polished with a metal polish. Remove the rags or masking tape from the other two cylinders and turn the crankshaft so that the two pistons which were at the bottom are now at the top. Place a rag or mask the cylinders which have been decarbonised and proceed as just described.

32 Oil pump driveshaft (Hi-Lux 8R-C and 18R-C engines) - servicing

1   The oil pump driveshaft bearings should be inspected for scoring or scratches.

2   The correct running clearances between the shaft and bearings is between 0.0010 and 0.0026 in (0.025 and 0.066 mm). Where the clearance exceeds 0.003 in (0.08 mm) the bearing must be renewed.

3   To do this, remove the plug at the back of the rear shaft bearing and using a suitably stepped mandrel, drive out the old and drive in the new bearings.

4   Check the endfloat of the driveshaft; this must not exceed 0.012 in (0.03 mm). If it does, renew the thrust plate to provide the standard endfloat of between 0.002 and 0.005 in (0.06 and 0.13 mm).

33 Flywheel - servicing

1   Examine the clutch driven plate contact surface of the flywheel for scoring or grooves. If they are deep or tiny cracks are visible, it is recommended that the flywheel is renewed.

2   Check the starter ring gear for cracks or chipped teeth.

3   On *8R-C, 18R-C and 12R engines,* remove the ring and fit a new one or preferably exchange the flywheel for a reconditioned unit.

4   Either split the ring with a cold chisel after making a cut with a hacksaw blade between two teeth, or use a soft headed hammer (not steel) to knock the ring off, striking it evenly and alternately at equally spaced points. Take great care not to damage the flywheel during this process.

5   Heat the new ring in either an electric oven to about 200°C (392°F) or immerse in a pan of boiling oil.

6   Hold the ring at this temperature for five minutes and then quickly fit it to the flywheel so the chamfered portion of the teeth faces the gearbox side of the flywheel.

7   The ring should be tapped gently down onto its register and left to cool naturally when the contraction of the metal on cooling will ensure that it is a secure and permanent fit. Great care must be taken not to overheat the ring (indicated by the ring turning light metallic blue) as if this happens the temper of the ring will be lost.

8   On *20R engines,* if the starter ring gear is worn, renew the flywheel complete.

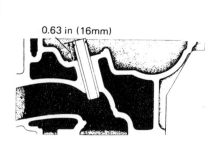

Fig. 1.54. Valve guide installation diagram (8R-C, 18R-C engines)

35.2 Installing crankshaft rear oil seal to retainer (Hi-Lux 8R-C/18R-C)

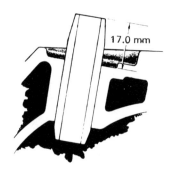

Fig. 1.55. Valve guide installation diagram (12R engine)

34 Driveplate (automatic transmission) - servicing

1 Examine the starter ring gear for worn or broken teeth; where these are evident, renew the driveplate complete.
2 Check the torque converter securing bolt holes for elongation and if apparent, renew the driveplate.

35 Oil seals - renewal

1 During a major overhaul, always discard the old oil seals and install new ones during reassembly.
2 Renew the timing cover and crankshaft rear oil seals on 8R-C, 18R-C and 12R engines. Renew the oil pump oil seal and crankshaft rear oil seal on 20R engines (photo).

36 Cylinder block - examination and renovation

1 Examine the crankcase and cylinder block for cracks especially around bolt holes and between the cylinders.
2 Probe waterways and oil galleries to ensure that they are not blocked.
3 Check the security and condition of the core plugs. To renew a core plug, first drill a hole in its centre and lever it out. If it is particularly stubborn, tap a thread in the hole and screw in a bolt, using a piece of tubing and a large washer to act as a point of leverage and extract the plug as the bolt is tightened.
4 Where the cooling system has frozen due to the use of a weak anti-freeze mixture, it is quite likely that one or more of the core plugs will have been partially dislodged from their seats by the expansion of the ice. In such an event, drive the plug fully home or better still, renew it. The engine side cover can be removed to gain access to the threaded type core plug located behind the oil pump driveshaft on 8R-C and 18R-C engines.

37 Tappets and pushrods (Hi-Ace and Hi-Lux 12R engines) - examination and renovation

1 Examine the tappets (cam followers) for pitting or scoring and renew if necessary.
2 It is rare for the tappets to be worn in their bore but if they are, oversize tappets can be fitted after the bores have been reamed out. This is a job for your Toyota dealer.
3 Check the pushrods to make sure that they are not bent or distorted. Renew if they are.

38 Engine reassembly - general

1 To ensure maximum life with minimum trouble from a rebuilt engine, not only must everything be correctly assembled but everything must be spotlessly clean, all the oilways must be clear, locking washers and spring washers must always be fitted where indicated and all bearing and other working surfaces must be thoroughly lubricated during assembly.

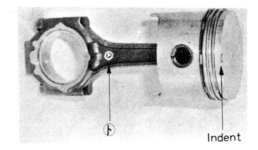

Fig. 1.56. Piston/connecting rod reconnection (8R-C/18R-C engine)

Indent

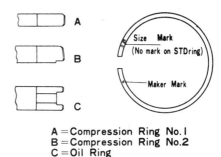

A = Compression Ring No.1
B = Compression Ring No.2
C = Oil Ring

Fig. 1.57. Piston ring fitting diagram (8R-C/18R-C engine)

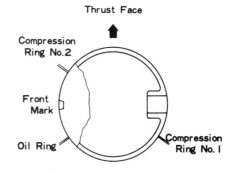

Fig. 1.58. Piston ring end gap staggering diagrams (8R-C/18R-C engines)

39.1 Installing and lubricating main bearing shells (Hi-Lux 8R-C/18R-C)

39.2 Installing crankshaft (Hi-Lux 8R-C/18R-C)

39.3 Main bearing cap directional mark and number (Hi-Lux 8R-C/18R-C)

39.4 Centre main bearing shell (Hi-Lux 8R-C/18R-C)

39.5 Tightening a main bearing bolt (Hi-Lux 8R-C/18R-C)

39.6a Crankshaft rear oil seal retainer gasket (Hi-Lux 8R-C/18R-C)

39.6b Installing crankshaft rear oil seal retainer (Hi-Lux 8R-C/18R-C)

39.10 Piston ring compressor in position (Hi-Lux 8R-C/18R-C)

39.11 Installing a big-end cap (Hi-Lux 8R-C/18R-C)

39.14 Installing the oil pump (Hi-Lux 8R-C/18R-C)

39.15 Installing engine front plate and gasket (Hi-Lux 8R-C/18R-C)

39.16a Installing oil pump driveshaft (Hi-Lux 8R-C/18R-C)

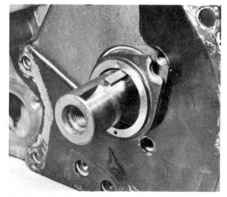

39.16b Oil driveshaft thrust plate (Hi-Lux 8R-C/18R-C)

39.17 Timing chain lower tensioner (Hi-Lux 8R-C/18R-C)

39.18 Timing chain and sprockets correctly installed (Hi-Lux 8R-C/18R-C)

2 Before assembly begins renew any bolts or studs the threads of which
are in any way damaged and whenever possible use new spring washers.
3 Apart from your normal tools, a supply of clean rags, an oil can filled
with engine oil, a supply of new assorted spring washers, a set of new
gaskets and a torque spanner, should be collected together.

39 Engine reassembly (Hi-Lux 8R-C and 18R-C)

Crankshaft and main bearings
1 Locate the main bearing shells in their crankcase recesses and lubricate them with engine oil (photo).
2 Carefully lower the crankshaft into position (photo).
3 Fit the main bearing caps complete with shell bearings, noting that
the caps (previously numbered 1 to 5) should have their arrows
pointing towards the front of the engine (photo).
4 Note that the centre bearing incorporates the thrust washers (photos).
5 Tighten the main bearing cap bolts to the specified torque (photo).
6 Bolt on the crankshaft rear oil seal retainer complete with new seal
and gasket (photos). Tighten the securing bolts to the specified torque.
Check that the crankshaft turns freely.

Pistons, rings and connecting rods
7 Assemble the piston to the connecting rod so that the marks on the
connecting rod and the piston crown are in alignment. These marks
face the front of the engine when installed.
8 Connect the two components by pushing in the gudgeon pin by
thumb pressure only (immerse the piston in hot water if necessary). Fit
new circlips, one at each end of the gudgeon pin.
9 Fit the rings to the pistons, using the same method as for removal. It
is vital that the rings are fitted in the correct order with their tapers
running the correct way. This will be achieved if the ring markings face
upwards. Stagger the piston ring gaps as indicated in Fig. 1.58.
10 Lubricate the piston rings liberally and the piston bore, fit a piston
ring compressor to the piston and place the assembly into a cylinder
bore until the ring compressor meets the block surface. Using the

handle of a hammer, tap the piston/connecting rod assembly into the
cylinder bore so that the directional mark on the piston crown is
towards the front of the engine (photo).
11 Rotate the crankshaft so that the crankpin is at the lowest point,
engage the connecting rod big-end with the crankpin and then fit the
big-end bearing cap so that the marks made prior to dismantling on the
rod and cap are adjacent and on the same side (photo).
12 Preferably renew the big-end bolts and tighten the big-end cap nuts
to the specified torque.
13 Repeat the procedure with the other three piston/connecting rod
assemblies and then check that the crankshaft turns smoothly.

Oil pump and timing gear
14 Fit the oil pump to the crankcase using a new joint gasket (photo).
15 Fit the front plate complete with new gasket (photo).
16 Insert the oil pump driveshaft and the thrust plate, tightening to the
specified torque (photos).
17 Fit the lower chain tensioner, so that the projection on the slipper
is visible when installed (photo).
18 Locate the crankshaft sprocket and the oil pump driveshaft sprocket
within the loops of their chain and fit the complete assembly to
crankshaft and oil pump driveshaft simultaneously. During this
operation, take care not to drive the sprocket onto the oil pump driveshaft with too much force or the plug at the back of the rear bearing
may be displaced. It is a nut and a distance piece. Ignore any timing
marks visible on the chain sprockets (photo).
19 Fit the timing cover gasket, sticking it in position with jointing
compound.
20 Fit the upper chain tensioner so that the projection on the slipper
is at the rear. Note that one securing bolt of each chain tensioner is
drilled with an oil hole, ensure that they are correctly located (photo).
21 Bend up the lockplate tabs to secure the tensioner bolts.
22 Fit the camshaft drive sprocket to the oil pump driveshaft and
tighten the retaining bolt to the specified torque. If the engine is in the
car, or the correct way up, use a hooked piece of wire to keep the
chain engaged with the sprocket teeth pending fitting the timing cover
and cylinder head (photo).

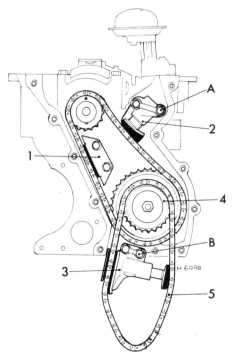

Fig. 1.59. Layout of timing gear (engine inverted) 8R-C/18R-C

1 Slipper
2 Lower chain tensioner
3 Upper timing tensioner
4 Camshaft drive sprocket
5 Upper timing chain
A and B securing bolts drilled with an oil hole

39.22 Tightening camshaft drive sprocket bolt (Hi-Lux 8R-C/18R-C)

39.20 Timing chain upper tensioner (Hi-Lux 8R-C/18R-C)

39.23 Fitting timing cover (Hi-Lux 8R-C/18R-C)

39.26 Tightening crankshaft pulley bolt (Hi-Lux 8R-C/18R-C)

39.27 Installing engine rear plate (Hi-Lux 8R-C/18R-C)

39.28 Tightening flywheel bolts (Hi-Lux 8R-C/18R-C)

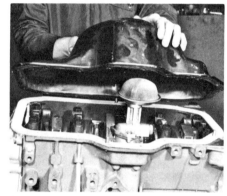
39.31 Installing the sump (Hi-Lux 8R-C/18R-C)

39.39 Cylinder head gasket correctly installed (Hi-Lux 8R-C/18R-C)

39.45 Camshaft bearing cap correctly installed (Hi-Lux 8R-C/18R-C)

39.47 Crankshaft pulley timing marks (Hi-Lux 8R-C/18R-C)

39.49 Camshaft driven sprocket correctly set for installing to camshaft (Hi-Lux 8R-C/18R-C)

39.50 Camshaft sprocket installed (Hi-Lux 8R-C/18R-C)

23 Fit the timing cover, using gasket cement on its mating faces (photo).
24 Tighten the timing cover bolts to the specified torque.
25 Fit the crankshaft pulley. A piece of tubing may be used to drive it into position.
26 Tighten the pulley securing bolt, with its washer, to the specified torque.

Flywheel (or driveplate - automatic transmission)
27 Bolt on the engine rear plate (photo).
28 Refitting either the flywheel or driveplate is a reversal of removal but tighten the securing bolts to the specified torque, and bend up the tabs of the locking plates (photo).

Sump
29 Ensure that the mating faces of the sump and crankcase are quite clean and free from old pieces of gasket.
30 Smear the crankcase flange with jointing compound and stick a new gasket into position.
31 Smear the sump flange with jointing compound and bolt it into position. Do not overtighten the sump securing bolts (photo).

Cylinder head and valves
32 Install the first valve into its respective guide, having first lubricated its stem with engine oil.
33 Fit the valve stem oil seal, plate and the double valve springs. Note that the closer coils of the spring are fitted nearer the cylinder head (photo).
34 Fit the valve spring retainer, and then compress the valve springs with a compressor and install the split collets. Gently release the compressor and check that the collets are correctly seated (photo).
35 Repeat the operations on the remaining valves making sure that each valve is returned to its original guide or, if a new valve has been fitted, into the seat into which it has been ground.
36 When all the valves have been reassembled into the cylinder head, tap the end of each valve stem using a block of hardwood and a hammer in order to settle the valve components.
37 Check that the surfaces of the cylinder head and block are scrupulously clean.
38 Smear the top of the block with a thin film of gasket cement, making sure that none runs down into the oil or water passages or the bolt holes.
39 Lay a new gasket carefully into position on the block (photo).
40 Smear the face of the cylinder head with a film of gasket cement and then lower the head straight down onto the block so that the positioning dowels engage first time. Do not slide the head about to position it as this will damage the gasket.
41 Make sure that the threads of the cylinder head bolts are clean and screw them in finger tight.

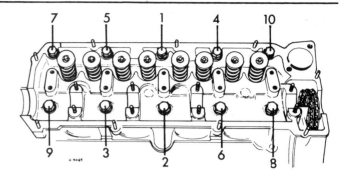

Fig. 1.60. Cylinder head bolt tightening sequence (8R-C/18R-C engines)

Fig. 1.61. Rocker shaft support pillars front facing markings

A Pillars 1 - 2 - 4 - 5 have recess on top of boss
B Pillar No. 3 has projection on top of boss

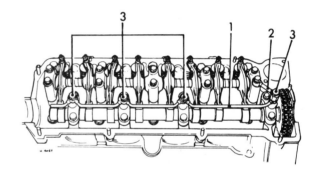

Fig. 1.62. Oil feed pipe installation (8R-C/18R-C engine)

1 Oil delivery pipe   3 Union bolts
2 Connecting pipe

39.33 Installing valve springs (Hi-Lux 8R-C/18R-C)

39.34 Valve spring retainer and collets correctly installed (Hi-Lux 8R-C/18R-C)

42 Tighten the bolts progressively (½ turn at a time) and in the sequence indicated in Fig. 1.60 to the specified torque. The timing chain should have been pulled through the aperture in the cylinder head with the hooked wire.

Camshaft and rocker gear

43 Install the camshaft lower bearing shells into their recesses on the top of the cylinder head.
44 Lubricate the bearings with engine oil and lower the camshaft into position.
45 Fit the bearing caps, complete with shell bearings. The caps should be numbered 1 to 4 (counting from the front of the engine) and the flat portion of their upper bosses must face the front (photo).
46 Tighten the camshaft bearing cap bolts to the specified torque.
47 Rotate the crankshaft by means of the pulley bolt until No. 1 piston is at TDC on its compression stroke. To ascertain this position, place a finger over No. 1 spark plug hole and feel the compression being generated. When the second (TDC) notch in the crankshaft pulley is opposite the pointer on the timing cover, the setting is correct (photo).
48 Turn the crankshaft so that the dowel pin and punch marks are uppermost. Pull the timing chain upwards with the hooked piece of wire previously used to retain it on its drive sprocket.
49 Engage the camshaft sprocket within the upper loop of the chain so that the sprocket will fit on the dowel of the camshaft mounting flange without moving, **even fractionally,** the camshaft or the crankshaft. A certain amount of repositioning of the camshaft sprocket within the chain will probably be required before exact alignment with the dowel can be achieved (photo).
50 Tighten the camshaft sprocket bolts to the specified torque (photo).
51 Install the rocker shaft assembly. If the rocker gear has been dismantled, refit the components in their original order and make sure that the rocker shaft support pillars have their front facing markings correctly set (photo).
52 Tighten the pillar bolts to the specified torque.
53 Install the oil feed pipe assembly and tighten the union bolts to the specified torque.

---

40 Valve clearances (Hi-Lux 8R-C and 18R-C engines) - adjustment

1   Adjust the valve clearances in the following manner. The clearances will have to be readjusted when the engine has been fully reassembled and run to normal operating temperature.
2   Set No. 1 piston at TDC on its compression stroke and adjust valves 1, 2, 3 and 5. The inlet valves should be adjusted to give a clearance of 0.007 in (0.18 mm) and the exhaust valves to 0.013 in (0.33 mm). Turn the adjusting screw until the feeler blade is a stiff sliding fit between the end of the screw and the end of the valve stem. Tighten the locknut without moving the adjusting screw (photo).
3   Rotate the crankshaft one complete turn so that the notch in the pulley is opposite to the TDC mark and adjust the valves 4, 6, 7 and 8. Numbering from the front of the engine, inlet valves are 2 - 3 - 6 - 7 and exhaust valves 1 - 4 - 5 - 8.
4   Install the rocker cover (photo).

41 Engine reassembly (Hi-Lux 20R)

Crankshaft and main bearings
1   Carry out the operations described in Section 39, paragraphs 1 to 6.

Pistons, rings, connecting rods, sump and flywheel
2   Carry out the operations described in Section 39, paragraphs 7 to 13.
3   Install the oil pick-up tube and screen, and the sump, using a new gasket and applying jointing compound to the covers as shown in Fig. 1.63.
4   Install the flywheel (or driveplate - automatic transmission) and tighten the bolts to the specified torque.

Timing gear, chain and cover
5   Install the chain guides and the chain tensioner.
6   Rotate the crankshaft until the Woodruff key at its front end is at its highest point (pointing upwards).
7   Engage the timing chain so that its single bright link is opposite the mark on the crankshaft sprocket.
8   Engage the camshaft sprocket within the loop of the timing chain so that the mark on the sprocket is between the two bright links on the chain.
9   Install the oil pump drive gear onto the front end of the crankshaft.
10 Install the timing cover gasket and then gently turn the camshaft sprocket in an anticlockwise direction to remove any slack from the chain.
11 Install the timing cover complete with oil pump onto the locating dowels, refit the bolts and tighten to the specified torque.
12 Install the crankshaft pulley. When tightening the retaining bolt, do not turn the crankshaft but either jam one of the crankshaft webs with a block of wood or refit the flywheel and jam the starter ring gear.

Cylinder head
13 Refer to Section 39, paragraphs 32 to 36, but note that single valve springs are used on this engine.
14 Install the camshaft and the bearing caps, in their correct sequence with arrows pointing to the front of the engine. Make sure that all the bearing surfaces are oiled before reassembly. Tighten the cap bolts to the specified torque wrench settings.
15 Install the thermostatic valve, the inlet manifold, the EGR valve, the exhaust manifold, the heat insulator to the cylinder head.
16 Make sure that the surfaces of the cylinder head and block are quite clean; smear jointing compound at the locations indicated in Fig. 1.67, and then install a new cylinder head gasket.
17 Install the cylinder head onto its locating dowels.
18 Without moving the head, rotate the camshaft so that the dowel on its flange is at the top.
19 Apply tension upwards to retain the timing chain and sprocket in engagement, and then turn the crankshaft by means of its pulley retaining bolt until the hole in the camshaft sprocket is in alignment with the flange dowel on the camshaft.
20 If the rocker gear has been dismantled, reassemble it, making sure that the arrows on the shaft support pillars face towards the front of

39.51 Installing rocker shaft (Hi-Lux 8R-C/ 18R-C)

40.2 Adjusting a valve clearance (Hi-Lux 8R-C/18R-C)

40.4 Installing rocker cover (Hi-Lux 8R-C/ 18R-C)

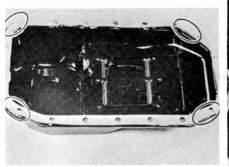

Fig. 1.63. Sump jointing application points (20R engine)

Fig. 1.64. Installing timing chain (20R engine)

Fig. 1.65. Camshaft sprocket and chain alignment marks (20R engine)

Fig. 1.66. Installing oil pump drive gear to crankshaft (20R engine)

Fig. 1.67. Cylinder block jointing compound application points (20R engine)

Fig. 1.68. Setting camshaft (20R engine)

the engine when installed.

21 Install the rocker assembly, and insert the combined cylinder head/ rocker pillar bolts, tightening them to the specified torque in the reverse sequence to that shown in Fig. 1.23.

22 Screw in the chain cover bolt. Fig. 1.22.

23 Install the camshaft sprocket/chain assembly to the dowel on the camshaft flange, and then push on the distributor drive gear and tighten the securing bolt to the specified torque.

42 Valve clearances (Hi-Lux 20R engine) - adjustment

1 Set No. 1 piston to TDC on its compression stroke. This can be ascertained by placing a finger over No. 1 spark plug hole and, as the crankshaft is turned, feeling the compression being generated. The TDC mark on the pulley should be aligned with the pointer on the timing cover.

2 Using a feeler blade, inserted between the end of the valve stem and the rocker arm adjust the clearance on the valves indicated in Figs. 1.71 and 1.72. The feeler blade should be a stiff sliding fit, otherwise release the locknut and turn the adjuster screw as necessary.

3 Now turn the crankshaft one complete turn (360°), and check and adjust the remaining valve clearances. Inlet valves clearances should be adjusted to 0.008 in (0.2 mm), exhaust valve clearances to 0.012 in (0.3 mm).

4 Install the semi-circular rubber plugs and fit the rocker cover.

43 Engine reassembly (Hi-Lux and Hi-Ace 12R)

Crankshaft and main bearings

1 Install the rear main bearing half section oil seal to its groove in the crankcase. Cut the ends of the seal flush.

2 Install the other half section oil seal into the groove in the rear main bearing cap. Cut the ends of the seal flush.

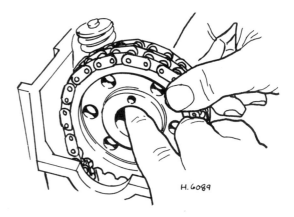

H.6089

Fig. 1.69. Installing camshaft sprocket (20R engine)

Fig. 1.70. Adjusting a valve clearance (20R engine)

48

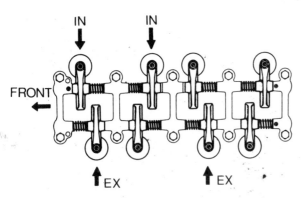

Fig. 1.71. Valves to be adjusted with crankshaft pulley mark at TDC on compression (No. 1 piston) - 20R engine

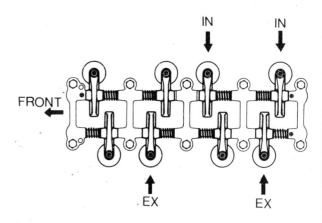

Fig. 1.72. Valves to be adjusted with crankshaft turned 360° from TDC mark - 20R engine

Fig. 1.73. Thrust washer installed to main bearing cap (12R engine)

Fig. 1.74. Installing sealing strips to crankcase grooves (12R engine)

Fig. 1.75. Timing sprocket alignment (12R engine) (engine inverted)

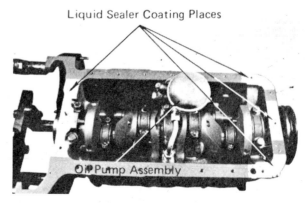

Fig. 1.76. Jointing compound application points on crankcase flange (12R engine)

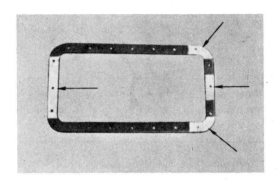

Fig. 1.77. Jointing compound application points on sump gasket
(12R engine)

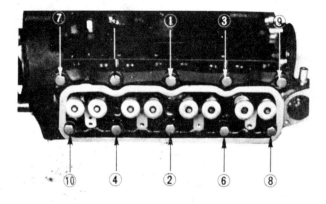

Fig. 1.78. Cylinder head bolt tightening sequence (12R engine)

3   Drive the cap packings into their recesses in the end of the block.
4   Install the main bearing shells into their crankcase seats. Oil them
liberally and install the crankshaft.
5   Insert the upper halves of the crankshaft thrust bearings. These go
either side of the centre main bearing so that the oil grooves are visible
when installed.
6   Install the main bearing caps, numbered 1 to 3 in their correct order
and with the arrows towards the front of the engine. Make sure that the
centre bearing incorporates the lower half thrust washers, again with
the oil grooves visible and with their tags engaged in the cap cut-outs.
7   Tighten the main bearing bolts to the specified torque. Check that
the crankshaft turns freely.
8   Drive the sealing strips into their crankcase grooves, having first
applied jointing compound to them.

Pistons and connecting rods
9   Repeat the operations described in Section 39, paragraphs 7 to 13.

Timing gear
10   Install the engine front plate with a new gasket.
11   Oil the camshaft bearings and install the camshaft carefully. It is
easier to carry out these operations if the engine block is inverted and in
view of this, the illustrations concerned are shown with the engine in
this upside down attitude.
12   Before pushing the camshaft fully home, turn the crankshaft so that
the key on the front of the crankshaft is vertically downwards. Push the
camshaft fully home so that when the camshaft sprocket engages with
the crankshaft sprocket, the timing marks are adjacent and in alignment
with a line drawn through the centres of both sprockets.
13   Tighten the thrust plate retaining bolts.
14   If the oil nozzle was removed, screw it into position and locate the
oil hole so that it discharges onto the timing gears. Stake the nozzle to
prevent it from moving.
15   Install the timing gear cover using a new gasket.
16   Grease the lip of the timing cover oil seal, fit the crankshaft pulley
and insert and tighten the securing bolt.

Oil pump and sump
17   Install the oil pump and oil pick-up tube into the crankcase.
18   Apply jointing compound as shown in Fig. 1.77, and then install a
new sump gasket and refit the sump.

Cylinder head and valves
19   Refer to Section 39, paragraphs 32 to 36, and repeat the operations
noting that single type valve springs are used.
20   Make sure that the mating faces of the cylinder block and head are
absolutely clean, and then place a new gasket on the cylinder block.
21   Install the cylinder head bolts and tighten to the specified torque in
two or three stages, half a turn at a time, and in the sequence shown in
Fig. 1.78.

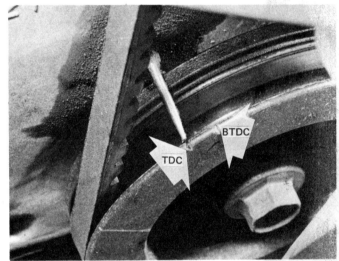

44.1 Crankshaft pulley timing marks on Hi-Lux 12R engine

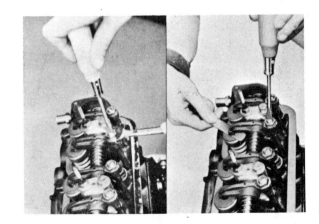

Fig. 1.79. Adjusting a valve clearance (12R engine)

45.2 Tightening a thermostat housing bolt (Hi-Lux 8R-C/18R-C)

45.3 Water pump/fan unit installed (Hi-Lux 8R-C/18R-C)

45.4 Left-hand engine mounting (Hi-Lux 8R-C/18R-C)

45.5 Installing alternator (Hi-Lux 8R-C/18R-C)

45.6 Correctly tensioned driving belt (Hi-Lux 8R-C/18R-C)

45.7 Water pump by-pass hose (Hi-Lux 8R-C/18R-C)

45.8a Location of engine rear lifting hook (Hi-Lux 8R-C/18R-C)

45.8b Location of engine front lifting hook (Hi-Lux 8R-C/18R-C)

45.9 Installing manifold complete with carburettor (Hi-Lux 8R-C/18R-C)

45.11 Location of oil pressure switch (Hi-Lux 8R-C/18R-C)

45.12a Fuel pump mounting flange gaskets and insulator

Tappets, pushrod and rocker gear
22 Oil the tappets (cam followers) and install them into their original positions.
23 Oil the pushrods and insert them in their original order.
24 Install the rocker shaft assembly, insert the pillar bolts and tighten progressively to the specified torque.
25 Fit the tappet chamber cover using a new gasket.

44 Valve clearances (Hi-Lux and Hi-Ace 12R engine) - adjustment

1 Turn the crankshaft until No. 1 piston is at TDC on its compression stroke. This can be ascertained by removing No. 1 spark plug and placing a finger over the plug hole and, as the crankshaft is turned, feeling the compression being generated. Continue turning until the TDC notch (rearmost mark in direction of pulley rotation) on the pulley is opposite the mark on the timing cover (photo).
2 Adjust the following valve clearances: Exhaust 1 and 5 and inlet 2 and 3. Turn the crankshaft one complete turn (360°) and adjust inlet 6 and 7 and exhaust 4 and 8. Inlet valves are 2 - 3 - 6 -7, and exhaust valves 1 - 4 - 5 -8 numbering the valves from the front of the engine.
3 The clearances should be (HOT):

> *Inlet*   *0.008 in (0.2 mm)*
> *Exhaust 0.014 in (0.3 mm)*

4 Insert the feeler blade between the end of the valve stem and the rocker arm. It should be a stiff sliding fit. Adjust by releasing the locknut and turning the adjuster screw in or out.
5 Install the rocker cover and gasket.

45 Engine ancillary components - refitting

1 This is largely a reversal of the removal operations but the following check list will prove a useful guide. The photographs used in this Section relate to the 8R-C series engine.
2 Install the thermostat and thermostat housing (photo).
3 Install the water pump and fan assembly (photo).
4 Bolt on the engine mounting brackets. It is a good idea, at this stage, to check the condition of the flexible mountings, and to renew them if they have deteriorated (photo).
5 Fit the alternator mounting bracket, the alternator itself and the adjustment link (photo).
6 Install the drivebelt and adjust to give a deflection of ½ in (12 mm) at the centre of the longest run of the belt (photo).
7 Fit the water pump bypass hose (photo).

8 Install the manifold assembly remembering to incorporate any engine lifting hooks (photos).
9 Refit the carburettor complete with heat insulator (photo).
10 Fit the crankcase ventilation hoses and the automatic choke heater pipes.
11 Screw in the oil pressure switch (photo).
12 Bolt on the fuel pump, making sure that the gaskets and insulator are correctly located (photos).
13 Install the distributor after reference to Chapter 4.
14 Fit the spark plugs and connect the HT leads between the distributor cap and the spark plug terminals (see Chapter 4 for sequence of fitting) (photo).
15 Insert the dipstick and connect the fuel pipe between the pump and carburettor.
16 An air pump is used in conjunction with the emission control system (8R-C engines before March 1971 only), refit it and tension the driving belt.
17 Install the clutch mechanism to the flywheel ensuring that the driven plate is centralised as described in Chapter 5.
18 The power unit is now ready for coupling to the gearbox or automatic transmission unit prior to installation of the combined assembly.

46 Engine to manual gearbox - reconnection

1 This is a reversal of separation described in Section 11.

47 Engine to automatic transmission - reconnection

1 This is a reversal of separation described in Section 12, but observe the following points.
2 Check that the two projections on the torque converter key with the slots in the transmission fluid pump impeller, particularly if the torque converter has been partially withdrawn during dismantling operations.
3 Make sure that the driveplate is bolted to the torque converter with the marks made prior to dismantling in alignment.
4 Tighten all bolts to the specified torque, and check the security of the transmission drain plug.

45.12b Installing the fuel pump

45.14 Ignition leads reconnected (Hi-Lux 12R)

48 Engine (Hi-Lux) - installation complete with automatic transmission

1   Locate slings or chains round the engine and support the weight of the combined unit on suitable lifting tackle. Where a fixed hoist is being used, raise the power unit and roll the car under it.
2   Lower the unit into the engine compartment, ensuring that nothing fouls during the operation.
3   With the front engine mountings roughly aligned, jack-up the transmission so that the rear crossmember and mounting can be installed. Remove the jack.
4   With the hoist still supporting the weight of the engine, the engine/transmission can be moved fractionally so that the front mountings can be aligned and bolted up.
5   Refit the propeller shaft, making sure that the rear driving flanges have their marks (made before dismantling) in alignment.
6   Reconnect the handbrake linkage.
7   Refit the fluid filler tube to the transmission, making sure that the 'O'-ring seals are correctly located.
8   Reconnect the speedometer drive.
9   Reconnect the speed selector mechanism.
10 Reconnect the exhaust pipe.
11 Refit the radiator.
12 Reconnect the transmission fluid cooler lines.
13 Reconnect all leads, controls and hoses to the engine and transmission.
14 Refill the engine with oil.
15 Refill the transmission with the correct grade and quantity of fluid.
16 Refill the cooling system.

50.1 Installing the engine (Hi-Lux 12R)

49 Engine (Hi-Lux) - installation, having left automatic transmission in vehicle

1   With a hoist and slings attached to the engine, lower it into the engine compartment and move it rearward to mate with the torque converter housing.
2   Reconnection of the engine to the automatic transmission is as described in Section 46, but if the tool described in Section 7, paragraph 6 has been used, remember to remove it.
3   Reconnect the engine front mountings and then remove the hoist.
4   Reconnect the throttle to transmission kick-down rod.
5   Install the radiator and reconnect the transmission fluid cooler lines.
6   Reconnect the exhaust pipe.
7   Reconnect all leads, controls and hoses to the engine and transmission.
8   Refill the engine with oil.
9   Refill the cooling system.

50 Engine (Hi-Lux) - installation complete with manual gearbox

1   Using the hoist and slings, lower the combined engine/gearbox at an angle into the engine compartment (photo).
2   Jack-up the rear of the gearbox and connect the rear mounting and crossmember.
3   Reconnect the engine front mountings and then remove the hoist.
4   Reconnect the propeller shaft and the gearshift lever.
5   Reconnect the speedometer cable.
6   Reconnect the handbrake linkage.
7   Reconnect the exhaust pipe.
8   Reconnect the clutch operating cylinder and pushrod.
9   Reverse the operations described in Section 5, paragraphs 2 to 14.

51 Engine (Hi-Lux) - installation (manual gearbox to be fitted later)

1   Reverse the removal operations as described in Section 5.
2   Refer to Chapter 6 for gearbox installation operations.

52 Engine (Hi-Ace) - installation complete with gearbox

1   Position the engine/gearbox under the vehicle and then using the method applied to remove it, raise it up into the engine compartment and while supporting its weight, reconnect the front and rear mountings.
2   Reconnect the exhaust pipe.
3   Reconnect the LT and HT ignition leads.
4   Reconnect the leads to the starter motor, oil pressure switch and water temperature transmitter.
5   Reconnect the accelerator cable and choke cable to the carburettor.
6   Reconnect the heater hoses.
7   Reconnect the fuel pipe to the fuel pump.
8   Refit the air cleaner.
9   Install the radiator from beneath the vehicle and reconnect the upper and lower hoses.
10 Reconnect the speedometer cable to the gearbox.
11 Reconnect the reversing lamp switch leads.
12 Reconnect the gearshift control rods and levers.
13 Refit the propeller shaft.
14 Refit the clutch operating cylinder and check the clutch pedal adjustment.
15 Refill the engine with the correct quantity and grade of oil.
16 Refill the cooling system.
17 Reconnect the battery.

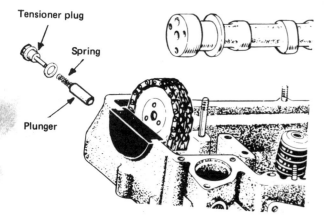

Fig. 1.80. Camshaft chain tensioner on very late type 18R-C engine

53 Engine (Hi-Ace) - installation (gearbox to be fitted later)

1   Position the engine under the vehicle and then using the method which was applied to remove it, raise it up into the engine compartment and reconnect the mountings.
2   Install the gearbox as described in Chapter 6, Section 4.
3   Carry out the operations described in the preceding Section, paragraphs 2 to 17 inclusive.

54 Starting up after major overhaul

1   Start the engine and check for oil or water leaks. None should be apparent, if new gaskets have been used throughout and the specified torque wrench settings adhered to.
2   Where an air conditioning system is installed, have the system professionally recharged with refrigerant gas.
3   Run the vehicle until normal operating temperature is reached and check the following:

a) Carburettor and emission control settings (Chapter 3).
b) Ignition timing (with a stroboscope) Chapter 4.
c) Check the valve clearances using the HOT clearances given in the Specifications provided the engine is at normal operating temperature.
d) Recheck and top up all oil levels.
e) Carry out the following work on cast-iron cylinder heads when the engine is hot but on alloy cylinder heads when the engine is cold. Check the torque of the cylinder head bolts (unscrew each bolt a quarter-turn and retighten to specified figure and in correct sequence). Check them again after 500 miles (800 km). On late model 18 R-C engines, the camshaft must first be removed before the cylinder head bolts can be retorqued. Take great care when doing this so that the chain tensioner plunger does not eject into the chain case. In order to obviate this, unscrew and remove the chain tensioner plug and spring first.

4   If a number of new internal components have been fitted to the engine, restrict engine and roadspeeds for the first few hundred miles.

55 Fault diagnosis - engine

Symptom	Reason/s
Engine will not turn over when starter switch is operated	Flat battery. Bad battery connections. Bad connections at solenoid switch and/or starter motor. Starter motor jammed. Defective solenoid. Starter motor defective.
Engine turns over normally but fails to start	No spark at plugs. No fuel reaching engine. Too much fuel reaching the engine (flooding)
Engine starts but runs unevenly and misfires	Ignition and/or fuel system faults. Incorrect valve clearances. Burnt out valves. Worn out piston rings.
Lack of power	Ignition and/or fuel system faults. Incorrect valve clearances Burnt out valves. Worn out piston rings.
Excessive oil consumption	Oil leaks from crankshaft rear oil seal, timing cover gasket and oil seal, rocker cover gasket, oil filter gasket, sump gasket sump plug washer. Worn piston rings or cylinder bores resulting in oil being burnt by engine. Worn valve guides and/or defective valve stem seals.
Excessive mechanical noise from engine	Wrong valve to rocker clearances. Worn crankshaft bearings. Worn cylinders (piston slap). Slack or worn timing chain and sprockets or gears.
Poor idling	Leak in inlet manifold gasket. Perforated or leaking PCV connecting pipe. Perforated or leaking brake servo pipe.

Note: When investigating starting and uneven running faults, do not be tempted into snap diagnosis. Start from the beginning of the check procedure and follow it through. It will take less time in the long run. Poor performance from an engine in terms of power and economy is not normally diagnosed quickly. In any event, the ignition and fuel systems must be checked first before assuming any further investigation needs to be made.

In addition to the foregoing, reference should also be made to the fault finding chart for emission control equipment which is to be found at the end of Chapter 3. Such a fault can have an immediate effect upon engine performance.

Chapter 2 Cooling system

Contents

Specifications

System type	Radiator, belt driven water pump and thermostat

Coolant capacity

8R-C, 18R-C engines	13¼ Imp. pints, 9 US qts., 7.5 litres
12R engine	12½ Imp. pints, 7¼ US qts., 7 litres
20R engine	14 Imp. pints, 8.5 US qts., 8 litres

Radiator pressure cap rating	12.8 lb/in^2 (0.9 kg/cm^2)

Thermostat

Type	Wax pellet
Opens	177 to 182°F (80.5 to 83.5°C)
Fully open	203°F (95°C)

1 General description

1 The cooling systems of all four engine types are similar although, as shown in the illustrations, the coolant circuit varies slightly.

2 The cooling system comprises the radiator, top and bottom water hoses, water pump, cylinder head and block water jackets, radiator cap with pressure relief valve and flow and return heater hoses. Later models are fitted with a coolant reservoir (expansion tank). The thermostat is located in a recess at the front of the cylinder head. The principle of the system is, that cold water in the bottom of the radiator circulates upwards through the lower radiator hose to the water pump, where the pump impeller pushes the water round the cylinder block and head, through the various cast-in passages, to cool the cylinder bores, combustion surfaces and valve seats. When sufficient heat has been absorbed by the cooling water, and the engine has reached an efficient working temperature, the water moves from the cylinder head past the now open thermostat into the top radiator hose and into the radiator header tank.

3 The water then travels down the radiator tubes where it is rapidly cooled by the in-rush of air when the vehicle is in forward motion. A four bladed fan, mounted on the water pump pulley, assists this cooling action. The water, now cooled, reaches the bottom of the radiator and the cycle is repeated.

4 When the engine is cold the thermostat remains closed until the coolant reaches a pre-determined temperature (see Specifications). This assists rapid warming-up.

5 On all models except those fitted with the 12-R engine, the fan is of variable speed type having its central hub of fluid coupling design (photo). At high engine speeds, the charge of silicone oil within the casing is thrown outwards by centrifugal force causing the disengagement of the fan so that it free-wheels and does not absorb any engine power. As the engine speed drops to a pre-determined level, the fluid coupling is re-engaged and the fan resumes its rotation.

The heater is supplied with hot water from the engine cooling system and a water temperature transmitter unit and gauge are fitted.

2 Cooling system - draining

1   With the car on level ground drain the system as follows:

2   If the engine is cold remove the filler cap from the radiator by turning the cap anti-clockwise. If the engine is hot, having just been run, then turn the filler cap very slightly until the pressure in the system has had time to disperse. Use a rag over the cap to protect your hand from escaping steam. If, with the engine very hot, the cap is released suddenly, the drop in pressure can result in the water boiling. With the pressure released the cap can be removed.

3   If anti-freeze is in the radiator drain it into a clean bucket or bowl for re-use.

4   Place the heater control in the 'HOT' position and unscrew the radiator drain plug and the one on the left-hand side of the cylinder block.

3 Cooling system - flushing

1   After some time the radiator and waterways in the engine may become restricted or even blocked with scale or sediment which reduces the efficiency of the cooling system. When this condition occurs or the coolant appears rusty or dark in colour the system should be flushed. In severe cases reverse flushing may be required as described later.

2   Place the heater controls to the 'HOT' position and unscrew fully the radiator and cylinder block drain taps.

3   Remove the radiator filler cap and place a hose in the filler neck. Allow water to run through the system until it emerges from both drain taps quite clean. **Do not flush a hot engine with cold water.**

4   In severe cases of contamination of the coolant or in the system, reverse flush by first removing the radiator cap and disconnecting the lower radiator hose at the radiator outlet pipe.

5   Remove the top hose at the radiator connection end and remove the radiator as described in Section 6.

6   Invert the radiator and place a hose in the bottom outlet pipe. Continue flushing until clean water issues from the radiator top tank.

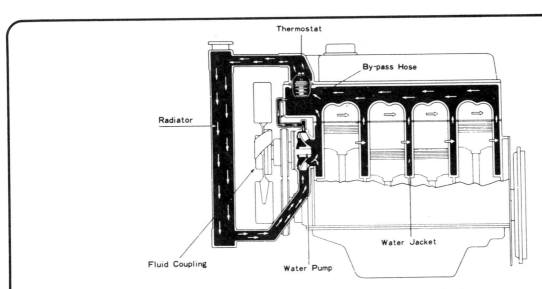

Fig. 2.1. Cooling system (8R-C, 18R-C, 12R series engines)

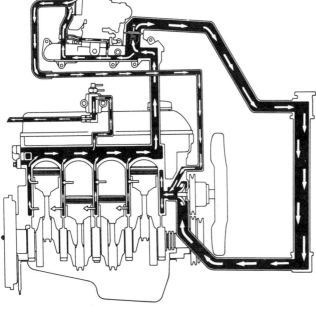

Fig. 2.2. Cooling system (20R engine)

1.5 Fan/fluid coupling assembly on 8R-C and 18R-C series engine

4 Cooling system - filling

Vehicles without a coolant reservoir/expansion tank
1 Place the heater control to 'HOT' and check that the radiator and cylinder block taps are closed.
2 Pour coolant slowly into the radiator filler neck until it is 1 in (25 mm) below the filler neck. Refit the cap.

Vehicles with a coolant reservoir/expansion tank
3 Place the heater control in the 'HOT' position and check that the radiator and cylinder block taps are closed. Pour coolant slowly into the radiator filler neck until it is full to the brim.
4 Run the engine at idling speed and watch the level of coolant at the filler neck drop, continuing to top up until the level no longer falls. Switch off the engine and refit the radiator pressure cap.
5 Remove the cap from the radiator reservoir tank and fill to the 'FULL' level with similar coolant.
6 Refit the reservoir cap.

5 Antifreeze and corrosion inhibiting mixtures

1 It is recommended that the system is filled with an antifreeze mixture where climatic conditions warrant its use. The cooling system should be drained, flushed and refilled every Autumn. The use of antifreeze solutions for periods of longer than a year is likely to cause damage and encourage the formation of rust and scale, due to the corrosion inhibitors gradually losing their efficiency. If the use of an antifreeze mixture is not necessary because of favourable climatic conditions, never use ordinary water but always fill the system with a corrosion inhibiting mixture of a recommended brand.
2 Before adding antifreeze to the system, check all hose connections and check the tightness of the cylinder head bolts as such solutions are searching. The cooling system should be drained and refilled with clean water as previously explained, before adding antifreeze.
3 The quantity of antifreeze which should be used for various levels of protection is given in the table below, expressed as a percentage of the system capacity.

Antifreeze volume	Protection to		Safe pump circulation	
25%	−26°C	(−15°F)	−12°C	(10°F)
30%	−33°C	(−28°F)	−16°C	(3°F)
35%	−39°C	(−38°F)	−20°C	(−4°F)

4 Where the cooling system contains an antifreeze or corrosion inhibiting solution any topping-up should be done with a solution made up in similar proportions to the original in order to avoid dilution.

6.4 Removing radiator (Hi-Lux)

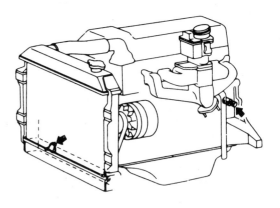
Fig. 2.3. Cooling system drain plugs

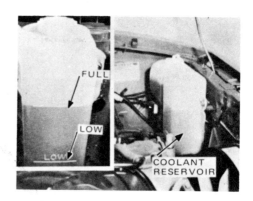
Fig. 2.4. Coolant reservoir tank and markings

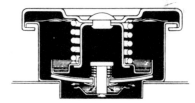
Vacuum valve operation

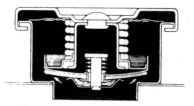
Pressure regulating valve operation

Fig. 2.5. Sectional views of radiator pressure cap

6 Radiator - removal, inspection and refitting

Hi-Lux
1 Drain the engine coolant.
2 Remove the lower shield to gain access to the bottom hose clamps. Remove the fan shroud.
3 Disconnect the top and bottom radiator hoses.
4 Unbolt the radiator and lift it from the engine compartment (photo).
5 *On vehicles equipped with automatic transmission,* before the radiator can be removed, the oil cooler hoses will first have to be disconnected from the bottom of the unit.
6 *On vehicles equipped with an air conditioning system,* the condenser is mounted in front of the radiator and this must not be disconnected or damaged during the radiator removal operations.
7 Radiator repair is best left to a specialist but minor leaks may be temporarily rectified with a proprietary sealant.
8 With the radiator removed, brush accumulations of flies and leaves from the fins and examine and renew, if necessary, any hoses or clips which have deteriorated.
9 The radiator can be flushed as described in Section 3.
10 Check the pressure rating of the radiator cap and have its operation tested by a service station.

Hi-Ace
11 To remove the radiator from the vehicles, drain the coolant and disconnect the radiator top and bottom hoses.
12 Unbolt the radiator and withdraw it downwards from the engine compartment. Make sure that there is sufficient clearance for this to be done by jacking up the front of the vehicle or placing it over an inspection pit.

7 Thermostat - removal, testing and refitting

1 A faulty thermostat can cause overheating or prolong the engine warming-up period. It can also affect the performance of the heater.
2 Drain off enough coolant through the radiator drain tap so that the coolant level is below the thermostat housing joint face. An indication that the correct level has been reached is when the cooling tubes are exposed when viewed through the radiator filler cap.
3 Unscrew and remove the two retaining bolts and withdraw the thermostat cover sufficiently to permit the thermostat to be removed

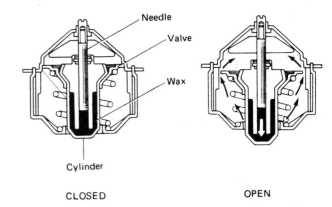

CLOSED   OPEN

Fig. 2.6. Operational diagrams of the thermostat

from its seat in the cylinder head.
4 To test whether the unit is serviceable, suspend the thermostat by a piece of string in a pan of water being heated. Using a thermometer, and referring to the opening and closing temperature in Specifications, its operation may be checked. The thermostat should be renewed if it is stuck open or closed or it fails to operate at the specified temperature. The operation of a thermostat is not instantaneous and sufficient time must be allowed for movement during testing. Never refit a faulty unit - leave it out if no replacement is available immediately.
5 Refitting the thermostat is a reversal of the removal procedure. Ensure the mating faces of the housing are clean. Use a new gasket with jointing compound. The word 'TOP' which appears on the thermostat face must be visible from above.

8 Water pump - removal and refitting

1 Drain the cooling system.
2 Remove the radiator.
3 Slacken the alternator mountings and remove the adjustment strap. Push the alternator in towards the engine and remove the driving belt.
4 On vehicles equipped with an air conditioning system, remove the driving belt in a similar manner to that described for the alternator/

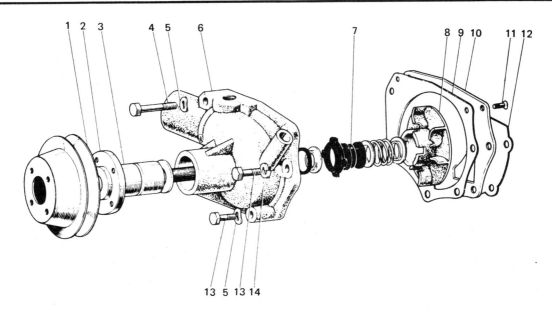

Fig. 2.7. Exploded view of water pump (12R engine)

1 Pulley	4 Bolt	7 Seal assembly	11 Screw
2 Pulley mounting flange	5 Lockwasher	8 Impeller	12 Gasket
3 Water pump bearing	6 Pump body	9 Gasket	13 Bolts
		10 Plate	14 Lockwasher

water pump drive belt.
5   Remove the fan from the fluid coupling assembly according to type.
6   Disconnect the water pump by-pass hose and the heater hose.
Unscrew and remove the water pump securing bolts and lift the pump
and fan assembly from the front face of the cylinder block.
7   Refitting is a reversal of removal but always use a new gasket and
check that pieces of old gasket are not adhering to the mating faces
of either the pump or the cylinder block.
8   Adjust the drivebelt tension as described in Section 10.

9   Water pump (12R engine) - overhaul

1   Withdraw the pulley mounting flange using a suitable extractor.
2   Remove the plate from the rear face of the water pump.
3   Withdraw the impeller using a suitable extractor.
4   Remove the seal assembly.
5   Press the water pump bearing assembly out of the pump body so
that it emerges from the pulley side of the pump. It is recommended
that the pump body is heated in boiling water before attempting to
press out the bearing.
6   Reassembly is a reversal of dismantling but observe the following.
7   Heat the pump body before pressing in the bearing and ensure that
the end of the bearing is flush with the pulley side of the pump body.
Always apply pressure to the bearing casing, never to the end of the
bearing shaft.
8   Coat the seal assembly with silicone grease before fitting it.
9   Press the impeller onto the shaft so that a clearance exists between
the impeller and the water pump body of between 0.012 and 0.030 in
(0.3 and 0.7 mm).
10 Use a new gasket when installing the rear plate.

10 Water pump (8R-C and 18R-C engine) - overhaul

1   Remove the fan coupling assembly.
2   Remove the impeller using an extractor or by pressing the bearing
shaft from it.
3   Remove the seal assembly.
4   Heat the water pump body in boiling water and press the bearing
assembly from it.
5   Extract the screws and remove the fluid coupling case.
6   Press the bearing shaft out of the fluid coupling bearing sub-assembly.
7   Reassembly is a reversal of dismantling, but heat the body before
installing the bearing assembly and apply pressure only to the bearing
casing, never to the end of the bearing shaft. Make sure that the end
of the bearing casing is flush with the water pump body.
8   When installing the fluid coupling/pulley assembly, make sure that
the end face of the bearing shaft is 1.2 in (30.0 mm) below the front
face of the coupling. Use a depth gauge to measure this.
9   When installing the water pump cover, make sure that the drain
hole is at the bottom.

11 Water pump (20R engine) - overhaul

1   Overhaul of this type of water pump is not recommended and any
fault should be rectified by renewal of the pump after the fan, fluid
coupling and pulley have first been removed for installation on the
new pump.

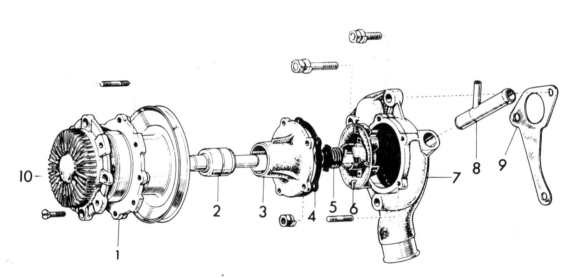

Fig. 2.8. Exploded view of water pump (8R-C and 18R-C series engines)

1   Fan fluid coupling
2   Shaft/bearing assembly
3   Cover
4   Cover gasket
5   Seal assembly
6   Impeller
7   Body
8   Union
9   Gasket
10 Fluid coupling case

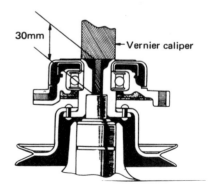

Fig. 2.9. Pulley/fluid coupling installation diagram (8R-C and 18R-C engines)

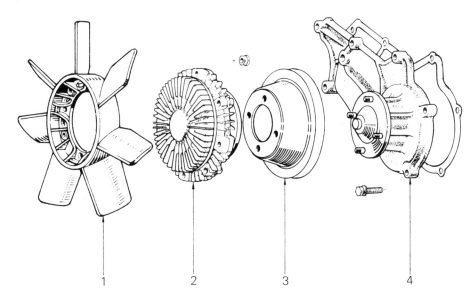

Fig. 2.10. Exploded view of water pump (20R engine)

1 Fan	2 Fluid coupling	3 Pulley	4 Water pump

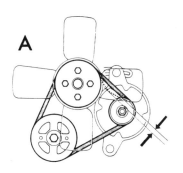

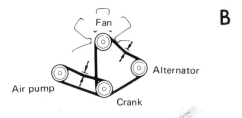

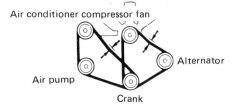

Fig. 2.11. Drivebelt tensioning diagrams

A *Water pump and alternator*
B *Water pump, alternator and air pump (emission control)*
C *Water pump, alternator, air pump and compressor (air conditioning)*

12 Fluid coupling - inspection

1   Any sign of fluid leakage or damage should be rectified by renewal of the coupling assembly.
2   Dismantling is not recommended even for earlier types which can be recharged with silicone fluid.

13 Drivebelts - tensioning and renewal

1   Depending upon the equipment fitted (emission control air pump, alternator, air conditioning compressor, water pump), so the drivebelt arrangement will differ.
2   All belts should have a deflection at the centre point of their longest run when depressed with the thumb, of ½ in (12 mm).
3   Adjustment is carried out by releasing the mounting and adjustment link bolts on the alternator (and air pump if the second belt requires attention) and moving the units towards or away from the engine as required. Retighten the bolts on completion.
4   If a drivebelt requires renewal, always push the alternator or air pump towards the engine as far as it will go, so that the new belt can be fitted without straining it excessively, over the pulley rims.

13.2 Checking tension of drivebelt

14 Fault diagnosis - cooling system

Symptom	Reason/s
Overheating	Insufficient water in cooling system. Fan belt slipping (accompanied by a shrieking noise on rapid engine acceleration). Radiator core blocked or radiator grille restricted. Bottom water hose collapsed, impeding flow. Thermostat not opening properly. Ignition advance and retard incorrectly set (accompanied by loss of power, and perhaps, misfiring). Carburettor incorrectly adjusted (mixture too weak). Exhaust system partially blocked. Oil level in sump too low. Blown cylinder head gasket (water/steam being forced down the radiator overflow pipe under pressure). Engine not yet run-in. Brakes binding.
Cool running	Thermostat jammed open. Incorrect thermostat fitted allowing premature opening of valve. Thermostat missing.
Loss of cooling water	Loose clips on water hoses. Top, bottom, or by-pass water hoses perished and leaking. Radiator core leaking. Thermostat gasket leaking. Radiator pressure cap spring worn or seal ineffective. Blown cylinder head gasket (pressure in system forcing water/steam down the overflow pipe. Cylinder wall or head cracked.

Chapter 3 Carburation, fuel and emission control systems

Contents

Specifications

Fuel pump type
12R engine ... ... Mechanical
8R-C, 18R-C ... ... Mechanical
20R engine ... ... Electric
Delivery pressure
(12R engine) ... ... 2.8 to 4.3 lb/in^2 (0.2 to 0.3 kg/cm^2)
(8R-C, 18R-C engines) ... ... 2.8 to 4.3 lb/in^2 (0.2 to 0.3 kg/cm^2)
(20R engine) ... ... 2.1 to 4.3 lb/in^2 (0.15 to 0.3 kg/cm^2)

Fuel tank capacity
Hi-Ace
  Van models ... ... 11.4 Imp. gals   52 litres   13.7 US gals
  Other models ... ... 9.9 Imp. gals   43 litres   11.5 US gals
Hi-Lux (early) ... ... 11.4 Imp. gals   52 litres   13.7 US gals
Hi-Lux (late) standard wheelbase ... ... 10.1 Imp. gals   46 litres   12.2 US gals
  long wheelbase ... ... 13.3 Imp. gals   61 litres   16 US gals

Carburettor type ... ... Aisan, dual barrel downdraught

*Carburettor specifications	Hi-Ace 12R	Hi-Lux 12R
Main jet (primary)	0.041 in (1.04 mm)	0.042 in (1.06 mm)
Main jet (secondary)	0.064 in (1.62 mm)	0.064 in (1.62 mm)
Slow jet (primary)	0.019 in (0.48 mm)	0.019 in (0.48 mm)
Slow jet (secondary)	0.026 in (0.65 mm)	0.026 in (0.65 mm)
Power jet	0.021 in (0.53 mm)	0.020 in (0.50 mm)
Pump jet	0.020 in (0.50 mm)	0.020 in (0.50 mm)
Thermostatic valve opening temperature	140°F (60°C)	140°F (60°C)

Setting and adjustment clearances are contained in the relevant overhaul sections of the text.

	Hi-Lux 8R-C
Main jet (primary)	0.046 in (1.18 mm)
Main jet (secondary)	0.053 in (1.35 mm)
Slow jet (primary)	0.022 in (0.55 mm)
Slow jet (secondary)	0.024 in (0.60 mm)
Power jet	0.032 in (0.80 mm)
Pump jet	0.032 in (0.80 mm)
Economic jet	0.042 in (1.06 mm)
Main air bleed (primary)	0.020 in (0.50 mm)
Main air bleed (secondary)	0.020 in (0.50 mm)
Slow air bleed (1)	0.051 in (1.30 mm)
Slow air bleed (2)	0.051 in (1.30 mm)
Idling speed	650 rev/min

	Hi-Lux 18R-C without EGR	Hi-Lux 18R-C with EGR
Main jet (primary)	0.0457 in (1.16 mm)	0.0457 in (1.16 mm)
Main jet (secondary)	0.0638 in (1.62 mm)	0.0661 in (1.68 mm)
Slow jet (primary)	0.0207 in (0.525 mm)	0.0213 in (0.5 mm)
Slow jet (secondary)	0.0335 in (0.85 mm)	0.0335 in (0.85 mm)
Power jet	0.0236 in (0.60 mm)	0.0236 in (0.60 mm)
Pump jet	0.0197 in (0.50 mm)	0.0197 in (0.50 mm)
Thermostatic valve opening temperature	140°F (60°C)	140°F (60°C)

Idling speed (manual)	...	...	...	...	...	...	...	...	650 rev/min
Idling speed (automatic)	...	...	...	...	...	...	...	...	850 rev/min (in 'N')
									Hi-Lux 20R engine
Main jet (primary)	...	...	...	...	...	...	...	...	0.0476 in (1.21 mm)
Main jet (secondary)	...	...	...	...	...	...	...	...	0.0697 in (1.77 mm)
Slow jet (primary)	..	...	...	...	...	...	...	...	0.0201 in (0.51 mm)
Power jet	...	...	...	...	...	...	...	...	0.020 in (0.5 mm)
Pump jet	...	...	...	...	...	...	...	...	0.020 in (0.5 mm)
Idling speed (manual)	...	...	...	...	...	...	...	...	850 rev/min
Idling speed (automatic)	...	...	...	...	...	...	...	...	850 rev/min (in 'N')
Fast idle speed	...	...	...	...	...	...	...	...	2400 rev/min

Torque wrench settings

								lb f ft	Nm
Carburettor to manifold	...	...	...	...	...	...	...	25	35
Fuel pump to crankcase	...	...	...	...	...	...	...	30	41
Manifold bolts	...	...	...	...	...	...	...	35	48

1 General description

1   All vehicles have a rear-mounted fuel tank (side-mounted to chassis frame on some Hi-Ace body styles), a dual barrel, downdraught carburettor, and a mechanically or electrically (20R engine) operated fuel pump.
2   An in-line fuel filter is fitted and all models have some emission control devices, although the complexity of the system depends upon the operating territory for which the vehicle is destined.

2 Air cleaners - description and servicing

1   One of three different types of air cleaner may be encountered. On the 12R engine, a fixed intake type paper element air cleaner is fitted (photos).
2   On larger capacity engines, either a variable position intake type or, an automatic temperature controlled air cleaner may be fitted.
3   At the intervals specified in the Routine Maintenance section, remove the central wing nut on the lid of the air cleaner, release the rim clamps and remove the lid.
4   Extract the filter element and tap it on a block of hardwood to remove any adhering dirt or dust. If an air line is available, remove the dust by applying the air nozzle to the internal surface of the element. Refit the element, so that a fresh surface is presented to the intake spout.
5   Renew the element at the specified intervals and, when doing so, clean the interior of the air cleaner casing, and check that the rubber seals are in good condition.
6   The automatic temperature controlled type on the 20R engines incorporates a sensor and valve device which 'mixes' the air being drawn into the carburettors to maintain the air temperature at a predetermined level thus preventing icing of the carburettor, reduction of exhaust emission and reduced condensation within the rocker box cover.
7   Hot air is drawn from the interior of a deflector plate attached to the exhaust manifold.
8   When the engine is operating under full load, a vacuum diaphragm connected to the inlet manifold opens the control valve fully to exclude hot air and override the sensor 'mixing' device.
9   On other engines equipped with this type of air cleaner, the temperature of the intake air is maintained by a simple deflector valve controlled by a thermostat and linkage.
10 Correct operation of either type of temperature controlled air cleaner is best checked by observing the position of the intake spout deflector valve under (i) cold engine operational temperature and (ii) normal engine operating temperature. The deflector should be open to warm air immediately after the engine has been started and closed when the engine is thoroughly hot.

3 Mechanical type fuel pumps - testing, and overhaul

1   On 12R engines, the fuel pump is actuated by an eccentric cam on the camshaft.
2   On 8R-C and 18R-C engines, the fuel pump is actuated by an eccentric cam on the oil pump (auxiliary) driveshaft.
3   Presuming that the fuel lines and unions are in good condition and that there are no leaks anywhere, check the performance of the fuel pump in the following manner: Disconnect the fuel pipe at the carburettor inlet union, and the high tension lead to the coil, and with a suitable container or a large rag in position to catch the ejected fuel, turn the engine over on the starter motor. A good spurt of petrol should emerge from the end of the pipe every second revolution.
4   If the pump does not operate correctly, disconnect the inlet and outlet pipes from the pump by unscrewing the two unions (photo).
5   Unscrew and remove the two bolts which secure the pump to the cylinder block. Withdraw the pump, together with insulator and gaskets.
6   Remove the securing screws and lift off the cover (1) (Fig. 3.1).
7   Remove the gasket (2).

2.1a Air cleaner body (12R engine)

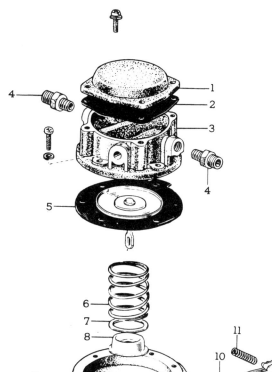

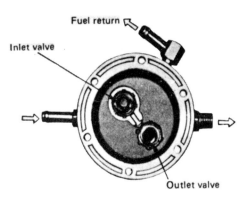

4
1
2
3
4
5

Fuel return
Inlet valve
Outlet valve

Fig. 3.2. Valves (mechanical type fuel pump)

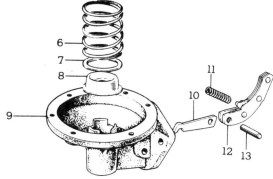

6
7
8
9
11
10
12
13

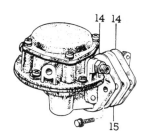

14 14
15

Fig. 3.1. Exploded view of mechanical type fuel pump

1 Cover	9 Lower body
2 Gasket	10 Rocker arm link
3 Upper body	11 Spring
4 Unions	12 Rocker arm
5 Diaphragm/rod assembly	13 Pivot pin
6 Spring	14 Gaskets
7 Oil seal retainer	15 Insulator
8 Oil seal	

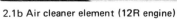

2.1b Air cleaner element (12R engine)

3.4 Mechanical type fuel pump

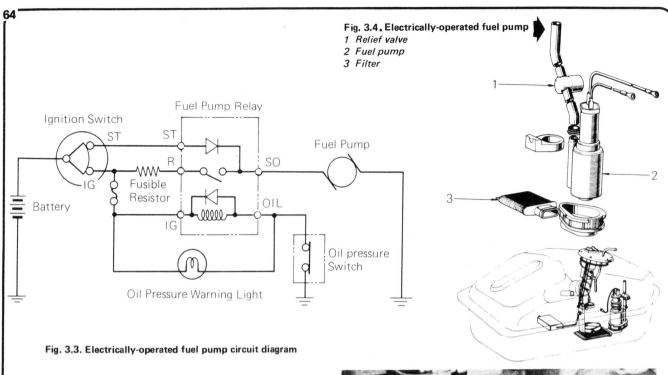

Fig. 3.4. Electrically-operated fuel pump
1 *Relief valve*
2 *Fuel pump*
3 *Filter*

Fig. 3.3. Electrically-operated fuel pump circuit diagram

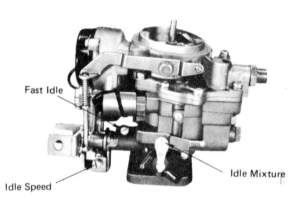

Fig. 3.5. Location of adjusting screws (all carburettors except 20R type)

Fig. 3.6. Location of adjusting screws (20R engine type carburettor)

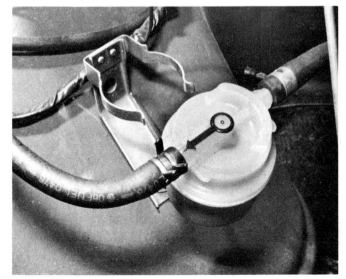

5.2 Fuel filter (typical)

6.3 Fuel tank drain plug

8 Scratch an alignment mark on the flange edges of the upper and lower halves of the pump body and then remove the flange securing screws and separate the two halves.
9 From the lower body, unhook the diaphragm operating rod from the rocker arm by depressing the rod and twisting it sideways. Withdraw the diaphragm/rod assembly.
10 Remove the oil seal, retainer and spring.
11 If essential, due to a worn rocker arm, the pin (13) may be removed and the arm and spring removed.
12 Examine all components for wear. If this is severe, it will probably be more economical to renew the pump complete, on an exchange basis.
13 Check the operation of the valves in the upper body, by alternately sucking and blowing with the mouth at the inlet and outlet ports. When blowing (through the inlet port), the valve should open and close positively when sucked. When blowing (through the outlet port), the valve should close and open when sucked. The valves are staked in position and in the event of a fault occuring, it is recommended that a new upper body complete with valves is obtained.
14 If the pump components are in good order, obtain a repair kit which will contain all the necessary renewable items. The diaphragm/rod assembly cannot be dismantled and is renewed complete.
15 Reassembly is a reversal of dismantling. Align the flange mating marks and tighten the flange securing screws evenly and in opposite sequence. Final tightening should be carried out with the rocker arm fully depressed.
16 Refitting is a reversal of removal but use a new gasket on each face of the insulating block.

4 Electrically-operated type fuel pump (20R engine) - checking, removal and refitting

1 This type of fuel pump is located in the fuel tank.
2 In the event of lack of fuel at the carburettor, first check that there is fuel in the tank, and that the filter is not clogged.
3 Check the electrical supply lead to the pump terminal, also the earth lead from the pump to the bodyframe for security and good contact.
4 It is possible for a faulty oil pressure switch to cause a fault in the fuel pump as they operate on an integrated circuit.
5 Assuming that the oil pressure was normal when the engine was last operating, pull off the lead from the oil pressure switch so that the fuel pump relay will actuate when the ignition is switched on.
6 Switch on the ignition and the pump should operate smoothly and quietly. If the pump does not run, the pump relay, resistor or pump itself may be faulty, and should be renewed after the individual components have first been tested by your dealer.
7 To renew the pump, first remove the fuel tank as described in Section 6, and then unscrew and withdraw the pump.
8 When installing the new fuel pump, always use a new gasket.

5 In-line fuel filter - renewal

1 The fuel filter used on most models is of the disposable type and it should be renewed as specified in the Routine Maintenance section.
2 It is located within the engine compartment or under the battery on Hi-Ace models. Renewal is carried out by disconnecting the inlet and outlet pipes from it and pulling the filter from its retaining clip (photo).
3 When fitting the new filter, make sure that the flow directional arrow is pointing in the direction of fuel supply (towards the carburettor).

6 Fuel tank - removal, servicing and refitting

1 On most models, the fuel tank is located under the load-carrying platform and is accessible from below the vehicle.
2 On certain Hi-Ace models, the tank is side-mounted on the chassis member.
3 Drain the fuel from the tank into a suitable (capped) container (photo).
4 Disconnect the fuel outlet pipe from the tank.
5 Disconnect the lead from the terminal of the fuel contents sender unit.

6 On vehicles fitted with the 20R engine, disconnect the leads from the tank-mounted electric fuel pump.
7 *On models with a vented filler cap,* remove the cap, the filler pipe grommet and the tank securing bolts and withdraw the tank.
8 *On models with a non-vented filler cap,* disconnect the vent pipes from the tank and also the flexible section of the filler tube before removing the tank securing bolts and the tank itself.
9 *On models with a fuel evaporative emission control system,* the breather hose from the tank contains a pressure equalising valve which must not be damaged or refitted the wrong way round. Fuel tanks on such models cannot be removed until the two hoses which run to the separator have been disconnected.
10 Over a period of time, sediment and water may accumulate in the bottom of the fuel tank. It is a good idea periodically when there is very little fuel left in the tank to remove the drain plug and drain the fuel and discard it.
11 If the tank is severely contaminated, withdraw the tank as previously described and remove the fuel level transmitter unit (also the pump on 20R engined models).
12 Use two or three changes of fuel and shake the tank vigorously until it is clean.
13 Should a leak develop, do not be tempted to solder over the hole. Fuel tank repair is a specialist job and unless lengthy safety precautions are observed, it can be a very dangerous procedure. It will probably be as economical to purchase a new tank as to have the original repaired.

7 Carburettors - general description

1 The carburettors used in conjunction with the different type of engine are basically very similar, and are of the dual barrel, downdraught, but they do vary in design of the cold start device.
2 The carburettor fitted to the 12R engine has a manual choke, that fitted to the 8R-C and 18R-C engines has an automatic choke heated bypass from the exhaust manifold.
3 The carburettor fitted to the 20R engine has a water-heated automatic choke connected to the engine cooling system.

8 Carburettor (8R-C, 18R-C and 12R engines) - idling adjustment

1 The use of a vacuum gauge and a tachometer will be required for this operation.
2 Run the engine until normal temperature is reached.
3 Check that the valve clearances are correctly adjusted, the ignition timing is correct and all emission control settings are as specified.
4 Connect the tachometer in accordance with the maker's instructions and connect the vacuum gauge to the tapped hole in the inlet manifold.
5 Preset the mixture control screw by first screwing it into its seat and then unscrewing it between 2 and 2½ turns. **Do not force the screw into its seat.**
6 Start the engine and adjust the idle speed control screw until the engine speed is 700 rev/min. (12R engine) 650 rev/min (8R-C and 18R-C manual gearbox) or 800 rev/min (18R-C automatic transmission).
7 Turn the mixture control screw until the maximum vacuum reading is obtained on the gauge, then turn the screw until the vacuum reading just starts to drop.
8 Readjust the throttle speed screw to attain the specified idling speed.
9 Switch off the engine, remove the vacuum gauge and the tachometer.
10 On later carburettors, the mixture control screw is fitted with a travel limiter cap. The adjustment should therefore be restricted to moving the screw within the confines of its stops, unless of course, the cap has been broken during any dismantling operations.
11 An alternative method of setting the idling speed is to use a device such as a Colortune.

9 Carburettor (20R engine) - idling adjustment

1 Connect a tachometer in accordance with the maker's instructions

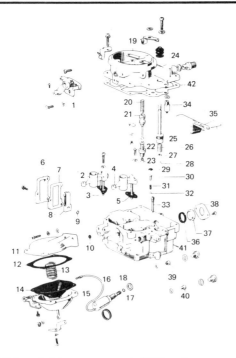

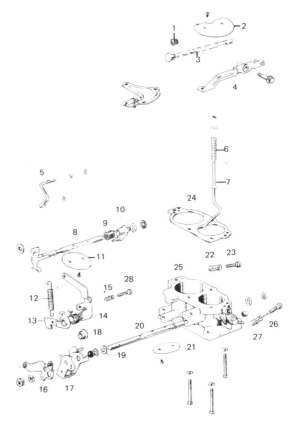

10.3 Accelerator cable connection to carburettor (12R engine)

Fig. 3.7. Body and air horn components (12R engine type carburettor)

1	Choke lever	22	Power valve
2	Secondary small venturi	23	Power jet
3	Gasket	24	Flexible boot
4	Primary small venturi	25	Accelerator pump plunger
5	Gasket	26	Spring
6	Thermostatic valve cover	27	Ball retainer
7	Gasket	28	Ball
8	Thermostatic valve	29	Gasket
9	'O' ring	30	Discharge weight
10	Gasket	31	Spring
11	Diaphragm housing cap	32	Ball
12	Gasket	33	Slow jet
13	Spring	34	Fuel inlet needle valve
14	Secondary throttle valve actuating diaphragm	35	Float
15	Diaphragm housing	36	Gasket
16	Solenoid fuel cut off valve (anti-run on)	37	Sight glass
17	Gasket	38	Plate
18	'O' ring	39	Secondary main jet
19	Air horn	40	Primary main jet
20	Spring	41	Body
21	Power piston	42	Gasket

10.4 Choke cable connection to carburettor (12R engine)

Fig. 3.8.   Throttle valve chamber components
(12R engine type carburettor)

1	Spring	15	Spring
2	Choke valve plate	16	Primary throttle lever
3	Choke spindle	17	Primary throttle spindle arm
4	Accelerator pump lever	18	Collar
5	Connecting link	19	Shim
6	Spring	20	Primary throttle spindle
7	Connecting rod	21	Primary throttle valve plate
8	Secondary throttle spindle	22	Spring
9	Spring	23	Idle speed screw
10	Diaphragm relief lever	24	Gasket
11	Secondary throttle valve plate	25	Throttle valve housing
12	Return spring	26	Idle mixture screw
13	Secondary kick lever	27	Spring
14	Fast idle lever	28	Fast idle screw

and run the engine to normal operating temperature, and set the gear-shift lever in neutral ('N' automatic transmission).
2   Turn the idle mixture screw until the engine reaches its fastest speed. Now turn the idle speed screw until the engine speed is 900 rev/min.
3   Repeat the operations described in the preceding paragraphs until further movement of the idle mixture screw will not cause any further rise in engine speed.
4   Now turn the idle mixture screw until the engine speed drops to 850 rev/min.
5   Where the engine is equipped with full emission control systems, the foregoing procedure must be regarded as an emergency tuning method only. Precise adjustment should be carried out using a CO meter until the reading is in accordance with that specified on the sticker attached to the particular vehicle.

10 Carburettor - removal and installation

1   Remove the air cleaner. To do this, remove the lid and element, as described in Section 2, mark and disconnect the vacuum and breather pipes from the underside of the air cleaner body, and then lift the assembly off the central mounting stud.
2   Disconnect the fuel inlet pipe. On 20R engines also disconnect the fuel return pipe.
3   Disconnect the throttle control linkage (photo).
4   On 12R engines, disconnect the choke control cable (photo).
5   On 8R-C and 18R-C engines, disconnect the choke stove pipes which run between the exhaust manifold and the carburettor.
6   On 20R engines, drain the cooling system and disconnect the hoses which run between the intake manifold and the carburettor.
7   Unscrew and remove the carburettor mounting flange nuts and lift the carburettor from the intake manifold.
8   Installation is a reversal of removal but make sure that the mating flanges are clean and free from old pieces of gasket and always use a new gasket when installing.
9   With mechanical type fuel pumps, it will take some time to fill the carburettor bowl when attempting to start the engine after the carburettor has been removed for overhaul and is now refitted. To overcome this, pour some fuel through the inlet nozzle of the carburettor until it overflows using a piece of tubing and a small funnel.
10 Once installed, check the slow-running adjustment, as described in earlier Sections. Basic settings for the idle mixture screws should be:

12R engine	*1½ turns out from fully closed*
8R-C and 18R-C engines	*2½ turns out from fully closed*
20R engine	*1¾ turns out from fully closed*

11 Carburettor (12R engine) - overhaul and adjustment

1   With the carburettor removed from the engine, clean away all external dirt and oil.

2   Refer to the illustration which indicates clearly the components and their relationship to each other. Remove only those components which are worn or damaged.
3   If complete dismantling is to be undertaken, then remove the parts in the following sequence.

   a) *The air horn, having first disconnected the accelerator pump lever and rod.*
   b) *The float and fuel inlet needle valve.*
   c) *The accelerator pump.*
   d) *Power piston assembly.*
   e) *Venturi, jets and solenoid valve.*
   f) *The diaphragm assembly.*

Do not remove the valve plates or spindles, unless essential, and then the peened ends of the screws, which secure the valve plates, must first be filed off before they can be unscrewed.
4   Renew any worn components and obtain a repair kit which will contain all the necessary gaskets.
5   While the jets are out of the carburettor, take the opportunity of checking their calibration marks with those listed in the Specifications at the beginning of this Chapter.
6   Reassemble in the reverse order to dismantling, but carry out the following checks and adjustments as the work proceeds.

Float level
7   Turn the air horn upside down, so that the float hangs by its own weight. The clearance between the lowest point on the float and the surface of the air horn should be 0.14 in (3.5 mm) (Fig. 3.10) otherwise bend tag A on the float lip (Fig. 3.9).
8   Now raise the float gently with the finger, and check the clearance between the end of the needle valve and the float lip. Adjust by bending the tag B of the float lip, if the clearance deviates from 0.05 in (1.2 mm). (See Fig. 3.11).

Valve plate opening
9   Open the throttle (butterfly) valve plates separately, and check that they lie at right angles to the carburettor mounting flange surface when fully open. If necessary, bend the throttle lever stoppers (1 and 2) (See Fig. 3.12).

Valve plate kick-up
10 Set the primary throttle valve plate to an angle of 62° to the venturi bore. This can easily be done if a piece of card is cut to the required angle and used as a template.
11 Adjust the clearance between the edge of the secondary throttle valve (Fig. 3.13) and the wall of the venturi, to 0.008 in (0.2 mm). Bend the secondary throttle lever if necessary to achieve this. Use a twist drill as a clearance gauge.

Fast idle
12 Close the choke valve plate with the fingers, and then check the clearance between the edge of the primary throttle valve plate and the venturi wall. Adjust the clearance to 0.05 in (1.2 mm) by turning the fast idle screw. Use a twist drill as a clearance gauge.

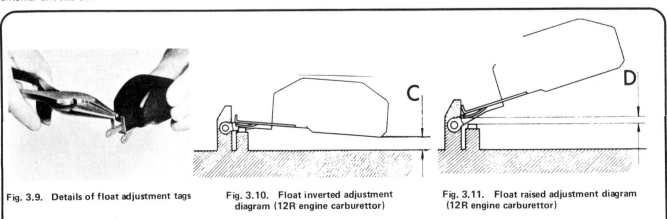

Fig. 3.9. Details of float adjustment tags

Fig. 3.10. Float inverted adjustment diagram (12R engine carburettor)

C = 3.5 mm (0.14 in)

Fig. 3.11. Float raised adjustment diagram (12R engine carburettor)

D = 1.2 mm (0.05 in)

Accelerator pump

13 Move the accelerator pump lever with the fingers, and measure the pump stroke. This should be 0.20 in (5.0 mm). Adjust if necessary, by bending the neck of the connecting rod to give a more acute or less acute angle as required.

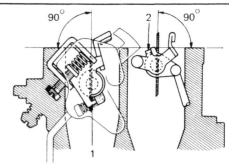

Fig. 3.12. Throttle valve plate opening adjustment diagram (12R engine carburettor)

12 Carburettor (8R-C and 18R-C engines) - overhaul and adjustment

1 This carburettor is very similar to the one used on the 12R engine, except that it has an automatic choke heated from the exhaust manifold.

2 The dismantling procedure follows the sequence given in Section 11.

3 Adjustments to the carburettor after overhaul are as described in Section 11, paragraphs 7 to 13, but the following clearances apply to this carburettor.

> *Float setting (air horn inverted) 0.20 in (5.0 mm)*
> *Float setting (float raised with finger) 0.04 in (1.0 mm)*
> *Valve plate kick-up. Primary valve plate setting 64°*
> > *Secondary throttle valve plate clearance*
> > *0.0079 in (0.2 mm)*
> *Fast idle. Primary throttle valve plate clearance 0.04 in (1.0 mm)*
> *Accelerator pump stroke 0.18 in (4.5 mm)*

4 Two additional adjustments may be required with this type of carburettor.

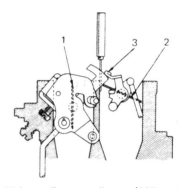

Fig. 3.13. Kick up adjustment diagram (12R engine carburettor)

1 *Primary throttle valve plate*   3 *Secondary throttle lever*
2 *Secondary throttle valve plate*

Choke unloader

5 Open the primary throttle valve plate fully with the fingers. The angle of the choke valve plate to the venturi bore should be 47°. This can be checked with a protractor or a cardboard template. Adjust if necessary by bending one or both of the interconnecting tags at (2 - Fig. 3.17).

Fig. 3.15. Body and air horn components (8 R-C, 18 R-C engine carburettors)

1	*Automatic choke coil housing*	23	*'O' ring*
2	*Gasket*	24	*Throttle positioner diaphragm unit*
3	*Plate*	25	*Air horn*
4	*Thermostat case*	26	*Spring*
5	*Piston link*	27	*Power piston*
6	*Vacuum piston*	28	*Power valve*
7	*Secondary small venturi*	29	*Power jet*
8	*Gasket*	30	*Flexible boot*
9	*Primary small venturi*	31	*Accelerator pump plunger*
10	*Gasket*	32	*Spring*
11	*Thermostatic valve cover*	33	*Ball retainer*
12	*Gasket*	34	*Ball*
13	*Thermostatic valve*	35	*Gasket*
14	*'O' ring*	36	*Discharge weight stop*
15	*Gasket*	37	*Pump discharge weight*
16	*Secondary throttle actuating diaphragm housing cap*	38	*Ball*
		39	*Slow jet*
17	*Gasket*	40	*Fuel inlet needle valve*
18	*Spring*	41	*Float*
19	*Diaphragm*	42	*Gasket*
20	*Diaphragm housing*	43	*Sight glass*
21	*Fuel cut (anti-run on) solenoid valve*	44	*Plate*
		45	*Secondary main jet*
22	*Gasket*	46	*Primary main jet*
		47	*Body*
		48	*Gasket*

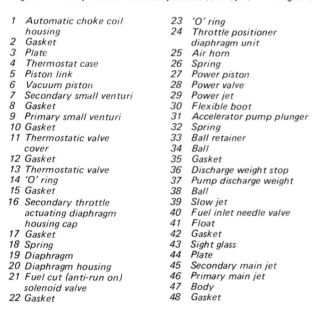

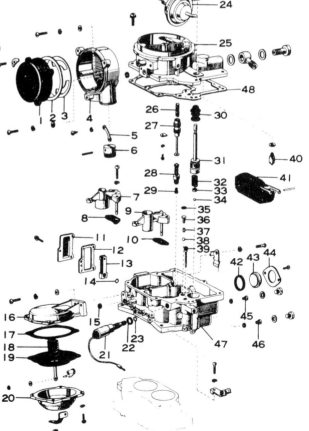

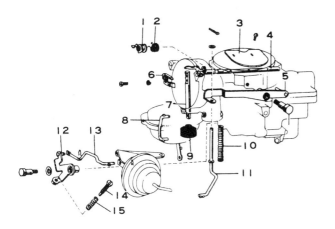

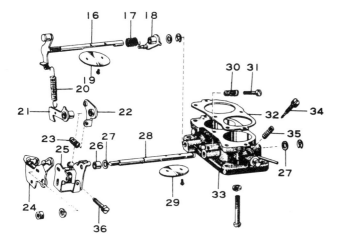

Fig. 3.16. Throttle valve chamber components (8R-C, 18R-C engine type carburettor)

1	Fast idle cam	19	Secondary throttle valve
2	Spring	20	Return spring
3	Choke valve plate	21	Secondary kick lever
4	Choke spindle	22	Fast idle adjusting lever
5	Accelerator pump lever	23	Spring
6	Fast idle cam follower	24	Primary throttle lever
7	Sliding rod	25	Primary throttle spindle arm
8	Connecting link	26	Collar
9	Flexible boot	27	Shim
10	Spring	28	Primary throttle spindle
11	Connecting rod	29	Primary throttle valve plate
12	Lever	30	Spring
13	Connecting rod	31	Idle speed screw
14	Throttle positioner adjusting screw	32	Gasket
15	Spring	33	Valve plate chamber
16	Secondary throttle spindle	34	Idle mixture screw
17	Spring	35	Spring
18	Diaphragm relief lever	36	Fast idle screw

Fig. 3.17. Choke unloader adjustment diagram (8R-C, 18R-C carburettor)

2   Point of adjustment

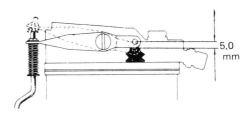

Fig. 3.14. Accelerator pump adjustment diagram (12R engine carburettor)

Automatic choke

6   The normal setting for the choke housing is for the mark on the coil housing to be opposite the centre line on the scale of the thermostat housing. In extremes of temperature, which may cause weak or overrich starting conditions, the coil housing may be turned one graduation of the scale at a time and starting performance evaluated before turning any further. Turning the housing in a clockwise direction weakens the mixture. Turning it anticlockwise richens the mixture.

7   Each graduation of the scale represents a change of 9°F (5°C).

13 Carburettor (20R engine) - overhaul and adjustment

1   Refer to the illustrations and commence dismantling by disconnecting the accelerator pump arm and connecting rod. (See Figs. 3.19, 3.20 and 3.21).

2   Remove the connecting links and choke opener and lift the air horn assembly from the carburettor body after having extracted the seven securing screws.

3   Remove the float assembly and the fuel inlet valve.

4   Remove the accelerator pump plunger and power piston assembly.

5   Remove the automatic choke housing (three screws).

6   Remove the choke lever now exposed and coil housing body.

7   Remove the choke breaker and relief lever.

8   The choke valve plate and spindle should only be dismantled if essential, in which case, file off the peened ends of the valve plate screws before unscrewing them.

9   From the carburettor body, remove the venturis, the pump jet assembly, including the 'O' ring, spring and ball and then extract the slow jet and the power valve.

10 Remove the plugs and the main jets.

11 Unscrew the cover and extract the thermostatic valve and the 'O'-ring. Do not dismantle the thermostatic valve.

12 Remove the sight glass from the float chamber and then remove the throttle positioner and link.

Fig. 3.18. Automatic choke adjustment (8R-C, 18R-C carburettor)

70

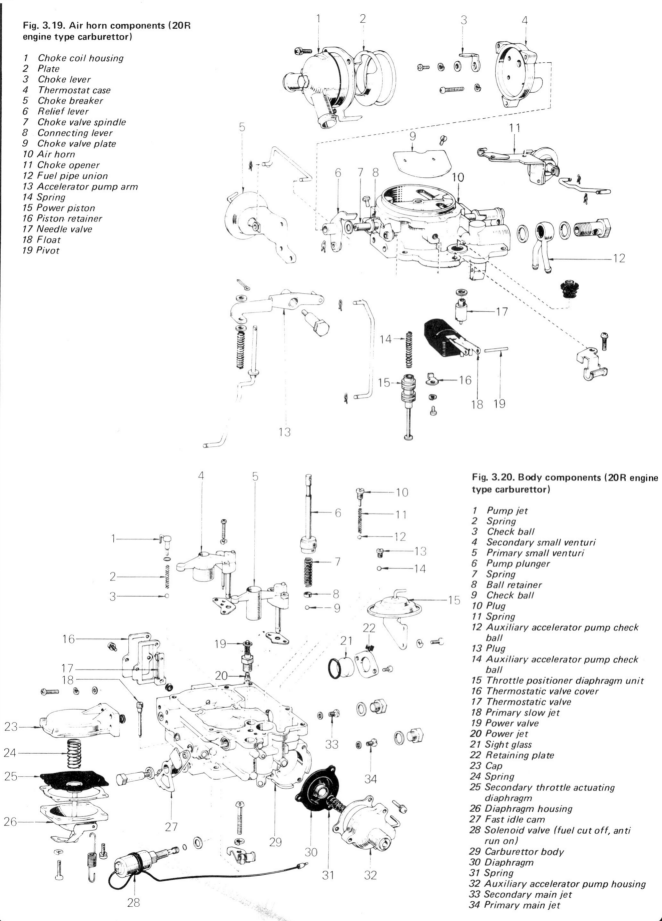

Fig. 3.19. Air horn components (20R engine type carburettor)

1 Choke coil housing
2 Plate
3 Choke lever
4 Thermostat case
5 Choke breaker
6 Relief lever
7 Choke valve spindle
8 Connecting lever
9 Choke valve plate
10 Air horn
11 Choke opener
12 Fuel pipe union
13 Accelerator pump arm
14 Spring
15 Power piston
16 Piston retainer
17 Needle valve
18 Float
19 Pivot

Fig. 3.20. Body components (20R engine type carburettor)

1 Pump jet
2 Spring
3 Check ball
4 Secondary small venturi
5 Primary small venturi
6 Pump plunger
7 Spring
8 Ball retainer
9 Check ball
10 Plug
11 Spring
12 Auxiliary accelerator pump check ball
13 Plug
14 Auxiliary accelerator pump check ball
15 Throttle positioner diaphragm unit
16 Thermostatic valve cover
17 Thermostatic valve
18 Primary slow jet
19 Power valve
20 Power jet
21 Sight glass
22 Retaining plate
23 Cap
24 Spring
25 Secondary throttle actuating diaphragm
26 Diaphragm housing
27 Fast idle cam
28 Solenoid valve (fuel cut off, anti run on)
29 Carburettor body
30 Diaphragm
31 Spring
32 Auxiliary accelerator pump housing
33 Secondary main jet
34 Primary main jet

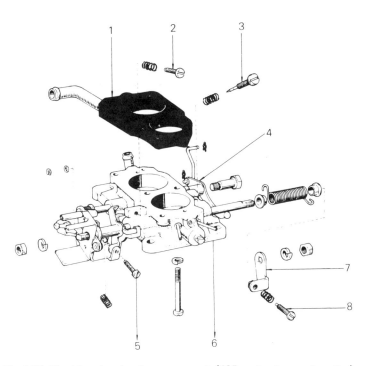

Fig. 3.22. Choke lever (1) and thermostat case screws (20R carburettor)

Fig. 3.23. Removing choke breaker (1) and relief lever (2) from 20R engine type carburettor

Fig. 3.21. Throttle valve chamber components (20R engine type carburettor)

1 Insulator
2 Idle speed screw
3 Idle mixture screw
4 Throttle positioner lever

5 Fast idle screw
6 Valve chamber
7 Throttle lever
8 Throttle positioner adjusting screw

Fig. 3.24. Auxiliary accelerator pump details (20R engine carburettor)

1 Inlet plug
2 Outlet plug
3 Housing

Fig. 3.25. Installing choke breaker and relief lever (20R engine type carburettor)

Fig. 3.26. Installing choke housing plate (20R engine type carburettor)

Fig. 3.27. Installing choke coil housing (20R engine type carburettor)

Fig. 3.28. Choke housing alignment marks (20R engine type carburettor)

1 Body seal
2 Vee notch on plate
3 Coil housing

Fig. 3.29. Throttle valve plate lever stops (20R engine type carburettor)

1 Primary
2 Secondary

13 Remove the auxiliary accelerator pump components.
14 Remove the diaphragm assembly, unscrew the fuel cut off solenoid valve and the fast idle cam.
15 Disconnect the carburettor body from the flange (three screws). The flange should be dismantled only if necessary.
16 Clean and inspect all components for wear, particularly the diaphragm. Suck the nozzle on the choke breaker; if the connecting rod does not move, renew the choke breaker complete. Check jet calibrations with those given in the Specifications in case a previous owner has substituted any for ones of a different size.
17 Reassembly is a reversal of dismantling, but the following detailed instructions are given where any confusion might arise.
18 Install the choke breaker and relief lever as shown (Fig. 3.25).
19 Fit the choke housing plate and gasket so that the hole in the plate is in alignment with the pin.
20 As the choke housing is offered up, make sure that the bimetal spring engages with the choke lever. Tighten the three securing screws after the Vee notch in the choke housing plate is in alignment with the centre line on the body scale and the line on the coil housing.
21 Once the float has been installed, turn the air horn upside down and measure the distance between the lowest point of the float and the surface of the air horn (no gasket) while the float is hanging under its own weight. The measurement should be 0.20 in (5.0 mm). Adjust if necessary by bending the straight tag on the float arm.
22 Now raise the float gently with the finger, and check the clearance between the end face of the fuel inlet valve plunger, and the float arm at the joint where it bears upon the valve. The clearance should be 0.04 in (1.0 mm). Adjust if necessary by bending the right-angled tags on the float arm.
23 When reassembly is complete, carry out the following checks and adjustments.

Valve plate opening
24 Open each throttle valve plate independently with the fingers and check that they lie absolutely parallel with the venturi bores when they are fully open. Any adjustment necessary can be made by bending the throttle lever stops.

Kick-up
25 Open the primary throttle valve fully with the fingers. The edge of the secondary throttle valve plate should be open so that there is a clearance between its edge and the venturi bore of 0.008 in (0.2 mm). Adjust if necessary by bending the secondary throttle lever.

Fast idle
26 Close the choke valve plate fully with the finger. The clearance between the edge of the primary throttle valve plate and the venturi bore should be 0.047 in (1.2 mm). Adjust if necessary by turning the fast idle screw.

Choke unloader
27 Close the primary throttle valve plate fully with the fingers and check the angle of the choke valve plate in relation to the vertical centre line of the carburettor throat. This should be 50°, otherwise bend the fast idle lever.

Choke opener
28 Push the connecting rod on the choke opener vacuum capsule so that the choke valve plate moves as far as it will go. Check the choke valve plate angle which should be 55° to the centre line through the carburettor throat. Adjust if necessary by bending the connecting rod to make the cranked sections of the rod more or less acute as required.

Choke breaker
29 Push the connecting rod into the choke breaker vacuum capsule to actuate the choke valve plate as far as it will go. Check the choke valve plate angle which should be 40° from the vertical centre line through the carburettor throat. Adjust if necessary by bending the relief lever.

Throttle positioner
30 With the throttle released, the clearance between the edge of the primary throttle valve plate and the venturi bore should be:

Fig. 3.30. Kick up adjustment details (20 R engine type carburettor)

1 Primary throttle valve   *3 Secondary throttle lever*
2 Secondary throttle valve

Manual gearbox	0.024 in (0.6 mm)
Automatic transmission	0.020 in (0.5 mm)

Adjust by turning the throttle positioner adjusting screw.

Accelerator pump
31 The pump stroke should be 0.177 in (4.5 mm). To increase or decrease the stroke, bend the cranked connecting rod.
32 If the idle mixture screw has been removed, screw it in fully, but gently, and then unscrew it 1¾ turns from the closed position. This will give a basic starting position pending precise setting of the idling speed as described in Section 9.

14 Emission control - general description

1 To prevent pollution of the atmosphere, a number of (fume) emission control systems are fitted to all vehicles. Their complexity depends upon the operating territory, but as a general rule, vehicles with the larger capacity engines and destined for North America have the most comprehensive and sophisticated systems.
2 All vehicles have a *Crankcase Ventilation System*, as described in Chapter 1, Sections 17, 20 and 23.
3 Many vehicles have a *Fuel Evaporative Emission Control System*, which is designed to restrict the fuel vapour from leaving the fuel tank and to direct it to be consumed during the normal engine combustion cycle (see Section 15).
4 Some vehicles have one or more of the following systems in order to reduce the emission of noxious gases from the exhaust system.

   a) Transmission Controlled Spark System (TCS).
   b) Throttle Positioner (Delay) System (TPS).
   c) Air Injection System (AIS).
   d) Exhaust Gas Recirculation System (EGR).

5 It must be emphasised that correct tuning and adjustment of the vehicles' fuel system and ignition system are extremely important in the maintenance of low levels of exhaust fume emission.

15 Fuel evaporative emission control system - description and maintenance

1 The system is designed to reduce the emission of fuel vapour to the atmosphere by directing the vapour from the fuel tank through a non-return valve into an absorbent charcoal canister. At vehicle speeds above 11 mph (17.7 kph) the vacuum switching valve operates and the vapour stored in the canister is drawn into the inlet manifold where it is then burned as a controlled fuel/air mixture within the engine combustion chambers.
2 The fuel tank filler cap incorporates a valve which opens to admit air should a partial vacuum be created within the tank due to vapour removal.
3 The non-return valve maintains pressure in the fuel tank to prevent fuel entering the vapour extraction line when the tank is being filled.

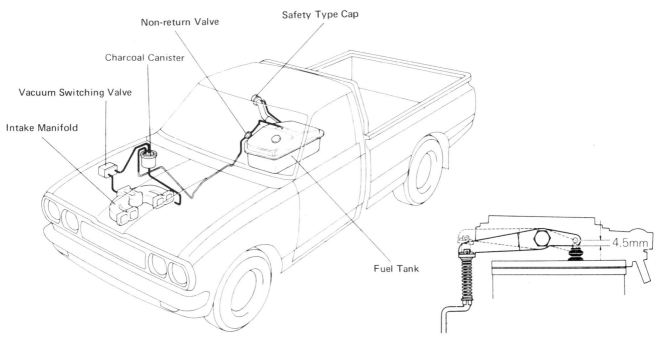

Fig. 3.32. Fuel evaporative emission control system (Hi-Lux)

Fig. 3.31. Accelerator pump stroke
adjustment diagram (20R carburettor)

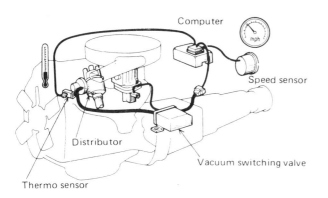

Fig. 3.33. TCS system components

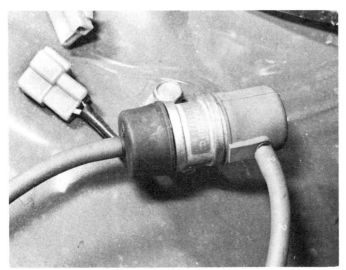

16.7 Vacuum switching valve (TCS system - emission control)

4   Regularly inspect the condition and security of the system connecting hoses and the filler cap seal and renew as necessary.
5   Renew the non-return valve as specified in the Routine Maintenance
Section.
6   Renew the charcoal canister every 5 years or at 50,000 miles
(80,000 km) intervals, whichever occurs sooner.
7   Refer to Section 22 of this Chapter, for fault symptoms and their
rectification.

16 Transmission Controlled Spark System (TCS) - description and testing of components

1   The Transmission Controlled Spark System (TCS) is a system which
will reduce emissions of oxides of nitrogen. Basically, the system
controls the distributor advance and retard characteristics, precisely,
according to engine heat and vehicle speed. The TCS system includes a
thermosensor, a computor, speed sensor and a vacuum switching valve.
2   *The thermosensor circuit* monitors the temperature of the engine
coolant. If it is not within specified limits the information is relayed
to the computer and the TCS system will not be actuated.
3   *The TCS circuit* controls the ignition timing to ensure optimum
combustion at low speeds. This is achieved by the use of a vacuum
switching valve (controlling the distributor through the diaphragm unit)
and a speed sensor. This is essentially a top gear position switch which
is screwed into the side of the gearbox. The distributor does not advance
at speeds below 36 mph (58 kmh) unless the vehicle has just
decelerated from a higher speed to not below 17 mph (27.4 kmh). At
speeds below 17 mph (27.4 kmh) the TCS system is operational and
the distributor is operating at the static timing position. At speeds
over 36 mph (58 kmh) the TCS system is off and normal distributor
advance characteristics are in operation.
4   *The thermosensor* is screwed into the side of the cylinder head. To
test its operation, have the engine idling at normal operating temperature and then disconnect the lead. Accelerate the engine and observe
if the vernier adjuster on the distributor moves inwards (ignition
advanced). This test simulates the conditions when engine coolant
temperature is below 122°F (50°C) and the TCS system is off. Now
reconnect the lead to the thermosensor and repeat the operation, the
vernier adjuster on the distributor should move outwards (ignition
retarded), indicating that the TCS system is on at temperature of over
122°F (50°C).
5   The following tests can only be carried out if you are in possession
of a tachometer, vacuum gauge, ohmmeter and test lamp.

6   With the engine running at normal operating temperature, disconnect and connect the lead from the thermosensor terminal several
times. With the hand resting on the vacuum switching valve, actuation
of the valve will be felt.

7   If the valve does not actuate, disconnect the lead from the thermosensor and insert the test lamp probe in the terminal of the vacuum
switching valve connector plug. Withdraw and insert the test lamp
probe several times and feel whether the vacuum switching valve
actuates and the test lamp lights up. If neither happens, renew the
switching valve (photo).

8   Switch off the engine and disconnect the thermosensor wire. Use an
ohmmeter to check the resistance of the thermosensor, this should be
2000 ohms (coolant temperature 178°F/81°C). If outside the specified
resistance, drain the cooling system and renew the thermosensor. If the
vacuum switching valve still does not actuate then the computer
(mounted below the instrument panel on the driver's side) must be
faulty and should be renewed.

17 Throttle Positioner System (TPS) - description and testing of components

1   This system controls the emission of exhaust gases during
deceleration.

2   This circuit is designed to open the throttle valve plate very slightly
when the accelerator pedal is released in order to increase the fuel/air
supply to ensure complete combustion and minimize the discharge of
exhaust contaminants.

3   When the vehicle is operating at medium and high speeds, the speed
sensor causes the vacuum switching valve to be energized. The valve
operates and allows air to be introduced into the throttle positioner
diaphragm. The throttle positioner is then retained in this position by
the tension of the return spring. If the accelerator pedal is now released,
the throttle valve plate is held slightly open by the positioner
mechanism instead of returning to the idling position.

4   When the vehicle speed enters the low speed range 20 to 24 mph
(32 to 39 kmh) the speed sensor causes the vacuum switching valve to
be de-energised and with the vacuum in the inlet manifold acting on the
throttle positioner diaphragm, the positioner is released from the
throttle valve plate, which then returns to the normal idling position.

5   The TPS system can be tested as follows. Have the engine running at
idling speed and then disconnect the vacuum hose from the throttle
positioner diaphragm capsule. Increase the engine speed and then
release the accelerator pedal.

6   The throttle positioner adjusting screw should be hard against the
throttle valve lever giving the engine a rather higher speed than normal
idling level.

7   Immediately connect the vacuum capsule *directly* to the intake
manifold, which should have the effect of releasing the throttle
positioner screw and to permit the engine to return to normal idle. If
this does not happen, check for faulty linkage, and if this is satisfactory,
renew the vacuum capsule unit.

8   With the engine at normal operating temperature, and the vacuum
hose disconnected from the throttle positioner vacuum capsule,
accelerate the engine and then release the accelerator. The engine
speed (checked on a tachometer) should be between 1300 and 1500
rev/min for vehicles with manual gearbox, and between 950 and 1150
rev/min for vehicles with automatic transmission. Turn the positioner
adjusting screw as necessary and then reconnect the vacuum hose.

18 Air Injection System (AIS) - description and maintenance

1   This system is designed to reduce the emission of toxic exhaust
gases by mixing pressurised air, (injected near each exhaust valve) with
the gases as they leave the engine combustion chambers.

2   The required air pressure is generated by an air pump which is
driven by a belt from the crankshaft pulley.

3   Normal maintenance consists of checking the tension of the belt
and keeping the connecting hoses tight and in good order. Adjust the
tension of the driving belt to give a deflection of ½ in (12.7 mm) at the
centre of the belt between the air pump and crankshaft pulleys. Adjustment is carried out by slackening the air pump mountings and adjustment strap and moving the air pump as required.

4   Occasionally test the operation of the air bypass valve. To do this,
run the engine at idling speed and listen for a hiss of escaping air from
the valve. If evident, renew the valve. Run the engine at about half
throttle, and then suddenly release the accelerator control rod. A
single ejection of air should be heard from the valve. If no air is released
or air keeps on escaping, then the valve must be renewed.

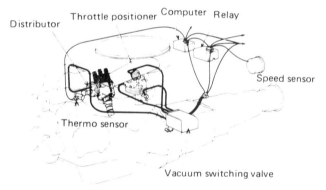

Fig. 3.34. TPS components fitted to 18R-C engine

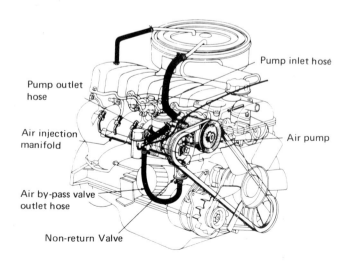

Fig. 3.35. AIS components

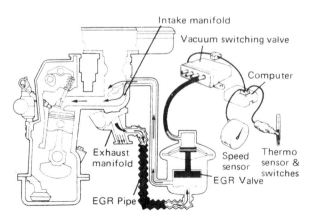

Fig. 3.36. EGR system components

21.2a Exhaust pipe flexible mounting

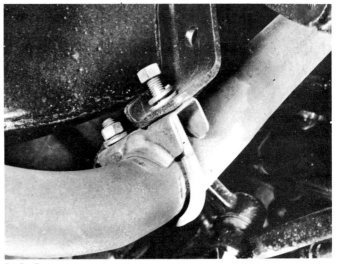

21.2b Exhaust downpipe clamp bracket

5   The non-return valve can be tested simply by blowing air in both directions and ensuring that air flow is restricted in one direction but not in the other.

6   A fault in the air pump can only be rectified by renewal of the pump.

19 Exhaust Gas Recirculation System (EGR) - description and maintenance

1   This system recirculates a proportion of the exhaust gases into the intake manifold in order to reduce the combustion temperature and so help to decrease the volume of nitrogen oxides which are produced.

2   The valve which controls the admission of gas into the intake manifold is actuated from a computer which receives signals from engine temperature and vehicle speed sensors.

3   Periodically, check the operation of the EGR valve. To do this, warm up the engine and then remove the cover from the air cleaner.

4   Let the engine idle and connect the EGR valve directly to the intake manifold with a length of vacuum hose. A bubbling noise should be heard coming from the carburettor. Disconnect the hose from the EGR valve when the bubbling noise should immediately cease.

5   Maintenance consists of periodically checking the security of all electrical leads and hose connections. A faulty EGR valve should be renewed complete.

20 Accelerator pedal and linkage

1   The accelerator cable and linkage should not normally require adjustment unless the cable has stretched or new components have been fitted.

2   Adjustment should be carried out by moving the position of the cable on the rocker box cover clamp and if essential, altering the length of the link connecting rod by pulling the socket joints from their ball connectors and screwing the sockets in or out.

3   Ensure that with the pedal released, the throttle valve plate lever is against the throttle speed screw and when the pedal is fully depressed, the throttle valve plates are fully open. This is best checked by removing the air cleaner.

4   There are minor differences in the layout and components of the accelerator linkage as fitted to the different vehicle models but the adjustment procedure is similar.

21 Exhaust system and manifolds

1   The layout of the exhaust system is similar on all models although the individual components may vary in detail design.

2   The system is supported on flexible mountings and incorporates a main silencer and a front and a rear pipe section (photos).

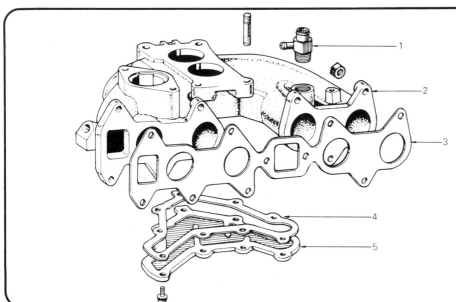

Fig. 3.37. Intake manifold (20R engine)

1 Automatic choke water connection
2 Manifold
3 Gasket
4 Gasket
5 Cover

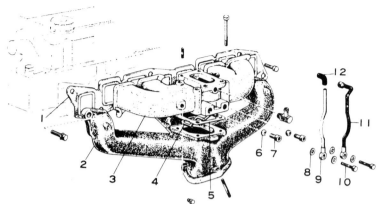

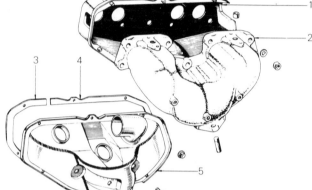

Fig. 3.38. Manifold assembly (8R-C, 18R-C engines)

1 Gasket
2 Exhaust manifold
3 Intake manifold
4 Automatic choke heater pipe
5 Gasket
6 Olive
7 Union
8 Gasket
9 Automatic choke inlet heater pipe
10 Bolt
11 Automatic choke outlet heater pipe
12 Connector

Fig. 3.40. Exhaust manifold (20R engine)

1 Inner heat insulator
2 Exhaust manifold
3 Gasket
4 Gasket
5 Outer heat insulator

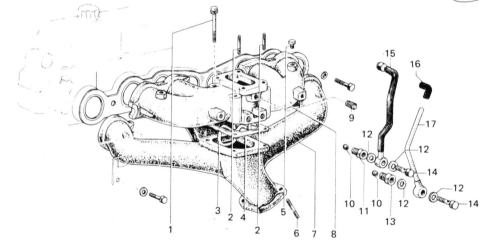

Fig. 3.39. Manifold assembly (12R engine)

1 Bolt
2 Stud
3 Automatic choke heater pipe
4 Gasket
5 Plug
6 Stud
7 Exhaust manifold
8 Intake manifold
9 Plug
10 Olive
11 Union
12 Gasket
13 Union
14 Bolt
15 Automatic choke heater outlet pipe
16 Connector
17 Automatic choke heater inlet pipe

3   Examination of the exhaust pipe and silencer at regular intervals is worthwhile as small defects may be repairable when, if left, they will almost certainly require renewal of one of the sections of the system. Also, any leaks, apart from the noise factor, may cause poisonous exhaust gases to get inside the car which can be unpleasant, to say the least, even in mild concentrations. Prolonged inhalation could cause sickness and giddiness.

4   As the sleeve connections and clamps are usually very difficult to separate, it is quicker and easier in the long run to remove the complete system from the car when renewing a section. It can be expensive if another section is damaged when trying to separate a bad section from it.

5   To remove the system, jack-up the car at the front and rear and then disconnect the front downpipe from the exhaust manifold.

6   Disconnect all the flexible mountings and withdraw the complete system from below and to the rear of the vehicle.

7   Cut away the bad sections, taking care not to damage the good sections which are to be retained.

8   File off any burrs at the ends of the new sections of pipe and smear them with grease. Slip the clamps over the pipes and connect the

sockets, but do not tighten the clamps at this stage.

9   Push the complete system under the vehicle and jack it up so that the front pipe can be bolted to the manifold and the rear tail pipe mounting connected.

10   Now turn the silencer sections to obtain their correct attitudes so that they will not touch or knock against any adjacent parts when the system is deflected to one side or the other.

11   Tighten all clamps and flexible mountings.

12   The inlet and exhaust manifolds vary slightly between models, the main difference being that the inlet manifold on the 20R type engine is heated from the engine cooling system and in turn, passes coolant through a short hose to the automatic choke housing on the carburettor. On 8R-C and 18R-C engines, the automatic choke is heated by gas from the exhaust manifold.

13   The manifolds on the 20R engine are on opposite sides of the cylinder head in accordance with the crossflow design of the unit.

14   When removing or refitting the manifolds, always use new gaskets and do not tighten the inlet to exhaust manifold bolts (8R-C, 18R-C and 12R engines) until the bolts holding the assembly to the cylinder head have been fully tightened.

22 Fault diagnosis - carburation, fuel and emission control systems

Fuel system and carburation

Symptom	Cause
Excessive fuel consumption	Air filter choked. Leakage from pump, carburettor or fuel lines or fuel tank. Float chamber flooding. Distributor condenser faulty. Distributor weights or vacuum capsule faulty. Mixture too rich. Contact breaker gap too wide. Incorrect valve clearances. Incorrect spark plug gaps. Tyres under inflated. Dragging brakes.
Fuel starvation or mixture weakness	Clogged fuel line filter. Float chamber needle valve clogged. Faulty fuel pump valves. Fuel pump diaphragm split. Fuel pipe unions loose. Fuel pump cover leaking. Inlet manifold gasket or carburettor flange gasket leaking. Incorrect adjustment of carburettor.

Emission control system

System or circuit	Symptom	Cause
Crankcase ventilation	Oil fume seepage from engine	Stuck or clogged PCV valve. Split or collapsed hoses.
Fuel Evaporative Emission Control	Fuel odour	Choked canister. Stuck filler cap valve.
	Vapour will not be drawn into manifold	Collapsed or split hoses. Vacuum switching valve defective. Speed sensor defective.
	Rough running engine	Defective non-return valve.
Transmission Controlled Spark (TCS)	TCS off when engine cold and raced	Defective distributor vacuum capsule, defective thermosensor or vacuum switching valve.
	TCS on when engine hot and raced	Defective thermosensor or vacuum switching valve.
	TCS off at incorrect speed ranges with engine hot	Defective vacuum switching valve or speed sensor.
Air Injection System (AIS)	Fume emission from exhaust pipe	Slack or broken air pump drive belt. Split or broken hoses. Clogged air filter. Defective air pump.
Throttle Positioner (Delay) System (TPS)	System fails to operate during acceleration System fails to turn off during deceleration	Adjust linkage, check vacuum hose to diaphragm unit. Defective diaphragm. Defective vacuum switching valve. Defective sensor.
Exhaust Gas Recirculation System (EGR)	Erratic idling Reduced power	Faulty valve. Faulty valve.

Note: The efficiency of the fume emission control system is also dependent upon the correct setting and adjustment of all other engine components. These include the ignition, cooling and lubrication systems, the valve clearances and the condition generally of the engine. Refer to the appropriate Sections and Chapters of this manual for servicing procedures.

Chapter 4 Ignition system

Contents

Specifications

System type ... ... 12 volt negative earth, battery, coil and distributor

Firing order ... ... 1 — 3 — 4 — 2

Distributor

	Hi-Ace Hi-Lux with 12R engine	8R-C engine	Hi-Lux 18R-C engine	20R engine
Contact points gap	0.016 to 0.020 in (0.4 to 0.5 mm)	0.016 to 0.020 in (0.4 to 0.5 mm)	0.016 to 0.020 in (0.4 to 0.5 mm)	0.018 in (0.45 mm)
Dwell angle	50 to 54°	50 to 54°	50 to 54°	50 to 54°
Rotor rotational direction	Clockwise	Clockwise	Clockwise	Clockwise
Static timing - degrees before top-dead-centre ... ... (BTDC) at idling speed (rev/min)	8° BTDC @ 700 rev/min	0° (TDC) @ 650 rev/min	Manual gearbox 7° BTDC @ 650 rev/min Auto. transmission 7° BTDC @ 800 rev/min in 'N'	Auto. transmission 8° BTDC @ 850 rev/min Manual transmission 8° BTDC @ 800 rev/min (high altitude - over 4000 ft 13° BTDC)

Vacuum advance angle (8R-C engine)
Advance begins ... ... 2.56 to 3.94 in Hg (65 to 100 mm Hg)
1.0 to 3.0° ... ... 4.72 in Hg (120 mm Hg)
3.0 to 5.0° ... ... 7.09 in Hg (180 mm Hg)
5.0 to 7.0° ... ... 9.84 in Hg (250 mm Hg)

Centrifugal advance angle (8R-C engine)
Advance begins ... ... 400 to 600 rev/min
12.5 to 14.5° ... ... 1100 rev/min
19.0 to 21.0° ... ... 2300 rev/min

Vacuum advance angle (12R engine)
Advance begins ... ... 4.33 to 5.12 in Hg (110 to 130 mm Hg)
5.5 to 7.5° ... ... 7.87 in Hg (200 mm Hg)
10.0 to 12.0° ... ... 11.02 in Hg (280 mm Hg)

Centrifugal advance angle (12R engine)
Advance begins ... ... 400 to 600 rev/min
8.5 to 10.5° ... ... 1400 rev/min
15.0 to 17.0° ... ... 2500 rev/min

Vacuum advance angle (18R-C engine)
Advance begins ... ... 2.28 to 4.02 in Hg (58 to 102 mm Hg)
1 to 3° ... ... 4.72 in Hg (120 mm Hg)
4 to 6° ... ... 7.88 in Hg (200 mm Hg)
7 to 9° ... ... 11.8 in Hg (300 mm Hg)

Centrifugal advance angle (18R-C engine)

Advance begins	510 to 690 rev/min (N. America 750 to 950)
4.6 to 6.4°	1030 to 1070 rev/min
10 to 12° (N. America)	1850 rev/min
12 to 14°	2600 rev/min

Vacuum advance angle (20R engine)

Advance begins	3.39 to 4.49 in Hg (86 to 114 mm Hg)
1.7 to 4.3°	5.51 in Hg (140 mm Hg)
6.5 to 7.5°	8.66 in Hg (220 mm Hg)
9 to 11°	11.81 in Hg (300 mm Hg)

Centrifugal advance angle (20R engine)

Advance begins	480 to 620 rev/min
7.8 to 9.3°	1350 rev/min
11.5 to 13.5°	2500 rev/min
11.2 to 13.2°	3000 rev/min

Condenser

Capacity	0.20 to 0.24 mf

Spark plugs

	8R-C	12R	18R-C	20R
Type	W20EP	W16EX BP5EZ	W20EP BP6ES	W16EX-U or W16EP BP5ESL or BP5EA-L
Gap	0.027 to 0.031 in (0.7 to 0.8 mm)	0.035 to 0.039 in (0.9 to 1.0 mm)	0.027 to 0.031 in (0.7 to 0.8 mm)	0.31 in (0.8 mm)

Torque wrench settings

	lb f ft	Nm
Spark plug	15	20
Distributor clamp plate bolt	15	20

1 General description

The ignition system comprises the following components:
The battery, which provides a current of 2.3 amps to the coil when the engine is running.
The ignition/starter switch.
The coil, which acts as a transformer to step up the 12 volt battery voltage to many thousands of volts, sufficient to jump the spark plug gaps.
The distributor, which comprises the contact breaker, condenser, rotor arm, distributor cap with brush and centrifugal and vacuum advance and retard mechanism, and is driven by the oil pump driveshaft at half crankshaft speed on 8R-C, 18R-C and 12R engines and from a gear on the front end of the camshaft on 20R engines.
The spark plugs, which ignite the compressed mixture in the combustion chambers.
Low and high tension leads connecting the various components.

When the ignition is switched on a current flows from the battery live terminal to the ignition switch through the coil primary winding to the moving contact breaker inside the distributor cap and to earth, when the contact breaker points are in the closed position. During this period of points closure, the current flows through the primary windings of the coil and magnetises the laminated iron core which in turn creates a magnetic field through the coil primary and secondary windings.

Each time the points open due to the rotation of the distributor cam, the current flow through the primary winding of the coil is interrupted. This causes the induction of a very high voltage (25000 volts) in the coil secondary winding. This HT (high tension) current is distributed to the spark plugs in the correct firing order sequence by the rotor arm and by means of the cap brush and HT leads.

A condenser is fitted to the distributor and connected between the moving contact breaker and earth to prevent excessive arcing and pitting of the contact breaker points.

The actual point of ignition of the fuel/air mixture which occurs a few degrees before TDC is determined by correct static setting of the ignition timing as described in Section 6. The ignition is advanced to meet the varying operating conditions by the centrifugal counterweights fitted in the base of the distributor body and by vacuum from the inlet manifold operating through a capsule linked to the movable distributor baseplate.

Slight variations of the static ignition setting may be made by means of the vernier adjuster to compensate for different fuel qualities. To improve the intensity of the spark at the spark plug electrodes during high speed running, an external resistor is included in the ignition primary circuit of all models except Hi-Ace (photo). After 1975, Hi-Ace models are also fitted with a resistor and earlier models can be modified to improve starting from cold.

Hi-Lux vehicles equipped with the 20R type engine incorporate an igniter device (see Section 6).

2 Contact breaker - adjustment

1 Pull off the HT leads from the spark plugs and mark them 1 to 4 for easy refitting.
2 Spring back the distributor cover securing clips and lift the cover to one side. Withdraw the rotor and the dustproof cover (photo).
3 Using a spanner on the crankshaft pulley securing bolt, rotate the engine in its normal direction of rotation until the heel of the movable contact breaker arm is on one of the 4 high points of the cam. Removal of the spark plugs will make turning the engine easier.
4 Examine the contact faces of the (now open) points and if they are pitted or burned then they must be removed and dressed as described in the next Section.
5 If the points are in good order, check the gap by inserting a feeler gauge of between 0.016 and 0.020 in (0.4 and 0.5 mm) in thickness. Insert the feeler blade in a vertical position and if the gap is correct, it will just fall by its own weight. If the gap is incorrect, adjust the fixed contact arm by loosening the retaining screw and moving it, as necessary, by means of a screwdriver blade inserted in the cut-out in the contact arm.
6 When the gap is correct, tighten the contact arm screw, remove the feeler blade, replace the dust proof cover, rotor arm and distributor cap. **Check that the ring spanner has been removed from the crankshaft pulley bolt.** Reconnect the HT leads.
7 Setting the contact breaker gap with a feeler blade must be regarded as the initial setting operation only, and the dwell angle must then be checked using a dwell meter.
8 The dwell angle is the number of degrees through which the distributor cam turns during the period between the instants of closure and opening of the contact breaker points.

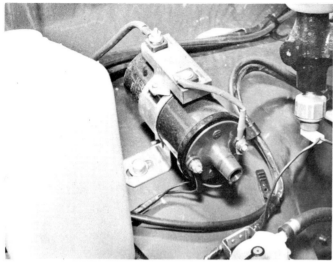

1.12 Coil with ballast resistor (Hi-Lux)

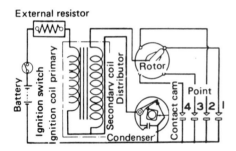

Fig. 4.1. Ignition circuit diagram (not 20R engine)

9   The correct dwell angle is as specified in Specifications Section. With the engine idling, connect a dwell meter between the negative terminal of the coil and a good earth on the engine or bodyframe.
10 If the indicated dwell angle is too large, increase the contact breaker points gap, if too small, reduce the contact breaker points gap.

3   Contact breaker points - removal and refitting (except 20R engines)

1   Carry out operations 1 and 2 of the preceding Section.
2   Detach the spring retaining clip from the top of the contact breaker arm pivot post.
3   Unscrew the nuts on the LT terminal on the outside of the distributor body just enough to enable the contact arm lead and spade terminal to be withdrawn, then lift the movable arm from the baseplate (early models).
4   Remove the securing screw and lift the fixed contact breaker arm from the baseplate (early models). Later models have a contact set which cannot be dismantled.
5   Examine the points. After a period of operation, one contact face should have a pip and the other a crater caused by arcing. This is a normal condition which should be removed by dressing the faces squarely on an oilstone, or abrasive strip.
6   Excessive pitting of the contact points may be caused by operation with an incorrect gap, the voltage regulator setting too high, faulty or wrong type of condenser, loose distributor baseplate or battery terminals.
7   Where contact breaker points are so badly worn or the pitting so deep that excessive rubbing would be required to eliminate it, then they should be renewed.
8   Wipe the faces of the points with methylated spirit before installing, smear the high points of the cam with petroleum jelly. Adjust the points as described in Section 2.
9   Refit the rotor, cap and HT leads.

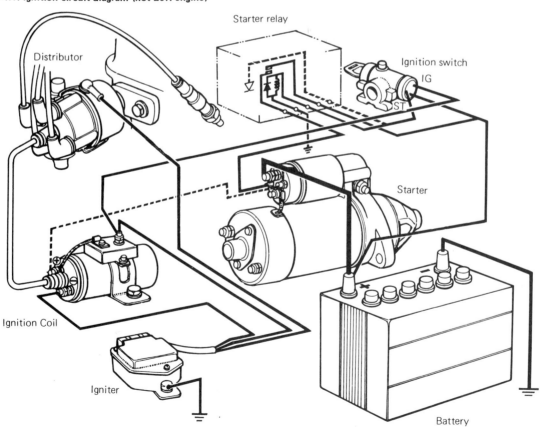

Fig. 4.2. Ignition circuit and component layout (20R engine)

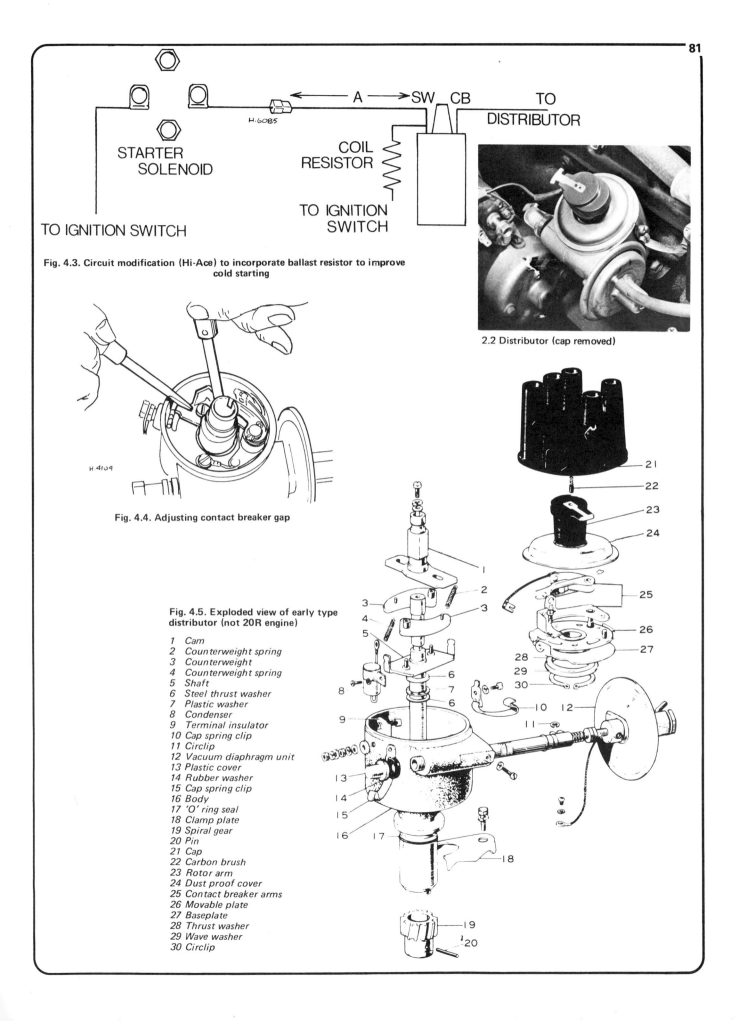

Fig. 4.3. Circuit modification (Hi-Ace) to incorporate ballast resistor to improve cold starting

2.2 Distributor (cap removed)

Fig. 4.4. Adjusting contact breaker gap

Fig. 4.5. Exploded view of early type distributor (not 20R engine)

1 Cam
2 Counterweight spring
3 Counterweight
4 Counterweight spring
5 Shaft
6 Steel thrust washer
7 Plastic washer
8 Condenser
9 Terminal insulator
10 Cap spring clip
11 Circlip
12 Vacuum diaphragm unit
13 Plastic cover
14 Rubber washer
15 Cap spring clip
16 Body
17 'O' ring seal
18 Clamp plate
19 Spiral gear
20 Pin
21 Cap
22 Carbon brush
23 Rotor arm
24 Dust proof cover
25 Contact breaker arms
26 Movable plate
27 Baseplate
28 Thrust washer
29 Wave washer
30 Circlip

4 Contact breaker points - removal and refitting (20R engine)

1 Remove the distributor cap, rotor and dustproof cover.
2 Remove the cap from the vernier adjuster and slide out the points cover.
3 Unbolt the LT terminal and withdraw the contact breaker set.
4 Repeat the operations described in paragraphs 5, 6 and 7 of the preceding Section.
5 Before installing the contact points, check the damper spring gap adjustment. With the contact face of the spring against one of the flats of the cam, the gap should be between 0.002 and 0.018 in (0.05 and 0.45 mm). Use a feeler blade to measure the gap and release the hold down screw if necessary, to move the position of the damping spring.
6 Refit the contact points by reversing the removal operations and adjust them as described in Section 2.

5 Condenser (capacitor) - removal, testing and refitting (except 20R engine)

1 The condenser ensures that with the contact breaker points open, the sparking between them is not excessive, as this would cause severe pitting. The condenser is fitted in parallel and its failure will automatically cause failure of the ignition system as the points will be prevented from interrupting the low tension circuit.
2 Testing for an unserviceable condenser may be effected by switching on the ignition and separating the contact points by hand. If this action is accompanied by a blue flash then condenser failure is indicated. Difficult starting, missing of the engine after several miles running or badly pitted points are other indications of a faulty condenser.
3 The surest test is by substitution of a new unit.
4 To remove the condenser, unscrew its retaining screw and detach its lead from the LT terminal on the distributor body. Refitting is a reversal of removal.

6 Igniter - testing (20R engine)

1 A misfire or failure to start may be due to a faulty igniter.
2 To test, switch on the ignition and, using a voltmeter, check for battery voltage at the resistor terminal as shown. If not, inspect the ignition switch leads for a break or disconnection.
3 Disconnect the LT lead from the distributor terminal and touch the

end of the lead against a clean earth surface on the engine or bodyframe. A spark should be visible each time this action is repeated. If not, switch off the ignition and renew the igniter.

7 Distributor - removal and overhaul (not 20R engine)

1 Remove the No. 1 spark plug and place a finger over the hole to feel the compression being generated as the engine is rotated by means of the crankshaft pulley bolt.
2 As soon as compression is felt this will indicate that No. 1 piston is rising on its compression stroke. Continue turning the engine until the advance timing mark (not TDC mark) on the crankshaft pulley is in line with the pointer on the timing cover.
3 Remove the distributor cap and mark the rim of the distributor body at a point opposite to the centre line of the contact end of the rotor arm. This is equivalent to alignment with No. 1 contact in the distributor cap.
4 Disconnect the LT wire from the terminal on the distributor body.
5 Disconnect the vacuum tube from the distributor advance diaphragm unit.
6 Unbolt the distributor clamp plate and withdraw the distributor from the recess in the crankcase.
7 The distributor cap may be withdrawn if the HT leads are first disconnected from the spark plugs and coil centre socket.

Early type distributor

8 Remove the contact breaker assembly and the cap from the vernier adjuster.
9 Remove the vacuum diaphragm unit by withdrawing the retaining screws (1 and 2) and the circlip (3) (Fig. 4.12).
10 Remove the distributor cap spring clips, the externally mounted condenser and the LT terminal from the distributor body.
11 Remove the contact breaker mounting plate (movable) and the baseplate (fixed) as an assembly. This is secured to the distributor body by screws.
12 Unscrew and remove the central cam screw and pull off the cam from the top of the distributor shaft.
13 Remove the mechanical advance counterweights and springs. Note carefully the positions of the two springs as they are not interchangeable.
14 Carefully drill out the rivetted end of the pin which secures the spiral gear/spacer to the bottom end of the distributor shaft.
15 Drive out the pin and withdraw the shaft upwards through the body, retaining any washers and shims.

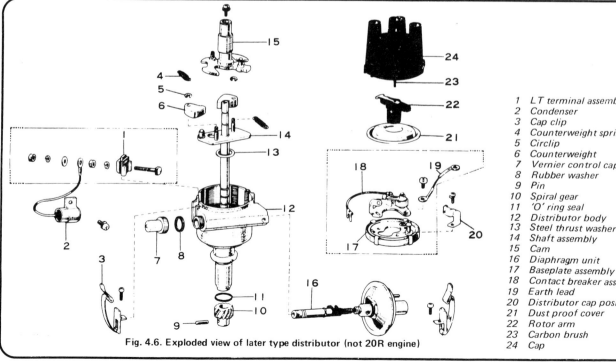

Fig. 4.6. Exploded view of later type distributor (not 20R engine)

1   LT terminal assembly
2   Condenser
3   Cap clip
4   Counterweight spring
5   Circlip
6   Counterweight
7   Vernier control cap
8   Rubber washer
9   Pin
10 Spiral gear
11 'O' ring seal
12 Distributor body
13 Steel thrust washer
14 Shaft assembly
15 Cam
16 Diaphragm unit
17 Baseplate assembly
18 Contact breaker assembly
19 Earth lead
20 Distributor cap positioner
21 Dust proof cover
22 Rotor arm
23 Carbon brush
24 Cap

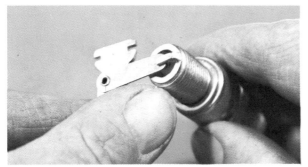

Measuring plug gap. A feeler gauge of the correct size (see ignition system specifications) should have a slight 'drag' when slid between the electrodes. Adjust gap if necessary

Adjusting plug gap. The plug gap is adjusted by bending the earth electrode inwards, or outwards, as necessary until the correct clearance is obtained. Note the use of the correct tool

Normal. Grey-brown deposits lightly coated core nose. Gap increasing by around 0.001 in (0.025 mm) per 1000 miles (1600 km). Plugs ideally suited to engine and engine in good condition

Carbon fouling. Dry, black, sooty deposits. Will cause weak spark and eventually misfire. Fault: over-rich fuel mixture. Check: carburettor mixture settings, float level and jet sizes; choke operation and cleanliness of air filter. Plugs can be re-used after cleaning

Oil fouling. Wet, oily deposits. Will cause weak spark and eventually misfire. Fault: worn bores/piston rings or valve guides; sometimes occurs (temporarily) during running-in period. Plugs can be re-used after thorough cleaning

Overheating. Electrodes have glazed appearance, core nose very white - few deposits. Fault: plug overheating. Check: plug value, ignition timing, fuel octane rating (too low) and fuel mixture (too weak). Discard plugs and cure fault immediately

Electrode damage. Electrodes burned away; core nose has burned, glazed appearance. Fault: initial pre-ignition. Check: as for 'Overheating' but may be more severe. Discard plugs and remedy fault before piston or valve damage occurs

Split core nose (may appear initially as a crack). Damage is self-evident, but cracks will only show after cleaning. Fault: pre-ignition or wrong gap-setting technique. Check: ignition timing, cooling system, fuel octane rating (too low) and fuel mixture (too weak). Discard plugs, rectify fault immediately

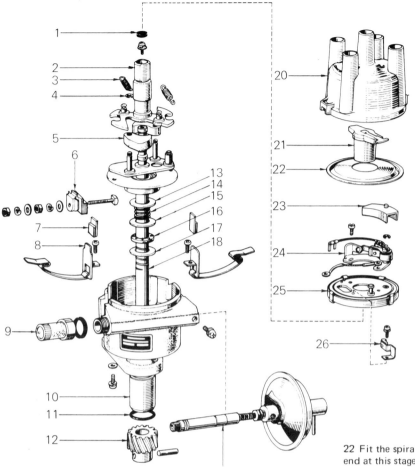

Fig. 4.7. Exploded view of distributor used in 20R engine

1	Lubrication pad	14	Spring
2	Cam	15	Washer
3	Spring	16	Bearing
4	'E' ring	17	Washer
5	Counterweight	18	Shaft
6	Terminal insulator	19	Vacuum unit
7	Rubber pad	20	Distributor cap
8	Cap clip	21	Rotor
9	Vernier control cap	22	Dustproof cover
10	Body	23	Contact points cover
11	'O' ring	24	Contact breaker assembly
12	Gear	25	Contact breaker baseplate
13	Washer	26	Damper spring

16 Check for wear between the shaft and the body. If evident it will be more economical to exchange the complete distributor unit for a reconditioned one rather than attempt to repair the old unit.
17 Check the fit of the counterweights on their pivot posts. The maximum clearance is 0.007 in (0.2 mm).
18 Examine the distributor cap for cracks and for burnt or eroded contacts. Check the carbon brush in the centre of the cap interior; if it has worn below 0.28 in (7 mm) in length, renew it.
19 Separate the contact breaker swivel plate from the baseplate. Do this by removing the circlip and carefully detaching the small components. Do not lose the rolling balls. Renew any items which are worn or distorted. When the movable and fixed plates are assembled, prise them apart with the fingers; if the clearance is greater than 0.008 in (0.2 mm) adjust by means of different adjusting washers. A force of between 7.1 and 17.6 oz (200 and 500g) should be needed to turn the movable plate.
20 Check the teeth on the spiral gear and renew the gear if it is worn or chipped.
21 Lubricate the shaft with clean engine oil, locate the washers on the shaft (plastic between two steel ones) and then insert it into the distributor body.

Fig. 4.8. Withdrawing contact points cover (20R type engine)

Fig. 4.9. Checking damper spring adjustment (20R type engine)

22 Fit the spiral gear and insert the retaining pin but do not peen its end at this stage as the shaft endfloat must be checked. The correct endfloat is between 0.006 and 0.020 in (0.15 and 0.5 mm) tested with feeler gauges inserted between the spiral gear and the distributor body. Where the endfloat is outside that specified, add or remove the steel thrust washers as necessary.
23 When the correct endfloat is achieved, peen over the end of the spiral gear securing pin.
24 Apply engine oil to the counterweight pivot posts and then fit the counterweights and springs. Note particularly the position of the spring with the shorter number of coils and the longer hook.
25 Smear the distributor shaft with grease, fit the cam and secure with the central screw.
26 Refit the distributor cap spring clips.
27 Install the breaker plate assembly into the distributor body making sure that the diaphragm actuating link pivot is positioned correctly to receive the link.
28 Fit the vacuum diaphragm engaging its link with the baseplate pivot post and securing it with the circlip.
29 Fit the contact breaker assembly to the baseplate but do not tighten the securing screws at this stage.
30 Connect the diaphragm unit earth lead. The contact breaker lead and condenser lead should then be connected to the terminal on the distributor body.

Later type distributor
31 Although there are detail differences in the components of the later type distributor, dismantling is very similar to the procedure described earlier in this Section, except that the cap securing clips are secured by internally located screws, the contact breaker assembly must not be dismantled and circlips are used to secure the counterweights.
32 Inspection of components for wear is similar to that described for the earlier type distributor except that if the force required to turn the movable baseplate exceeds 2.2 lbs (1.0 kg) when lubricated with engine oil, then the assembly must be renewed complete.
33 Reassembly is similar to the earlier type distributor, but if endfloat of the distributor shaft is outside that specified (0.006 to 0.020 in - 0.15 to 0.50 mm) a new single thrust washer must be selected from

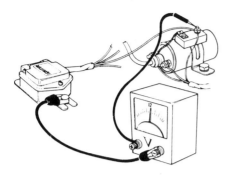

Fig. 4.10. Testing igniter (20R type engine)

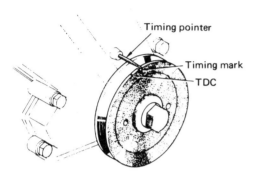

Fig. 4.11. Ignition timing marks (not 20R engine) - Larger Vee notch is BTDC mark

Fig. 4.12. Distributor vacuum unit retaining screw (1) earth lead (2) and circlip (3) on early type distributor (not 20R engine)

Fig. 4.13. Location of counterweight springs on early type distributor (not 20R engine). (1 and 2) counterweights, (3 and 4) springs

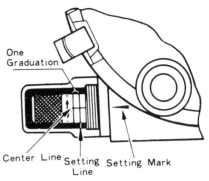

Fig. 4.14. Distributor vernier adjuster

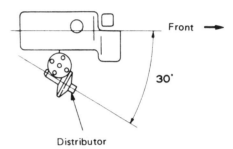

Fig. 4.15. Distributor installation diagram (not 20R engine)

those available in thicknesses of 0.098 in (2.5 mm), 0.106 in (2.7 mm), 0.114 in (2.9 mm).

34 The baseplate assembly is secured to the distributor body with clips. Note carefully the location of the distributor cap positioner and that the earth lead is secured under the cap clip screw nearest the LT terminal on the distributor body.

35 Adjust the contact points gap as described in Section 2 of this Chapter.

8 Distributor - installation (not 20R engine)

1 If the engine is turned while the distributor is removed, reset the crankshaft pulley timing mark opposite the timing cover pointer (No. 1 piston on compression stroke) as described in paragraphs 1 and 2 of the preceding Section.

2 Turn the rotor arm so that its centre line is in alignment with the mark made on the distributor body rim before removal. If a new distributor is being fitted then mark the rim of the body after the rotor arm has been aligned with No. 1 contact in the distributor cap (see Fig. 4.29).

3 Set the vernier adjuster so that its centre line is opposite the setting mark on the diaphragm unit.

4 Hold the distributor over its recess in the crankcase so that a line drawn through the vacuum diaphragm unit makes an angle of 30° with the centre line of the engine.

5 Using a screwdriver, turn the slot in the oil pump driveshaft (visible at the bottom of the distributor recess) so that it is in alignment with the tongue on the bottom of the distributor shaft.

6 Holding the distributor in the predetermined position, turn the rotor arm anticlockwise 30°.

7 Insert the distributor into the crankcase and as the gears mesh the rotor will rotate in a clockwise direction and become aligned with the mark made on the rim of the distributor body. The distributor should be pushed right down to fully engage the driveshaft tongue with the slot. The rotor will be opposite No. 1 spark plug contact in the distributor cap.

8 Rotate the distributor body until the contact breaker points are just about to open and then tighten the distributor clamp plate bolt.

9 Refit the distributor cap, connect the LT and HT leads and the vacuum pipe.

10 Check the timing with a stroboscope as described in Section 11.

Fig. 4.16. Rotor arm in alignment with No. 1 spark plug contact in distributor cap after correct installation (not 20R engine)

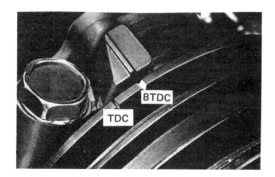

Fig. 4.17. Ignition timing marks (20R engine).

Fig. 4.18. Withdrawing distributor from 20R type engine

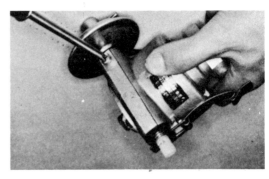

Fig. 4.19. Vacuum unit securing screw (20R type engine distributor)

Fig. 4.20. Removing contact breaker plate (20R type engine distributor)

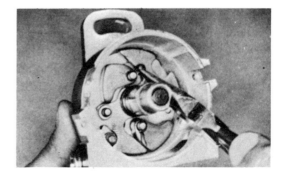

Fig. 4.21. Extracting 'E' clip (20R type engine distributor)

9 Distributor - removal and overhaul (20R engine)

1   The distributor on this type of engine is driven from a gear on the front end of the camshaft.

2   Repeat the operations described in Section 7, paragraphs 1 to 7 inclusive.

3   Remove the dustproof cover, vernier adjuster cap and withdraw the contact breaker points cover.

4   Remove the LT terminal.

5   Remove the contact breaker set and damping spring.

6   Release the securing screw and withdraw the vacuum diaphragm unit.

7   Extract the two rubber pads and unscrew the screws which hold the two cap clips.

8   Remove the contact breaker plate with a pair of pliers.

9   Disconnect the counterweight springs, noting their locations (use quick-drying paint to mark the ends of the springs and their respective anchorages).

10 Extract the 'E' clips and withdraw the counterweights and bearings.

11 Extract the lubrication felt pad from the top of the distributor shaft, remove the screw now exposed, and pull off the cam.

12 Drill out the gear securing pin.

13 Extract the two securing screws and withdraw the distributor shaft from the body.

14 Withdraw the bearing, spring and washers and extract the 'O' ring seal from the distributor body.

15 Clean and inspect all components for wear. Renew where necessary.

16 Reassembly is a reversal of dismantling but observe the following.

17 Smear shaft and cam interior with grease and match the 13.5 mark on the counterweight with the stopper (see Fig. 4.25).

18 Make sure that the bearing, washers and spring are fitted to the distributor shaft in the correct sequence.

19 Note that the cap clip which incorporates the locating tag must be fitted on the terminal side of the distributor body.

20 Fit a new gear and retaining pin and peen both ends of the pin.

21 Set the contact points gap and the damper spring gap as described in Sections 2 and 4 of this Chapter.

Fig. 4.22. Removing cam screw (20R type engine distributor)

Fig. 4.23. Removing shaft retaining screws (20R type engine distributor)

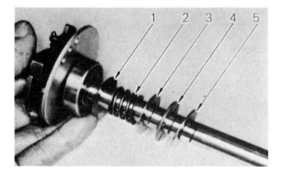

Fig. 4.24. Distributor shaft details (20R type engine distributor)

1 Blue washer   4 Bearing
2 Spring   5 Thick washer
3 Thin washer

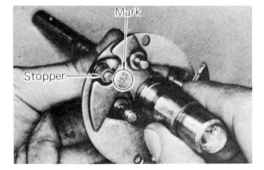

Fig. 4.25. Matching counterweight mark with stopper (20R engine type distributor)

Fig. 4.26. Position of rotor after correct installation of distributor (20R engine type distributor)

10 Distributor - installation (20R engine)

1 If the crankshaft has been turned while the distributor has been removed from the engine, set the pulley (static advance) mark opposite the pointer on the timing cover. This is not the TDC mark on the pulley. The method of doing this is described in Section 7, paragraphs 1 and 2.

2 Hold the distributor so that the vernier adjuster is pointing vertically upwards and then turn the rotor arm so that its contact end is in alignment with the uppermost distributor cap clip.

3 Insert the distributor and, as the gears mesh, the rotor arm will turn in an anti-clockwise direction and take up a position opposite No. 1 cap contact or the mark made on the rim of the distributor body before removal.

4 Turn the distributor body until the contact points are just about to open and then insert and tighten the clamp plate bolt.

5 Refit the distributor cap, the HT and LT leads and the vacuum pipe.

6 Check the timing with a stroboscope as described in the next Section.

11 Ignition timing

1 Check the ignition timing using a stroboscope. First paint the timing cover pointer and the timing notch on the pulley (not the TDC notch) with white paint. The position of this slot will vary in accordance with engine type and static advance setting (see Specifications Section).

2 Disconnect the vacuum pipe from the distributor diaphragm unit.

3 Start the engine and set the slow running speed to that shown in Specifications according to engine type, preferably by using a tachometer.

4 Project the light from the stroboscope onto the timing cover pointer and pulley mark. Each flash of the stroboscope indicates that No. 1 cylinder has fired and if the timing is correct, the pulley mark will appear to be stationary and in alignment with the pointer.

5 Where the mark is not in alignment with the pointer, release the distributor clamp bolt and turn the distributor body until they do coincide. Tighten the clamp bolt.

A useful check on the correct operation of the vacuum advance mechanism may be made by replacing the vacuum pipe to the distributor and still using the stroboscopic light as for checking the timing (just described), slowly increase the speed of the engine. The timing mark on the pulley should now move out of alignment with the timing cover pointer and the amount of misalignment should increase in proportion to the increase in engine speed. This proves correct operation of the vacuum advance mechanism. No movement between the pulley mark and pointer indicates either a break in the vacuum pipe or an unserviceable diaphragm unit.

6 Slight alterations to the ignition timing should be carried out by means of the vernier adjuster. This may be required when fuels of different octane ratings are used.

7 To adjust, drive the vehicle at a steady road speed (in top gear — manual gearbox or 'D' — automatic transmission) at about 25 mph (40 km/h). Suddenly depress the accelerator pedal to the floor and listen for the sound of 'pinking' (pre-detonation). If evident, remove the plastic cap from the vernier adjuster and turn it in the 'R' direction only

enough to prevent pinking on retest. Where the ignition timing is thought to be retarded or a fuel or higher octane rating is being used, turn the vernier adjuster in the 'A' direction until any further movement would cause the engine to 'pink'. Turning the vernier control through one graduation is equivalent to altering the ignition timing by 10 degrees.
8   With the engine switched off, it is a good idea to check the operation of the centrifugal advance mechanism. To do this, remove the distributor cap and turn the rotor arm fully clockwise. Release the rotor arm and ensure that it returns all the way to its original position. If it fails to do so, the counterweights are sticking or the return springs are broken or stretched.

12 Coil polarity and testing

1   High tension current should be negative at the spark plug terminals. If the HT current is positive at the spark plug terminals then the LT leads to the coil primary terminals have been incorrectly connected. A wrong connection can cause as much as 60% loss of spark efficiency and can cause rough idling and misfiring at speed.
2   With a negative earth electrical system, the LT lead from the distributor connects with the negative (primary) terminal on the coil.
3   The simplest way to test a coil is by substitution. If an ohmmeter is available use it to carry out the following checks but first apply a 12 volt current to the coil to bring it to normal operating temperature.
4   Check the primary resistance between the coil (+) and (−) terminals which should be between 1.3 and 1.5 ohms.
5   Check the secondary resistance (secondary to primary terminals) this should be between 6500 and 10500 ohms.
6   Check the ballast resistor resistance which should be between 1.3 and 1.7 ohms.
7   Insulation breakdown can only be satisfactorily tested using a megohmmeter between the coil casing and the primary terminals. The resistance should be in excess of 50 megohms.

13 Spark plugs and HT leads

1   The correct functioning of the spark plugs is vital for the correct running and efficiency of the engine. The plugs fitted as standard are listed in the Specifications.
2   At intervals of 6000 miles (9600 km) the plugs should be removed, examined, cleaned and, if worn excessively, renewed. The condition of the spark plug will also tell much about the overall condition of the engine.
3   If the insulator nose of the spark plug is clean and white, with no deposits, this is indicative of a weak mixture, or too hot a plug.
4   If the top and insulator nose is covered with hard black looking deposits, then this is indicative that the mixture is too rich. Should the plug be black and oily, then it is likely that the engine is fairly worn, as well as the mixture being too rich.
5   If the insulator nose is covered with light tan to greyish brown deposits, then the mixture is correct and it is likely that the engine is in good condition.
6   If there are any traces of long brown tapering stains on the outside of the white portion of the plug, then the plug will have to be renewed, as this shows that there is a faulty joint between the plug body and the insulator, and compression is being allowed to leak away.
7   Plugs should be cleaned by a sand blasting machine, which will free them from carbon more thoroughly than cleaning by hand and wire brush. The machine will also test the condition of the plugs under compression. Any plug that fails to spark at the recommended pressure should be renewed.
8   The spark plug gap is of considerable importance, as, if it is too large or too small, the size of the spark and its efficiency will be seriously impaired. The spark plug gap should be set to 0.030 in (0.76 mm) for the best results.
9   To set it, measure the gap with a feeler gauge, and then bend open, or close, the outer plug electrode until the correct gap is achieved. The centre electrode should never be bent as this may cause plug failure.
10 The HT leads to the coil and spark plugs are of internal resistance, carbon core type. They are used in the interest of eliminating interference caused by the ignition system. They are much more easily damaged than copper cored cable and they should be pulled from the spark plug terminals by gripping the rubber end fitting at the end of

the cable. Occasionally wipe the external surfaces of the leads free from oil and dirt using a fuel moistened cloth.
11 Always check the connection of the HT leads to the spark plugs is in the correct firing order sequence, 1 − 3 − 4 − 2.

14 Ignition system - fault diagnosis

Failures of the ignition system will either be due to faults in the HT or LT circuits. Initial checks should be made by observing the security of spark plug terminals, switch terminals, coil and battery connections. More detailed investigation and the explanation and remedial action in respect of symptoms of ignition faults are described in next Section.

15 Ignition system - fault symptoms

Engine fails to start
1   If the engine fails to start and the car was running normally when it was last used, first check there is fuel in the tank. If the engine turns over normally on the starter motor and the battery is evidently well charged, then the fault may be in either the high or low tension circuits. First check the HT circuit. **Note:** If the battery is known to be fully charged; the ignition light comes on, and the starter motor fails to turn the engine, check the tightness of the leads on the battery terminals and also the secureness of the earth lead to its connection on the body. It is quite common for the leads to have worked loose, even if they look and feel secure. If one of the battery terminal posts gets very hot when trying to work the starter motor this is a sure indication of a faulty connection to that terminal.
2   One of the commonest reasons for bad starting is wet or damp spark plug leads and distributor. Remove the distributor cap. If condensation is visible internally, dry the cap with a rag and also wipe over the leads. Replace the cap.
3   If the engine still fails to start, check that current is reaching the plugs, by disconnecting each plug lead in turn at the spark plug end, and hold the end of the cable about 3/16th inch (5 mm) away from the cylinder block. Spin the engine on the starter motor.
4   Sparking between the end of the cable and block should be fairly strong with a regular blue spark. (Hold the lead with rubber to avoid electric shocks). If current is reaching the plugs, then remove them and clean and regap them. The engine should now start.
5   If there is no spark at the plug leads take off the HT lead from the centre of the distributor cap and hold it to the block as before. Spin the engine on the starter once more. A rapid succession of blue sparks between the end of the lead and the block indicate that the coil is in order and that the distributor cap is cracked, the rotor arm faulty, or the carbon brush in the top of the distributor cap is not making good contact with the spring on the rotor arm. Possibly the points are in bad condition. Clean and reset them as described in this Chapter.
6   If there are no sparks from the end of the lead from the coil, check the connections at the coil end of the lead. If it is in order start checking the low tension circuit.
7   Use a 12v voltmeter or a 12v bulb and two lengths of wire. With the ignition switched on and the points open test between the low tension wire to the coil (it is marked +) and earth. No reading indicates a break in the supply from the ignition switch. Check the connections at the switch to see if any are loose. Refit them and the engine should run. A reading shows a faulty coil or condenser, or broken lead between the coil and the distributor.
8   Take the condenser wire off the points assembly and with the points open, test between the moving point and earth. If there is a reading now, then the fault is in the condenser. Fit a new one and the fault is cleared.
9   With no reading from the moving point to earth, take a reading between earth and the (−) terminal of the coil. A reading here shows a broken wire which will need to be renewed between the coil and distributor. No reading confirms that the coil has failed and must be renewed, after which the engine will run once more. Remember to refit the condenser wire to the points assembly. For these tests it is sufficient to separate the points with a piece of dry paper while testing with the points open.

Engine misfires
10 If the engine misfires regularly, run it at a fast idling speed. Pull off each of the plug caps in turn and listen to the note of the engine. Hold

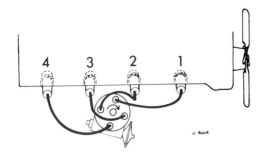

Fig. 4.27. Spark plug lead connection diagram (not 20R engine)

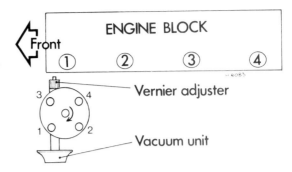

Fig. 4.28. Spark plug lead connection diagram (20R engine)

the plug cap in a dry cloth or with a rubber glove as additional protection against a shock from the HT supply.

11 No difference in engine running will be noticed when the lead from the defective circuit is removed. Removing the lead from one of the good cylinders will accentuate the misfire.

12 Remove the plug lead from the end of the defective plug and hold it about 3/16 in (5 mm) away from the block. Restart the engine. If the sparking is fairly strong and regular, the fault must lie in the spark plug.

13 The plug may be loose, the insulation may be cracked, or the points may have burnt away giving too wide a gap for the spark to jump. Worse still, one of the points may have broken off. Either renew the plug, or clean it, reset the gap, and then test it.

14 If there is no spark at the end of the plug lead, or if it is weak and intermittent, check the ignition lead from the distributor to the plug. If the insulation is cracked or perished, renew the lead. Check the connection at the distributor cap.

15 If there is still no spark, examine the distributor cap carefully for tracking. This can be recognised by a very thin black line running between two or more contacts, or between a contact and some other part of the distributor. These lines are paths which now conduct

electricity across the cap, thus letting it run to earth. The only answer is a new distributor cap.

16 Apart from the ignition timing being incorrect, other causes of misfiring have already been dealt with under the section dealing with the failure of the engine to start. To recap - these are that:

  a) *The coil may be faulty giving an intermittent misfire.*
  b) *There may be a damaged wire or loose connection in the low tension circuit.*
  c) *The condenser may be short circuiting.*
  d) *There may be a mechanical fault in the distributor (broken driving spindle or contact breaker spring).*

17 If the ignition timing is too far retarded, it should be noted that the engine will tend to overheat, and there will be a quite noticeable drop in power. If the engine is overheating and the power is down, and the ignition timing is correct, then the carburettor should be checked, as it is likely that this is where the fault lies.

18 Finally check the setting and adjustment of the fume emission control equipment, particularly the transmission controlled spark system (TCS) described in Chapter 3.

Chapter 5 Clutch

Contents

Specifications

Type

Hi-Lux (except 12R engine)	Single dry plate, diaphragm spring, hydraulic actuation
Early Hi-Ace (and Hi-Lux with 12R engine)	Single dry plate, coil springs, hydraulic actuation. Later Hi-Ace models have diaphragm spring clutch.

Dimensions

	Hi-Lux (except 12R engine)	Early* Hi-Ace (and Hi-Lux with 12R engine)
Disc outer diameter	8.80 in (224.0 mm)	8.35 in (212.0 mm)
Disc inner diameter	6.30 in (160.0 mm)	5.51 in (140.0 mm)
Lining thickness	0.13 to 0.14 in (3.3 to 3.5 mm)	0.14 in (3.5 mm)

Master cylinder

Bore diameter	0.6248 to 0.6265 in (15.870 to 15.913 mm)	0.75 in (19.05 mm)
Piston diameter	0.6225 to 0.6235 in (15.811 to 15.838 mm)	0.74 in (18.80 mm)
Piston clearance in bore	0.0013 to 0.0040 in (0.032 to 0.102 mm)	0.0012 in (0.0254 mm)
Spring free length	3.35 in (85.0 mm)	3.80 in (96.5 mm)
		* later models as column 1

Operating cylinder

Bore diameter	0.5906 to 0.5922 in (15.000 to 15.043 mm)	0.59 in (15.0 mm)
Piston diameter	0.5886 to 0.5896 in (14.950 to 14.975 mm)	0.58 in (14.9 mm)
Piston clearance in bore	0.0010 to 0.0037 in (0.025 to 0.093 mm)	0.0010 in (0.025 mm)
Number of pressure plate springs (coil)	—	6
Free length	—	1.90 in (48.2 mm)

Torque wrench settings

	lb f ft	Nm
Pressure plate to flywheel bolts		
Hi-Lux except 12R engine	16	22
Hi-Ace 12R engine	11	15
Clutch bellhousing to engine bolts:		
Hi-Ace 12R engine	32	44
Hi-Lux except 12R engine	50	68
Release arm pivot stud	22	30
Pedal pivot bolts	32	44
Reservoir securing bolt	22	30
Master cylinder end cap	145	197

1 General description

Early Hi—Ace models and Hi-Lux with 12R engine are fitted with a coil spring type clutch. All other models have a diaphragm spring type clutch.

Diaphragm spring type clutch

1 The unit comprises of a pressure plate assembly which contains the pressure plate, diaphragm spring and fulcrum rings. The assembly is bolted by means of its cover to the rear face of the flywheel.

2 The driven plate (friction disc) is free to slide along the gearbox input shaft and is held in place between the flywheel and pressure plate faces by the pressure exerted by the diaphragm spring. The friction lining material is rivetted to the driven plate which incorporates a rubber cushioned hub designed to absorb transmission rotational shocks and to assist in ensuring smooth take offs.

3 The circular diaphragm spring assembly is mounted on shouldered pins and held in place in the cover by two fulcrum rings. The spring itself is held in place by three spring steel clips.

4 Depressing the clutch pedal pushes the release bearing, mounted on its hub retainer, forward, to bear against the fingers of the diaphragm spring. This action causes the diaphragm spring outer edge to deflect and so move the pressure plate rearwards to disengage the pressure plate from the driven plate.

5 When the clutch pedal is released, the diaphragm spring forces the pressure plate into contact with the friction linings of the driven plate and at the same time pushes the driven plate fractionally forward on its splines to ensure full engagement with the flywheel. The driven plate is now firmly sandwiched between the pressure plate and the flywheel and so the drive is taken up.

Coil spring type clutch

6 The operation of this type of clutch mechanism is similar to the diaphragm spring type, but it requires rather higher pedal pressures to compress the coil springs used in its construction.

7 Clutch actuation on all models is hydraulic.

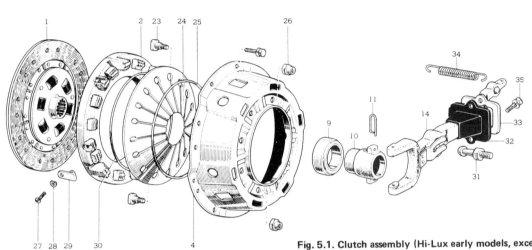

Fig. 5.1. Clutch assembly (Hi-Lux early models, except 12R engine)

1	Driven plate (disc)	26	Nut
2	Pressure plate	27	Screw
4	Cover	28	Spring washer
9	Release bearing	29	Retracting spring
10	Hub	30	Fulcrum ring
11	Clip	31	Ball pivot stud
14	Release arm/fork assembly	32	Boot
23	Bolt	33	Boot retainer plate
24	Diaphragm spring	34	Return spring
25	Fulcrum ring	35	Bolt

Fig. 5.2. Clutch assembly (Hi-Lux later models, except 12R engine)

1 Driven plate (disc)
2 Pressure plate
6 Diaphragm spring/cover assembly
7 Release bearing
8 Hub
9 Clip
10 Release arm/fork assembly
13 Boot
14 Return spring
15 Release fork retaining spring hanger
16 Ball pivot stud
17 Retracting spring

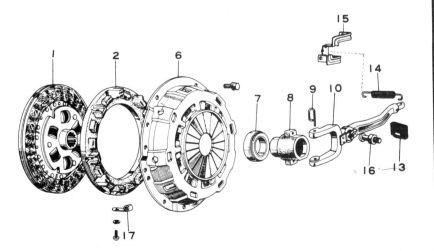

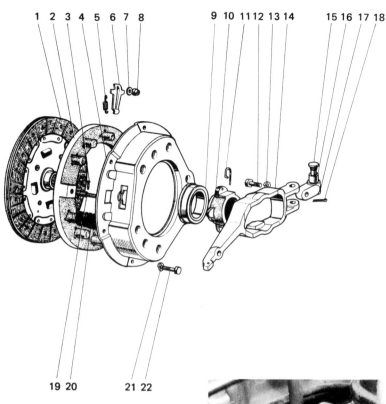

Fig. 5.3. Clutch assembly (Hi-Ace (early model) and Hi-Lux with 12R engine)

1 Driven plate (disc)
2 Pressure plate
3 Rivet
4 Cover
5 Lever spring
6 Release lever
7 Washer
8 Nut
9 Release bearing
10 Hub
11 Clip
12 Bolt
13 Lockwasher
14 Release arm/fork assembly
15 Pivot pin
16 Bush
17 Support
18 Split pin
19 Bolt
20 Clutch coil spring
21 Lockwasher
22 Bolt

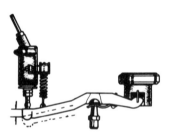

Fig. 5.4. Diagram showing clutch release arm free movement

3.2 Master cylinder to operating cylinder hydraulic hose and bracket

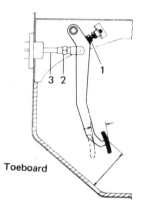

Toeboard

Fig. 5.5. Clutch pedal adjustment diagram
1 Pedal stop bolt   3 Pushrod
2 Locknut

2 Clutch - adjustment

1 For correct clutch operation, adjustment must be carried out to the pedal and to the hydraulic operating cylinder. Free-play at the clutch pedal is essential to ensure that the clutch engages and disengages fully, otherwise difficult gear changing or clutch slip can occur.
2 Adjust the pedal return stop bolt until the distance between the centre of the upper surface of the pedal pad and the floor (surface of anti-drumming sheet - carpet removed) is as shown in the following table according to model.
3 Working underneath the vehicle, check that the free movement between the end of the clutch operating cylinder pushrod and the release fork arm is also as shown in the table. Establish this movement by detaching the release fork arm return spring and gently moving the arm back and forth. If necessary, adjust the clearance by loosening the locknut on the pushrod and rotating the pushrod.
4 Now measure the clutch pedal free movement which should be in accordance with the figure shown in the table according to model. If it is not, loosen the locknut on the master cylinder pushrod and rotate the pushrod until the free movement is correct.
5 Tighten all lock nuts without altering the adjustment and reconnect the return springs.

	Hi-Lux up to 1971 except those with 12R engine	Hi-Lux 1972 on except those with 12R engine
a) Free play at release arm	0.145 in (2.4 mm)	0.08 to 0.14 in (2.0 to 3.5 mm)
b) Pedal height from floor	6.024 in (153 mm)	6.3 in (160 mm)
c) Pedal free play	1.30 in. (33.0 mm)	1 in. (25.4 mm)

	Early Hi-Ace and Hi-Lux 12R (coil spring)	Later Hi-Ace and Hi-Lux 12R (Diaphragm spring)
a) Free play at release arm	0.15 in (3.8 mm)	0.138 to 0.20 in (3.5 to 5.0 mm)
b) Pedal height from floor	7.20 to 7.24 in (183 to 184 mm)	7.28 in (185.0 mm)
c) Pedal free play	1.30 in. (33.0 mm)	1.0 in. (25.4 mm)

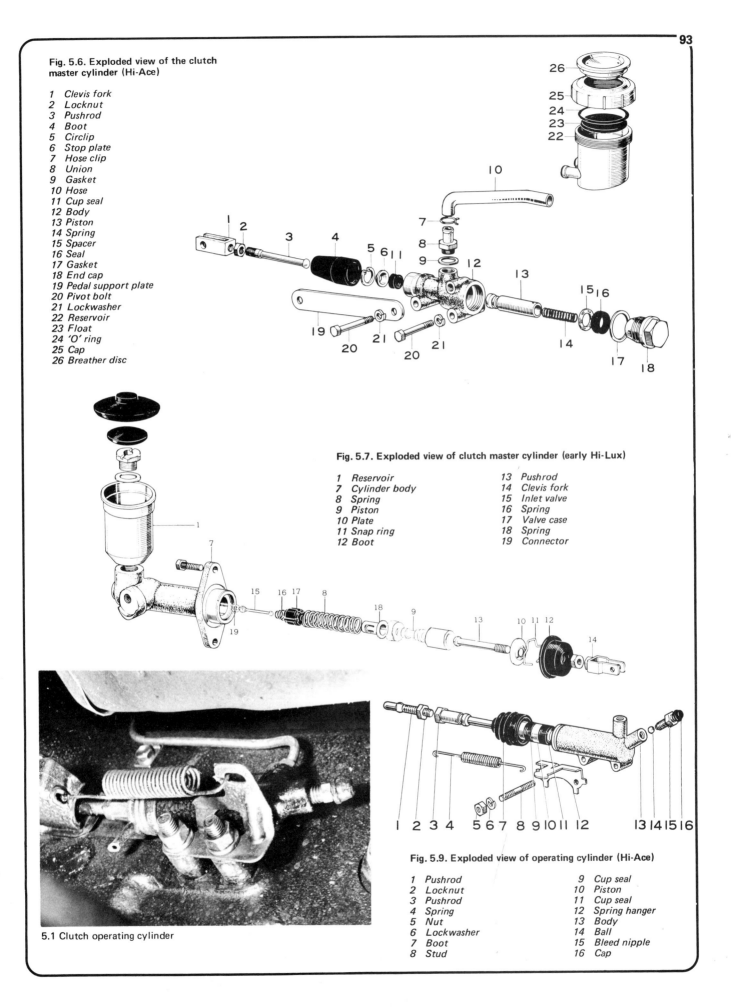

Fig. 5.6. Exploded view of the clutch master cylinder (Hi-Ace)

1 Clevis fork
2 Locknut
3 Pushrod
4 Boot
5 Circlip
6 Stop plate
7 Hose clip
8 Union
9 Gasket
10 Hose
11 Cup seal
12 Body
13 Piston
14 Spring
15 Spacer
16 Seal
17 Gasket
18 End cap
19 Pedal support plate
20 Pivot bolt
21 Lockwasher
22 Reservoir
23 Float
24 'O' ring
25 Cap
26 Breather disc

Fig. 5.7. Exploded view of clutch master cylinder (early Hi-Lux)

1   Reservoir
7   Cylinder body
8   Spring
9   Piston
10 Plate
11 Snap ring
12 Boot
13 Pushrod
14 Clevis fork
15 Inlet valve
16 Spring
17 Valve case
18 Spring
19 Connector

5.1 Clutch operating cylinder

Fig. 5.9. Exploded view of operating cylinder (Hi-Ace)

1 Pushrod
2 Locknut
3 Pushrod
4 Spring
5 Nut
6 Lockwasher
7 Boot
8 Stud
9   Cup seal
10 Piston
11 Cup seal
12 Spring hanger
13 Body
14 Ball
15 Bleed nipple
16 Cap

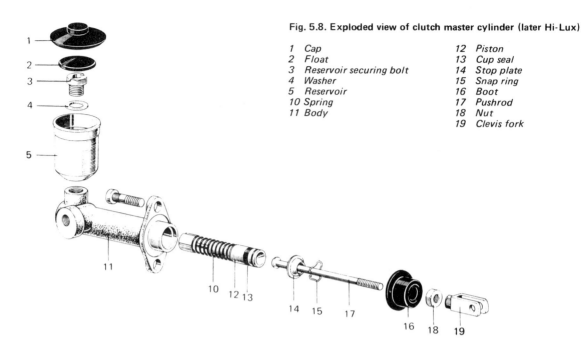

Fig. 5.8. Exploded view of clutch master cylinder (later Hi-Lux)

1	Cap	12	Piston
2	Float	13	Cup seal
3	Reservoir securing bolt	14	Stop plate
4	Washer	15	Snap ring
5	Reservoir	16	Boot
10	Spring	17	Pushrod
11	Body	18	Nut
		19	Clevis fork

3 Master cylinder - removal and refitting

1   Disconnect the master cylinder pushrod from the clutch pedal
2   Disconnect the flexible hydraulic hose at its junction with the rigid fluid line. Plug or cap both the open hoses to prevent dirt entering the system. On models with a separate reservoir, disconnect the supply hose (photo).
3   Unbolt the master cylinder from the engine rear bulkhead taking care not to spill any hydraulic fluid onto the vehicle paintwork.
4   Refitting is a reversal of removal but after installation is complete, check the pedal free movement as described in the preceding Section and bleed the hydraulic system (Section 7).

4 Master cylinder - dismantling and reassembly

1   The design of the master cylinder varies between models and date of manufacture but the operations described in this Section apply to all types.
2   Remove the reservoir cap and float and tip out the fluid (integral reservoir types only).
3   Operate the pushrod two or three times to eject any fluid from the cylinder.
4   Unscrew the reservoir securing bolt (accessible within the reservoir) and remove the reservoir (integral reservoir types only).
5   Unscrew the flexible hose from the master cylinder (integral reservoir types only).
6   Peel back the rubber boot from the end of the cylinder and remove the circlip.
7   On master cylinders with a threaded end cap at the forward end, secure the master cylinder body in a vice and unscrew the cap.
8   Extract the piston/seal assembly from the cylinder.
9   Wash all components in clean fluid and discard all rubber seals. If there are any 'bright' wear areas on the piston or cylinder bore surfaces, renew the complete unit.
10 If the components are in good condition, obtain a repair kit which will contain all the necessary seals and other items requiring renewal.
11 Reassembly is a reversal of dismantling, but locate the rubber seals using the fingers only, to avoid damaging them, and noting that their lips face the cap end of the master cylinder. Dip each component in clean hydraulic fluid before fitting it into the cylinder. Tighten the end cap and reservoir securing bolt to the torque specified in the Specifications section.

5 Operating cylinder - removal and refitting

1   Disconnect the hydraulic pipe at its union on the operating cylinder body (photo).
2   Disconnect the return spring.
3   Unscrew and remove the securing bolts and withdraw the cylinder.
4   Refitting is a reversal of removal but check the pushrod to release arm free movement after the hydraulic system has been bled (Sections 2 and 7).

6 Operating cylinder - dismantling and reassembly

1   The design of the operating cylinder may vary slightly according to model and date of manufacture, but the operations described in this Section apply to all types.
2   Depress the pushrod two or three times to eject any hydraulic fluid and then pull out the pushrod assembly complete with rubber boot.
3   Eject the piston assembly by applying air pressure at the fluid inlet or by tapping the end of the cylinder on a block of wood.
4   Wash components in clean hydraulic fluid and discard all rubber seals. If there are any 'bright' wear areas on the piston or cylinder bore surfaces, renew the complete unit.
5   If the components are in good condition, obtain a repair kit which will contain all the necessary seals and other items requiring renewal.
6   Reassembly is a reversal of dismantling but manipulate the seals into position using the fingers only to avoid damaging them. Dip each component in clean hydraulic fluid before inserting it into the cylinder.

7 Hydraulic system - bleeding

1   Gather together a clean glass jar, a length of rubber tubing which fits tightly over the bleed nipple on the operating cylinder, a tin of hydraulic brake fluid and someone to help.
2   Check that the master cylinder reservoir is full. If it is not, fill it and cover the bottom two inches of the jar with hydraulic fluid.
3   Remove the rubber dust cap from the bleed nipple on the operating cylinder, and with a suitable spanner open the bleed nipple approximately three quarters of a turn.
4   Place one end of the tube securely over the nipple and insert the other end into the jar so that its open end will remain submerged in the fluid.

5 Have your assistant depress the clutch pedal to the limit of its travel and then remove his foot so that the pedal can return to its normal position without being obstructed.

6 Repeat this operation until no more air can be seen being expelled from the end of the tube submerged in the jar. Keep the reservoir well topped-up with fluid to prevent air being drawn into the system again.

7 With the pedal fully depressed, tighten the bleed nipple.

8 Refit the dust cap. Always use new hydraulic fluid for topping-up the reservoir, which has been stored in an air tight tin and has not been shaken during the preceding 24 hours. Always discard fluid which has been bled from the system or retain it for bleed jar purposes only.

8 Clutch pedal - removal and refitting

1 On all Hi-Ace and Hi-Lux right-hand drive vehicles, the clutch and brake pedals operate on a common pivot bolt.

2 On Hi-Lux left-hand drive vehicles, separate pivot bolts are used.

3 Where the brake pedal must be removed because of the common pivot bolt, first detach the leads from the stop lamp switch and then disconnect the pedal return springs.

4 Withdraw the split pins and cotter pins which connect the brake and clutch master cylinder pushrods to the pedals.

5 Unscrew and remove the nut from the end of the pivot bolt and withdraw the pivot bolt from the clutch pedal side.

6 Examine all bushes and components for wear and renew as necessary.

7 Refitting is a reversal of removal, but apply grease to the pivot bolt and pedal bushes.

8 Check the pedal heights (see Section 2 of this Chapter).

9 Clutch - removal

1 Access to the clutch assembly and to the clutch release mechanism (Section 11) may be gained in one of two ways; (i) by removing the gearbox leaving the engine in position in the vehicle as described in Chapter 6 or (ii) by removing the engine/gearbox as one unit (at the time of major overhaul) and then separating the gearbox from the engine (Chapter 1).

2 Scribe a mating line from the clutch cover to the flywheel to ensure identical positioning on replacement and then remove the cover from the rear face of the flywheel. Unscrew the bolts diagonally half a turn at a time to prevent distortion to the cover flange.

3 With all the bolts and spring washers removed, lift the clutch assembly off the locating dowels. The driven plate (clutch disc) may fall out at this stage as it is not attached to either the clutch cover assembly or the flywheel.

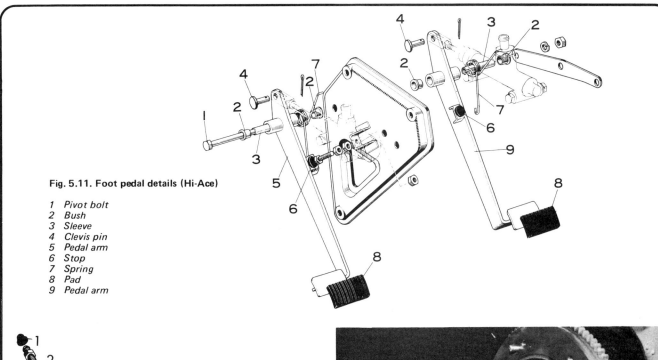

Fig. 5.11. Foot pedal details (Hi-Ace)

1   *Pivot bolt*
2   *Bush*
3   *Sleeve*
4   *Clevis pin*
5   *Pedal arm*
6   *Stop*
7   *Spring*
8   *Pad*
9   *Pedal arm*

Fig. 5.10. Exploded view of operating cylinder (Hi-Lux)

1	*Dust cap*	6	*Piston*
2	*Bleed nipple*	7	*Boot*
3	*Body*	8	*Pushrod*
4	*Cup seal*	9	*Nut*
5	*Seal*	10	*Pushrod*

12.2 Installing clutch assembly to flywheel

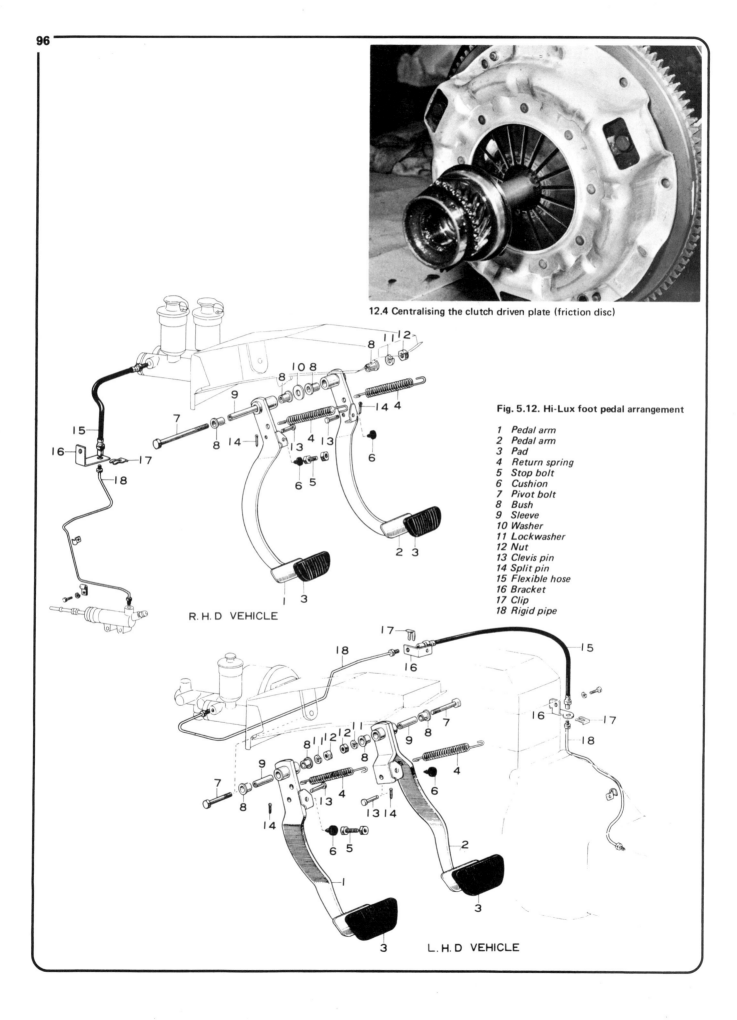

12.4 Centralising the clutch driven plate (friction disc)

Fig. 5.12. Hi-Lux foot pedal arrangement

1 Pedal arm
2 Pedal arm
3 Pad
4 Return spring
5 Stop bolt
6 Cushion
7 Pivot bolt
8 Bush
9 Sleeve
10 Washer
11 Lockwasher
12 Nut
13 Clevis pin
14 Split pin
15 Flexible hose
16 Bracket
17 Clip
18 Rigid pipe

R. H. D VEHICLE

L. H. D VEHICLE

10 Clutch - inspection and renovation

1 Examine the clutch disc friction linings for wear and loose rivets and the disc for rim distortion, cracks, perished torsion rubbers and worn splines. The surface of the friction linings may be highly glazed, but as long as the clutch material pattern can be clearly seen this is satisfactory. Compare the amount of lining wear with a new clutch disc at the stores in your local garage, and if the linings are more than three quarters worn renew the disc.

2 It is always best to renew the clutch driven plate as an assembly to preclude further trouble but if it is wished to merely renew the linings, the rivets should be drilled out and not knocked out with a punch. The manufacturers do not advise that only the linings are renewed and personal experience dictates that it is far more satisfactory to renew the driven plate complete than to try and economise by only fitting new friction linings.

3 Check the machined faces of the flywheel and the pressure plate. If either are grooved they should be machined until smooth, or renewed.

4 If the pressure plate is cracked or split it is essential that an exchange unit is fitted, also if the pressure of the diaphragm (or coil springs) is suspect. It is not practical to dismantle the pressure plate assembly as it will have been accurately set up and balanced to very fine limits.

11 Clutch release bearing - renewal

1 Check the release bearing for smoothness of operation. There should be no harshness and no slackness in it. It should spin reasonably freely bearing in mind it has been pre-packed with grease.

2 If a new clutch disc is being fitted it is a false economy not to renew the release bearing at the same time. This will preclude having to replace it at a later date, when wear on the clutch linings is still very small.

3 From the open front of the clutch bellhousing, unscrew and remove the release fork pivot bolt (Hi-Ace). On Hi-Lux vehicles, slide the release fork sideways off its pivot ball stud.

4 Detach the clips which secure the bearing/hub assembly to the release fork.

5 Using a distance piece of suitable diameter, press the hub from the bearing inner track and press on the new one ensuring that it seats fully on the hub and that it is fitted the right way round: contact plate facing the clutch release fingers.

6 Refitting is a reversal of removal, but use new clips to retain the bearing/hub to the release fork and check the condition of the release fork arm rubber dust excluder at the clutch bellhousing aperture.

7 Finally check the condition of the input shaft spigot bearing which is located in the centre of the flywheel. If it is worn, remove it and fit a new one.

12 Clutch - installation

1 Before the driven plate and pressure plate assembly can be refitted to the flywheel, a centralising guide tool must be obtained or made up. This may be either an old input shaft from a dismantled gearbox or a stepped mandrel similar to the one shown (photo).

2 Locate the driven plate against the face of the flywheel ensuring that its flatter side is against the flywheel (photo).

3 Offer up the pressure plate assembly to the flywheel, aligning the marks made prior to dismantling, and insert the retaining bolts finger-tight only. Where a new pressure plate assembly is being fitted, locate it to the flywheel in a similar relative position to the original by reference to the index marking and dowel positions.

4 Insert the guide tool through the splined hub of the driven plate so that the end of the tool locates in the flywheel spigot bush. This action of the guide tool will centralise the driven plate by causing it to move in a sideways direction (photo).

Insert and remove the guide tool two or three times to ensure that the driven plate is fully centralised and then tighten the pressure plate securing bolts a turn at a time and in a diametrically opposite sequence, to the specified torque, to prevent distortion of the pressure plate cover.

5 Install the gearbox (Chapter 6) or connect it to the engine and install the engine/gearbox (Chapter 1).

6 When installation is complete, check the pedal and release arm free movement and adjust to the Specification (see Section 2 of this Chapter).

13 Fault diagnosis - clutch

Symptom	Reason/s
Judder when taking up drive	Loose engine or gearbox mountings. Badly worn friction linings or contaminated with oil. Worn splines on gearbox input shaft or driven plate hub. Worn input shaft spigot bush in flywheel.
Clutch spin (failure to disengage) so that gears cannot be meshed	Incorrect release bearing to pressure plate clearance due to rust. May occur after vehicle standing idle for long periods. Damaged or misaligned pressure plate assembly. Fault in hydraulic system.
Clutch slip (increase in engine speed does not result in increase in vehicle road speed - particularly on gradients)	Incorrect release bearing to pressure plate finger clearance. Friction linings worn out or oil contaminated.
Noise evident on depressing clutch pedal	Dry, worn or damaged release bearing. Insufficient pedal free-travel. Weak or broken pedal return spring. Weak or broken clutch release lever return spring. Excessive play between driven plate hub splines and input shaft splines.
Noise evident as clutch pedal released	Distorted driven plate. Broken or weak driven plate cushion coil springs. Insufficient pedal free travel. Weak or broken clutch pedal return spring. Weak or broken release lever return spring. Distorted or worn input shaft. Release bearing loose on retainer hub.

Chapter 6/Part 1: Manual gearbox

Contents

Specifications

Application and identification

Hi-Ace (early) ... ...
Four forward speeds (all synchromesh) and one reverse. Steering column mounted gearshift control

Ratios:
1st	4.400 : 1
2nd	2.750 : 1
3rd	1.681 : 1
4th	1.000 : 1
Reverse	5.009 : 1
Oil capacity	1.6 Imp qts (1.8 litres) 1.9 US qts

Hi-Ace (later)
Type L42 gearbox ... ...
Four forward speeds (all synchromesh) and one reverse. Steering column mounted gearshift control

Gear ratio specifications are as for the Hi-Lux models fitted with the type L42 gearbox.

Oil capacity ... ...
1.7 Imp qts (1.9 litres) 2 US qts

Hi-Lux (up to 1971) with early OHV or 8R type engine ... ...
Four forward speeds (all synchromesh) and one reverse.

Gear ratio specifications were not available at the time of publication of this manual. Consult your Toyota dealer if necessary.

Oil capacity ... ...
1.7 Imp qts (1.9 litres) 2 US qts

Hi-Lux (1971 to 1975) with 8R-C or 18R-C series engines
Type L40 gearbox ... ...
Four forward speeds (all synchromesh) and one reverse. Floor-mounted gearshift

Ratios:
1st	4.016 : 1
2nd	2.509 : 1
3rd	1.534 : 1
4th	1.000 : 1
Reverse	4.571 : 1
Oil capacity	1.7 Imp qts (1.9 litres) 2 US qts

Hi-Lux (1975 on) with 20R engine
Type L43 gearbox ... ...
Four forward speeds (all synchromesh) and one reverse. Floor-mounted gearshift.

Ratios:
1st	3.674 : 1
2nd	2.114 : 1
3rd	1.403 : 1
4th	1.000 : 1
Reverse	4.183 : 1
Oil capacity	1.7 Imp qts (1.9 litres) 2 US qts

Hi-Lux (all models with 12R engine)

Type L42 gearbox	Four forward speeds (all synchromesh) and one reverse. Steering-column mounted gearshift.

Ratios:

1st	4.862 : 1
2nd	2.991 : 1
3rd	1.681 : 1
4th	1.000 : 1
Reverse	5.009 : 1
Oil capacity	1.7 Imp qts (1.9 litres) 2 US qts

Hi-Lux (1975 on - option) with 20R engine

Type W50 gearbox	Five forward speeds (all synchromesh) and one reverse. Floor-mounted gearshift

Ratios:

1st	3.287 : 1
2nd	2.043 : 1
3rd	1.394 : 1
4th	1.000 : 1
5th	0.853 : 1
Reverse	4.039 : 1
Oil capacity	2.3 Imp qts (2.7 litres) 2.6 US qts

Torque wrench settings

	lb f ft	Nm
Hi-Ace gearbox		
Front bearing retainer bolts	5	7
Extension housing bolts	33	45
Side cover bolts	16	22
Clutch bellhousing to engine bolts	30	41
Hi-Lux (four-speed gearbox)		
Side cover bolts	16	22
Front bearing retainer bolts	5	7
Extension housing bolts	32	44
Rear mounting bracket to extension housing	32	44
Drain plug	32	44
Bellhousing to gear case bolts	50	68
Bellhousing to engine bolts	33	45
With 20R type engine	50	68
Output flange nut (long wheelbase)	72	98
Hi-Lux (five-speed gearbox)		
Detent plug	22	30
Mainshaft rear bearing retainer bolts	15	20
Reverse gearshift pivot nut	11	15
Restrictor pin plugs	30	41
Extension housing bolts	32	44
Bellhousing to gear casing	50	68
Bellhousing to engine	33	45
Front bearing retainer bolts	6	8
Gearshift lever retainer bolts	13	18
Reversing lamp switch	30	41
Output flange nut (long wheelbase models)	72	98

1 General description

1 *Hi-Lux models* are equipped with a four-speed manual gearbox as standard equipment. From 1975, a five-speed manual gearbox is available as an option. With all gearboxes, except the one fitted in conjunction with the 12R engine, gearshift control is floor-mounted, but a column-mounted shift is employed where the 12R engine is used.

2 Automatic transmission was introduced as an option in conjunction with the 18R-C engine as from 1973 and continues to be available with the 20R engine.

3 *Hi-Ace models* are equipped with a four-speed manual gearbox having column shift. No options are available. Hi-Ace gearboxes fitted to later models are similar in appearance to earlier types, but differ considerably in internal details. Reference should be made to the appropriate Section.

2 Repair without removing gearbox

1 The only repair which can be carried out without first removing the gearbox from the car is renewal of the extension housing oil seal.

2 To do this, disconnect the front end of the propeller shaft (see Chapter 7) and draw the defective oil seal from the extension housing using a suitable extractor. The dust seal will come out with the oil seal.

3 Apply grease to the lips of the oil seal and drive it into position with a piece of tubing.

4 Soak the dust seal in gear oil and then tap it carefully into position against the oil seal.

5 Reconnect the propeller shaft.

3 Gearbox (Hi-Lux) - removal and installation

1 Either position the vehicle over a pit or raise the rear end sufficiently

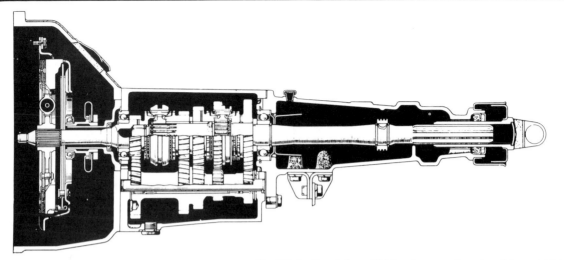

Fig. 6.1. Sectional view of Hi-Lux four-speed gearbox (Types L40, L43)

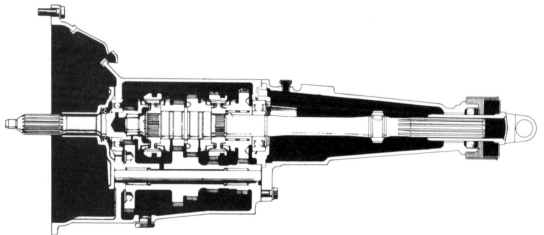

Fig. 6.2. Sectional view of Hi-Lux four-speed gearbox (Type L42)

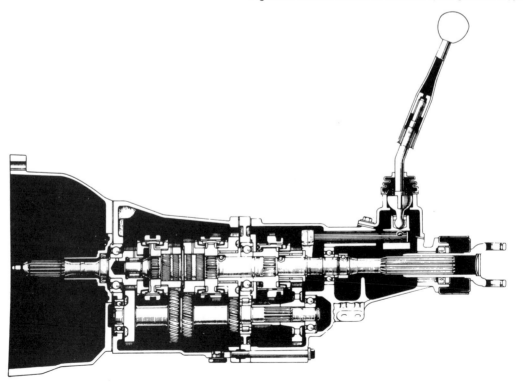

Fig. 6.3. Sectional view of Hi-Lux five-speed gearbox (Type W50)

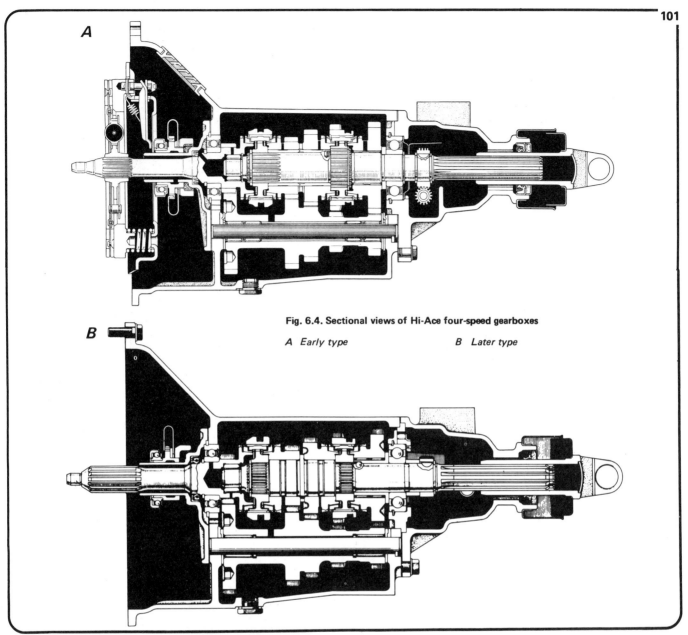

Fig. 6.4. Sectional views of Hi-Ace four-speed gearboxes

A Early type   B Later type

3.3 Control link coupling (Hi-Lux L42 gearbox)

3.12 Reversing lamp and TCS (emission control) top gear switch on L42 type gearbox

high to permit withdrawal of the gearbox from below and to the rear of the vehicle.

With floor-mounted gearshift

2   Working inside the driving compartment, remove the floor mat and the gearshift lever flexible boot retainer. Release the gearshift lever retaining cap which has a bayonet type fixing on four-speed models. Depress and turn to release it and withdraw the gearshift lever. On five-speed models, the gearshift lever retainer is secured by screws.

With a column-mounted gearshift

3   Disconnect the control link coupling (photo).
4   Disconnect the leads from the battery negative and positive terminals, then drain the cooling system and retain the coolant for further use if it is in a good clean condition.
5   Disconnect the radiator upper hose.
6   Disconnect the accelerator torque rod (lhd vehicle).
7   Remove the starter motor mounting nuts and draw the starter motor forward a few inches.
8   Disconnect the clutch hydraulic line clip, unbolt the clutch operating cylinder and tie it up out of the way. There is no need to disconnect the hydraulic line during this operation.
9   Disconnect the exhaust downpipe from the manifold and from the support bracket on the gearbox.
10 Remove the cover plate from the lower front face of the clutch bellhousing. On 12R engines, unbolt the lower cover from the flywheel housing (photo).
11 Disconnect the parking brake primary cable from the intermediate lever under the gearbox extension housing. Disconnect the lever from its pivot and let the parking brake secondary cables and equaliser hang down under the rear of the vehicle.
12 Disconnect the speedometer cable by unscrewing the knurled ring which secures it to the gearbox extension housing. Disconnect the leads from the reversing lamp switch on the gearbox, also the leads from the top gear switch (emission control) (photo).
13 Disconnect the propeller shaft from the gearbox (see Chapter 7). Some loss of oil may occur from the rear of the extension housing during removal operations. To prevent this, slip a plastic bag over the end of the housing and secure it tightly with an elastic band.
14 Support the gearbox on a jack, preferably of the trolley type, and unbolt and remove the gearbox rear support crossmember. Slip a block of wood between the engine sump and the front crossmember.
15 Lower the jack slightly and remove the bolts which secure the clutch bellhousing to the engine crankcase.
16 Lower the jack as necessary until the gearbox can be withdrawn downwards and towards the rear of the vehicle. Do not allow the weight of the gearbox to hang upon the primary shaft whilst the latter is engaged with the clutch mechanism.
17 Installation is a reversal of removal, but, if the clutch has been dismantled, make sure that the driven plate has been centralised before offering the gearbox to the engine (see Chapter 5).
18 Refill the gearbox with the correct grade and quantity of lubricant and check the clutch adjustment (see Chapter 5).
19 Make sure that all nuts and bolts are tightened to the specified torque wrench settings.

---

4   Gearbox (Hi-Ace) - removal and installation

1   Raise the front of the vehicle and support it securely under the suspension lower arms.

On early model vehicles

2   Disconnect the return spring and then disconnect the gearshift rods from the cross-shaft at the side of the gearbox.
3   Release the locking pin which secures the cross-shaft to the gear casing and disconnect the cross-shaft.
4   Unbolt the cross-shaft bracket from the chassis frame and withdraw the cross-shaft/bracket assembly. Disconnect the upper gearshift rod from its lever on the gearbox.

On later model vehicles

5   Disconnect the shift and selector control rods from the levers on the outside of the gearcase.
6   Disconnect the leads from the reversing lamp switch on the gear casing.
7   Disconnect the speedometer cable from the gear case.

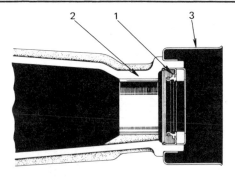

Fig. 6.5. Sectional view of extension housing oil seal

1   *Oil seal*   3   *Dust deflector*
2   *Bush*

Fig. 6.6. Disconnecting coupling (Hi-Lux column gearshift)

2   *Clutch release cylinder*   5   *Flywheel housing cover*
3   *Exhaust pipe*   6   *Control link coupling*

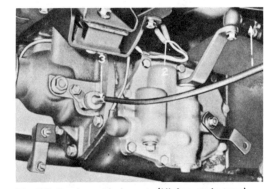

Fig. 6.7. Gearbox attachments (Hi-Ace, early type)

1   *Gearshift rod*   3   *Speedometer*
2   *Reversing lamp switch leads*   *cable*

Fig. 6.8. Gearbox attachments (Hi-Ace, early type)

1   *Engine oil pressure switch*   3   *Clutch operating cylinder*
2   *Clutch hydraulic line support* 4   *Exhaust clamp*
    bracket

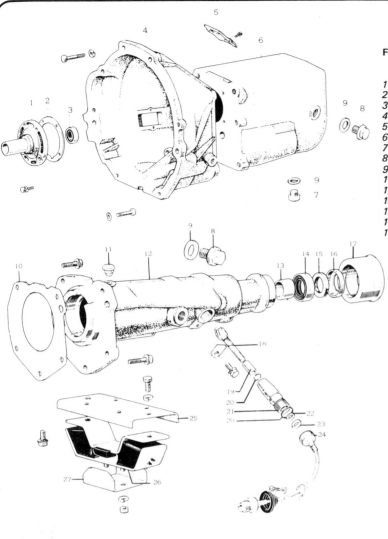

Fig. 6.10. Gear casing and external components (Hi-Lux up to 1971)

1	Front bearing retainer	16	Dust excluder retainer
2	Gasket	17	Dust deflector
3	Oil seal	18	Speedometer driven gear
4	Clutch bellhousing	19	Bush
5	Inspection plate	20	'O' ring
6	Gear case	21	Sleeve
7	Drain plug	22	Collar
8	Filler plug	23	Gasket
9	Gaskets	24	Drive cable
10	Gasket	25	Mounting bracket
11	Breather	26	Insulator
12	Extension housing	27	Stabiliser
13	Bush		
14	Oil seal		
15	Dust excluder		

Fig. 6.9. Removing Hi-Ace gearbox (early type shown)

6.10 Removing lower cover from clutch housing (Hi-Lux 12R)

Fig. 6.11. Gearbox internal components (Hi-Lux, up to 1971)

1	Circlip	22	Mainshaft
2	Input shaft bearing	23	Woodruff key
3	Input shaft	24	1st gear
4	3rd/4th synchro ring	25	Bush
5	Needle rollers	26	Spacer
6	Circlip	27	Circlip
7	Circlip	28	Bearing
8	Shift key	29	Circlip
9	Spring	30	Oil baffle
10	3rd/4th synchro hub	31	Circlip
11	3rd/4th synchro sleeve	32	Speedometer drive gear
12	3rd gear	38	Countergear thrust washer
13	Bush	39	Counter gear
14	Thrust washer	40	Needle roller bearing
15	Bush	41	Spacer
16	2nd gear	42	Countershaft
17	Shift key	43	End-float adjusting washer
18	1st/2nd synchro hub	44	Reverse idler assembly
19	Reverse gear	45	Bush
20	Circlip	46	Reverse idler shaft
21	Lock pin		

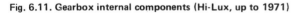
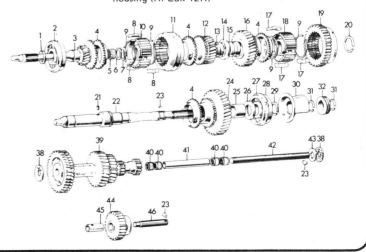

8 Disconnect the return spring from the clutch release lever, unbolt the clutch operating cylinder and hydraulic line support bracket and tie the cylinder to one side out of the way. There is no need to disconnect the hydraulic line during this operation.
9 Disconnect the oil pressure switch lead from its clip at the top of the clutch bellhousing.
10 Disconnect the exhaust pipe supporting 'U' bolt.
11 Drain the gearbox oil.
12 Remove the propeller shaft (see Chapter 7).
13 Unbolt and remove the cover from the lower part of the flywheel housing and then, using a jack and a block of wood as an insulator, support the weight of the engine/gearbox under the teeth of the starter ring gear on the flywheel.
14 Support the gearbox on a second jack, preferably of the trolley type, and then remove the bolts which secure the clutch bellhousing to the engine crankcase.
15 Unbolt the gearbox rear mountings from the chassis frame.
16 Lower both jacks carefully together until the gearbox can be withdrawn towards the rear of the vehicle. **Do not** allow the weight of the gearbox to hang upon the primary shaft whilst the latter is engaged with the clutch mechanism.
17 Installation is a reversal of removal, but if the clutch has been dismantled, make sure that the driven plate has been centralised before offering the gearbox to the engine (see Chapter 5).
18 Refill the gearbox with the correct grade and quantity of lubricant and finally check the clutch adjustment (see Chapter 5).

---

5 Gearbox (Hi-Lux four-speed up to 1971) - overhaul

1 Unscrew the side cover bolts, half a turn at a time and in diagonal sequence and then tap off the cover with a soft faced mallet. Do not lever it off by inserting a screwdriver between the joint faces or the light alloy surfaces will be damaged.
2 From within the clutch bellhousing, remove the clutch release mechanism and bearing.

3 Unbolt the clutch bellhousing from the gearbox and remove it. Remove the speedometer drive gear from the extension housing.
4 From the front face of the gearbox, unbolt and remove the bearing retainer.
5 Unscrew and remove the bolts which secure the extension housing to the gearbox casing and then turn the extension housing in a clockwise direction (viewed from the rear) until the end of the countershaft is exposed. Measure the countershaft gear assembly endfloat and record it for reference during reassembly.
6 From the front face of the gearbox, drive the countershaft out towards the rear. Use a rod for this purpose, which is slightly less in diameter than the countershaft so that it will retain the countershaft needle roller bearing and thrust washers in position as it passes through.
7 Withdraw the dummy countershaft and lower the countershaft gear to the bottom of the gearbox.
8 Withdraw the extension housing together with the mainshaft assembly from the rear of the gearbox. During this operation, hold the countergear assembly to one side of the gearbox casing.

Fig. 6.13. Extension housing rotated to expose end of countershaft (Hi-Lux gearbox, up to 1971)

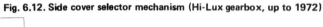

Fig. 6.12. Side cover selector mechanism (Hi-Lux gearbox, up to 1972)

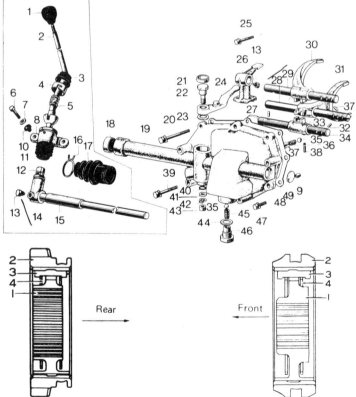

1	Knob	26	Shift/select lever
2	Gearshift lever	27	Interlock pins
3	Boot	28	2nd/3rd selector shaft
4	Cap	29	1st/2nd selector shaft
5	Spring	30	1st/2nd shift fork
6	Bolt	31	3rd/4th shift fork
7	Washer	32	Interlock pin
8	Retainer	33	Reverse selector dog
9	Dowel	34	Reverse selector shaft
10	Bush	35	Detent ball
11	Boot	36	Detent spring
12	Bush	37	Seat
13	Lockbolt	38	Tension pin
14	Housing	39	Bolt
15	Remote control rod	40	'O' ring
16	Clip	41	Washer
17	Boot	42	Lock washer
18	Oil seal	43	Nut
19	Side cover assembly	44	Gasket
20	Bolt	45	Spring
21	Plug	46	Reverse restrictor
22	Shift arm pivot		ball holder
23	Washer	47	Bolt
24	Reverse shift arm	48	Gasket
25	Bolt	49	Plug

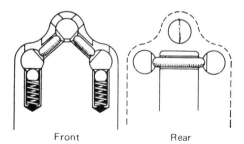

Fig. 6.14. Correct assembly of 1st/2nd synchro unit (Hi-Lux gearbox, up to 1971)

1 Synchro hub   3 Shift key
2 Synchro sleeve   4 Spring

Fig. 6.15. Correct assembly of 3rd/4th synchro unit (Hi-Lux gearbox, up to 1971)

1 Synchro hub   3 Shift key
2 Synchro sleeve   4 Spring

Fig. 6.16. Diagrams showing location of detent balls and interlock pins on Hi-Lux gearbox (up to 1971)

5.22 Example of wear in shift fork

5.28a 1st/2nd synchro circlip fitted to mainshaft
(Hi-Lux four-speed up to 1971)

5.28b Installing 1st gear to rear end of
mainshaft (Hi-Lux four-speed, up to 1971)

5.28c Installing mainshaft rear bearing
(Hi-Lux four-speed, up to 1971)

5.29 Measuring 1st gear to spacer clearance
(Hi-Lux four-speed, up to 1971)

5.30 Mainshaft rear bearing circlip (Hi-Lux
four-speed, up to 1971)

9   Remove the input shaft by tapping it gently, with a soft faced
hammer, out of the front face of the gearbox in a forward direction. If
necessary, remove the bearing, using a two legged extractor, after withdrawing the securing circlip.

10 Using a thin drift, drive the reverse idler gear shaft to the rear, far
enough to enable the reverse idler gear to be removed from the shaft.
Extract the shaft complete with Woodruff key.

11 Lift the countergear assembly complete with needle rollers from the
bottom of the gearbox and also remove the two thrust washers.

12 From the front end of the mainshaft (still attached to the extension
housing) remove the circlip and draw off the 3rd/4th synchro unit, third
gear and bush, thrust washer, 2nd gear and bush, and 1st/2nd synchro
unit.

13 Remove the mainshaft bearing outer track circlip and tap the mainshaft forward out of the extension housing.

14 If necessary, the speedometer drive gear with its retaining clips can
now be withdrawn from the mainshaft, retaining the Woodruff key.
Remove the oil deflector and if the bearing is to be removed, a press
will have to be used. Draw off the circlip, bearing, 1st gear bush and
spacer from the rear end of the mainshaft.

15 If the shift fork and selector mechanism is to be dismantled, secure
the side cover in a vice and move 3rd/4th gear shift fork to the 4th
gear positon. Drive out the tension pin and then remove the selector
shaft and fork taking care to retain the detent ball and spring which
will be ejected.

16 Remove the 1st/2nd selector shaft and fork in a similar manner and
remove the interlock pins during the process.

17 From the lower face of the side cover, unscrew and remove the
reverse restrictor plug, spring and ball.

18 Cut the locking wire and remove the shift lever lock bolt. Withdraw
the remote control rod.

19 Remove the reverse shift arm and pivot bolt and then drive out the
securing tension pin and withdraw the reverse selector shaft and fork.
Again, take care that the detent ball and spring are not lost. Remove
the reversing lamp switch if necessary.

20 Wash all components in paraffin and dry them. Check the gears for
worn or chipped teeth and the shafts for scoring or grooving.

21 Fit the synchro rings to the gear wheel cones and check the clearance.
It should not be less than 0.047 in (1.2 mm).

22 With the shift forks located in the synchro sleeve grooves, check the
side clearance. This should be between 0.006 and 0.042 (0.15 and 1.25
mm) otherwise renew the components (photo). Also test the fit of the
shift lever shaft in the shift fork. The clearance should be between
0.008 and 0.024 in (0.2 and 0.6 mm).

23 Renew the oil seals in the front bearing retainer, the rear extension
housing and the shift lever shaft housing. A piece of tubing can be used
as a drift for these operations.

24 Examine the gearbox casing and extension housing for cracks. These
components are of light alloy and should be treated with respect.

25 Inspect the condition of the synchroniser units. If there has been a
history of noisy gearchanging or the synchromesh could easily be
'beaten', renew the unit complete.

26 Correct assembly of the two synchro units must be carried out
before installing them on the mainshaft. Ensure that the spring ends do
not engage in the same gaps on opposite sides of the unit.

27 Commence reassembly by fitting the selector and shift mechanism
to the side cover by reversing the dismantling process. Use new tension
pins and 'O' ring seals and check carefully that the detent balls and
interlock pins are correctly located. Do not tighten the shift arm pivot
locknut until the side cover is fitted to the gearbox and the pivot
adjusted (see paragraph 51).

28 Ensure that the 1st/2nd synchro retaining circlip is in position on
the mainshaft and then, to the rear end of the mainshaft, slide on the
1st gear and the spacer, and then press on the new bearing, applying
pressure only to the centre track (photos). Make sure that the outer
track circlip groove is nearer the front of the shaft.

29 Measure the clearance between the 1st gear and the spacer which
should be between 0.004 and 0.008 in (0.10 and 0.20 mm).

30 Fit a bearing retaining circlip which will give the minimum groove
clearance from the six thicknesses available (photo).

31 To the mainshaft, fit the oil baffle, the first circlip, the speedometer
drive gear with Woodruff key, and the second speedo drive gear circlip
(photo).

5.31a Fitting oil baffle to mainshaft (Hi-Lux four-speed, up to 1971)

5.31b Speedometer drive gear Woodruff key (Hi-Lux four-speed, up to 1971)

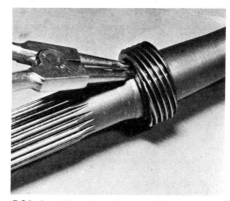
5.31c Installing a speedometer drive gear circlip (Hi-Lux four-speed, up to 1971)

5.32a Installing mainshaft rear bearing outer circlip to extension housing (Hi-Lux four-speed, up to 1971)

5.32b Installing mainshaft assembly into extension housing (Hi-Lux four-speed, up to 1971)

5.33a Installing speedometer driven gear (Hi-Lux four-speed, up to 1971)

5.33b Speedometer driven gear lockplate and bolt (Hi-Lux four-speed, up to 1971)

5.34a Installing 1st/2nd synchro unit to mainshaft (Hi-Lux four-speed, up to 1971)

5.34b Installing 2nd gear bush to mainshaft (Hi-Lux four-speed up to 1971)

5.34c Installing 2nd gear to mainshaft (Hi-Lux four-speed, up to 1971)

5.34d Installing 2nd gear thrust washer to mainshaft (Hi-Lux four-speed, up to 1971)

5.34e Installing 3rd gear bush to mainshaft (Hi-Lux four-speed, up to 1971)

5.36 Installing 3rd/4th synchro unit to mainshaft (Hi-Lux four-speed, up to 1971)

5.37 Fitting circlip to front end of mainshaft (Hi-Lux four-speed, up to 1971)

5.38 Installation of reverse idler gear and shaft (Hi-Lux four-speed, up to 1971)

5.43 Needle rollers retained in input shaft (Hi-Lux four-speed, up to 1971)

5.44 Installing input shaft (Hi-Lux four-speed, up to 1971)

5.45 Assembling extension housing to gear casing (Hi-Lux four-speed, up to 1971)

5.46 Countershaft key (Hi-Lux four-speed, up to 1971)

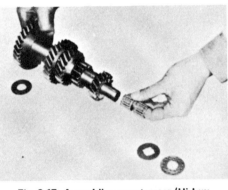

Fig. 6.17. Assembling countergear (Hi-Lux gearbox, up to 1971)

5.48 Installing front bearing retainer (Hi-Lux four-speed, up to 1971)

32 Assemble the mainshaft into the extension housing after installing a bearing outer track circlip to provide minimum endfloat, from the six thicknesses available (photo).

33 Fit the speedometer driven gear to the extension housing (photos).

34 To the front of the mainshaft, fit the 1st/2nd synchro unit, 2nd gear and its bush, the thrust washer and 3rd gear bush (photos).

35 Measure the endfloat between 2nd gear and the 2nd/3rd gear thrust washer. Where this is not within 0.004 to 0.008 in (0.10 to 0.20 mm) change the second gear bush for one of different length.

36 Onto the mainshaft install 3rd gear and 3rd/4th gear synchro unit, then measure the endfloat between 3rd gear and the thrust washer. If the clearance is outside that specified, 0.004 to 0.008 in (0.10 to 0.20 mm), change the 3rd gear bush for one of different length (photo).

37 Fit a new circlip to the front end of the mainshaft, ensuring that the correct endfloat of between 0 and 0.0020 in (0 and 0.05 mm) is obtained by selecting one of suitable thickness from the ten thicknesses available (photo).

38 Install the reverse idler gear and shaft into the gearbox, aligning the Woodruff key correctly with the keyway. Note the direction of

installation of the reverse idler gear (photo).

39 Using a dummy shaft, insert the needle roller bearings into each end of the countergear using thick grease to hold them and their spacers.

40 Stick the countergear thrust washers into their recesses on the internal faces of the gearbox casing, again, using a dab of thick grease for the purpose.

41 Lower the countergear assembly into the bottom of the gearbox taking care not to displace the thrust washers.

42 If the input shaft bearing has been removed, press on the new one and select an outer track circlip to give the minimum clearance in the groove from the two sizes available.

43 Stick the needle rollers into the recess in the rear face of the input shaft using thick grease to retain them and then fit the internal type circlip (photo).

44 Install the input shaft into the gearbox and fit the synchro ring to the input shaft cone (photo).

45 Use a new gasket and assemble the extension housing to the gearbox, rotating the housing to expose the countershaft hole. (photo).

46 Insert a hand through the side cover aperture and raise the counter-

5.49a Side cover/selector mechanism (Hi-Lux four-speed, up to 1971)

5.49b Installing side cover (Hi-Lux four-speed, up to 1971)

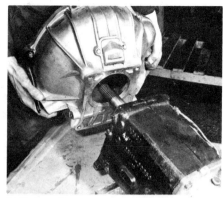

5.50a Installing clutch bellhousing to gear casing (Hi-Lux four-speed, up to 1971)

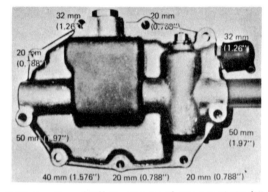

Fig. 6.18. Location of differing lengths of side cover bolts (Hi-Lux gearbox, up to 1971)

5.50b Clutch release bearing and springs correctly installed (Hi-Lux four-speed, up to 1971)

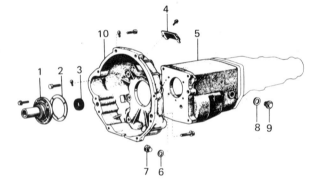

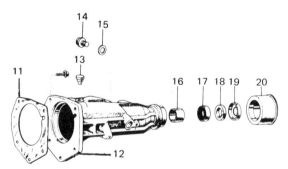

Fig. 6.20. Gear casing and external components (Hi-Lux four-speed gearbox, 1972 on)

1 Bearing retainer	11 Gasket
2 Gasket	12 Extension housing
3 Oil seal	13 Breather
4 Inspection cover	14 Drain plug
5 Gear casing	15 Gasket
6 Gasket	16 Bush
7 Drain plug	17 Oil seal
8 Gasket	18 Dust seal
9 Filler plug	19 Dust seal retainer
10 Bellhousing	20 Dust deflector

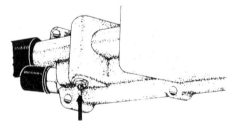

Fig. 6.19. Location of reverse gear pivot adjuster screw on Hi-Lux gearbox, up to 1971

Fig. 6.23. Speedometer driven gear retaining bolt (Hi-Lux four-speed gearbox, 1972 on)

Fig. 6.21. Gearbox internal components (Hi-Lux four-speed, 1972 on)

RN 25, 28 Series

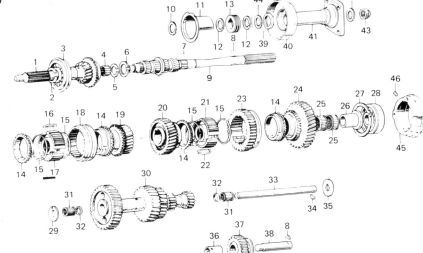

1   Input shaft
2   Circlip
3   Bearing
4   Needle rollers
5   Circlip
6   Circlip
7   Reverse restrictor ball
8   Woodruff key
9   Mainshaft
10 Circlip
11 Oil baffle
12 Circlip
13 Speedometer drive gear
14 3rd/4th synchro ring
15 Spring
16 Shift key
17 3rd/4th synchro hub
18 3rd/4th synchro sleeve
19 3rd gear
20 2nd gear
21 1st/2nd synchro hub
22 Shift key
23 Reverse gear
24 1st gear
25 Needle roller bearings
26 1st gear bush
27 Circlip
28 Mainshaft bearing
29 Countergear thrust washer
30 Countergear
31 Needle roller bearing
32 Spacer
33 Countershaft
34 Woodruff key
35 Thrust washer
36 Bush
37 Reverse idler gear

38 Reverse idler shaft
39 *Spacer
40 *Dust deflector
41 *Output shaft flange
42 *Washer
43 *Nut
44 *Circlip
45 Mainshaft rear bearing retainer
46 Tension spring

*   Apply to long wheelbase models only.

Fig. 6.24. Output flange nut (Hi-Lux long wheelbase models)

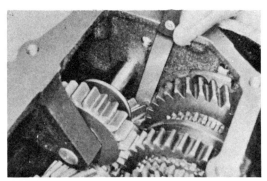

Fig. 6.25. Measuring countergear end-float (Hi-Lux four-speed, 1972 on)

Fig. 6.26. Withdrawing mainshaft (Hi-Lux four-speed, 1972 on)

Fig. 6.27. Removing reverse idler shaft (Hi-Lux four-speed, 1972 on)

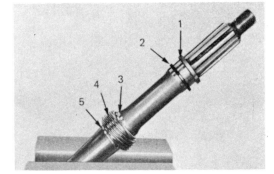

Fig. 6.28. Mainshaft rear end details (Hi-Lux four-speed, 1972 on)

1   *Spacer
2   *Circlip
3   Circlip
4   Speedometer drive gear
5   Circlip
*   Long wheelbase models only.

gear so that the countershaft can be installed from the rear face of the gearbox, displacing the dummy shaft but not the needle rollers or thrust washers. Check that the countershaft is secured by the Woodruff key which is positioned at the extension housing end of the shaft. Check the countershaft gear endfloat which should lie within 0.002 to 0.006 (0.05 to 0.15 mm), and as measured before dismantling. Where it is outside the correct tolerance, the thrust washers will have to be changed for ones of alternative thickness from the thirteen available thicknesses (photo).

47 Turn the extension housing back to its correct position and tighten the securing bolts, having applied jointing compound to their threads.

48 Fit the front bearing retainer using a new gasket and making sure that the oil return groove is correctly aligned. Apply jointing compound to the bolt threads (photo).

49 Fit the side cover using a new gasket. Make sure that the shift forks engage correctly with the synchro unit grooves. Apply jointing compound to both sides of the gasket and to the bolt threads. Note that the side cover securing bolts are of different lengths and must be refitted exactly as indicated in Fig. 6.18 (photos).

50 Refit the clutch bellhousing and release mechanism (photos).

51 With the gearbox completely reassembled, adjust the reverse gear pivot. To do this, release the shift arm pivot locknut and using the slot in the end of the shift arm pivot, turn it in a **clockwise** direction so that reverse idler gear is moved into contact with 1st gear. Now, by means of the slot, turn the shift arm pivot through 90° **anti-clockwise** and secure it in this position with the locknut.

6 Gearbox (Hi-lux four-speed, L40, L42 and L43) - overhaul

1 With the gearbox removed from the car, clean away all external dirt.

2 Unscrew the side cover bolts, half a turn at a time and in a diagonal sequence, then, tap off the cover with a soft-faced mallet. Do not lever it off by inserting a screwdriver between the joint faces or the light alloy surfaces will be damaged.

3 From within the clutch bellhousing, remove the clutch release mechanism and bearings.

4 Unbolt the clutch bellhousing from the gearbox and remove it. On type L42 gearboxes, the bellhousing is integral with the gearcase. Remove the speedometer driven gear from the extension housing.

5 From the front face of the gearbox, unbolt and remove the bearing retainer.

6 On long wheelbase versions having a three-joint type propeller shaft, relieve the staking on the nut which secures the output flange and drive off the flange.

7 Unbolt and remove the extension housing.

8 Measure the countershaft gear assembly endfloat and record it for reference during reassembly.

9 From the front face of the gearbox, drive the countershaft out towards the rear. Use a rod for this purpose which is slightly less in diameter than the countershaft so that it will retain the countershaft needle roller bearings and thrust washers in position as it passes through.

10 Withdraw the dummy countershaft and lower the countershaft gear to the bottom of the gearbox.

11 Push the 3rd/4th synchro sleeve towards 4th gear and withdraw the mainshaft assembly.

12 Remove the synchroniser ring and drive out the input shaft by tapping it gently, with a soft-faced hammer, out of the front face of the gearbox in a forward direction. If necessary, remove the bearing using a two legged extractor after withdrawing the securing circlip.

13 Using a thin drift, drive the reverse idler gear shaft to the rear, far enough to enable the reverse idler gear to be removed from the shaft. Extract the shaft complete with Woodruff key.

14 Lift the countergear assembly complete with needle rollers from the bottom of the gearbox and also remove the two thrust washers.

15 Secure the mainshaft in the jaws of a vice suitably protected with blocks of wood or aluminium plates.

16 *On long wheelbase models,* remove the spacer (1) and shaft circlip (2) (Fig. 6.28).

17 Remove the circlip (3), speedometer drive gear (4), Woodruff key and second circlip (5).

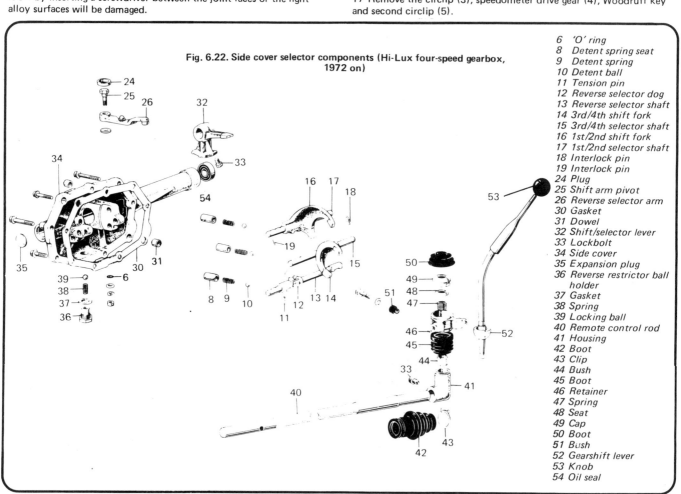

Fig. 6.22. Side cover selector components (Hi-Lux four-speed gearbox, 1972 on)

6 'O' ring
8 Detent spring seat
9 Detent spring
10 Detent ball
11 Tension pin
12 Reverse selector dog
13 Reverse selector shaft
14 3rd/4th shift fork
15 3rd/4th selector shaft
16 1st/2nd shift fork
17 1st/2nd selector shaft
18 Interlock pin
19 Interlock pin
24 Plug
25 Shift arm pivot
26 Reverse selector arm
30 Gasket
31 Dowel
32 Shift/selector lever
33 Lockbolt
34 Side cover
35 Expansion plug
36 Reverse restrictor ball holder
37 Gasket
38 Spring
39 Locking ball
40 Remote control rod
41 Housing
42 Boot
43 Clip
44 Bush
45 Boot
46 Retainer
47 Spring
48 Seat
49 Cap
50 Boot
51 Bush
52 Gearshift lever
53 Knob
54 Oil seal

Fig. 6.29. Extracting 3rd/4th synchro circlip (Hi-Lux four-speed, 1972 on)

Fig. 6.30. Pressing off 1st gear and bearing (Hi-Lux four-speed, 1972 on)

1   Bearing   2   1st gear

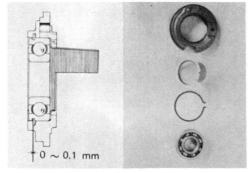

Fig. 6.31. Circlip to mainshaft rear bearing retainer clearance (Hi-Lux four-speed, 1972 on)

18 Extract the circlip and withdraw 3rd/4th synchro sleeve and hub and 3rd gear.
19 Extract the circlip and press out the bearing (1), together with 1st gear (2). Catch the restrictor ball (Fig. 6.30).
20 Withdraw the 1st/2nd synchro rings and hub, together with reverse gear and 2nd gear.
21 Using feeler blades, measure the clearance between the circlip and the bearing retainer and record the measurement for use at reassembly.
22 If the mainshaft rear bearing is to be renewed, press it from its retainer and withdraw the oil baffle.
23 If the shift fork and selector mechanism is to be dismantled, unscrew the reversing lamp switch, then secure the side cover in a vice and move 3rd/4th gear shift fork to the 4th gear position. Drive out the tension pin (No 2, Fig. 6.32) and then remove the selector shaft (3) and fork (1) taking care to retain the detent balls and spring which will be ejected (Fig. 6.33).
24 Remove the 1st/2nd selector shaft and fork in a similar manner and remove the interlock pins during the process.
25 From the lower face of the side cover, unscrew and remove the detent ball, spring and two interlock pins.
26 Drive out the tension pin from the 1st/2nd shift fork, withdraw the selector shaft and extract the detent ball and spring from the cover.
27 Release the shift arm pivot locknut and remove the washers and 'O' ring seal.

With floor-mounted gearshift
28 Unscrew and remove the reverse restrictor ball holder, spring and ball. Cut the locking wire and unscrew the shift lever lock bolt. Pull the remote control rod out of the cover (reversing lamp switch side).

With column gearshift
29 Remove the selector outer lever (1) and the shaft (2). Extract the lockbolt (3) and slide out the shift outer lever (4) from the cover. Watch for ejection of the spring-loaded detent ball. Remove the sliding shift lever, detent ball and spring (Fig. 6.38).
30 Wash all components in paraffin and dry them. Check the gears for worn or chipped teeth and the shafts for scoring or grooving.
31 Fit the synchro rings to their gear wheel cones and, while pressing them into contact with the fingers and at the same time turning them, check that the clearance for 1st, 2nd and 3rd gears is 0.0453 to 0.0728 in (1.10 to 1.90 mm) and for 4th gear 0.0433 to 0.0748 in (1.10 to 1.90 mm). The minimum clearance should be 0.03 in (0.8 mm) and if below this figure renew the components.
side clearance. This should not exceed 0.4 in (1.0 mm), otherwise renew the components. Also test the fit of the shift lever shaft in the shift fork. The clearance should be between 0.008 and 0.024 in (0.2 and 0.6 mm).
33 Inspect the condition of the synchroniser units. If there has been a history of noisy gearchanging or the synchromesh could easily be 'beaten', renew the unit complete.
34 Correct assembly of the two synchro units must be carried out before installing them on the mainshaft. Ensure that the spring ends do not engage in the same gaps on opposite sides of the unit. The diagrams show the assembly of the synchro units and the sides which face the front of the gearbox when installed to the mainshaft (Fig. 6.39 and 6.40).

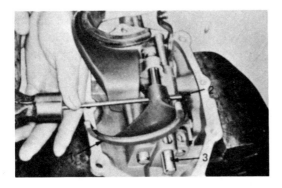

Fig. 6.32. Removing 3rd/4th shift fork tension pin (Hi-Lux four-speed, 1972 on)

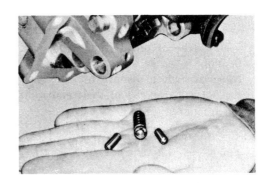

Fig. 6.33. Removing interlock pins (Hi-Lux four-speed, 1972 on)

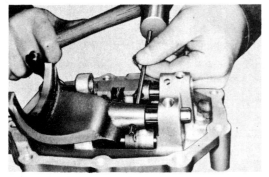

Fig. 6.34. Removing 1st/2nd shift fork tension pin (Hi-Lux four-speed, 1972 on)

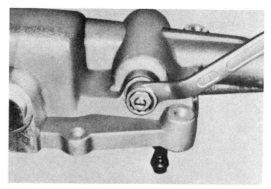

Fig. 6.35. Releasing shift arm pivot locknut (Hi-Lux four-speed, 1972 on)

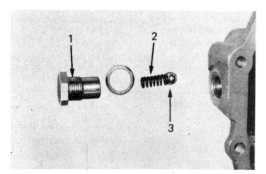

Fig. 6.36. Reverse restrictor components (Hi-Lux four-speed, 1972 on)

1 Ball holder   2 Spring   3 Locking ball

Fig. 6.37. Cutting shift lever bolt locking wire (Hi-Lux four-speed, 1972 on)

Fig.6.38. Selector components (Hi-Lux column shift)

1 Selector outer lever   *4 Shift outer lever*
2 Shaft   *5 Detent ball*
3 Lockbolt

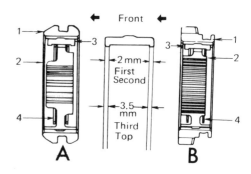

Fig. 6.39. Synchro assembly diagram (Hi-Lux four-speed, 1972 on)

A 3rd/4th   *B 1st/2nd*
1 Sleeve   *3 Shift key*
2 Hub   *4 Springs*

Fig. 6.40. Synchro spring arrangement diagram

Fig. 6.41. Gears assembled to rear end of mainshaft (Hi-Lux four-speed, 1972 on)

1 2nd gear   *2 Reverse gear*

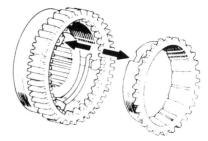

Fig. 6.42. Synchro ring alignment (Hi-Lux four-speed, 1972 on)

Fig. 6.43. Assembling 1st gear to mainshaft (Hi-Lux four-speed, 1972 on)

1 Locking ball   4 1st gear
2 1st gear bush   5 Synchro ring
3 Bearing

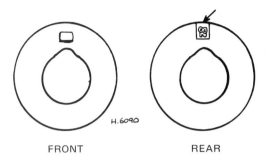

Fig. 6.44. Countergear thrust washer markings (Hi-Lux four-speed, 1972 on)

Fig. 6.45. Installing reverse idler gear (Hi-Lux four-speed, 1972 on)

1 Reverse idler gear   3 Woodruff key
2 Reverse idler shaft

Fig. 6.46. Selecting an input shaft circlip (Hi-Lux four-speed, 1972 on)

35 Renew the oil seals in the front bearing retainer, the rear extension housing and the shift lever shaft housing. A piece of tubing can be used as a drift for these operations.
36 Examine the gearbox casing and extension housing for cracks. These components are of light alloy and should be treated with respect.
37 Commence reassembly by smearing the mainshaft with oil and installing the 2nd gear onto the rear end of the shaft.
38 Install the synchro ring followed by reverse gear. Make sure that the sliding keys are aligned with the slots in the synchro ring.
39 Apply grease to the locking ball and fit it into the mainshaft bolt slot.
40 Install the bearing (3) into the bush (2) and insert both of them into 1st gear (4). Install the synchro ring (5) and then assemble the gear onto the mainshaft, making sure that the locking ball (1) aligns with the groove in the gear.
41 If the mainshaft rear bearing has been removed, install the baffle and circlip into the bearing retainer. Press on the bearing while the circlip is being expanded. Apply pressure to the bearing inner track only. Select a circlip from the five available thicknesses which will provide a clearance between the circlip and the retainer of between 0 and 0.004 in (0 and 0.1 mm).
42 Press the bearing/retainer assembly onto the mainshaft, applying pressure to the inner bearing track only.
43 Select a circlip from the five thicknesses available which will give a clearance between the circlip and rear bearing of between 0 and 0.006 in (0 and 0.15 mm). Install the selected circlip to the mainshaft.
44 Install the speedometer drive gear with its two securing circlips. Make sure that the Toyota mark on the gear is facing towards the rear of the mainshaft.
45 Fit the circlip and spacer to the end of the mainshaft.
46 Fit 3rd gear onto the mainshaft from the front end.
47 Install the 3rd/4th synchro assembly making sure that the sliding keys align with the slots in the synchro ring. Select a circlip from the three thicknesses available which will provide a clearance between the end face of the synchro hub and the circlip, of between 0 and 0.006 in (0 and 0.15 mm). Install the selected circlip.

48 Measure the endfloat of all gears. This should be between 0.004 and 0.010 in (0.1 and 0.25 mm).
49 Assemble the countergear complete with bearings and spacers. Insert the dummy shaft into the countergear. If no new components have been fitted, and the countergear endfloat was within the tolerance specified (0.004 to 0.010 in/0.1 to 0.25 mm) when measured before dismantling, the original thrust washers can be installed. Where the end-float was excessive or new components have been fitted, check and establish the correct endfloat of the countergear at this stage and adjust it, if necessary, by changing the rear thrust washer for one of the five thicknesses available. Note that the face of the thrust washer which has the small oil retaining depressions goes against the face of the countergear. The front and rear thrust washers are marked to identify them as shown (Fig. 6.44).
50 Lower the countergear complete with dummy shaft into the bottom of the gearcase.
51 Stick the countergear thrust washers into position in the gearcase using a dab of thick grease to retain them. Make sure that the tab on the washer engages in the groove in the casing.
52 Install reverse idler gear and drive in the shaft (complete with key) from the rear end of the casing.
53 If the bearing was removed from the input shaft, press on a new one so that the outer circlip groove of the bearing is nearer the front of the shaft. Select a bearing securing circlip from the six thicknesses available which will provide a clearance between the face of the circlip and the face of the bearing inner track of between 0 and 0.02 in (0 and 0.05 mm). Renew the input shaft internal roller bearings if worn. To remove them, release the circlip.
54 Install the input shaft into the front face of the gear casing, tapping the bearing outer track gently with a soft-faced mallet. Set the cutaway part of the input shaft as shown in the diagram.
55 Install the mainshaft assembly and then push 3rd/4th synchro sleeve towards 4th gear. As the mainshaft mates with the input shaft, make sure that the synchro sliding keys align with the synchro ring slots, and that the slotted spring pin in the mainshaft rear bearing retainer is aligned with the groove in the gear casing.

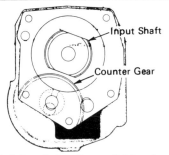

Fig. 6.47. Input shaft installation diagram (Hi-Lux four-speed, 1972 on)

Fig. 6.48. Installing mainshaft (Hi-Lux, four-speed, 1972 on)

1 3rd/4th synchro sleeve   2 Bearing retainer spring pin

Fig. 6.49. Front bearing retainer (Hi-Lux four-speed, 1972 on)

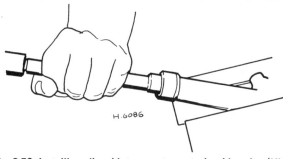

Fig. 6.50. Installing oil seal into remote control rod housing (Hi-Lux four-speed, 1972 on)

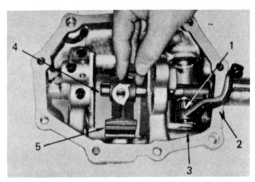

Fig. 6.51. Installing reverse shift arm (Hi-Lux four-speed, 1972 on)

1 Shift arm pivot   4 Selector lever shaft
2 Shift arm   5 Shift/select lever
3 Washer

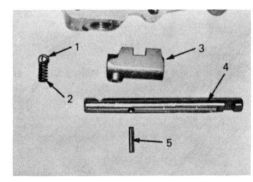

Fig. 6.52. Reverse selector shaft details (Hi-Lux four-speed, 1972 on)

1 Detent ball   4 Selector shaft
2 Detent spring   5 Tension pin
3 Dog

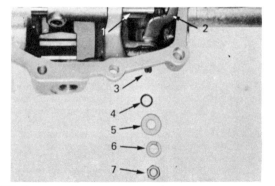

Fig. 6.53. Reverse shift arm pivot details (Hi-Lux four-speed, 1972 on)

1 Selector shaft   5 Washer
2 Shift arm   6 Washer
3 Pivot   7 Nut
4 'O' ring

Fig. 6.54. Installing interlock pin into side cover (Hi-Lux four-speed, 1972 on)

Fig. 6.55. Installing 1st/2nd shift fork (Hi-Lux four-speed, 1972 on)

1 Shift fork   3 Tension pin
2 Selector shaft

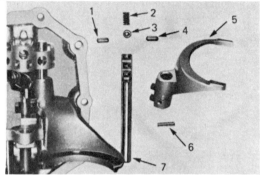

Fig. 6.57. 3rd/4th shift fork details (Hi-Lux four-speed, 1972 on)

1 Interlock pin   5 Shift fork
2 Detent spring   6 Tension pin
3 Detent ball   7 Selector shaft
4 Interlock pin

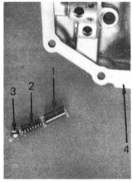 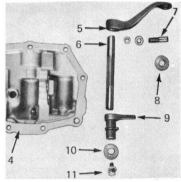

Fig. 6.58. Installing shift lever components (Hi-Lux column gearshift)

1 Spring seat   4 Side cover   7 Pin   10 Washer
2 Spring   5 Outer lever   8 Washer   11 Bolt
3 Detent ball   6 Shaft   9 Shift lever

Fig. 6.59. Selector lever components (Hi-Lux, column gearshift)

1 Lever   3 Outer lever
2 Washer   4 Pin

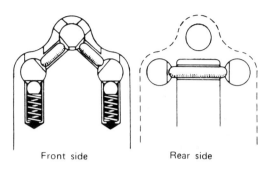

Front side   Rear side

Fig. 6.56. Detent ball and interlock pin installation diagram (Hi-Lux four-speed, 1972 on)

56 Raise the countergear carefully, and drive in the countershaft from the rear of the gear casing. The countershaft will displace the dummy shaft which has been retaining the alignment of the thrust washers, spacers and roller bearings for entry of the countershaft itself. Install the Woodruff key, ensuring that it engages correctly in the casing groove.

57 Use a new gasket and fit the bearing retainer to the front face of the gearbox. Make sure that the oil slot and hole are in alignment and apply sealing compound to the bolt threads to prevent oil seepage.

58 Use a new gasket and install the extension housing. Apply sealing compound to the bolt threads to prevent oil seepage.

59 Install the speedometer gear and bush.

With floor-mounted gearshift

60 If the side cover was dismantled, drive in a new oil seal into the remote control rod housing.

61 Install the shift arm pivot (1) to the reverse shift arm (2) with washer (3) and fit into the cover. (Fig. 6.51).

62 Install the remote control rod (4) and selector dog (5), insert the lock bolt and secure with wire.

63 Fit the reverse shift fork selector shaft (4), detent spring (2) and ball (1) into the gear casing. Be sure to push in the selector shaft (4) from the rear edge of the cover. Secure the selector dog (3) with a new tension pin (5) (Fig. 6.52).

64 Align reverse selector arm (2) with reverse selector shaft (1) and then install the 'O' ring, washers and nut to the selector arm pivot. Tighten the nut with the fingers only, pending adjustment (see paragraph 74). (Fig. 6.53).

65 Install the reverse ball, spring and ball holder complete with a new gasket to the side cover.

66 Install the interlock pin into the rear section of the cover.

67 Install the detent ball and spring into the front section of the cover and fit the 1st/2nd shift fork and selector shaft. Secure with a new tension pin.

68 Insert the two interlock pins into the front section of the cover.

69 Install the spring (2), locking ball (3), and fit 3rd/4th shift fork and selector shaft. Secure with a new tension pin.

With column-mounted gearshift

70 Install a new oil seal to the side cover.

71 Fit the shift lever and shaft to the side cover.

72 Insert the spring seat (1), spring (2), and detent ball (3), into the side cover (4) (Fig. 6.58).

73 Assemble the outer lever (5), to the shaft (6), and secure with the pin (7).

74 Locate the shift lever (9), inside the side cover and then insert the shaft (6) from the top of the cover over the washer (8). Make sure that the missing spline teeth of the lever and shaft are in alignment.

75 Tighten the bolt (11) having passed it through its washer (10).

76 Align the tip of the select lever (1) (Fig. 6.59) with the groove in the shift lever and install the select lever into the side cover. Assemble the washer (2) and outer lever (3) onto the select lever and secure with pin (4).

77 Install the spring seat (1), the spring (2) and detent ball (3) into the lower hole in the side cover. Position the reverse shift head (4) inside the side cover and install the shaft (5). Make sure that the detent ball groove on the shaft is nearer the front. Secure the reverse shift dog to the shaft with the pin (Fig. 6.61).

Fig. 6.60. Selector lever installed (Hi-Lux column gearshift)

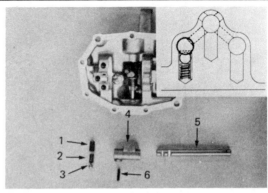

Fig. 6.61. Reverse shift details (Hi-Lux column gearshift)

1 Spring seat   4 Reverse dog
2 Spring   5 Selector shaft
3 Detent ball   6 Pin

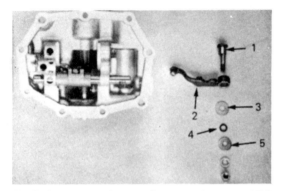

Fig. 6.62. Reverse shift details (Hi-Lux, column gearshift)

1 Pivot   4 'O' ring
2 Arm   5 Washer
3 Washer

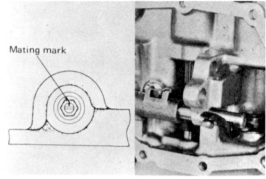

Fig. 6.63. Reverse shift arm pivot alignment mark

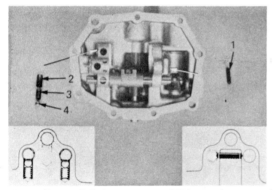

Fig. 6.64. 1st/2nd shift fork components (Hi-Lux, column gearshift)

1 Interlock pin   3 Spring
2 Spring seat   4 Detent ball

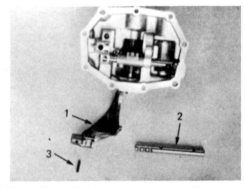

Fig. 6.65. 1st/2nd shift fork and selector shaft (Hi-Lux, column gearshift)

1 Fork   3 Pin
2 Shaft

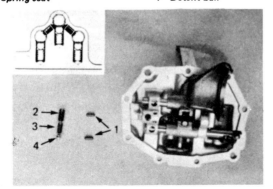

Fig. 6.66. 3rd/4th shift fork components (Hi-Lux, column gearshift)

1 Interlock pin   3 Spring
2 Spring seat   4 Detent ball

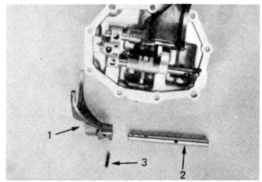

Fig. 6.67. 3rd/4th shift fork and selector shaft (Hi-Lux, column gearshift)

1 Fork   3 Pin
2 Shaft

78 Install the reverse shift arm by placing it on the pivot (1), fitting the washer (3), and inserting the assembly into the side cover. Fit the 'O' ring, washer and nut and make sure that the mark on the pivot is as shown in the diagram (Figs. 6.62 and 6.63).

79 Install the 1st/2nd shift fork, having first moved the reverse shaft to neutral and inserted the interlock pin. Install the spring seat (2), detent spring (3), and ball (4), into the upper hole in the side cover. (Fig. 6.64).

80 Install 1st/2nd shift fork to the side cover and insert the shaft (2). Make sure that the detent ball grooves are towards the front of the cover (Fig. 6.65). Secure the shift fork to the shaft with a new pin. .

81 Move reverse selector shaft and 1st/2nd shift fork to neutral and insert the interlock pins.

82 Insert the spring seat (2), spring (3), and detent ball (4), into the

centre hole in the side cover (Fig. 6.66).

83 Place 3rd/4th shift fork in the side cover and insert the shaft (2). Secure the fork to the shaft with a new pin (Fig. 6.67).

84 Fit the side cover using a new gasket. Make sure that the shift forks engage correctly with the synchro unit grooves. Apply jointing compound to both sides of the gasket and to the bolt threads. **Note**: the side cover securing bolts are of different lengths and must be refitted exactly as indicated (Fig. 6.68).

85 Screw in the reversing lamp switch using a new gasket.

86 Refit the clutch bellhousing and the clutch release mechanism.

Long wheelbase models

87 Install the output flange to the end of the mainshaft, tighten the nut to the specified torque and stake the nut.

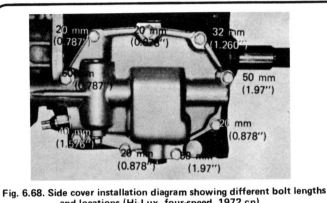

Fig. 6.68. Side cover installation diagram showing different bolt lengths and locations (Hi-Lux, four-speed, 1972 cn)

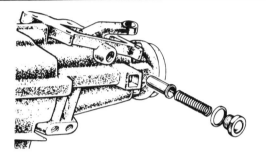

Fig. 6.69. Removing a restrictor pin assembly from the extension housing (Hi-Lux five-speed)

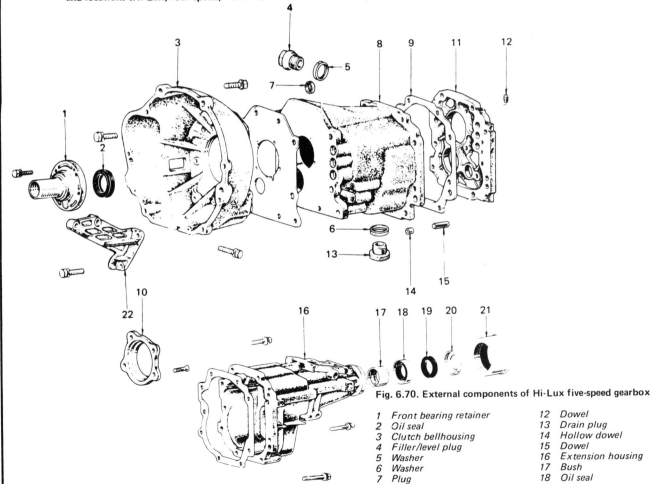

Fig. 6.70. External components of Hi-Lux five-speed gearbox

1	Front bearing retainer	12	Dowel
2	Oil seal	13	Drain plug
3	Clutch bellhousing	14	Hollow dowel
4	Filler/level plug	15	Dowel
5	Washer	16	Extension housing
6	Washer	17	Bush
7	Plug	18	Oil seal
8	Casing	19	Dust seal
9	Gasket	20	Dust seal retainer
10	Mainshaft rear bearing retainer	21	Dust deflector
11	Intermediate plate	22	Reinforcement bracket

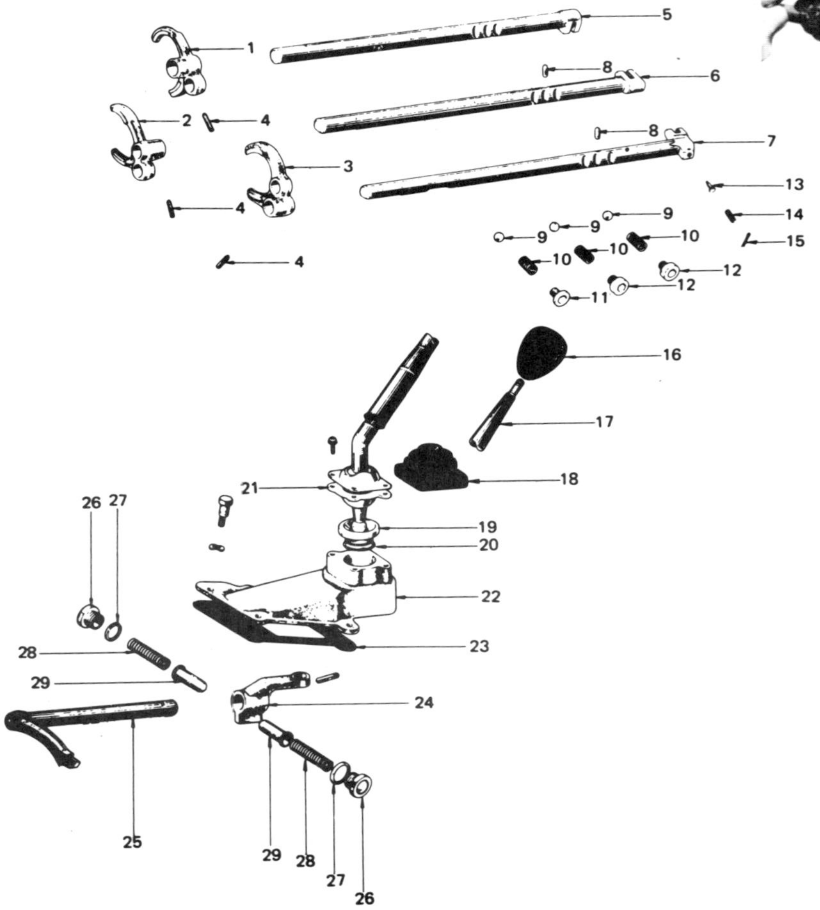

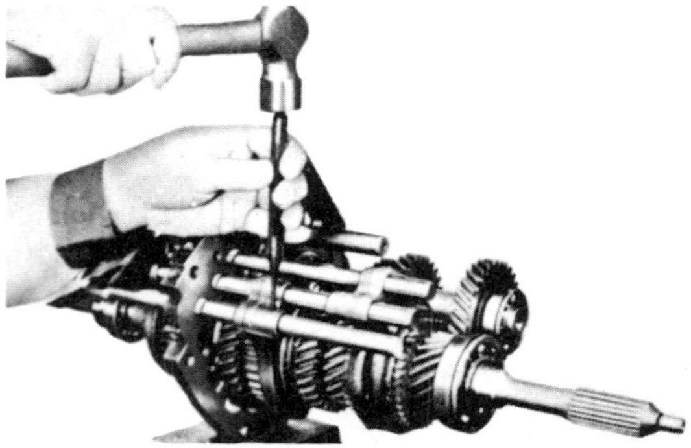

Fig. 6.74. Removing a shift fork tension pin (Hi-Lux five-speed)

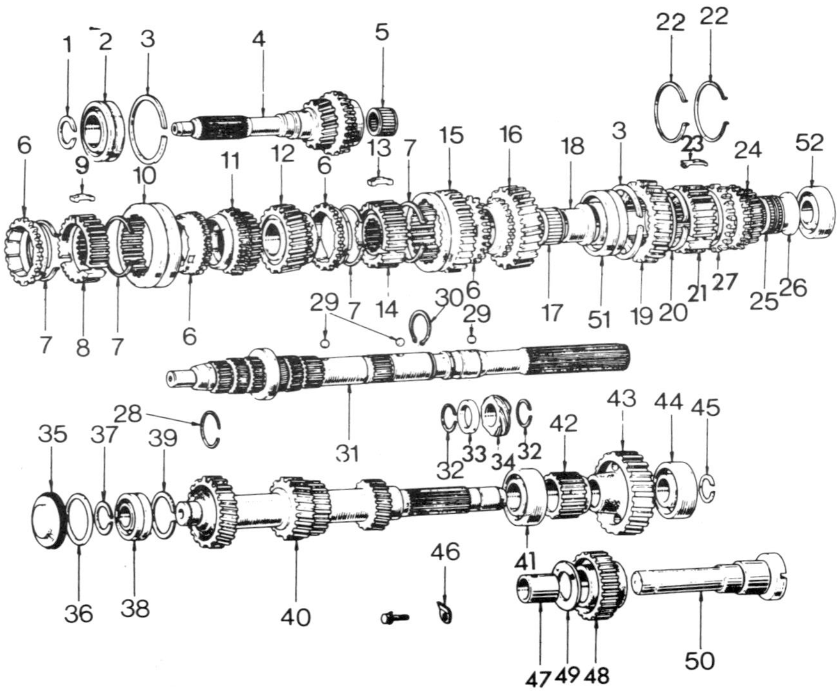

Fig. 6.73. Removing a detent socket screw (Hi-Lux five-speed)

Fig. 6.75. Removing 5th gear from mainshaft (Hi-Lux five-speed)

Fig. 6.76. Removing countershaft bearing outer track (Hi-Lux five-speed)

Fig. 6.77. Removing 3rd gear from front of mainshaft (Hi-Lux five-speed)

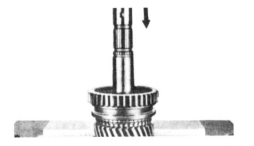

Fig. 6.78. Removing mainshaft rear bearing (Hi-Lux five-speed)

Fig. 6.71. Selector mechanism (Hi-Lux five-speed gearbox)

1 3rd/4th shift fork
2 1st/2nd shift fork
3 5th/reverse shift fork
4 Tension pin
5 1st/2nd selector shaft
6 3rd/4th selector shaft
7 5th/reverse selector shaft
8 Interlock pin
9 Detent ball
10 Detent spring
11 and 12 socket screws
13 Reverse restrictor pin
14 Spring
15 Split pin
16 Knob
17 Gearchange lever
18 Boot
19 Seat
20 Spring
21 Gasket
22 Remote control housing
23 Oil deflector
24 Swing arm
25 Remote control shaft
26 Plug
27 Washer
28 Spring
29 Restrictor pin

Fig. 6.72. Internal components of Hi-Lux five-speed gearbox

1 Circlip
2 Input shaft bearing
3 Bearing outer track circlip
4 Input shaft
5 Needle roller bearing
6 Synchro ring
7 Spring
8 3rd/4th synchro hub
9 Blocker bar
10 3rd/4th synchro sleeve
11 3rd gear
12 2nd gear
13 Blocker bar
14 1st/2nd synchro hub
15 Reverse gear
16 1st gear
17 Needle bearing
18 Needle bearing inner track
19 Reverse gear
20 Circlip
21 5th gear synchro hub
22 Spring
23 Blocker bar
24 5th gear
25 Needle roller bearing
26 Needle bearing inner track
27 Synchro ring
28 Circlip
29 Lock balls
30 Mainshaft rear bearing circlips
31 Mainshaft
32 Circlip
33 Spacer
34 Speedometer drive gear
35 Countershaft cover
36 Spacer
37 Circlip
38 Countershaft front bearing
39 Bearing outer track circlip
40 Countergear
41 Bearing
42 Reverse gear
43 Fifth gear
44 Bearing
45 Circlip
46 Stop
47 Bush
48 Reverse idler gear
49 Spacer
50 Reverse idler gear shaft
51 Mainshaft bearing
52 Mainshaft bearing

Fig. 6.79. Removing 1st gear from mainshaft (Hi-Lux five-speed)

Fig. 6.80. Pressing off reverse and 2nd gears from mainshaft (Hi-Lux five-speed)

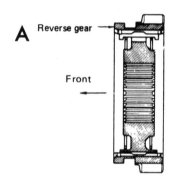

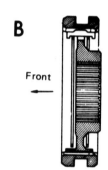

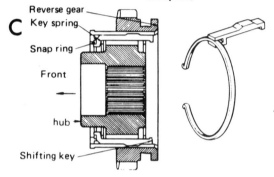

Fig. 6.81. Correct assembly of synchro units (Hi-Lux five-speed)

A   1st/2nd
B   3rd/4th
C   5th

88 With the gearbox completely reassembled, adjust the reverse gear pivot. To do this, release the shift arm pivot locknut and using the slot in the end of the shift arm pivot, turn it in a **clockwise** direction so that reverse idler gear is moved into contact with 1st gear. Now, by means of the slot, turn the shift arm pivot through 90° **anti-clockwise** and secure it in this position with the locknut (Fig. 6.19).

7   Gearbox (Hi-Lux five-speed, 1975 on) - overhaul

1   Unbolt the clutch bellhousing from the gearbox casing.
    Remove the speedometer driven gear and two restrictor pin assemblies from the extension housing.
    Unscrew and remove the reverse gear restrictor pin and then unbolt and remove the exhaust housing, making sure that the swing arm is moved in an anti-clockwise direction (when viewed from the rear) to disengage the remote control rod from the selector rods.
    With the extension housing removed, drive out the tension pin and remove the remote control rod and swing arm.
    Remove the reversing lamp switch.
2   From the front face of the gearbox, remove the front bearing retainer, the countershaft cover and spacer.
    Remove the circlips from the outer tracks of the input shaft and countershaft front bearings.
3   Separate the casing from the intermediate plate and pull off the casing leaving all the gear assemblies attached to the intermediate plate. Secure the intermediate plate in the jaws of a vice using jaw protectors to prevent damaging the plate.
4   Using a socket wrench, unscrew and remove the plugs from the edge of the intermediate plate and extract the springs and detent balls.
5   Drive out the tension pins from the shift forks and withdraw the selector shafts taking care not to lose the two interlock pins.
6   Remove the speedometer drive gear and its spacer from the mainshaft after the shaft circlips have been removed. Take care not to lose the locking ball.
7   Using a two legged puller, draw off the bearing from the rear end of the mainshaft.
8   Remove the circlip from the mainshaft.

9   From the rear end of the countershaft, remove the circlip and draw off the bearing.
10 Withdraw the countershaft 5th gear and reverse gear.
11 From the mainshaft, remove the circlip and withdraw 5th gear, the synchro ring, needle roller bearing and 5th gear inner bearing track, taking care not to lose the track locking ball.
12 Remove the reverse gear and 5th gear synchro unit.
13 Slacken the bolt which secures the reverse idler shaft stop to the intermediate plate, withdraw the shaft to the rear and remove the reverse idler gear and spacer.
14 Unbolt the mainshaft rear bearing retainer and remove the circlip from the bearing.
15 From the rear end of the countershaft, push the bearing outer track to the rear and withdraw the bearing components The countershaft assembly may now be removed from the intermediate plate.
16 Remove the input shaft and synchro ring from the mainshaft and then withdraw the mainshaft assembly from the intermediate plate.
17 To service the mainshaft, extract the circlip and remove the 3rd/4th synchro unit, the synchro ring and third gear from the front end of the mainshaft.
18 From the rear end of the mainshaft draw off the bearing. A press will be required for this operation.
19 Remove first gear, the needle roller bearing, bearing inner track and synchro ring. Take care not to lose the inner track locking ball.
20 Press off the second gear complete with synchro ring and reverse gear.
21 Clean all components thoroughly and examine for worn or chipped teeth and grooving or scoring of the shaft. The gears should have a running clearance between their internal bores and the shaft of between 0.0008 and 0.0020 in (0.02 and 0.05 mm) for 1st and 5th gears, and 0.0014 and 0.0039 in (0.06 and 0.10 mm) for 2nd and 3rd gears.
22 Inspect the condition of the synchro units. If there has been a history of noisy gearchanging or the synchromesh could easily be 'beaten', renew the unit complete. In any event, fit the synchro ring onto the gear and measure the clearance. This should not be less than 0.031 in (0.8 mm) otherwise renew the ring.
    Fit the shift forks to the synchro sleeves and check for side clearance. If this exceeds 0.039 in (1.0 mm) renew one or both components as necessary.

Correct assembly of the three synchro units must be carried out before installing them to the mainshaft. Ensure that the spring ends do not engage in the same gaps on opposite sides of the unit.

23 Commence reassembly of the mainshaft by installing the 3rd/4th synchro ring to third gear and then fitting them to the shaft.

24 Fit the 3rd/4th synchro unit, positioning it tight against the mainshaft shoulder. Secure it with a circlip to give a groove clearance of between 0 and 0.002 in (0 and 0.05 mm) from the range of thicknesses available.

25 Using feeler blades, measure the third gear endfloat, which should be between 0.0059 and 0.0098 in (0.15 and 0.25 mm) with a maximum of 0.0118 in (0.30 mm).

26 Install 2nd gear complete with synchro ring onto the mainshaft.

27 Using a press, install the 1st/2nd synchro unit and reverse gear assembly onto the mainshaft.

28 Measure 2nd gear endfloat which should be within the tolerance specified for 3rd gear in paragraph 25.

29 Using a dab of thick grease, stick the needle bearing inner track locking ball into its shaft recess.

30 Slide 1st gear, 3rd/4th synchro ring, needle bearing and inner track, (held as an assembly) onto the shaft. Check that the inner track slot aligns with the locking ball and that the synchro ring slots are aligned with the shift keys.

31 Press the mainshaft rear bearing onto the shaft end, making sure that the outer track circlip groove is nearer the rear end of the mainshaft.

32 Measure first gear endfloat which again should be as specified for third gear in paragraph 25.

33 To service the input shaft, carry out the following operations.

34 Inspect the gear teeth for chipping and the splines and shaft surfaces for wear.

35 Locate the synchro ring to the rear end of the input shaft and check the clearance between the two components. It should be between 0.039 and 0.079 in (1.0 and 2.0 mm) with a maximum of 0.031 in (0.8 mm), otherwise renew the ring.

36 Check the internal bore of the needle bearing recess and the condition of the bearing itself.

37 If the main bearing requires renewal, it will have to be removed on a press. When pressing on the new one, make sure that the outer circlip groove is nearer the front of the shaft. Select a shaft circlip to give the minimum side clearance in the shaft groove from the range of thicknesses available.

38 The countershaft assembly cannot be dismantled and must be renewed if the gears are chipped or worn. The bearings can be renewed using an extractor and press.

39 The reverse idler gear should be renewed if the teeth are worn or chipped; also the shaft if scored or grooved.

40 If the reverse gear bush is worn, it must be pressed out and the new one fitted so that the oil holes are in alignment and then the bush reamed, if necessary, to achieve a finished internal diameter of between 0.9858 and 1.0260 in (25.04 and 26.06 mm).

41 When fitting the countershaft cylindrical roller bearing inner track, position it so that its flanged side is towards the front of the gearbox.

42 When carrying out a major overhaul of the gearbox, it is recommended that all oil seals and 'O' rings are renewed as a matter of routine.

43 Renew the speedometer driven gear, 'O' rings and any worn components of the drive or driven gear.

44 Renew the oil seal in the front bearing retainer, using a tubular drift.

45 Renew the oil seal at the end of the rear extension housing in a similar manner to that described in the preceding paragraph. Should the metal bush be worn, it can be renewed after heating the rear end of the extension housing in boiling water. When installing the new bush, make sure that the oil feed grooves are in alignment.

46 Commence reassembly by checking that the intermediate plate dowel pins project by between ¼ and 5/16 in (6.0 and 8.0 mm) from the the front face of the intermediate plate and then secure the plate in a vice fitted with jaw protectors.

47 Install the needle roller bearing assembly to the input shaft and then fit the 3rd/4th synchro ring to the cone on the end of the input shaft.

48 Fit the mainshaft assembly to the intermediate plate and then fit the input shaft to the mainshaft.

49 Install the countershaft assembly onto the intermediate plate and then fit the roller bearing onto the shaft from the rear side of the plate and then fit the spacer.

50 Fit the circlip to the outer track of the mainshaft rear bearing.

51 Install the mainshaft rear bearing retainer onto the intermediate plate.

52 Assemble the reverse idler gear spacer onto the reverse idle shaft and then insert the assembly into the intermediate plate from the rear side. The oil holes in the reverse idler gear must face to the rear.

53 Lock the reverse idler shaft with the stop plate and bolt, then check the reverse idler gear endfloat. This should be between 0.0059 and 0.0098 in (0.15 and 0.25 mm) with a maximum of 0.0118 in (0.30 mm).

54 Locate the 5th gear synchro unit (assembled with the reverse gear) onto the mainshaft until it is tight against the inner track of the bearing in the intermediate plate.

55 Fit the locking ball into the mainshaft recess. Use a dab of thick grease to retain it.

56 To the mainshaft, fit the fifth gear, synchro ring, needle roller bearing and inner track, (all assembled together) until the assembly rests against the face of the synchro unit.

57 Secure the assembly to the mainshaft by selecting a circlip from the thirteen available thicknesses to give the minimum clearance.

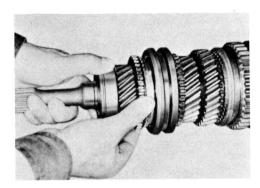

Fig. 6.82. Fitting input shaft to the mainshaft (Hi-Lux five-speed)

Fig. 6.83. Installing mainshaft rear bearing retainer (Hi-Lux five-speed)

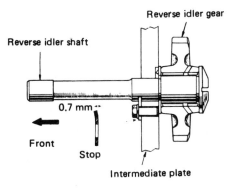

Fig. 6.84. Reverse idler gear assembly diagram (Hi-Lux five-speed)

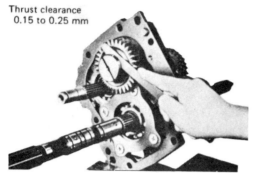

Thrust clearance
0.15 to 0.25 mm

Fig. 6.85. Measuring reverse idler gear end-float (Hi-Lux five-speed)

Fig. 6.86. Fitting 5th gear to mainshaft (Hi-Lux five-speed)

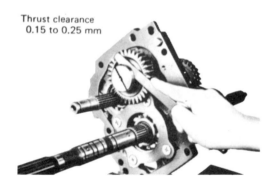

Thrust clearance
0.15 to 0.25 mm

Fig. 6.87. Measuring 5th gear end-float (Hi-Lux five-speed)

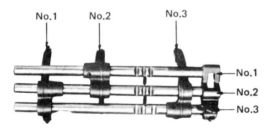

No.1   No.2   No.3

No.1
No.2
No.3

Fig. 6.88. Correct assembly of selector shafts and shift forks (Hi-Lux
five-speed)

1 1st/2nd   3 5th/reverse
2 3rd/4th

58 Check fifth gear endfloat; this should be between 0.0039 and
0.0098 in (0.10 and 0.25 mm) with a maximum clearance of 0.0118 in
(0.30 mm)
59 Fit the countershaft reverse gear, fifth gear and drive on the bearing
using a piece of tubing as a drift.
60 Fit a circlip to the countershaft and another to the mainshaft. Select
the circlips from the four available thicknesses.
61 Drive the rear bearing onto the mainshaft, again using a piece of
tubing as a drift and making sure that it rests against the inner track of
the bearing.
62 To the mainshaft, fit the spacer, locking ball and speedometer drive
gear and secure them with a circlip.
63 Locate the shift forks in their respective synchro hub grooves,
ensuring that the bosses of the forks face the correct way as shown.
64 Insert the 1st/2nd selector shaft and the 5th/reverse selector shaft.
The gears should be in neutral when assembling each shaft and the
interlock pins correctly inserted.
65 Insert the 3rd/4th selector shaft.
66 Insert the detent balls and springs into their holes in the edge of the
intermediate plate. Tighten the sockets screws to the specified torque
and, in order to prevent oil leaks, ensure that their threads are coated
with jointing compound.
67 Secure the shift forks to the selector shafts by driving in the tension
pins.
68 Position a new gasket to the front face of the intermediate plate and
locate the gearbox casing on the plate.
69 Fit the circlips to the input shaft and countershaft front bearings.
70 Assemble the remote control rod and swing arm into the extension
housing by driving in the connecting tension pin.
71 Locate a new gasket on the rear face of the intermediate plate and
offer up the extension housing until it is within an inch (25.4 mm) of
its installed position. Move the swing arm clockwise to engage the
remote control rod with the shift forks and push the extension housing
fully home.
72 Bolt the extension housing to the gearbox casing, sandwiching the
intermediate plate and two gaskets in between them. Tighten the bolts
to the specified torque.
73 Push the countershaft fully to the rear and measure the distance
between the front face of the countershaft front bearing, and the front
face of the gearbox, using a dial gauge or feeler blades. Select a spacer
to correspond with the dimension established from the thicknesses
available.
74 Fit the selected spacer to the front of the countershaft bearing,
followed by the cover.
75 Use a new gasket and bolt on the input shaft bearing retainer,
making sure that the oil return holes are in alignment.
76 Use a new gasket and bolt the clutch bellhousing to the front face of
the gearbox. Tighten the bolts to the specified torque.
77 Insert the restrictor pins and springs, one on each side of the
extension housing and tighten the plugs to the specified torque.
78 Refit the speedometer driven gear to the extension housing and the
reversing lamp switch to the gearbox casing.
79 The gearshift lever will normally be bolted to the extension housing
as the gearbox is offered up during installation.

8 Gearbox (Hi-Ace four-speed, early) - overhaul

1 Remove the clutch release bearing and mechanism from within the
bellhousing.
2 Unbolt and remove the front bearing retainer and gasket.
3 Unbolt and remove the transmission side cover and gaskets
4 Extract the bolts which retain the extension housing to the main
gear case. Rotate the extension housing until the cutaway on the
extension housing aligns with the end of the countershaft.
5 Using a dummy shaft slightly less in diameter than the countershaft, drive the countershaft out of the gearbox towards the rear.
6 Withdraw the extension housing complete with mainshaft assembly.
7 Withdraw the input shaft from the gearbox.
8 Remove the countergear assembly and thrust washers from the
interior of the gearbox.
9 Dismantle the countergear by pushing out the dummy shaft, spacer
and needle roller bearings.
10 Using a brass drift, drive the reverse idler gear shaft towards the
rear of the gearbox and remove it. Extract the reverse idler gear.

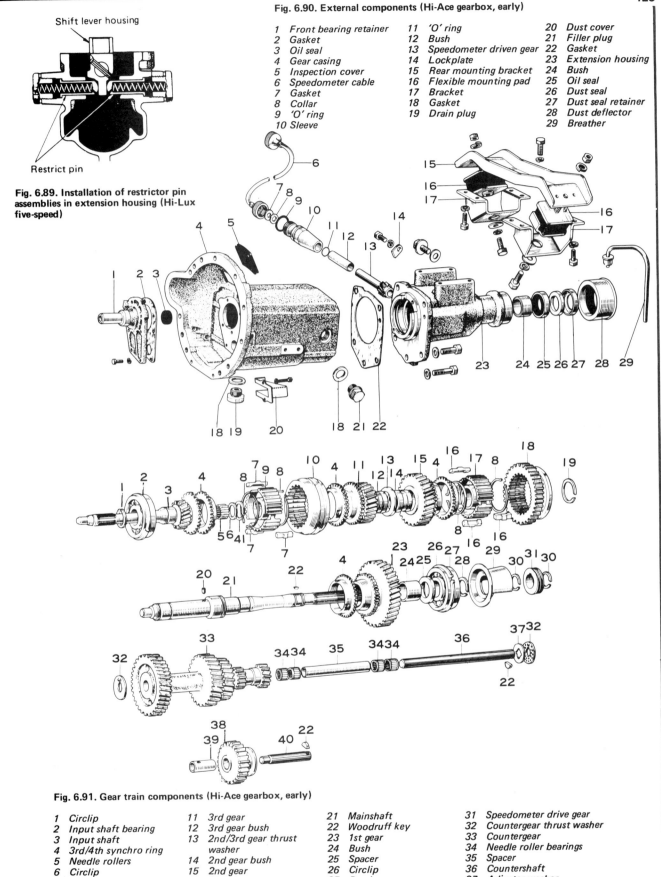

Shift lever housing

Restrict pin

Fig. 6.89. Installation of restrictor pin assemblies in extension housing (Hi-Lux five-speed)

Fig. 6.90. External components (Hi-Ace gearbox, early)

1	Front bearing retainer	11	'O' ring	20	Dust cover
2	Gasket	12	Bush	21	Filler plug
3	Oil seal	13	Speedometer driven gear	22	Gasket
4	Gear casing	14	Lockplate	23	Extension housing
5	Inspection cover	15	Rear mounting bracket	24	Bush
6	Speedometer cable	16	Flexible mounting pad	25	Oil seal
7	Gasket	17	Bracket	26	Dust seal
8	Collar	18	Gasket	27	Dust seal retainer
9	'O' ring	19	Drain plug	28	Dust deflector
10	Sleeve			29	Breather

Fig. 6.91. Gear train components (Hi-Ace gearbox, early)

1	Circlip	11	3rd gear	21	Mainshaft	31	Speedometer drive gear
2	Input shaft bearing	12	3rd gear bush	22	Woodruff key	32	Countergear thrust washer
3	Input shaft	13	2nd/3rd gear thrust washer	23	1st gear	33	Countergear
4	3rd/4th synchro ring	14	2nd gear bush	24	Bush	34	Needle roller bearings
5	Needle rollers	15	2nd gear	25	Spacer	35	Spacer
6	Circlip	16	Shift key	26	Circlip	36	Countershaft
7	Synchro shift key	17	1st/2nd synchro hub	27	Bearing	37	Adjuster washer
8	Spring	18	Reverse gear	28	Circlip	38	Reverse idler gear
9	3rd/4th synchro hub	19	Circlip	29	Oil baffle	39	Bush
10	3rd/4th synchro sleeve	20	Lock pin	30	Circlip	40	Reverse idler gear shaft
						41	Circlip

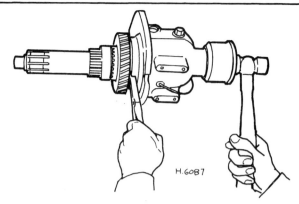

Fig. 6.93. Removing mainshaft from extension housing (Hi-Ace gearbox, early)

Fig. 6.94. Removing 3rd/4th shift fork (Hi-Lux gearbox, early)

1   Fork   3   Selector shaft
2   Tension pin

Fig. 6.95. Removing 1st/2nd shift fork tension pin (Hi-Lux gearbox, early)

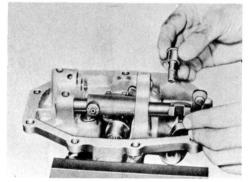

Fig. 6.96. Removing reverse shift arm pivot (Hi-Ace gearbox, early)

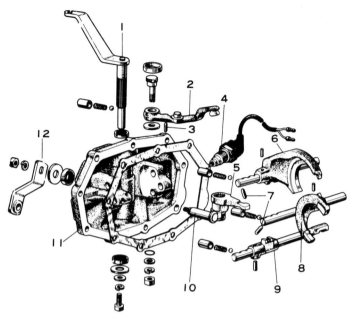

Fig. 6.92. Side cover selector components (Hi-Ace gearbox, early)

1   Selector rod/arm assembly   7   Interlock pin
2   Reverse shift arm   8   3rd/4th shift fork
3   Interlock pin   9   Reverse selector dog
4   Reversing lamp switch   10   Selector lever shaft
5   Sliding shift lever   11   Side cover
6   1st/2nd shift fork   12   External lever

11 Extract the circlip from the front end of the mainshaft and slide off the synchro unit, the synchro ring, 3rd gear, 3rd gear bush, the thrust washer, 2nd gear bush, 2nd gear, synchro ring, synchro hub, reverse gear and the last synchro ring.

12 Remove the lockplate and extract the speedometer gear assembly from the extension housing.

13 Expand the mainshaft rear bearing retaining circlip and then drive the mainshaft out of the extension housing using a plastic-faced mallet.

14 Extract the securing circlip and withdraw the speedometer drive gear, Woodruff key and the oil baffle from the mainshaft.

15 Extract the remaining circlips and press 1st gear, spacer and bearing from the mainshaft.

16 To dismantle the side cover, first unscrew and remove the reversing lamp switch.

17 Move 3rd/4th shift fork towards the front (4th speed position). Using a long drift, drive out the tension pin which secures the fork to the selector shaft.

18 Withdraw the selector shaft from the rear edge of the cover taking care to catch the spring-loaded detent ball. Remove the shift fork.

19 Extract the detent spring and the two interlock pins from the cover.

20 Drive the tension pin out of 1st/2nd shift fork and remove the shaft, fork, detent ball and spring in a similar manner to that just described.

21 Unscrew the shift arm pivot locknut and remove the pivot and reverse shift arm from the cover.

22 Drive out the tension pin and remove reverse selector dog and selector shaft. Extract the detent ball and spring.

23 Remove the selector outer lever and shaft.

24 Remove the selector rod lock bolt and slide the rod out of the side cover. Be prepared to catch the lock ball which will be ejected.

25 With the gearbox dismantled, clean all components in paraffin and examine them for wear or damage.

26 Check the bores of the gear wheels for roughness and the teeth for chipping. Where a dial gauge is available, gear back lash should be checked and compared with the following tolerances. Between all gears, except reverse idler to countergear, and reverse idler gear to mainshaft reverse gear, the tolerance should not exceed 0.004 in (0.10 mm). Reverse gear backlash 0.005 in (0.12 mm).

27 Check the synchroniser units for wear or damage. When a synchro ring is placed on the cone of a gear, the ring to cone gap should not be less than 0.047 in (1.2 mm), otherwise renew the ring (and gear if necessary).

28 Check the shafts for worn splines and the bearings for noisy or rough operation when turned with the fingers.

29 Test the clearance of the shift forks in the grooves of their respective synchro sleeves. The clearance should not exceed 0.04 in (1.0 mm), otherwise renew the shift fork or sleeve, or both, as necessary to correct the situation.

30 Renew all oil seals as a matter of routine and obtain the necessary gaskets.

31 Commence reassembly by sliding 1st gear onto the mainshaft so that the synchro side is towards the front of the shaft.

32 Fit the spacer and press the bearing onto the mainshaft, so that the outer circlip groove is nearer the front of the shaft.

33 Select a circlip from the available thicknesses to provide the minimum clearance in the shaft groove (0 to 0.002 in/0 to 0.05 mm). Install the oil baffle and then fit the selected circlip.

34 Fit the Woodruff key into its groove in the mainshaft, and then slide the speedometer drive gear into the shaft and secure it with circlips.

35 Locate the mainshaft circlip into its groove in the front end of the extension housing. Expand the circlip using circlip pliers and then install the mainshaft assembly to the extension housing. When carrying out this operation, it is a good idea to fit the propeller shaft universal joint sleeve yoke to the end of the mainshaft. This will help to prevent damage to the extension housing oil seal and bush and also centre the mainshaft. The mainshaft endfloat should be between 0 and 0.002 in (0 and 0.05 mm), otherwise change the rear bearing circlip for one of different thickness from the range of thicknesses available.

36 Assemble the synchro units. Fit the two springs into the synchro hub so that they are located as shown in Fig. 6.97. Engage the three shift keys with the slots in the synchro hub and with the springs. Note that the shift keys of the two synchroniser units are different. The longer keys belong to the 3rd/4th synchro unit.

37 Assemble the synchro sleeves and hubs as shown in Fig. 6.97.

38 Install 3rd/4th synchro assembly on the mainshaft. Align the cutaway parts of the synchro ring with the shift keys.

39 Slide 2nd gear bush onto the mainshaft and align the groove in the bush with the pin on the mainshaft.

40 Fit the 2nd gear onto the bush on the mainshaft and then fit 2nd/3rd gear thrust washer, making sure to engage the cut-outs in the washers with the tags on the bush.

41 Install 3rd gear bush, 3rd gear, 3rd/4th synchro ring and synchro assembly to the mainshaft. Select a circlip which will provide the minimum end-float (0 to 0.002 in/0 to 0.05 mm) between the face of the synchro hub at the circlip.

42 Using a feeler gauge, check the endfloat of 2nd and 3rd gears. This should be between 0.002 and 0.006 in (0.05 and 0.15 mm). If it is not, change the gear thrust washer.

43 If the bearing has been removed from the input shaft, press on the new one so that the outer circlip groove is nearer the front of the shaft. Select a circlip which will retain the bearing to the input shaft with minimum endfloat.

44 Install the needle roller bearings into the recess in the rear end of the input shaft, holding them in position with thick grease and then fit the circlip.

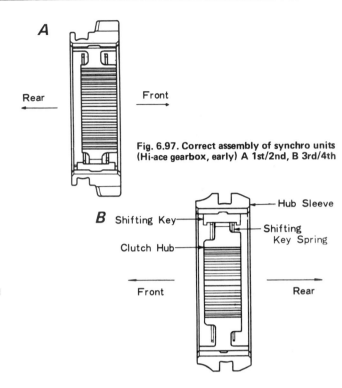

Fig. 6.97. Correct assembly of synchro units (Hi-ace gearbox, early) A 1st/2nd, B 3rd/4th

45 Install the reverse idler gear into the gear case so that the shift fork groove is towards the rear. Drive the reverse idler shaft through the gear so that the keyway in the shaft is in alignment with the cut-out in the casing. Fit the key.

46 Insert the spacer into the countergear followed by a needle roller bearing assembly at each end. Insert the dummy shaft used for dismantling and lay the countergear assembly in the gearbox.

47 Stick the countergear thrust washers and the single adjusting washer to the inside of the gear case using thick grease.

48 Install the input shaft.

49 Offer up the extension housing complete with mainshaft gear train to the main gear case. Make sure that a new joint gasket is used.

50 Rotate the extension housing so that the countershaft hole is exposed, lift the countergear and install the countershaft from the rear of the gear case. The countershaft will displace the dummy shaft during this operation and at the same time pick-up the thrust washers as it passes through them. Secure the countershaft with the Woodruff key. At this stage, check the countergear endfloat. This should be between 0.002 and 0.006 in (0.05 and 0.15 mm). If it is not, change the adjusting washer for one of different thickness.

51 Insert the extension housing bolts, not forgetting the exhaust pipe support bracket, and tighten the bolts to the specified torque wrench setting.

52 Fit the speedometer drive gear and lock plate.

53 Use a new gasket and fit the front bearing retainer. Apply jointing compound to the threads of the securing bolts to prevent oil seepage.

54 Install the clutch release bearing and mechanism.

55 If the side cover has been dismantled, commence reassembly by installing the selector rod detent spring and ball into the hole in the cover. Place the sliding shift lever onto the side cover so that the shift groove is towards reverse selector shaft. Depress the detent ball and fit the washer to the selector rod and insert it into the cover. Fit the remaining washers and secure the selector rod with its end bolt.

56 Install the selector lever shaft, washer and external lever to the side cover. Place reverse dog on the cover so that the shift fork slot is towards the rear.

57 Insert the detent spring and detent ball; depress the latter with a thin screwdriver then install reverse selector shaft into the side cover from the rear. Fit the reverse selector dog to the shaft and secure with a new tension pin.

58 Install reverse shift arm and washer and engage the centre pin of the arm with the slot at the rear end of the reverse selector shaft.

59 Install the reverse shift arm pivot using a new 'O' ring and tighten the securing nut.

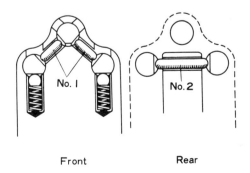

Fig. 6.98. Interlock pin locations (Hi-Ace gearbox, early)

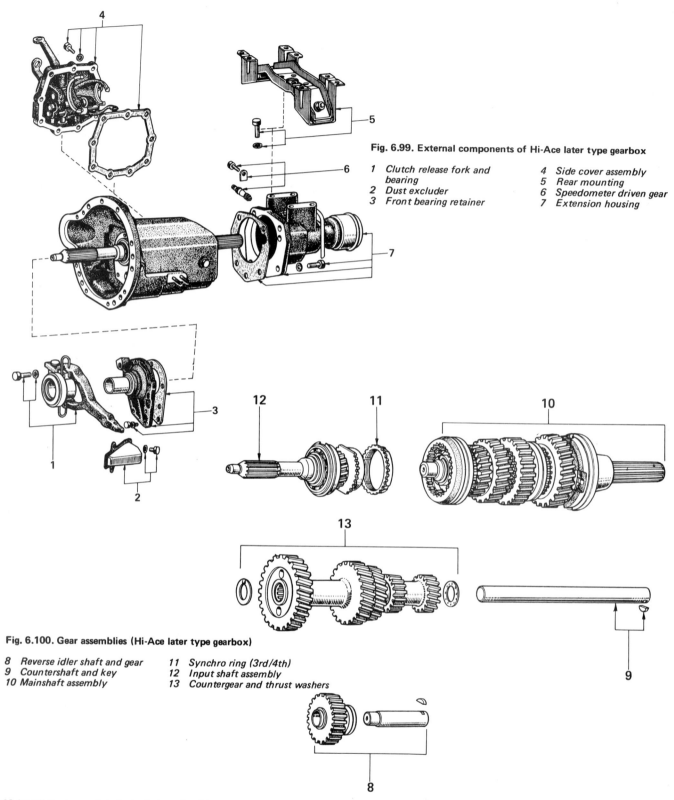

Fig. 6.99. External components of Hi-Ace later type gearbox

1	Clutch release fork and	4	Side cover assembly
	bearing	5	Rear mounting
2	Dust excluder	6	Speedometer driven gear
3	Front bearing retainer	7	Extension housing

Fig. 6.100. Gear assemblies (Hi-Ace later type gearbox)

8	Reverse idler shaft and gear	11	Synchro ring (3rd/4th)
9	Countershaft and key	12	Input shaft assembly
10	Mainshaft assembly	13	Countergear and thrust washers

60 Install the longer interlock pin into the side cover and then assemble 1st/2nd shift fork, selector shaft, detent spring and ball into the side cover. Secure the shift fork with a new tension pin.
61 Set reverse selector dog and 1st/2nd shift fork in the neutral position.
62 Insert the two shorter interlock pins into their holes in the side cover, and then assemble 3rd/4th shift fork, selector shaft, detent spring and ball. Secure the shift fork with a new tension pin.
63 Screw the reversing lamp switch into the cover.

64 Align the shift forks and reverse selector dog with their respective synchro sleeve grooves, or gear groove, and install the side cover using a joint gasket.
65 With the gearbox completely reassembled, adjust the reverse gear pivot. To do this, release the shift arm pivot locknut and using the slot in the end of the shift arm pivot, turn it in a **clockwise** direction so that reverse idler gear is moved into contact with 1st gear. Now by means of the slot, turn the shift arm pivot through 90° **anticlockwise** and secure it in this position with the locknut (Fig. 6.19).

Fig. 6.101. Side cover assembly (Hi-Ace later type gearbox)

21 *Reverse lamp switch*
22 *Tension pin*
23 *3rd/4th shift fork and shaft*
24 *Detent ball, spring and interlock pin*
25 *Tension pin*
26 *1st/2nd shift fork and shaft*
27 *Pin*
28 *Locknut, washers and 'O' ring*
29 *Reverse shift arm and pivot*
30 *Tension pin*
31 *Reverse selector shaft and dog*
32 *Detent ball and spring*
33 *Selector outer lever and shaft*
34 *Shift outer lever, shaft and sliding lever*
35 *Detent ball and spring*

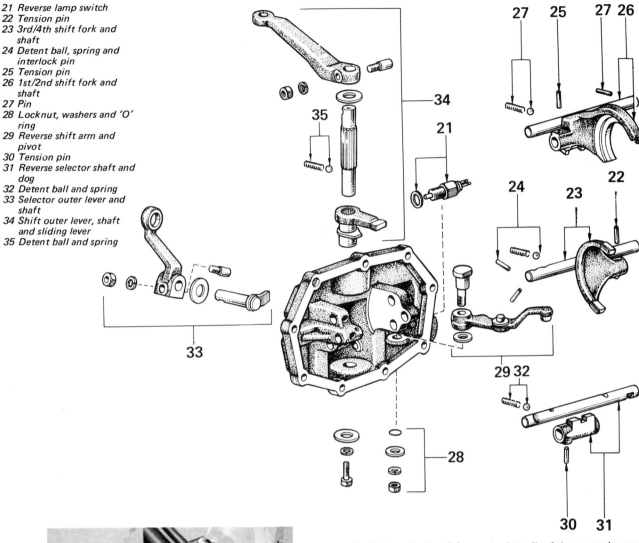

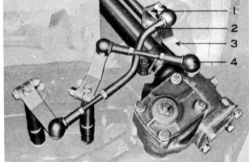

Fig. 6.102. Gearshift linkage at base of steering column (Hi-Ace gearbox, early)

1 *Shift control lever*   3 *Selector control lever*
2 *Shift control rod*   4 *Selector control rod*

9 Gearbox (Hi-Ace four-speed, later) - overhaul

1 Internally, this gearbox is very similar to the type L42 used on some Hi-Lux models, but the differences in the extension housing and the side cover selector mechanism will be observed from Figs. 6.99 and 6.101.

2 Refer to Section 6 for overhaul details of the gear train components and to Section 8, paragraphs 16 to 24 for details of the side cover selector mechanism, but noting the difference in the design of some of the components.

3 When checking the internal components, note that the following tolerances apply and not those given in Section 6. The other tolerances and clearances are as stated in Section 6.

Maximum shift fork to synchro sleeve groove clearance 0.039 in (1.0 mm)
Synchro ring to gear clearance 0.032 in (0.8 mm)
Gear to shaft running clearance (except reverse idler) 0.0024 to 0.0043 in (0.06 to 0.11 mm)
Gear to shaft running clearance (reverse idler) 0.0024 to 0.0039 in (0.06 to 0.10 mm)

10 Steering column gearshift (Hi-Ace, early) - overhaul and adjustment

1 Wear occurring in the steering column mounted gearshift linkage can normally only be overcome by renewal of the components concerned. However, adjustment of the two control rods which run between the lower end of the steering column and the levers on the support bracket may rectify any slackness in the linkage.

2 First adjust the length of shift rod (2) to set the hand control lever in the horizontal position.

3 Now adjust the length of the selecting rod (4) until the hand control lever moves smoothly in neutral (Fig. 6.102).

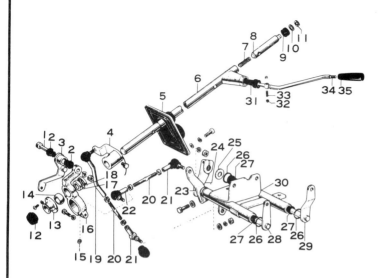

Fig. 6.103. Exploded view of steering column gearshift linkage (Hi-Ace, early)

Fig. 6.105. Gearshift selector cross shaft installed (Hi-Ace, early)

1 Pivot bolt
2 Bush
3 Selector control lever
4 Shift control lever
5 Cover plate
6 Control shaft
7 Spring
8 Control shaft upper section
9 Bush
10 Washer
11 'E' clip
12 Dust cover
13 Seat
14 Bush
15 Lockwasher
16 Lower bracket
17 Dust seal
18 Dust seal retainer

19 Shift rod
20 Adjusting rod
21 Balljoint
22 Balljoint
23 Relay lever
24 Relay lever
25 Washer
26 'O' ring
27 Bush
28 Selector lever
29 Shift lever
30 Relay bracket
31 Dust cover
32 Pin
33 Spring
34 Hand control lever
35 Knob

1 Selector rod/arm assembly
2 External lever
3 Balljoint
4 Link rod
5 Return spring
6 Selector rod
7 Cross shaft

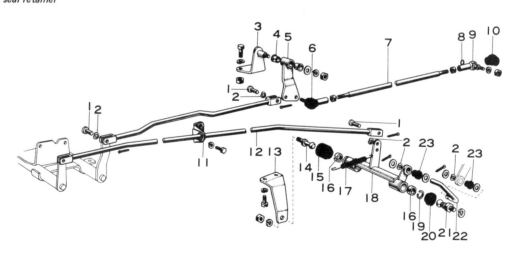

Fig. 6.104. Relay bracket to gearbox linkage (Hi-Ace, early)

1 Clevis pin
2 Wave washer
3 Bracket
4 Bush
5 Lever
6 Balljoint

7 Shift rod
8 Circlip
9 Balljoint
10 Dust seal
11 Guide
12 Selector rod

13 Cross shaft bracket
14 Pivot knob
15 Dust cover
16 Bush
17 Tension spring

18 Cross shaft
19 Circlip
20 Dust cover
21 Cross shaft pivot knob
22 Link rod
23 Bush

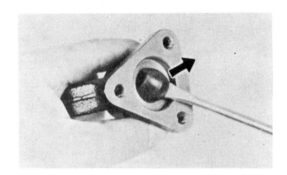

Fig. 6.109. Lower bracket bush (Hi-Ace, later type gearshift)

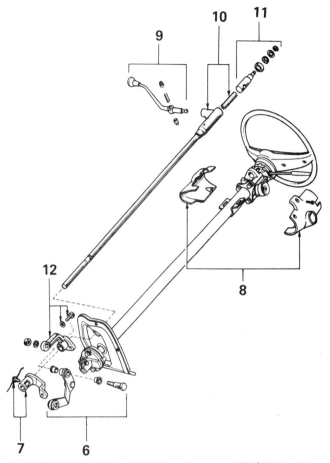

Fig. 6.106. Exploded view of steering column gearshift (Hi-Ace, later models)

6   Selector lever
7   Shaft lever
8   Steering column shrouds
9   Gearshift column

10   Control shaft and spring
11   Upper shaft components
12   Lower bracket

4   If the gearshift mechanism must be dismantled, first remove the steering wheel as described in Section 11 and the direction switch as described in Section 10.
5   Extract the 'E' clip from the top of the gearshift shaft and remove the bush and washer.
6   Remove the contact ring housing (two bolts) from the steering column.
7   Depress the hand control lever pins and withdraw the hand control lever from the gearshift shaft.
8   Extract the separate upper section of the gearshift shaft and the spring.
9   Remove the steering column upper support bracket.
10 Unbolt the cover plate at the base of the steering column and disconnect the ball-jointed shift-rod from the shaft lever.
11 Disconnect the other ball-jointed shift-rod in a similar way.
12 Remove the pinch bolt from the bracket clamp at the base of the shaft.
13 Pull the steering column upwards into the vehicle interior, at the same time, depressing the clutch fully to provide clearance for the steering column and gearshift shaft.
14 Cut the locking wire and remove the lever from the base of the gearshift shaft.
15 Remove the pivot bolt and withdraw the select lever from the clamp bracket at the base of the gearshift shaft. Remove the clamp bracket.
16 Dismantling of the linkage, which connects the levers on the side of the gearbox with the levers on the frame-mounted relay brackets, is quite straightforward as is also the cross-shaft and reference should be made to Figs. 6.104 and 6.105.
17 Reassembly is a reversal of dismantling, but apply grease to all metal friction surfaces before refitting.
18 Adjust as described at the beginning of this Section.

11 Steering column gearshift (Hi-Ace, later) - overhaul and adjustment

1   To dismantle this type of steering column gearshift, first disconnect the selector and shift control rods at the base of the steering column.
2   Make alignment marks on the steering wormshaft and flexible coupling yoke. Release the coupling pinch bolt and, after releasing the necessary securing bolts, withdraw the steering column complete. Full details of removal of the steering column are given in Chapter 11.
3   Cut the locking wire and remove the bolt and control shaft lever from the bottom end of the column.

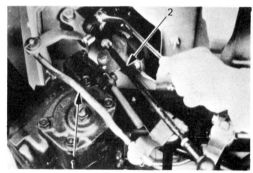

Fig. 6.107. Selector rod (1) and shift rod (2) at base of steering column (Hi-Ace later type gearshift)

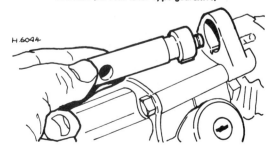

Fig. 6.108. Withdrawing upper shaft and bush (Hi-Ace, later type gearshift)

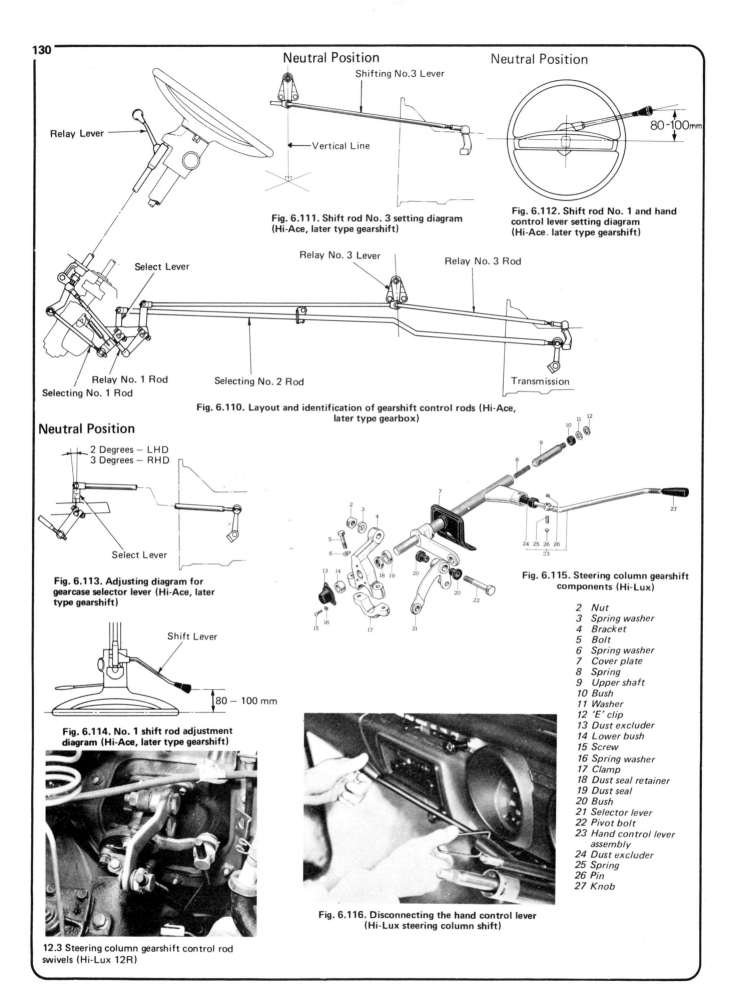

Relay Lever

Neutral Position

Shifting No.3 Lever

Vertical Line

Fig. 6.111. Shift rod No. 3 setting diagram
(Hi-Ace, later type gearshift)

Neutral Position

80 -100mm

Fig. 6.112. Shift rod No. 1 and hand
control lever setting diagram
(Hi-Ace. later type gearshift)

Select Lever

Relay No. 3 Lever

Relay No. 3 Rod

Relay No. 1 Rod

Selecting No. 2 Rod

Transmission

Selecting No. 1 Rod

Fig. 6.110. Layout and identification of gearshift control rods (Hi-Ace,
later type gearbox)

Neutral Position

2 Degrees – LHD
3 Degrees – RHD

Select Lever

Fig. 6.113. Adjusting diagram for
gearcase selector lever (Hi-Ace, later
type gearshift)

Shift Lever

80 – 100 mm

Fig. 6.114. No. 1 shift rod adjustment
diagram (Hi-Ace, later type gearshift)

Fig. 6.115. Steering column gearshift
components (Hi-Lux)

2   Nut
3   Spring washer
4   Bracket
5   Bolt
6   Spring washer
7   Cover plate
8   Spring
9   Upper shaft
10 Bush
11 Washer
12 'E' clip
13 Dust excluder
14 Lower bush
15 Screw
16 Spring washer
17 Clamp
18 Dust seal retainer
19 Dust seal
20 Bush
21 Selector lever
22 Pivot bolt
23 Hand control lever
      assembly
24 Dust excluder
25 Spring
26 Pin
27 Knob

Fig. 6.116. Disconnecting the hand control lever
(Hi-Lux steering column shift)

12.3 Steering column gearshift control rod
swivels (Hi-Lux 12R)

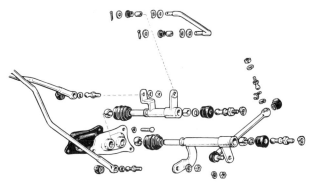

Fig. 6.117. Steering column gearshift arrangement at gearbox end
(Hi-Lux)

4   Depress the spring-loaded plungers and remove the hand control
lever from the upper end of the column.
5   Withdraw the upper shaft and bush.
6   Inspect all components for wear and renew as necessary. The bush
in the lower bracket is accessible for renewal after the seal and the
retainer have first been withdrawn.
7   Reassemble by reversing the dismantling operations, but apply
grease to all friction surfaces.
8   When reassembly is complete, carry out the following adjustments
which are critical, if smooth and positive gearshifting is to be achieved.
9   Set the levers on the gear casing at the hand control to the neutral
position.
10 Adjust the length of shift rod No. 3 so that the relay lever is vertical.
11 Adjust the length of shift rod No. 1 so that the hand control lever
is positioned as shown in Fig. 6.112.
12 Adjust the length of selector rod No. 2 so that the selector lever at
the base of the steering column is inclined from the vertical as shown
in Fig. 6.113.
13 Adjust the length of shift rod No. 1 so that the position of the hand
control lever is as shown.

12 Steering column gearshift (Hi-Lux) - overhaul and adjustment

1   Slackness in the gearshift linkage will probably be due to wear in
the components.
2   There are slight differences in design between the components used
in the steering column gearshift linkage, according to date of vehicle
production, but the dismantling operation for all models is similar.
3   Working within the engine compartment, disconnect the control
rod swivels at the base of the steering column.
4   Remove the control select lever.
5   Remove the control shaft lower bracket.
6   Disconnect the lead from the battery negative terminal.
7   Working within the driving compartment, disconnect the harness
multi-pin plugs and then remove the steering wheel (see Chapter 11).
8   Remove the direction indicator switch (Chapter 10).

13 Fault diagnosis - manual gearbox

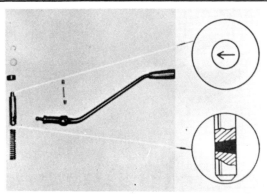

Fig. 6.118. Hand control lever and upper shaft alignment (Hi-Lux
steering column gearshift)

About 30mm(1.2")   About 25mm(0.9")

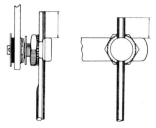

Selecting Rod   Shifting Rod

Fig. 6.119. Control rod and swivel nut setting diagram (Hi-Lux
steering column gearshift)

9   Depress the spring-loaded pins and withdraw the hand control lever
from the shift lever shaft.
10 Remove the upper shaft and spring.
11 Remove the upper clamp and stay from the steering column.
12 Release the cover plate at the base of the steering column and
withdraw the gearshift lever shaft into the vehicle interior.
13 Working under the vehicle, disconnect the rearmost control rod
from the shift lever on the outside of the transmission casing.
14 Extract the bolts and remove the cross-shaft assembly.
15 Inspect all components for wear or distortion and renew as necessary.
16 Reassembly is a reversal of dismantling, but apply grease to all metal
friction surfaces, and note particularly the direction of the tapered hole
in the upper shaft.
17 When reassembly is complete, place the hand control lever in
neutral and move it up and down to ensure that the action is smooth.
The select and shift rods should be set approximately in accordance
with the diagram, but final tightening of the swivel nuts should not be
carried out until the hand control lever is placed in each shift position
in turn, and the levers on the outside of the gearcase checked to see
that they are centred in the particular detent without any tendency to
be pulled one way or the other by the overriding force of the control
rods.

Symptom	Cause
Ineffective synchromesh on one or more gears	Worn baulk rings. Worn sliding keys.
Jumps out of one or more gears	Weak detent springs. Worn shift forks. Worn engagement dogs. Worn synchro hubs.
Whining, roughness, vibration allied to other faults	Bearing failure and/or overall wear. Incorrect gear endfloat or back lash.
Noisy and difficult gear engagement	Clutch not operating correctly.
Sloppy and impositive gear selection	Overall wear throughout the selector mechanism.

Chapter 6 Part 2: Automatic transmission

Contents

Specifications

Type ... ... A30 Three element, single stage, two phase torque converter with planetary gear train

Ratios

1st	2.400 : 1
2nd	1.479 : 1
3rd	1.000 : 1
Reverse	1.920 : 1

Fluid capacity ... ... 5.6 Imp qts (6.4 litres/6.80 US qts)

Torque wrench settings

	lb f ft	Nm
Driveplate bolts to crankshaft	45	62
Driveplate bolts to torque converter	32	44
Torque converter housing to engine bolts	55	77
Oil pan bolts	8	11
Extension housing bolts	15	21

14 General description and precautions

1 As from 1973, three-speed automatic transmission with a floor-mounted shift has been available as an option on Hi-Lux models using 18-R or 20R engines only.

2 In the event of breakdown, the vehicle must not be towed in excess of 30 mph (48 km/h) or further than 50 miles (80 km) unless the propeller shaft is disconnected. Failure to observe this requirement may cause damage to the transmission due to lack of lubrication. Due to the complexities of dismantling and reassembly of automatic transmission units, the operations described in this Chapter are limited to maintenance, adjustment and removal and installation of the unit.

15 Maintenance

1 If the transmission fluid is cold, withdraw the dipstick, wipe it, re-insert it and withdraw it again. The fluid level should be within the cold range. If the vehicle has travelled at least 5 miles (8 km) the fluid level should be within the hot range of the dipstick when the same checking procedure is followed. Top-up with fluid of the specified grade.

2 Keep the external surfaces of the transmission unit clean and free from mud and grease to prevent overheating. Check the fluid cooler and make sure that the connecting pipes are secure and in good condition.

16 Selector linkage - adjustment

1 The adjustments described in this and the following Sections are not to be considered as routine and should only be carried out when wear in the components or incorrect operation of the automatic transmission requires them.

2 The floor mounted speed selector lever operates in a six position gate, through a right-hand control rod and a cross-shaft to the hydraulic valve lever. On the left-hand side of the transmission unit a secondary control rod actuates the transmission parking lock.

3 It is essential that the hand control moves smoothly and positively through all positions and when a speed is selected, the valve lever should be in the centre of its detent and not under any overriding force from the control rod.

4 To synchronise the hand control and the valve lever positions, remove the swivel bolt which connects the hand lever to the control rod. Set the valve lever to the 'N' on the transmission speed range indicator and then set the hand lever to the 'N' position. Reconnect the swivel bolt and tighten fully.

5 Now loosen the adjusting nuts on the forward end of the parking lock rod, place the selector hand lever in 'P' and pull the parking lock shaft to the lock position. Tighten the adjusting nuts without disturbing the setting of the rod.

6 When adjustment of the parking lock rod is completed, check that with the selector lever in 'R', the parking pawl is completely disengaged. To do this push the vehicle backwards and forwards.

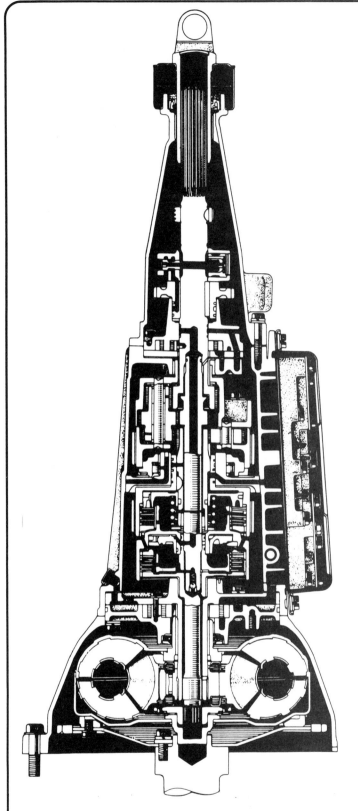

Fig. 6. 120. Sectional view of A30 automatic transmission

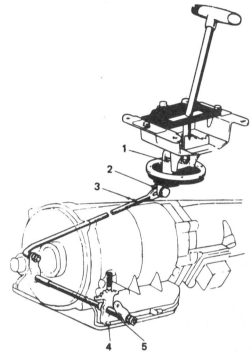

COLD   HOT

Fig. 6.121. Automatic transmission dipstick markings

Fig. 6.122. Automatic transmission speed selector linkage

1 *Selector lever*   4 *Valve lever*
2 *Swivel bolt*   5 *Cross shaft*
3 *Control rod*

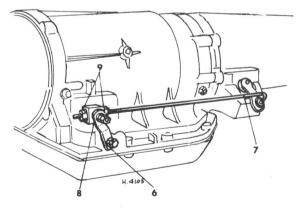

H.4105

Fig. 6.123. Parking lock control linkage on automatic transmission

6 *Shaft lever*   8 *Swivel*
7 *Lock rod*   9 *Locknuts*

17 Starter inhibitor/reversing lamp switch - adjustment

1   Remove the knob from the speed selector lever and withdraw the centre console.
2   With the switch now exposed, place the speed selector lever in 'N' and adjust the position of the switch (by moving it within the limits of its elongated bolt holes) until it corresponds with the illustrations shown in Figs. 6.124 and 6.125.

18 Throttle link connecting rod - adjustment and testing

1   The correct adjustment of this component is essential to ensure correct operation of the 'kick-down' facility when fast acceleration is required by immediate change to a lower speed.
2   Operate the throttle lever on the carburettor by hand so that the carburettor throttle butterfly valve is fully open. Have an assistant check that the throttle valve lever indicator is in alignment with the mark on the side of the transmission casing. Where this is not the case, loosen the turnbuckle locknut on the connecting rod, rotate the turn-buckle and when adjustment is correct, tighten the locknut.
3   Before road testing for correct operation of the 'kick-down', check the fluid level and run the vehicle to normal operating temperature over a distance of at least 6 miles (9 km) to ensure that the transmission fluid is fully warmed.
4   Accelerate gently but progressively and listen for the points of change (up) to the next speed. These should occur from 1 to 2 at between 6 and 10 mph (10 and 16 km/h) and from 2 to 3 between 11 and 18 mph (17 and 28 km/h). Repeat the test on the same stretch of road but accelerating at full throttle. The speed change points should occur from 1 to 2 at between 33 and 41 mph (53 and 66 km/h) and 2 and 3 at between 54 and 63 mph (86 and 100 km/h). If the shifts made are at a constant speed according to the degree of acceleration (throttle opening), then it can be assumed that the transmission and control gear are operating correctly.
5   Now check the 'kick-down' change points. With the throttle valve about half open at a road speed of 43 mph (68 km/h) in 3rd speed depress the accelerator pedal sharply and check that the transmission downshifts to 2nd speed.
6   Under similar conditions at a road speed of between 50 and 55 mph (80 and 88 km/h) move the selector lever to the '2' position. The transmission should immediately downshift to 2nd speed. As the road speed decreases to between 18 and 33 mph (29 and 52 km/h) the transmission will downshift to 1st speed.
7   If the preceding tests do not prove positive and the throttle link connecting rod has been correctly adjusted, a fault must lie in the governor, valve, throttle valve, or the shift valves; consult your Toyota dealer.

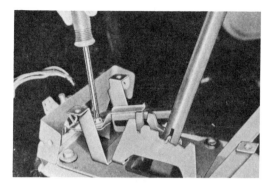

Fig. 6.124. Adjusting starter inhibitor/reversing lamp switch on automatic transmission

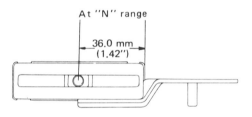

Fig. 6.125. Starter inhibitor switch setting diagram

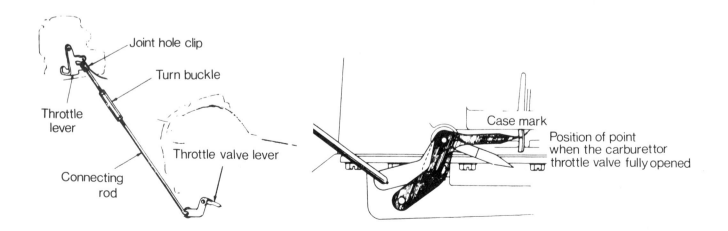

Fig. 6.126. 'Kick-down' rod adjustment diagram

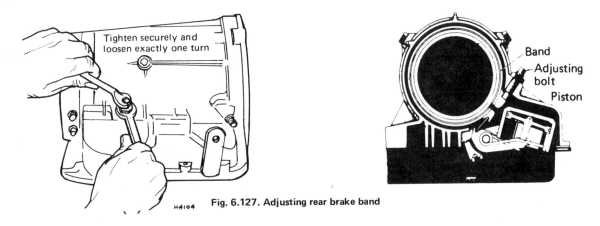

Fig. 6.127. Adjusting rear brake band

Fig. 6.128. Adjusting front brake band

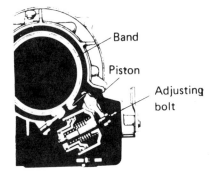

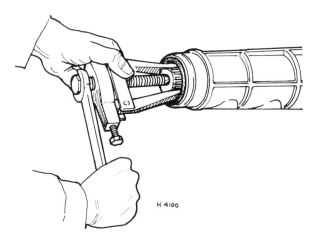

Fig. 6.129. Removing automatic transmission extension housing oil seal

19 Brake bands - adjustment

1   Adjustment of these components should only be carried out as the result of relevant fault symptoms occurring as described in Section 22.
2   The rear band adjuster is located on the right-hand inclined surface of the transmission casing. Loosen the locknut and tighten the anchor bolt to a torque of 3.6 lb f ft (0.5 kg f m) then unscrew it exactly one turn and tighten the locknut.
3   The front band adjuster is only accessible after draining the transmission unit and removing the oil pan. The clearance between the faces of the adjuster bolt and piston should be 0.0118 in (3.0 mm). Screw the bolt in or out as necessary.

20 Extension housing oil seal - renewal

1   Renewal of the oil seal may be carried out with the transmission unit in position in the vehicle.
2   Remove the propeller shaft as described in Chapter 7.
3   Knock off the dust deflector towards the rear and prise out the dust seal. Using a suitable extractor and levering against the end face of the mainshaft, extract the oil seal.
4   Drive in the new oil seal with a tubular drift, fit a new dust seal and refit the dust deflector.
5   Refit the propeller shaft after first greasing the front sliding sleeve both internally and externally. Make sure that the propeller shaft and pinion driving flanges have their mating marks aligned.

21 Automatic transmission - removal and installation

1   Disconnect the lead from the battery negative terminal.
2   Drain the cooling system and disconnect the radiator top hose.
3   Remove the air cleaner and disconnect the throttle control at the carburettor.
4   Unless the vehicle is over a pit or raised on a hoist, jack-up the front and rear so that there is an adequate working clearance between the underside of the body floor and the ground to permit the torque converter housing to be withdrawn.

5   Drain the fluid from the transmission unit.
6   Remove the starter motor.
7   Disconnect the propeller shaft from the rear axle (see Chapter 7) and withdraw it from the transmission rear extension housing.
8   Disconnect the speed selector linkage at the transmission unit, also the 'kick-down' rod.
9   Disconnect the exhaust downpipe from the manifold and remove the support bracket from the transmission unit.
10 Disconnect the fluid cooler pipes from the transmission and plug them. Remove the pipe supports from the transmission.
11 Disconnect the speedometer drive cable.
12 Pull the fluid filler tube from the transmission and retain the 'O' ring seal.
13 Disconnect the handbrake intermediate lever from the rear mounting crossmember.
14 Remove the cover plate from the lower half of the front of the torque converter housing.
15 Support the automatic transmission with a jack and then remove the rear crossmember and mounting. Through the open lower half of the torque converter housing, remove the six bolts which secure the drive plate and converter together. These can only be removed in turn by

rotating the drive plate. To do this, apply a ring spanner to the crankshaft pulley securing bolt.
16 When all bolts are withdrawn, remove one of the lower torque converter housing (to engine) bolts and fix a flat metal bar, so positioned that it will maintain pressure on the front face of the torque converter to prevent it being displaced from its engagement with the tangs of the oil pump when the transmission is withdrawn.
17 Place a jack under the engine sump (use a block of wood to protect it) and remove the bolts which secure the torque converter housing to the the engine.
    Lower both jacks progressively, until the transmission unit will clear the lower edge of the engine rear bulkhead.
18 Withdraw the transmission rearwards.
19 The drive plate can be removed, if necessary, by unbolting it from the crankshaft mounting flange.
20 If the starter ring gear is worn, renew the driveplate (to which it is attached) as an assembly.
21 Installation is a reversal of removal, but tighten all bolts to the specified torque and carry out the adjustments described earlier in this Chapter, after first having refilled the unit with the correct grade and quantity of fluid.

22 Fault diagnosis - automatic transmission

Symptom	Cause
Vehicle fails to move in any selector position	Low hydraulic pressure. Transmission locked by parking pawl.
Vehicle fails to move in 'D', '2' or 'L'	Front clutch inoperative.
No drive in 2nd speed with selector in 'D' or '2' with vehicle moving	Front band inoperative or requires adjustment.
No drive in 3rd speed with selector in 'D' and vehicle moving	Rear clutch inoperative. Low hydraulic pressure.
Vehicle fails to move in 'R'	Rear clutch inoperative. Low oil pressure. Rear brake band requires adjustment or rear servo piston not actuating.
No 1st/2nd speed upshift	Low governor pressure. Front servo piston inoperative or front brake band requires adjustment.
No 2nd/3rd speed upshift	Low governor pressure. Rear clutch inoperative. Low oil pressure to rear clutch and front servo.
No 3rd/2nd downshift	Low throttle valve pressure. High governor pressure. Front servo piston inoperative or front brake band requires adjustment.
No 2nd/1st downshift	High governor pressure. One-way clutch inoperative.
Incorrect speed shift points	Faulty shift valves. Throttle link connecting rod incorrectly adjusted. Line pressure abnormal.
Incorrect kick down point	Throttle pressure check ball faulty. Incorrect adjusted 'kick down' rod.
Jerky upshift and downshift throughout range	High hydraulic line pressure. Faulty internal control valve.
Jerky upshift or downshift to 2nd speed with selector in 'D' or '2'	High hydraulic line pressure. Front brake band worn.
Jerky 2nd/3rd upshift	High hydraulic line pressure.
Jerky 2nd/1st downshift	Faulty one way clutch.
Evidence of high fuel consumption	Incorrect grade of fluid. Faulty one way clutch. Friction or slipping between idle or operating clutches and bands.

Chapter 7 Propeller shaft

Contents

Specifications

Type	Tabular shaft with needle bearing universal joints and sliding sleeve. Long wheelbase models have centre bearing

Universal joint circlip thicknesses ...   .

0.047 in (1.20 mm)
0.049 in (1.25 mm)
0.051 in (1.30 mm)
0.053 in (1.35 mm)

Torque wrench settings

	lb f ft	Nm
Drive flange bolts	20	27
Centre bearing attachment bolts	20	27
Centre bearing castellated nut	140	190

1 General description

1 Hi-Ace models and standard wheelbase Hi-Lux models are equipped with a two-joint type propeller shaft.
2 The universal joints and the sliding sleeve which fits over the rear end of the gearbox mainshaft, absorb the varying angles and length of the propeller shaft which is caused by the up and down motion of the rear axle due to the deflection of the rear road springs.
3 Long wheelbase Hi-Lux models are equipped with a three-joint type propeller shaft. This type of shaft is connected to the output shaft of the transmission by means of a flange and it is attached to the bodyframe by means of a flexible-mounted centre bearing.
4 The universal joints each comprise a four way trunnion, or 'spider', each leg of which runs in a needle roller bearing race, prepacked with grease and fitted into the bearing journal yokes of the sliding sleeve and propeller shaft and flange. The universal joints are replaceable and the components are supplied in kit form.

2 Maintenance

1 No maintenance is required to the two-joint type shaft as the sliding sleeve at the front end of the shaft is lubricated by oil seepage from the gearbox.
2 With the three-joint type propeller shafts, apply the grease gun to the nipple on the sliding section at the intervals specified in Routine Maintenance at the beginning of this manual.
3 The universal joints are of lubricant sealed type and require no attention.
4 It is recommended that periodic inspection is carried out, however, whenever the car may be undergoing service, to check for any slackness in the universal joint bearings or at the flange bolts.

3 Propeller shaft (two-joint type) - removal and installation

1 Unless the vehicle is over a pit or supported on a hoist, jack up the rear to provide adequate working clearance.
2 Mark the edges of the propeller shaft rear driving flange and the rear axle pinion flange.
3 Unscrew and remove the four bolts from the rear driving flange. Separate the rear flanges by pulling the propeller shaft forward slightly and then withdraw the propeller shaft from the extension housing of the gearbox or automatic transmission. As the sliding joint is withdrawn from a manual type gearbox, be ready to catch a small quantity of oil.
4 Refitting is a reversal of removal but remember to align the rear flange mating marks.

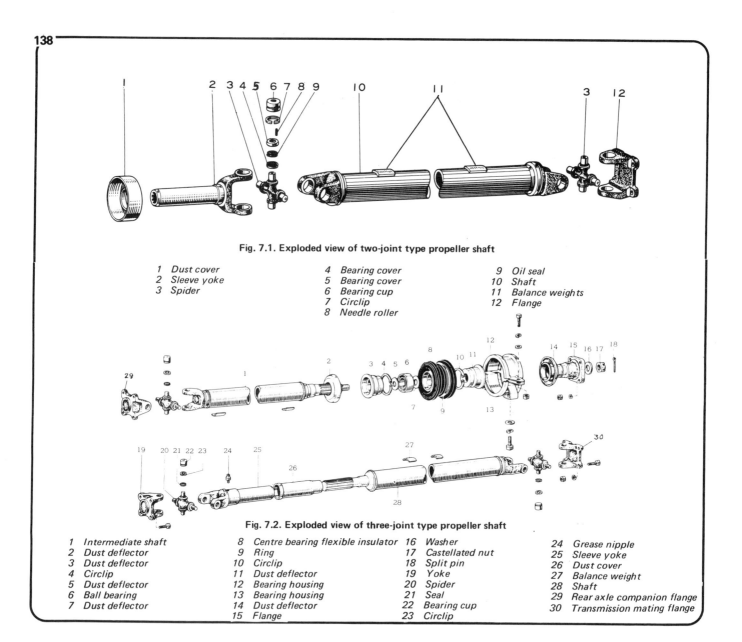

Fig. 7.1. Exploded view of two-joint type propeller shaft

1	Dust cover	4	Bearing cover	9	Oil seal
2	Sleeve yoke	5	Bearing cover	10	Shaft
3	Spider	6	Bearing cup	11	Balance weights
		7	Circlip	12	Flange
		8	Needle roller		

Fig. 7.2. Exploded view of three-joint type propeller shaft

1	Intermediate shaft	8	Centre bearing flexible insulator	16	Washer	24	Grease nipple
2	Dust deflector	9	Ring	17	Castellated nut	25	Sleeve yoke
3	Dust deflector	10	Circlip	18	Split pin	26	Dust cover
4	Circlip	11	Dust deflector	19	Yoke	27	Balance weight
5	Dust deflector	12	Bearing housing	20	Spider	28	Shaft
6	Ball bearing	13	Bearing housing	21	Seal	29	Rear axle companion flange
7	Dust deflector	14	Dust deflector	22	Bearing cup	30	Transmission mating flange
		15	Flange	23	Circlip		

4.2 Propeller shaft rear flange (Hi-Lux)

4.4 Propeller shaft centre bearing (Hi-Lux)

4 Propeller shaft (three-joint type) - removal and installation

1 Repeat the operations described in paragraphs 1 and 2 of the preceding Section.
2 Disconnect the propeller shaft rear flange from the rear axle pinion flange (photo).
3 Withdraw the rear section of the propeller shaft from the universal joint sleeve yoke.
4 Unbolt the centre bearing from the bodyframe crossmember (photo).
5 Disconnect the propeller shaft front flange from the output flange at the rear of the transmission.
6 Remove the front section of the propeller shaft.
7 Refitting is a reversal of removal, but make sure that the arrow marked on the propeller shaft is aligned with the grease nipple on the sleeve yoke.

5 Universal joints - inspection, dismantling and reassembly

1 Preliminary inspection of the universal joints can be carried out with the propeller shaft on the car.
2 Grasp each side of the universal joint, and with a twisting action, determine whether there is any play or slackness in the joint. Also try an up and down rocking motion for the same purpose. If there is any sign whatsoever of play, the joints need renewal.
3 Remove the propeller shaft as described in Section 3 or 4.
4 Dot punch adjacent edges of the yokes so that they will be refitted in their original positions. Remove the circlips which are located on the inner faces of the joint yokes, not on the ends of the bearing cups. They can be driven from their grooves with a pointed tool.
5 The bearing cups may be removed by one of two methods. Either hit the yoke (supported in the hand) adjacent to the bearing cup hole with a wooden or plastic mallet until the cup begins to emerge or press the cup out in a vice using an old bearing cup on one side and tubular spacer on the other to receive the ejected cup. With both methods, screw the cups out of their seats once they have emerged far enough to be able to grip them with a self-locking wrench.
6 Inspect the holes in the yokes for elongation. Evidence of this is only likely in the event of previous neglect or abuse, in which case the yokes must be renewed.
7 Obtain the appropriate repair kit for each joint. This will comprise spider, bearing cups, needle bearings and seals.
8 Locate the spider within the yoke and check that the 'O' ring seals are in position and that the dot punch marks mate.

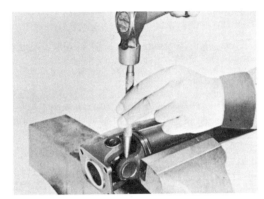

Fig. 7.3. Marking the relative positions of propeller shaft yokes

9 Fill the bearing cup 1/3rd full with grease and check that the needle bearings are correctly held in position (with grease) around the inside of the cup.
10 Using a vice and an old bearing cup, press the new bearing cup into the yoke at the same time holding the spider in alignment so that the cup will slide onto the trunnion.
11 Repeat the operations for the remaining three bearings of each universal joint.
12 Insert new circlips **which must be of the same thickness for each opposite pair of bearing cups** and must be selected from the sizes listed in Specifications to ensure an axial endfloat of not more than 0.002 in (0.05 mm).

6 Centre bearing - dismantling and reassembly

1 Make alignment marks on the intermediate shaft and the universal joint flange.
2 Extract the split pin and holding the flange quite still, unscrew the castellated nut.
3 Press the intermediate shaft from the universal joint flange.
4 Withdraw the centre bearing assembly from the intermediate shaft.
5 Remove the bearing housing from its flexible insulator.

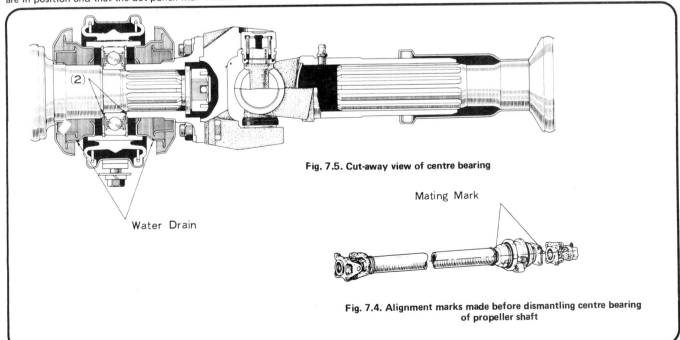

Fig. 7.5. Cut-away view of centre bearing

Fig. 7.4. Alignment marks made before dismantling centre bearing of propeller shaft

6 Remove the dust deflectors and then extract the circlips and remove the bearing from the flexible insulator.
7 Inspect all components and renew as necessary.
8 Commence reassembly by installing the circlip and bearing into the flexible insulator.
9 Apply multi-purpose grease to the dust deflectors, and also to both faces of the bearing.
10 Press the rearmost dust deflector into the insulator. Check the drain hole is correctly positioned.
11 Locate the bearing housing round the insulator, making sure that the drain hole in the dust deflector is at the lowest point.
12 Install the bearing assembly to the intermediate shaft, having located

the second dust deflector to its front face.
13 Match the alignment marks made before dismantling and install the universal joint flange to the intermediate shaft.
14 Tighten the castellated nut to specified torque and insert a new split pin.
15 Check the bearing for smooth rotation and then bolt the propeller shaft flange to the centre bearing flange, so that the grease nipple is in alignment with the marks made on the centre bearing flange and the intermediate shaft.
16 When connecting the rear propeller shaft section to the sleeve yoke, make sure that the arrow on the shaft is in line with the grease nipple.

7 Fault diagnosis - propeller shaft

Symptom	Cause
Vibration	Worn universal joints. Worn or loose centre bearing. Propeller shaft bent. Extension housing bush worn. Loose drive flange bolts. Propeller shaft out of balance.
Knocking during starting, deceleration, gear-changing, or at the moment of deceleration	Worn universal joints. Worn splines on shafts. Loose drive flange bolts.

Chapter 8 Rear axle

Contents

Specifications

Axle type	Semi-floating, hypoid

Ratios
Hi-Lux with 8R-C, 18R-C or 20R engine	4.111 : 1
Hi-Lux with 12R engine	4.875 : 1
Hi-Ace	Trucks 5.286 : 1, vans, campers 4.875 : 1

Oil capacity	1.4 Imp qt (1.6 litres), 1.7 US qt

Torque wrench settings

	lb f ft	Nm
Differential carrier to casing nuts	20	27
Axle casing end flange bolts	50	68
Drain plug	40	54
Filler plug	40	54
Pinion nut	150	204
Spring 'U' bolt nuts	75	102

1 General description

The rear axle is of the hypoid semi-floating type. The final drive ratio differs between the various models and reference should be made to the Specifications Section for precise details.

The crownwheel and pinion and differential are mounted as an assembly in the differential carrier and this is bolted to the front of the banjo type axle casing. The advantage of this type of differential carrier is that the differential carrier may be removed complete with crownwheel and pinion and differential after disconnection of the propeller shaft and partial withdrawal of the halfshafts (axle shafts).

Operations on the rear axle should be limited to those described in this Chapter. Dismantling and reassembly of the differential and crownwheel and pinion is not considered to be within the scope of the

home mechanic due to the need for special tools and gauges. When a fault develops through wear or damage, exchange the differential carrier complete for a factory reconditioned unit.

2 Halfshafts, bearings and oil seals - removal and refitting

1 Remove the hub cap from the roadwheel and loosen the roadwheel nuts.
2 Jack up the rear of the vehicle and support securely under the rear axle casing.
3 Remove the roadwheel.
4 Remove the brake drum.
5 Remove the brake shoes from the brake backplate as described in Chapter 9.

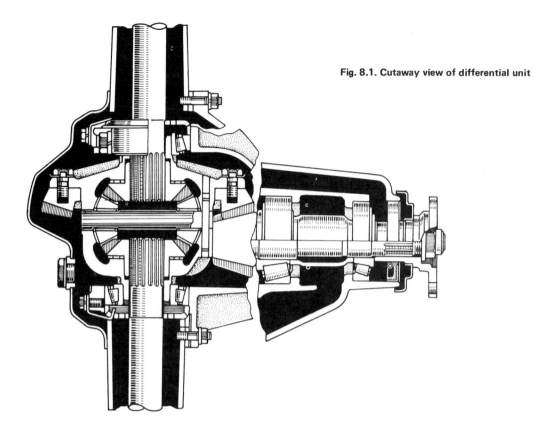

Fig. 8.1. Cutaway view of differential unit

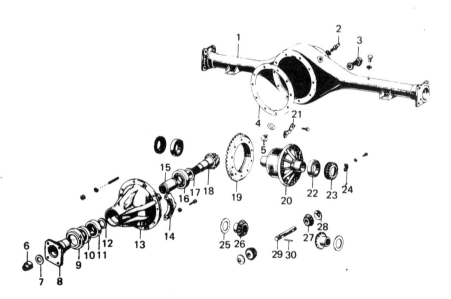

Fig. 8.2. Exploded view of rear axle

1   Casing
2   Breather
3   Filler plug
4   Gasket
5   Drain plug
6   Pinion nut
7   Washer
8   Pinion drive flange
9   Dust deflector
10 Oil seal
11 Bearing
12 Shim
13 Differential carrier
14 Bearing cap
15 Spacer
16 Bearing
17 Shim
18 Drive pinion
19 Crownwheel
20 Differential case
21 Lockplate
22 Tapered roller bearing
23 Bearing adjusting nut
24 Adjusting nut lock
25 Side gear thrust washer
26 Side gear
27 Pinion
28 Thrust washer
29 Pinion shaft
30 Locking pin

6 Disconnect the parking brake cable from the shoe lever and then withdraw the cable from the backplate.

7 Disconnect the brake hydraulic line from the wheel cylinder by unscrewing the union. Seal the hydraulic line by pushing on a rubber cap.

8 Unscrew and remove the four nuts which secure the brake backplate to the flange of the axle casing.

9 Pull the axle shaft complete with brake backplate from the axle casing.

10 Extract the bearing retaining circlip.

11 By supporting the axle shaft bearing case, the shaft can now be pressed through and out of the bearing/case assembly. A press should be used for this operation and unless one is available, it is best to leave this to your Toyota dealer.

12 Remove the bearing from the bearing case.

13 The serrated bolts which hold the bearing case and the brake backplate together can be driven out with a brass drift and the components separated.

14 If necessary, press out the roadwheel studs and remove the brake drum oil deflector.

15 Prise out and discard the oil seal from the bearing case.

16 Prise out the oil seal from the axle casing and discard it. Discard the axle casing flange 'O' ring.

17 Commence reassembly by installing the new oil seals into the axle casing and the bearing case. Apply grease to the lips of the oil seals.

18 Fit the bearing case and the backplate together and press in the serrated bolts.

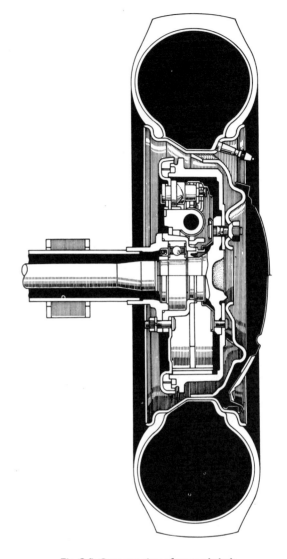

Fig. 8.3. Cutaway view of rear axle hub

Fig. 8.5. Withdrawing halfshaft from axle casing

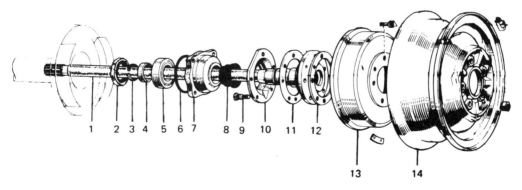

Fig. 8.4. Exploded view of halfshaft, hub assembly

1 Halfshaft	4 Bearing retainer	7 Bearing case	11 Gasket
2 Axle casing oil seal	5 Bearing	8 Bearing case oil seal	12 Gasket
3 Circlip	6 'O' ring	9 Roadwheel stud	13 Brake drum
		10 Oil deflector	14 Roadwheel

Fig. 8.6. Extracting rear axleshaft bearing circlip

Fig. 8.7. Rear axle casing oil seal

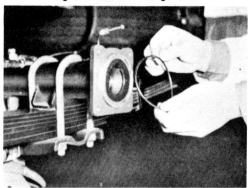

Fig. 8.8. Removing axle casing flange oil seal

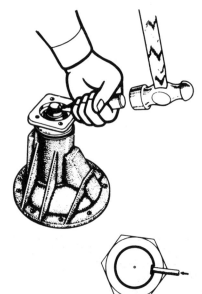

Fig. 8.9. Staking pinion nut

19 Install the oil deflector with gasket onto the flange of the halfshaft and then press the roadwheel studs into position to secure the oil deflector.

20 Insert the bearing into the bearing case and then support the bearing inner track while the halfshaft is pressed into position in the bearing and case.

21 Slide the bearing retainer onto the shaft and install the circlip.

22 Place a new 'O' ring seal onto the axle casing flange and install the axleshaft backplate. Hold the shaft horizontally and push it into the axle casing until the splines on the shaft can be felt to engage with those on the differential side gears. Take care not to damage the casing oil seal.

23 Tighten the backplate nuts.

24 Install the brake assembly and connect the parking brake cable as described in Chapter 9.

25 Reconnect the brake hydraulic line and bleed the hydraulic systems as described in Chapter 9.

26 Refit the brake drums and roadwheel and lower the vehicle to the ground.

3 Pinion oil seal - renewal

1 The pinion oil seal may be renewed with the differential carrier still in position on the rear axle casing and the casing still attached to the rear suspension.

2 Jack up the rear of the vehicle and mark the edges of the propeller shaft rear flange and the pinion driving flange. Then disconnect the flanges and tie the propeller shaft up out of the way.

3 Mark the pinion coupling in relation to the pinion splines and knock back the staking on the pinion nut with a drift or narrow chisel.

4 Hold the pinion coupling quite still by bolting a length of flat steel to two of the coupling flange holes and then unscrew the pinion nut. A ring spanner of good length will be required for this.

5 Remove the lever from the coupling flange and withdraw the coupling. If it is tight, use a two or three legged puller, but on no account attempt to knock it from the splined pinion. Withdraw the dust deflector.

6 Remove the defective oil seal using a two legged extractor.

7 Refit the new oil seal having first greased the mating surfaces of the seal and the axle housing. The lips of the oil seal must face inwards. Using a piece of brass or copper tubing of suitable diameter, carefully drive the new oil seal into the axle housing recess until the face of the seal is flush with the housing. Make sure that the end of the pinion is not knocked during this operation.

8 Refit the coupling to its original position on the pinion splines after first having located the dust cover.

9 Fit a new pinion nut and, holding the coupling still with the lever, tighten the nut to the specified torque wrench setting. A fixed spacer and shims are used in this type of rear axle and bearing pre-load will automatically be restored once the pinion nut has been tightened.

10 Stake the nut, refit the propeller shaft, making sure to align the mating marks.

11 Lower the vehicle and check the oil level in the axle.

4 Differential carrier - removal and refitting

1 Jack-up the car and support it on stands as for halfshaft removal. Drain the oil from the back axle by removing the drain plug. The halfshafts should then be removed sufficiently far for the inner ends to disengage from the differential side gears. The propeller shaft should then be disconnected from the rear axle pinion flange. It is not necessary to draw it out from the gearbox provided it can be conveniently rested out of the way on one side.

2 Undo the ten nuts and washers holding the differential carrier to the casing. The whole unit can be drawn forward off the studs and taken out.

3 When replacing the assembly ensure that the mating faces are perfectly clean and free from burrs. A new gasket coated with sealing compound should also be used. Otherwise refitting is a reversal of the removal operation. Tighten the nuts to the specified torque.

4 Refill the unit with the correct grade and quantity of oil.

5 Rear axle - removal and refitting

1 Jack-up the rear of the vehicle, place axle stands under the rear body frame side members and securely chock the front wheels. Place a jack under the differential and take its weight.

2 Remove the roadwheels and disconnect the propeller shaft at the rear axle pinion coupling flange. Remember to mark the edges of the flanges before disconnecting them so that they will be refitted in their original positions. Move the rear end of the propeller shaft to one side and support it to avoid strain on the centre universal joint or bearing.

3 Remove the brake drums and disconnect the handbrake cables from the actuating levers and then detach them from the brake backplate. Refit the drums to protect the brake shoe assemblies.

4 Disconnect the brake hydraulic line at the union on top of the axle casing. Plug both ends of the line to prevent loss of fluid or ingress of dirt.

5 Disconnect the rear shock absorber lower mountings from the road leaf spring support plates.

6 Unscrew and remove the four road spring 'U' bolts.

7 Remove each of the lower rear spring shackle bolts and lower the rear ends of the road springs to the ground.

8 Lower the jack previously placed under the differential until the rear axle assembly can be drawn out sideways from under the vehicle.

9 Refitting is a reversal of removal but bleed the brake hydraulic system on completion.

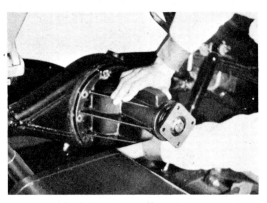

Fig. 8.10. Removing differential carrier

6 Fault diagnosis - rear axle

Symptom	Cause
Noisy differential	
(a) During normal running	Lack of oil, damaged or worn gears, incorrect adjustment.
(b) During deceleration	Incorrect adjustment or damage to drive pinion bearings.
(c) During turning of vehicle	Worn or damaged axle-shaft bearing, worn differential gears.
Noisy rear hub	Worn axle-shaft bearings, buckled roadwheel, defective tyre, bent axle shaft.
Oil leakage at hub and pinion oil seals	May be caused by blocked breather plug on axle casing or over-filled unit.

Chapter 9 Braking system

Contents

Specifications

System type

Except Hi-Lux with 20R engines from late 1974 on	Four wheel drum, hydraulic with servo unit (booster) on some models. Parking brake mechanically operated to rear wheels.
Hi-Lux late 1974 on with 20R engine	Similar to above but with disc front brakes and automatically adjusted rear drum brakes

Drum internal diameter

Hi-Ace and Hi-Lux (early models)	9.055 to 9.063 in (230.0 to 230.2 mm)
Hi-Ace later models	10.08 in (256.0 mm)
Hi-Lux later models	10.000 to 10.007 in (254.0 to 254.2 mm)

Disc (minimum) thickness

Hi-Lux late 1974 on	0.453 in (11.5 mm)

Disc maximum run-out ... ...   0.0059 in (0.15 mm)

Total lining area

Hi-Ace early models	233.76 in^2 (1766.4 cm^2)
All other models	189.6 in^2 (1094.0 cm^2)

Vacuum servo (booster) diameter ... ...   7.5 in (190.5 mm)

Vacuum servo push-rod to piston clearance ... ...   0.004 to 0.020 in (0.1 to 0.5 mm)

Torque wrench settings

	lb f ft	Nm
Rigid brake pipe union nut	13	18
Flexible hose union	18	25
Master cylinder stop bolt	9	12
Master cylinder outlet plug	100	136
Master cylinder banjo union bolt	40	54
Pressure switch	30	41
Wheel cylinder to backing plate bolt	11	15
Master cylinder reservoir to body	20	27
Disc caliper (Hi-Lux, 1974 on) bolts	80	109
Disc to hub bolts	35	48
Brake backplate bolts	9	12

1 General description

1 The braking system used on all models built up until late 1974 is of the four wheel drum type with hydraulic actuation. The parking brake operates through a mechanical linkage on the rear wheels only. On Hi-Lux vehicles fitted with the 20R engine built after late 1974, front disc brakes become standard fitting.

2 Depending upon the operating territory and the complexity of its safety regulations, a single or dual line hydraulic system may be encountered.

3 A vacuum servo (booster unit) is normally fitted in conjunction with dual line systems.

4 On the front wheels, if drum brakes are fitted, two leading shoes are used. These incorporate two separate wheel cylinders each having a single piston. If front disc brakes are fitted, these are of the Girling fixed caliper type.

5 On the rear wheels duo servo type shoes are used. These incorporate a single wheel cylinder which has two opposing pistons.

6 Drum brakes are manually adjusted except for Hi-Lux (1974 on) rear brakes which have automatic adjusters. Front disc brakes require no adjustment.

7 Some layouts include a brake warning lamp switch which illuminates a warning lamp on the instrument panel in the event of pressure loss in either of the hydraulic circuits.

8 On later Hi-Ace models, a load sensitive brake pressure regulating device may be installed as an option.

9 A parking brake 'on' switch is fitted to some late model vehicles.

10 Reference to 'early' models in this Chapter indicates vehicles which are equipped with finned brake drums.

2 Brakes - adjustment

1 Before adjusting the brakes, check that the brake pedal is correctly set as described in Section 14.

Front brakes

2 Jack-up one of the roadwheels at the front of the vehicle.

3 Remove the hole plugs from the brake backplate (photo).

4 Insert a suitable tool through the backplate hole and turn the star adjuster until the drum is locked (photo).

5 Back off the star adjuster until the drum rotates freely (photo).

6 Repeat the adjustment on the other wheel cylinder star adjuster.

7 Apply the foot brake hard and repeat the adjustment operations if the minimum shoe to drum clearance is to be obtained. Refit the backplate hole plugs.

8 Repeat the adjustment on the opposite front brake.

2.3 Brake backplate hole plug

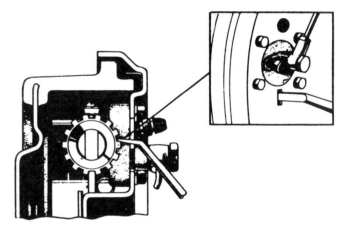

Fig. 9.1. Adjusting a front brake

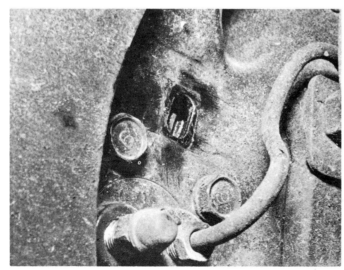

2.4 Brake backplate hole showing star wheel adjuster

2.5 A front wheel brake cylinder (Hi-Lux)

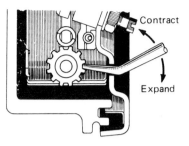

Fig. 9.2. Adjusting a rear brake

Fig. 9.3. Releasing a retracting spring clamp bolt on a rear brake (early Hi-Ace)

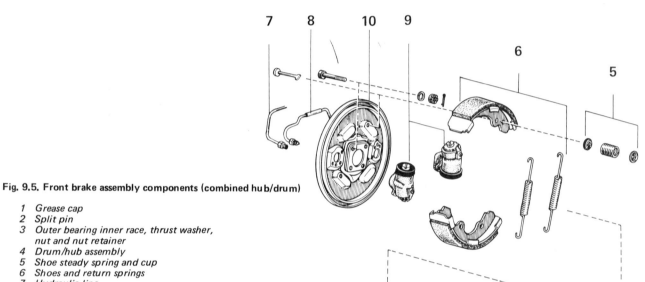

Fig. 9.5. Front brake assembly components (combined hub/drum)

1 Grease cap
2 Split pin
3 Outer bearing inner race, thrust washer, nut and nut retainer
4 Drum/hub assembly
5 Shoe steady spring and cup
6 Shoes and return springs
7 Hydraulic line
8 Wheel cylinder connecting pipe
9 Wheel cylinder
10 Backplate

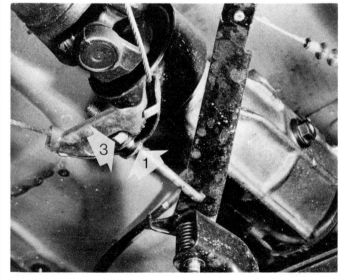

3.4 Parking brake cable equaliser and intermediate lever (Hi-Lux)

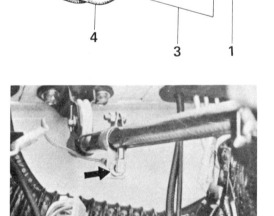

Fig. 9.4. Parking brake switch

Rear brakes

9 Check that the parking brake is fully released.

10 Jack-up one of the rear roadwheels and remove the hole plug from the brake backplate.

11 Unscrew the retracting spring clamp bolt which is located on the backplate just below the rear axle casing flange.

12 Insert a suitable tool through the hole in the backplate and turn the star adjuster until the drum is locked. Now tighten the retracting spring clamp bolt firmly.

13 Back off the star adjuster until the drum turns freely.

14 Refit the backplate hole plug and then repeat the adjustment operations on the opposite rear brake.

3 Parking brake - adjustment

1 Under normal conditions, the parking brake will automatically be adjusted when the shoes are adjusted. However, when excessive travel of the parking brake control lever occurs due to cable stretch, carry out the following operations.

2 Slacken the parking brake 'ON' switch bracket and push in the brake control handle until the handle is stopped by the switch pawl. At this stage, the switch should be in the 'OFF' position.

3 Push the parking brake control handle to the fully off position.

4 Working under the car, release the locknut (1) on the equaliser and adjust the second locknut (3) to remove any slack from the cables (photo).

5 Jack-up both rear wheels and check that they rotate freely.

6 The parking brake control should now lock the rear wheels when it is pulled on between 8 and 12 notches.

7 Re-set the parking brake switch.

4 Brake shoes - inspection and renewal

1 At the intervals specified in Routine Maintenance, jack-up each roadwheel in turn and remove the roadwheel.

2 *To remove a front drum* on vehicles built up until 1976, tap off the grease cap and extract the split pin and nut retainer. Unscrew and remove the nut and thrust washer. Withdraw the drum/hub assembly, catching the outer bearing as it is drawn off the stub axle. On 12R engined vehicles built after 1976, the drum is retained by a single screw and is removed independently.

3 *To remove a rear drum,* simply extract the drum securing screw (photo).

4 Brush away any accumulated brake lining dust **but take great care not to inhale it.**

5 Inspect the linings for wear. If they have worn down to a thickness of 1/16 in (1.6 mm) or less, in the case of bonded type linings, or level with, or nearly level with, the heads of the rivets in the case of rivetted linings, then they must be renewed.

6 If there is any evidence of oil staining or seepage, check the cause and rectify. With front wheel brakes, this is most likely to be due to hydraulic fluid leaking from a faulty wheel cylinder. With rear brakes, this may be due to a faulty wheel cylinder or worn axleshaft oil seal. Trace and rectify the fault by renewing the cylinder seal or oil seal before installing the new shoes.

7 Always fit shoes complete with factory fitted linings. Do not attempt to reline shoes yourself, they seldom produce satisfactory results.

8 Once the drums are removed do not depress the foot brake pedal.

9 *To renew the front shoes,* first remove the shoe steady springs. On early models, the spring also forms the securing clip at the end of the steady post, but on later vehicles, a circular cup is used to retain the

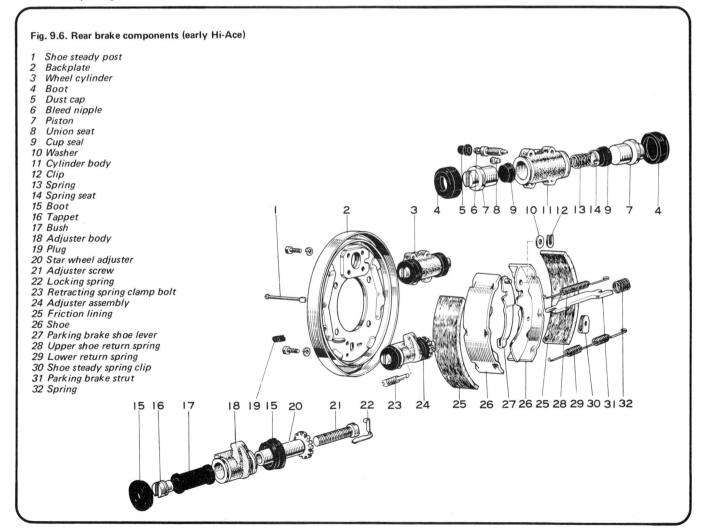

Fig. 9.6. Rear brake components (early Hi-Ace)

1 Shoe steady post
2 Backplate
3 Wheel cylinder
4 Boot
5 Dust cap
6 Bleed nipple
7 Piston
8 Union seat
9 Cup seal
10 Washer
11 Cylinder body
12 Clip
13 Spring
14 Spring seat
15 Boot
16 Tappet
17 Bush
18 Adjuster body
19 Plug
20 Star wheel adjuster
21 Adjuster screw
22 Locking spring
23 Retracting spring clamp bolt
24 Adjuster assembly
25 Friction lining
26 Shoe
27 Parking brake shoe lever
28 Upper shoe return spring
29 Lower return spring
30 Shoe steady spring clip
31 Parking brake strut
32 Spring

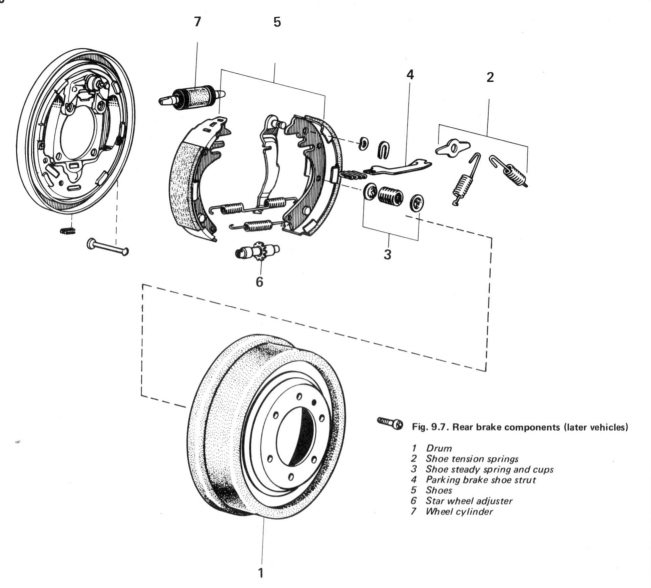

Fig. 9.7. Rear brake components (later vehicles)

1 Drum
2 Shoe tension springs
3 Shoe steady spring and cups
4 Parking brake shoe strut
5 Shoes
6 Star wheel adjuster
7 Wheel cylinder

4.2 Front brake (detachable drum removed from hub) - Hi-Lux 12R engine 1976 on

4.3 Rear brake assembly with drum removed

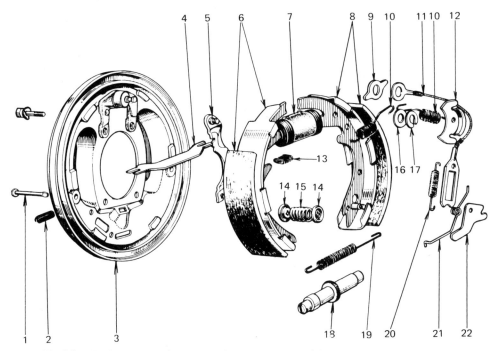

Fig. 9.8A. Exploded view of rear brake (automatic adjuster) fitted to Hi-Lux, late 1974 on

1 *Shoe steady post*	6 *Shoe (nearest front of vehicle*	11 *Automatic adjuster cable*	17 *'C' clip*
2 *Backplate plug*	*with short lining)*	12 *Cable guide*	18 *Star wheel adjuster*
3 *Backplate*	7 *Wheel cylinder*	13 *Parking brake strut spring*	19 *Shoe lower return spring*
4 *Parking brake shoe strut*	8 *Shoe (nearest rear of vehicle*	14 *Shoe steady spring seat*	20 *Spring*
5 *Parking brake shoe lever*	*with longest lining)*	15 *Shoe steady spring*	21 *Adjuster lever spring*
	9 *Guide plate*	16 *Wave washer*	22 *Adjuster lever*
	10 *Shoe upper spring*		

coil spring to the steady post. Depress the clip or cup and turn it through 90° to release it from the shoe steady post.

10 Grip the brake shoes and pull them apart against the tension of their return springs and lift them from the brake backplate.

11 Before dismantling the shoes from their return springs, note the holes in the shoe webs into which the return springs engage and the position of the shoes in respect of leading and trailing ends.

12 Clean the backplate and apply a trace of high melting point grease to the shoe sliding high points on the backplate.

13 Screw each of the star adjusters fully in to provide maximum shoe clearance in order to accommodate the new thicker friction linings.

14 Install the new shoes by reversing the removal operations.

15 Refit the drums and adjust the hub bearing pre-load as described in Chapter 11 (up to 1976). On 12R later vehicles refit the drum and secure with a single screw.

16 Adjust the brake shoes as described in Section 2.

17 Always renew front brake shoes as a complete axle set - never one side only.

18 *To renew the rear shoes (manually adjustable type),* remove the shoe steady clips or springs according to type (see paragraph 9).

19 Fully release the retracting spring clamp bolt.

20 On early Hi-Ace vehicles, detach the upper and lower shoe return springs. On other vehicles, remove the upper and lower tension springs (four in number).

21 Prise the shoes apart and extract the parking brake strut and short compression spring.

22 Withdraw the shoes complete with adjuster from the backplate.

23 Disconnect the lever on the shoe from the parking brake cable.

24 Detach the shoe lever from the shoe by first extracting the 'U' clip and washer.

25 Clean the backplate and apply a trace of high melting point grease to the shoe sliding high points on the backplate.

26 Screw the star adjuster fully in to provide the maximum shoe clearance in order to accommodate the new thicker friction linings.

27 Install the new shoes by reversing the removal operations. Check that the shoes are correctly located in respect of their leading and trailing ends.

28 Refit the drum and adjust the brake as described in Section 2.

29 Always renew rear brake shoes as a complete axle set - never one side only.

30 *To renew the rear shoes (automatically adjustable type) - Hi-Lux 1974 on),* remove the torsion spring (21) and the lever (22) (Fig. 9.8A).

31 From the upper end of the brake shoes, detach the springs (10), the adjusting cable (11), the shoe guide plate (9), and the cable guide (12).

32 Extract the parking brake strut (4) and spring (13) which lie between the shoes.

33 From the lower end of the shoes, remove the return spring (19) and the star wheel adjuster (18).

34 Remove the shoe steady springs and withdraw the shoes from the backplate. Disconnect the parking brake shoe lever from the end of the parking brake cable.

35 Remove the 'C' clip and detach the parking brake shoe lever from the brake shoe itself.

36 Refit the new shoes by reversing the removal operations, but make sure that the shoes are correctly located in respect of their leading and trailing ends.

37 When installing the star wheel adjuster, apply a little grease to the thread and make sure that the threaded end is facing towards the front of the vehicle. Set the adjuster to its fully retracted position. If both rear brakes are being dismantled at the same time, do not mix up the star wheel adjusters, as the left-hand rear wheel star wheel has a left-hand thread and the right-hand rear wheel one has a right-hand thread.

38 When the brake shoes are fully assembled, expand the shoes by turning the star wheel adjuster until the brake drum will just pass over the shoes. Fit the drum and then apply the foot brake hard to centralise the shoes. Now operate the parking brake several times to adjust the brake by means of the automatic adjuster mechanism.

5 Disc pads (Hi-Lux, late 1974 on) - inspection and renewal

1 Jack-up the front end of the vehicle and remove the roadwheels. Inspect the pad friction material thickness; if it is less than 0.08 in (2.0 mm) the pads must be renewed as an axle set of four.

2 Remove the spring clips and withdraw the pad retaining pins.

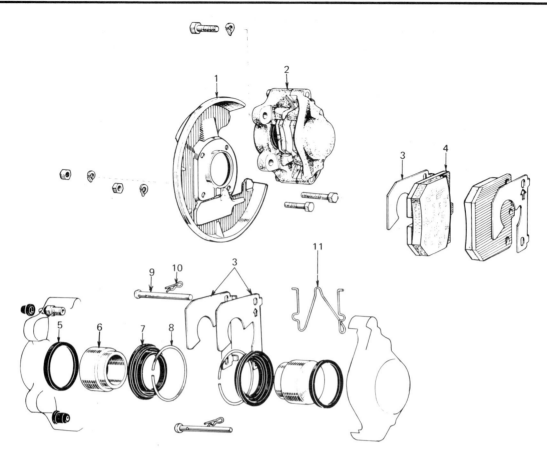

Fig. 9.8B. Exploded view of front disc brake (Hi-Lux, late 1974 on with 20R engine)

1 Disc shield	4 Pad	7 Dust excluder	10 Clip
2 Caliper	5 Piston seal	8 Dust excluder retainer	11 Pad anti-rattle spring
3 Anti-squeal shim	6 Piston	9 Pad retaining pin	

Fig. 9.8C. Disc/hub assembly (Hi-Lux, late 1974 on with 20R engine)

1 Disc
2 Oil seal
3 Inner bearing
4 Wheel stud
5 Hub
6 Outer bearing
7 Thrust washer
8 Nut
9 Nut retainer
10 Grease cap

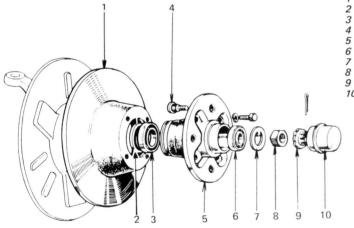

Fig. 9.9. Checking drum internal diameter

3 Extract the anti-squeal shims and then withdraw the disc pads, gripping their projections with a pair of pliers.

4 Wipe out any dust from the interior of the caliper unit and using a flat bar depress each of the pistons into its cylinder squarely. This action will cause the level of the fluid in the hydraulic reservoir to rise unless the bleed nipple on the caliper unit is released.

5 Insert the new pads with their anti-squeal shims correctly located at the rear of the pad backing plates and with the arrows pointing upwards.

6 Fit the anti-rattle springs, retaining pins and spring clips.

7 Apply the foot brake two or three times to bring the pads against the disc and then repeat all the foregoing operations on the opposite front brake.

6 Brake disc - examination, removal and refitting

1 Jack-up the front of the vehicle, remove the roadwheel and caliper.

2 Inspect the disc surfaces for deep scoring or grooves. Light scoring is normal.

3 Using a dial gauge or similar instrument, check for run-out (buckle). This should not exceed 0.0059 in (0.15 mm) otherwise the disc should be renewed.

4 The disc thickness should not be reduced below 0.453 in (11.5 mm) either by normal wear or if it is decided to surface grind it to remove scoring.

5 To remove the disc/hub assembly, tap off the grease cap (10), remove the split pin and nut retainer (9). Unscrew the nut (8) and extract the thrust washer (7) (Fig. 9.8C). Withdraw the disc/hub assembly taking care not to let the outer bearing drop out.

6 Unscrew the bolts which secure the disc to the hub and separate the two components.

7 Refitting is a reversal of dismantling but tighten the disc to hub bolts to the specified torque and adjust the front bearing pre-load as described in Chapter 11.

7 Brake drum - examination and renovation

1 Whenever the brake drums are removed, take the opportunity of examining them for scoring or grooving.

2 After high mileages, it is possible for the drum internal diameter to wear oval in shape. When this occurs, some brake chatter may be experienced when applying the foot brake, but an accurate vernier gauge will be needed to take exact measurements at several different points around the drum.

3 Where any of the foregoing conditions exist, the drum should either be renewed or machined out provided the internal diameter is not increased by more than 0.08 in (2.0 mm).

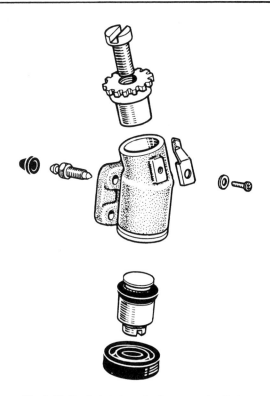

Fig. 9.10. Exploded view of a front wheel cylinder

Fig. 9.12. Removing master cylinder (Hi-Ace)

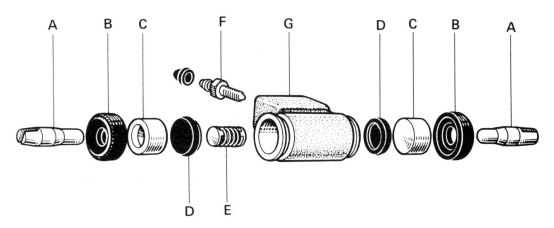

Fig. 9.11. Exploded view of a typical rear wheel cylinder

A Tappet   C Piston   E Spring   G Cylinder body
B Flexible boot   D Seal   F Bleed nipple

8 Front wheel cylinders - removal, servicing and refitting

1 Remove the brake shoes, as described in Section 4, according to type.
2 Although it is possible to dismantle the wheel cylinder while it is still attached to the backplate, it is recommended that the backplate is removed. To do this, disconnect the fluid line from the cylinder and either plug the line, or seal the reservoir filler neck with a sheet of polythene to prevent loss of fluid.
3 Remove the wheel cylinder from the brake backplate.
4 Remove the adjuster wheel and screw and the dust excluder, and then eject the piston by tapping the cylinder on a piece of wood or by applying air from a tyre pump to the fluid inlet.
5 Examine the mating surfaces of the piston and cylinder. If they are scored or any 'bright' wear areas are evident, renew the cylinder complete.
6 Where the components are in good order, discard the seals and wash all items in clean hydraulic fluid or methylated spirit.
7 Obtain a repair kit and manipulate the new seal into position using only the fingers.
8 Dip the piston assembly into clean hydraulic fluid and insert it into the cylinder. Fit the dust excluder, adjuster wheel and screw.
9 Bolt the wheel cylinders to the backplate, tightening the bolts to the specified torque wrench settings.
10 Reconnect the fluid line and bleed the brakes as described in Section 16.

9 Rear wheel cylinders - removal, servicing and refitting

1 The procedure is similar to that described for front wheel cylinders in the preceding Section.

10 Front disc caliper - removal and overhaul

1 Jack-up the front of the vehicle, support it securely and remove the front roadwheel.
2 Remove the disc pads as described in Section 5.
3 Disconnect the brake hydraulic line from the caliper and plug the line to prevent loss of fluid.

4 Unscrew and remove the caliper mounting bolts and withdraw the caliper off the disc.
5 Clean away external dirt and then extract the dust seal retainer and the dust seal. Insert a thin piece of wood between the pistons and apply air pressure from a tyre pump to the open fluid inlet hole on the caliper and eject the pistons.
6 Mark the pistons with a piece of masking tape to identify them in respect of their cylinders.
7 At this stage, examine the surfaces of the pistons and the cylinder bores. If they are scored or grooved or there is evidence of 'bright' wear areas, renew the caliper complete.
8 Where the components are in good condition then discard the rubber seals and obtain a repair kit which will contain all the necessary seals and other renewable items.
9 Install the new seals using the fingers only to manipulate them into position.
10 Install the pistons into their original bores and then fit the dust excluders and retainers.
11 Refit the caliper, the disc pads and bleed the hydraulic system as described in Section 16.

11 Master cylinder (single circuit type) - removal, overhaul and refitting

1 Disconnect the master cylinder pushrod from the brake pedal. On early Hi-Ace vehicles, this was unnecessary as the pushrod was an unsecured sliding fit in the master cylinder.
2 Disconnect the fluid line from the master cylinder body. Allow any fluid to drain into a container, taking care not to let any fluid come into contact with the vehicle paintwork or it will act as an effective paint stripper!
3 On Hi-Ace vehicles, the master cylinder is mounted under the instrument panel. On other vehicles, it is mounted on the engine compartment rear bulkhead. Unbolt and remove the master cylinder.
4 Clean away any external dirt, pull off the dust excluding boot and extract the circlip from the open end of the master cylinder body.
5 Withdraw the washer, piston and other internal components and wash them in clean hydraulic fluid or methylated spirit.
6 Inspect the surfaces of the piston and cylinder bore for scoring or 'bright' wear areas. If these are evident, renew the master cylinder complete.

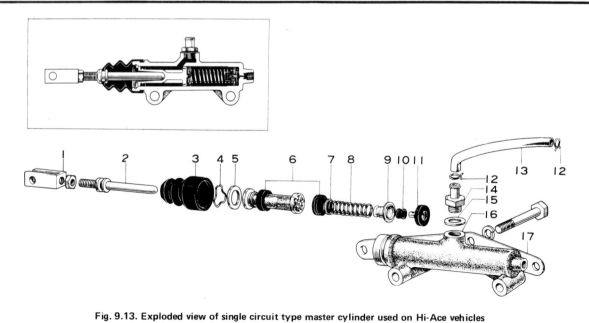

Fig. 9.13. Exploded view of single circuit type master cylinder used on Hi-Ace vehicles

1 Pushrod clevis	5 Stop washer	9 Outlet non-return valve seat	13 Tube to reservoir
2 Pushrod	6 Piston and cup seals	10 Non-return valve	14 Union
3 Flexible boot	7 Return spring retainer	11 Gasket	15 Gasket
4 Circlip	8 Return spring	12 Clip	16 Master cylinder body
			17 Support plate

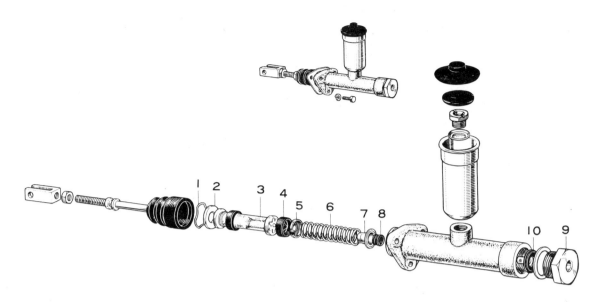

**Fig. 9.14. Exploded view of single circuit type master cylinder used on
Hi-Lux vehicles**

1	Circlip	6	Spring
2	Stop plate	7	Seat
3	Piston	8	Non-return valve
4	Cup seal	9	Plug
5	Retainer	10	Gasket

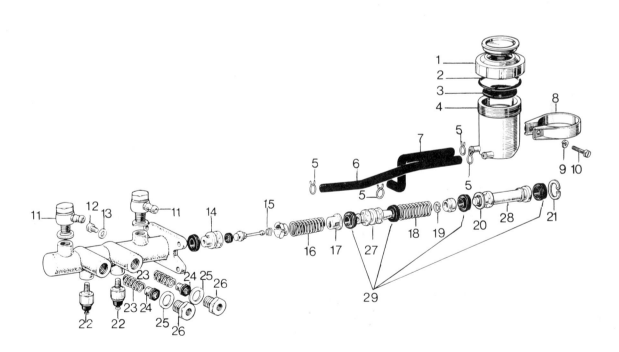

Fig. 9.15. Exploded view of tandem master cylinder used on early vehicles

1	Reservoir cap	8	Clamp	15	Retainer	22	Oil pressure switch
2	'O' ring	9	Lockwasher	16	Spring	23	Spring
3	Float	10	Screw	17	Return spring retainer	24	Outlet non-return valve
4	Reservoir	11	Banjo union	18	Spring	25	Gasket
5	Clip	12	Stop bolt	19	Circlip	26	Plug
6	Fluid supply pipe	13	Gasket	20	Spacer	27	Secondary piston
7	Fluid supply pipe	14	Inlet valve seat	21	Circlip	28	Primary piston
						29	Seals

7 Where the components are in good order, discard all rubber seals
and obtain a repair kit.
8 Install the new seals using the fingers only to manipulate them into
position.
9 Dip the internal components in clean hydraulic fluid before
reassembling them.
10 Installation of the master cylinder is a reversal of removal but check
and adjust the brake pedal height (see Section 17) and bleed the
hydraulic system (Section 16).

12 Master cylinder (tandem type) - removal, overhaul and refitting

1 *On vehicles without a booster,* disconnect the master cylinder
pushrod from the brake pedal.
2 Disconnect the fluid lines from the master cylinder body and let the
fluid drain into a suitable container (photo).
3 Disconnect the leads from the brake warning lamp switches on the
master cylinder.
4 *On vehicles without a booster,* unbolt and remove the master
cylinder from the engine compartment rear bulkhead (Hi-Lux) or from
the under fascia bracket (Hi-Ace).
5 *On vehicles with a booster,* unbolt and remove the master cylinder
from the front face of the booster.
6 Clean away all external dirt and then extract the circlip from the
open end of the master cylinder body.
7 Withdraw the primary piston and spring.
8 Unscrew and remove the stop bolt.
9 Extract the secondary piston assembly complete with inlet valve.
Wash components in hydraulic fluid or methylated spirit.
10 At this stage, inspect the surfaces of the pistons and cylinder bore.
If any scoring or 'bright' wear areas are evident, renew the master
cylinder complete.
11 Where the components are in good condition, discard all rubber
seals and obtain a repair kit.
12 Remove the outlet plugs and valves and reservoir connecting banjo
unions, if necessary.

13 Install the new seals using the fingers only to manipulate them into
position. Dip the internal components in clean hydraulic fluid before
reassembling them.
14 Installation of the master cylinder is a reversal of removal, but
check and adjust the brake pedal height (Section 17), the booster
pushrod adjustment (Section 23) and bleed the hydraulic system
(Section 16).

13 Flexible hoses - inspection and renewal

1 Inspect the condition of the flexible hoses leading from under the
front wings to the brackets on the front suspension units, and also the
single hose on the rear axle casing. If they are swollen, damaged or
chafed, they must be renewed.
2 Undo the locknuts at both ends of the flexible hoses and then,
holding the hexagon nut on the flexible hose steady, undo the other
union nut and remove the flexible hose and washer.
3 Replacement is a reversal of the removal procedure, but carefully
check that all the securing brackets are in a sound condition and that
the locknuts are tight. Bleed the hydraulic system.

12.2 Tandem type master cylinder (Hi-Lux)

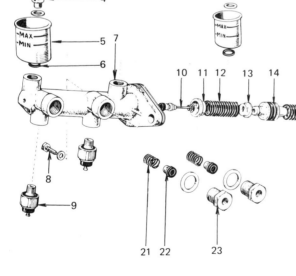

**Fig. 9.16. Exploded view of tandem master cylinder used on later
vehicles**

1 Reservoir cap	13 Spring retainer
2 Float	14 Secondary piston
3 Strainer	15 Spring
4 Reservoir securing bolt	16 Circlip
5 Reservoir	17 Spring retainer
6 Seal	18 Primary piston
7 Master cylinder body	19 Circlip
8 Stop bolt	20 Boot
9 Pressure warning switch	21 Spring
10 Inlet valve rod	22 Outlet non-return valve
11 Inlet valve	23 Outlet plug
12 Spring	

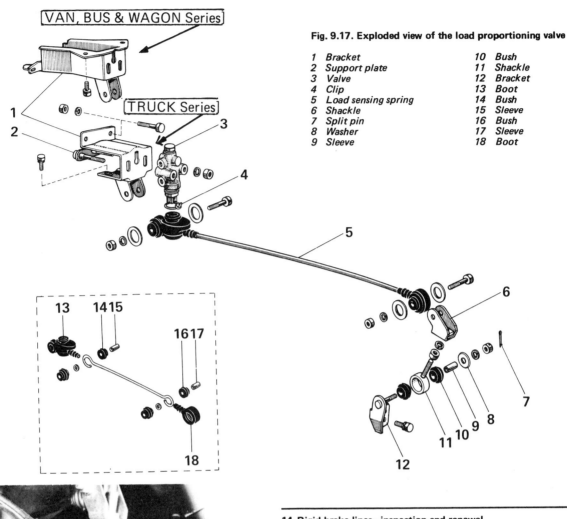

Fig. 9.17. Exploded view of the load proportioning valve

1	Bracket	10	Bush
2	Support plate	11	Shackle
3	Valve	12	Bracket
4	Clip	13	Boot
5	Load sensing spring	14	Bush
6	Shackle	15	Sleeve
7	Split pin	16	Bush
8	Washer	17	Sleeve
9	Sleeve	18	Boot

Fig. 9.18. Load proportioning valve shackle bracket (2) and bolts (1)

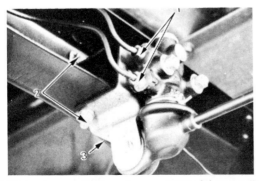

Fig. 9.19. Load proportioning valve connections (1) Hydraulic lines
(2) Valve bracket bolts (3) Bracket

14 Rigid brake lines - inspection and renewal

1 At regular intervals wipe the steel pipes clean and examine them for signs of rust or denting caused by flying stones.
2 Examine the securing clips. Bend the tongues of the clips if necessary to ensure that they hold the brake pipes securely without letting them rattle or vibrate.
3 Check that the pipes are not touching any adjacent components or rubbing against any part of the vehicle. Where this is observed, bend the pipe gently away to clear.
4 Any section of pipe which is rusty or chafed should be renewed. Brake pipes are available to the correct length and fitted with end unions from most Toyota dealers and can be made to pattern by many accessory suppliers. When installing the new pipes use the old pipes as a guide to bending and do not make any bends sharper than is necessary.
5 The system will of course have to be bled when the circuit has been reconnected.

15 Load sensing proportioning valve - removal, refitting and adjustment

1 This device is fitted to later Hi-Ace models to adjust the front and rear braking pressures according to the axle load at the time of braking.
2 Unscrew and remove the two bolts and disconnect the shackle bracket from the rear axle casing.
3 Disconnect the hydraulic lines from the valve body and cap the lines to prevent a loss of fluid.
4 Unbolt and remove the valve complete with bracket.
5 Any wear in the valve is likely to be found at the contacting surface of the piston pin. Renew as necessary.
6 Reassemble the valve, bracket and shackle exactly as shown in Fig. 9.21, noting that dimension A should be set to 3.07 in (78.0 mm).

7   Install the valve/bracket assembly and reconnect the shackle bracket.

8   Reconnect the hydraulic lines and bleed the system as described in Section 16.

9   Precise setting of the valve will require special equipment and also depends upon the vehicle body type. It is best left to your Toyota dealer. Varying the length of A (Fig. 9.21) at the shackle will alter the braking pressure between front and rear wheels while moving the valve assembly up or down will alter the hydraulic pressure in the rear wheel cylinders.

16 Hydraulic system - bleeding

1   Removal of all the air from the hydraulic system is essential to the correct working of the braking system, and before undertaking this, examine the fluid reservoir cap to ensure that both vent holes, one on top and the second underneath but not in line, are clear; check the level of fluid and top up if required.

2   Check all brake line unions and connections for possible seepage, and at the same time check the condition of the rubber hoses, which may be perished.

3   If the condition of the wheel cylinders is in doubt, check for possible signs of fluid leakage.

4   If there is any possibility of the incorrect fluid having been put into the system, drain the fluid out and flush through with methylated spirit. Renew all piston seals and cups since these will be affected and could possibly fail under pressure.

5   Gather together a clean glass jar, a length of tubing which fits tightly over the bleed nipples, and a tin of the correct brake fluid.

6   To bleed the system, clean the areas around the bleed valves, and

start on the rear brakes (furthest from the master cylinder), by removing the rubber cup over the bleed valve, and fitting a rubber tube in position.

7   Place the end of the tube in a clean glass jar containing sufficient fluid to keep the end of the tube underneath during the operation.

8   Open the bleed valve with a spanner and quickly press down the brake pedal. After slowly releasing the pedal, pause for a moment to allow the fluid to recoup in the master cylinder and then depress again. This will force air from the system. Continue until no more air bubbles can be seen coming from the tube. At intervals make certain that the reservoir is kept topped-up, otherwise air will enter at this point again.

9   Once the rear brakes have been bled, bleed the front brake furthest from the master cylinder, followed by the remaining front brake.

10 Tighten the bleed screws when the pedal is in the fully depressed position. Use only clean fluid for topping up purposes and discard fluid from the bleed jar. Fluid used for topping up should have been kept in an air tight container and remained unshaken for the previous 24 hours.

17 Brake pedal - removal, refitting and adjustment

1   Details of removal and refitting the brake pedal are given in conjunction with the clutch pedal in Chapter 5, Section 8.

2   Brake pedal adjustment should be in accordance with the appropriate diagram. In all cases, adjust the pedal height above the floor first by altering the position of the stop lamp switch. Then adjust the pedal free movement by releasing the locknut on the pushrod and altering its effective length.

3   On vehicles equipped with a booster, destroy the vacuum by repeatedly depressing the foot brake pedal before carrying out the pedal adjustments.

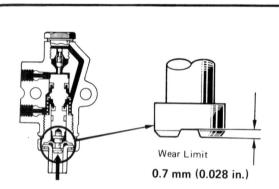

Fig. 9.20. Load proportioning valve wear diagram

Wear Limit
0.7 mm (0.028 in.)

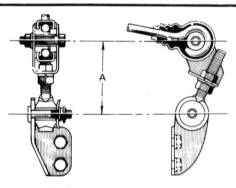

Fig. 9.21. Load proportioning valve setting diagram

A = 3.07 in (78.0 mm)

Fig. 9.22. **Topping up brake master cylinder reservoir on Hi-Ace vehicle**

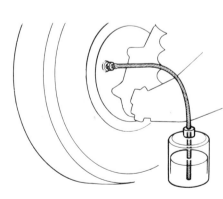

Fig. 9.23. **Brake bleed tube attached**

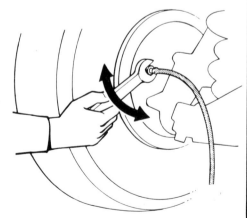

Fig. 9.24. **Opening and closing the brake bleed nipple**

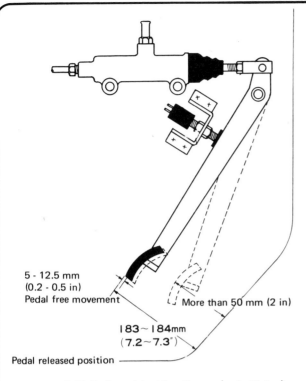

5 - 12.5 mm
(0.2 - 0.5 in)
Pedal free movement

More than 50 mm (2 in)

183~184mm
(7.2~7.3")

Pedal released position

Fig. 9.25. Brake pedal setting diagram (early Hi-Ace)

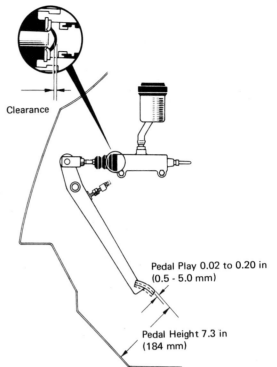

Clearance

Pedal Play 0.02 to 0.20 in
(0.5 - 5.0 mm)

Pedal Height 7.3 in
(184 mm)

Fig. 9.26. Brake pedal setting diagram (later Hi-Ace) single master cylinder

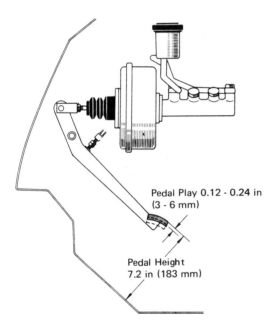

Pedal Play 0.12 - 0.24 in
(3 - 6 mm)

Pedal Height
7.2 in (183 mm)

Fig. 9.27. Brake pedal setting diagram (later Hi-Ace) tandem master cylinder with servo (booster) unit

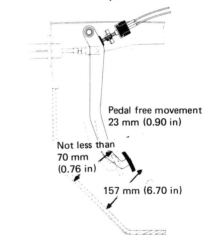

Pedal free movement
23 mm (0.90 in)

Not less than
70 mm
(0.76 in)

157 mm (6.70 in)

Fig. 9.28. Brake pedal setting diagram (early Hi-Lux)

Fig. 9.29. Brake pedal setting diagram (later Hi-Lux) with and without servo (booster) unit

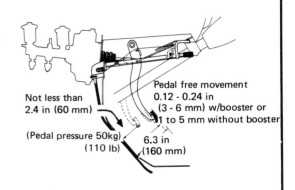

Not less than
2.4 in (60 mm)

(Pedal pressure 50kg)
(110 lb)

Pedal free movement
0.12 - 0.24 in
(3 - 6 mm) w/booster or
1 to 5 mm without booster

6.3 in
(160 mm)

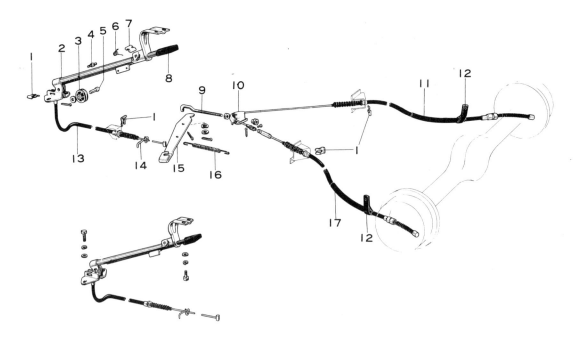

Fig. 9.31. Parking brake control handle removal points

1 Plunger pin   4 Pivot pin
2 Control handle   5 Cable pulley
3 Clip

Fig. 9.30. Parking brake components (early Hi-Ace)

1 Clip   10 Equaliser
2 Plunger guide   11 Secondary cable (right-hand)
3 Cable pulley   12 Guide
4 Pin   13 Primary cable
5 Clevis pin   14 Guide
6 Spring   15 Intermediate lever
7 Pawl   16 Return spring
8 Control handle   17 Secondary cable (left-hand)
9 Pull rod

18 Parking brake cables (Hi-Ace, early models) - renewal

1   If the cables are to be renewed or other worn components renewed, carry out the following operations.
2   Release the parking brake control handle and align the plunger pin (1) with the hole in the guide. Drive out the pin (Fig. 9.31).
3   Release the control handle fully and extract the clip (3) which secures the primary cable.
4   Remove the pivot pin (4) and the cable pulley (5).
5   Turn the control handle slightly anti-clockwise and disconnect the primary cable from the end of the control handle.
6   Working under the vehicle, disconnect the return spring from the intermediate lever and detach the primary cable from the intermediate lever. Remove the clip which secures the primary cable to the body.
7   To remove the secondary (rear) cables, first disconnect them from the levers on the brake shoes as described in Section 4.
8   Disconnect the equaliser from the pull rod, bend up the tabs on the equaliser and extract the cable. The secondary cable is in two sections which can be separated after extracting the joint pin.
9   Install the cables by reversing the removal operations and then adjust the mechanism as described in Section 3.

19 Parking brake cables (Hi-Ace, later models) - renewal

1   Removal and installation of the cables is similar to that described in the preceding Section, but note the following differences.
2   The primary cable and control handle are permanently joined and must be renewed as an assembly.
3   One of the primary cable retaining clips is only accessible after the radiator grille has been removed.

20 Parking brake cables (Hi-Lux) - renewal

1   The operations are very similar to those described in Section 18, but the primary cable can only be disconnected from the hand control after the pulley bracket has been unbolted from the engine compartment rear bulkhead.

21 Vacuum servo (brake booster) unit - description

1   The vacuum servo unit is designed to supplement the effort applied by the driver's foot to the brake pedal.

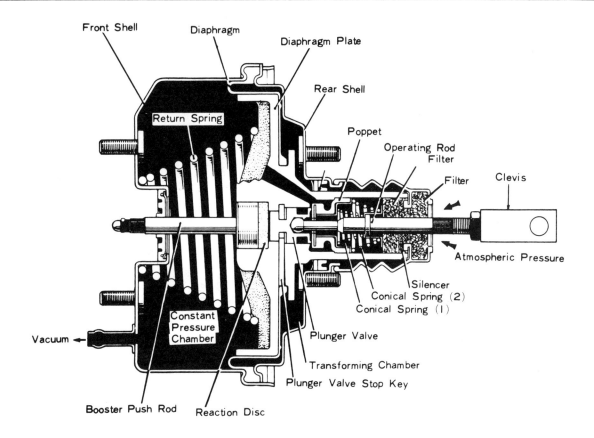

Fig. 9.32. Sectional view of vacuum servo (booster) unit

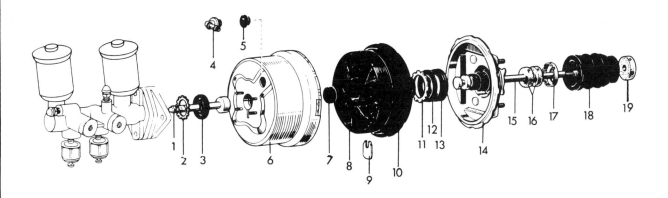

Fig. 9.33. Exploded view of JKK type vacuum servo unit

1	Pushrod	6	Front shell	11	Retainer	16	Air silencer
2	Retainer	7	Reaction disc	12	Bearing	17	Retainer
3	Plate/seal assembly	8	Valve body and diaphragm plate	13	Seal	18	Boot
4	Non-return valve	9	Plunger stop key	14	Rear shell	19	Filter
5	Grommet	10	Diaphragm	15	Valve rod and plunger		

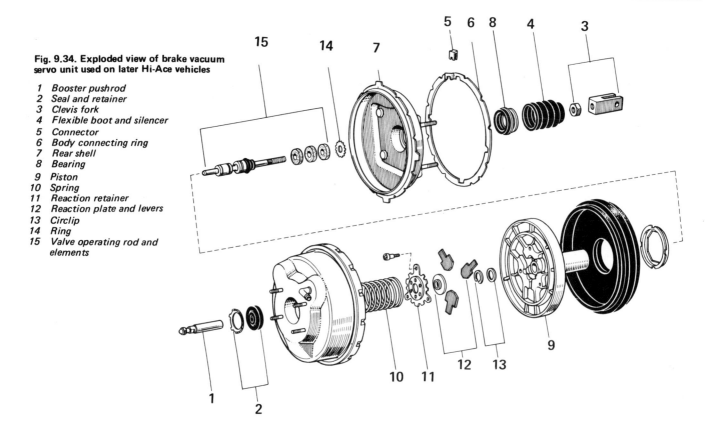

Fig. 9.34. Exploded view of brake vacuum servo unit used on later Hi-Ace vehicles

1   Booster pushrod
2   Seal and retainer
3   Clevis fork
4   Flexible boot and silencer
5   Connector
6   Body connecting ring
7   Rear shell
8   Bearing
9   Piston
10 Spring
11 Reaction retainer
12 Reaction plate and levers
13 Circlip
14 Ring
15 Valve operating rod and
    elements

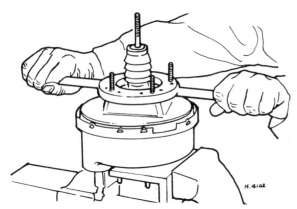

Fig. 9.35. Releasing servo rear shell

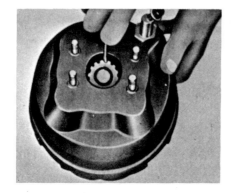

Fig. 9.36. Removing retainer from servo front shell

2   The unit is an independent mechanism so that in the event of its failure the normal braking effort of the master cylinder is retained. A vacuum is created in the servo unit by its connection to the engine inlet manifold and with this condition applying on one side of the diaphragm, atmospheric pressure applied on the other side of the diaphragm is harnessed to assist the foot pressure on the master cylinder. With the brake pedal released, the diaphragm is fully recuperated and held against the rear shell by the return spring. The operating rod assembly is also fully recuperated and a condition of vacuum exists each side of the diaphragm.

3   When the brake pedal is applied, the valve rod assembly moves forward until the control valve closes the vacuum port. Atmospheric pressure then enters the chamber to the rear of the diaphragm and forces the diaphragm plate forward to actuate the master cylinder pistons through the medium of the vacuum servo unit pushrod.

4   When pressure on the brake pedal is released, the vacuum port is opened and the atmospheric pressure in the rear chamber is extracted through the non-return valve. The atmospheric pressure inlet port remains closed as the operating rod assembly returns to its original position by action of the coil return spring.

5   The diaphragm then remains in its position with vacuum conditions on both sides until the next depression of the brake pedal when the cycle is repeated.

22 Vacuum servo unit - removal and installation

1   Destroy the vacuum effect in the servo unit by repeated applications of the foot pedal.

2   Disconnect the vacuum hose from the servo unit.

3   Disconnect the hydraulic circuit fluid pipes from the master cylinder unions and plug the pipes to prevent ingress of dirt.

4   Disconnect the leads from the master cylinder pressure switches.

5   From inside the vehicle disconnect the operating rod from the brake pedal arm and then unscrew and remove the four servo unit securing nuts from their studs.

6   Remove the vacuum servo unit complete with master cylinder and regulator valve from its location on the engine rear bulkhead.

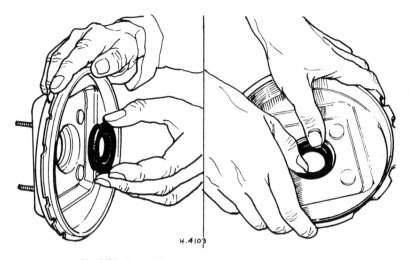

Fig. 9.37. Assembling servo rear shell

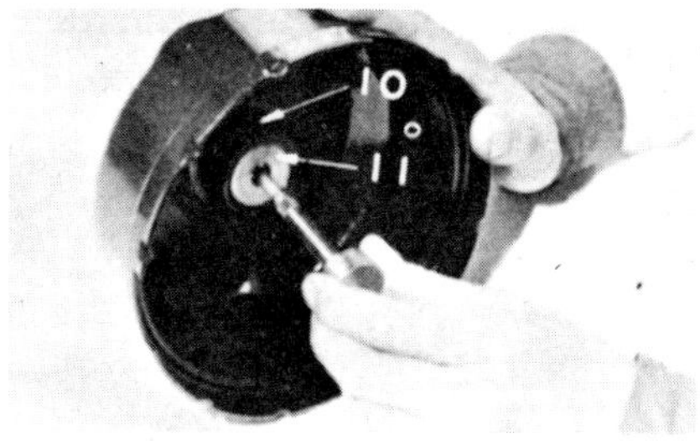

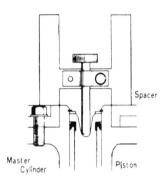

Fig. 9.38. Fitting the plate and seal assembly to servo front shell

10 Shell   11 Plate/seal

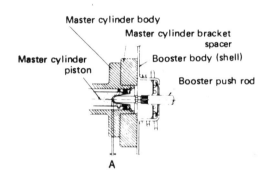

Fig. 9.39. Servo pushrod to master cylinder piston clearance diagram

A = clearance (see Specifications Section)

7 Unbolt the master cylinder from the face of the servo unit.
8 Installation is a reversal of removal, but on completion, check the pedal height and bleed the hydraulic system as described earlier in this Chapter.

23 Vacuum servo unit - dismantling and reassembly

1 If, as a result of checking the fault diagnosis Section the vacuum servo unit is found to be faulty, then it is recommended that a factory exchange unit is obtained rather than undertake the servicing of the unit yourself. However, where the necessary tools and skill are available, dismantling procedure should be carried out as described in this Section. The operations apply to a unit of JKK manufacture but where the other makes of unit are encountered, the information is generally applicable although the construction may differ in detail.
2 Scratch mating marks on the front and rear shells.
3 Holding the mounting studs of the front shell in a plate drilled to receive them, rotate the rear shell anti-clockwise to release it using a tool similar to the one shown. Remove the diaphragm return spring.
4 Withdraw the diaphragm plate from the rear shell and remove the retainer, bearing and seal. The diaphragm plate is made of brittle plastic and should be handled carefully.
5 Remove the diaphragm from the diaphragm plate.
6 Remove the filter/silencer retainer, then the key by pointing the keyhole downwards and pressing the valve operating rod. Withdraw the valve plunger assembly.
7 Remove the retainer, plate and seal and push the rod from the front shell.

Fig. 9.40. Suitable tool for measuring depth of master cylinder recess during pushrod clearance adjustment

8 Clean all components in methylated spirit and check for cracks, corrosion and distortion, and the diaphragm and seals for deterioration (these are best renewed in any event).
9 Smear silicone oil of the recommended grade to the seal and bearing and fit them into the rear shell, then secure them with a retainer.
10 Apply silicone oil to the plunger disc outer edge and assemble.
11 Fit a new air filter/silencer and press the retainer into the diaphragm plate.
12 Fit the diaphragm to the diaphragm plate and the reaction disc, first having smeared it with silicone oil.
13 Smear the outer edge of the diaphragm with silicone oil and then fit the diaphragm plate assembly and the valve body to the rear shell.
14 Fit the plate and seal assembly to the front shell using a smear of silicone oil and then install the pushrod.
15 Secure the front shell in the holding tool and insert the diaphragm return spring. Align the shell mating marks and engage the front and rear shells with a clockwise twisting motion. If they are difficult to engage, apply a smear of silicone oil to the diaphragm edges.
16 Using the tool which was required for dismantling the front and rear shells, tighten the rear shell until it comes up against the stop on the front shell.
17 Whenever the vacuum servo unit has been dismantled and reassembled, check that there will be a clearance, as specified in the Specifications Section according to booster type, between the end of the servo unit pushrod and the end of the master cylinder piston. Check by using the official tool or making up a depth gauge so that the projection of the servo unit pushrod can be compared with the depth of the recess to the end of the master cylinder piston. Carry out any adjustment by loosening the locknut and rotating the front section of the vacuum servo unit pushrod.

24 Fault diagnosis - braking system

Symptom	Cause
Brake grab	Brake shoe linings or pads not bedded in. Contaminated with oil or grease. Scored drums or discs. Servo unit faulty.
Brake drag	Master cylinder faulty. Brake foot pedal return impeded. Blocked filler cap vent on master cylinder reservoir. Master cylinder reservoir or compartments overfilled. Seized wheel caliper or cylinder. Incorrect adjustment of handbrake. Weak or broken shoe return springs. Crushed or blocked pipelines.
Brake pedal feels hard	Friction surfaces contaminated with oil or grease. Glazed friction material surfaces. Rusty disc surfaces. Seized caliper or wheel cylinder. Faulty servo unit.
Excessive pedal travel	Low fluid level in reservoir. Automatic rear shoe adjusters faulty (Hi-Lux, 1974 on). Excessive disc run-out. Worn front wheel bearings. System requires bleeding. Worn pads or linings.
Pedal creep during sustained application	Fluid leak. Faulty master cylinder. Faulty servo.
Pedal 'spongy' or 'springy'	System requires bleeding. Perished flexible hose. Loose master cylinder. Cracked brake drum. Linings not bedded-in. Faulty master cylinder.
Fall in master cylinder fluid level	Normal disc pad wear. Leak. Internal fluid leak from servo.

Servo unit fault diagnosis

Symptom	Cause
Hard pedal, lack of assistance when engine running	Lack of vacuum due to: Loose connections. Restricted hose. Blocked air filter/silencer. Major fault in unit.
Slow action of servo	Faulty vacuum hose. Blocked air filter/silencer.
Lack of assistance during heavy braking	Air leaks in: Non-return valve grommet. Non-return valve. Dust cover. Hoses and connections.
Loss of fluid	Major failure in unit.
Brake pedal pushes back against foot pressure	Hydraulic inlet and outlet pipes incorrectly connected at regulator valve. Major fault in unit.

Chapter 10 Electrical system

Contents

Specifications

System type	12 volt, negative earth
Battery	12V 35/40/60 AH depending upon operating territory

Alternator

	Vehicles with 12R engine	Vehicles with 8R-C or 18R-C engine	Vehicles with 20R engine
Output (A)	35	40	45
Rotor coil resistance	4.2 ohms		
Minimum (exposed) brush length	0.217 in (5.5 mm)		

Voltage regulator

Regulating voltage	13.8 to 14.8 volts
Relay operating voltage	4.5 to 5.8 volts

Starter (standard type)

	Vehicles with 12R engine	Vehicles with 8R-C or 18R-C engine	Vehicles with 20R engine
Output (kW)	0.8	0.9	0.9
Rating (seconds)	30	30	30
Minimum brush length	0.47 in (12.0 mm)		

Starter (reduction gear type)

Output (kW)	0.9
Rating (seconds)	30
Minimum brush length	0.39 in (10.0 mm)

Bulbs

Headlight (sealed beam):	Wattage
Inner	37.5
Outer	37.5/50
Front park/turn lamp	23/8
Side marker lamp	8
Stop/tail lamp	23/8
Rear turn lamp	23
Reversing lamp	23
Rear license plate lamp	8
Interior lamp	5
Courtesy lamp	5
Instrument panel	3.4

Fuses

Fuse holder marking	Circuit protected	Fuse rating (amperage)
Tail	Instrument panel lights, parking tail and licence plate lights	15
Stop	Horns and stop lights	20
Lighter	Cigarette lighter, interior and hazard warning lights	20
Wiper	Radio, windscreen wiper and washer	20
Heater	Reversing lights, heater blower, fuel and temperature gauges, ignition warning light, oil pressure and brake warning lights	20
Turn	Direction indicator and voltage regulator	15
Ignition coil *	Fuel cut-off solenoid	15
Engine *	High exhaust temperature warning light (California) and emission control system	15
SPARE		20

Only fitted to vehicles equipped with emission control systems

1 General description

The electrical system is of the 12 volt negative earth type. The major components comprise a battery, an alternator and a pre-engaged type starter motor.

The battery supplies a steady current to the ignition system and to the vehicle's electrical equipment. All electrical circuits incorporate fuses and a fusible link is inserted in the battery lead to the fuse block.

2 Battery - removal and installation

1 On Hi-Lux vehicles, the battery is located at the front of the engine compartment on the right-hand side.
2 On Hi-Ace vehicles, the exact location of the battery varies according to vehicle type and body style.
3 Disconnect the lead from the negative terminal by unscrewing the clamp bolt.
4 Disconnect the lead from the positive terminal and remove the battery securing bolts and frame.
5 Lift the battery carefully from its tray and avoid spilling electrolyte on the paintwork.
6 Installation is a reversal of removal, but when connecting the terminals, clean off any corrosion or white deposits, which may be present and when the clamp bolts are tight, smear the terminal and clamp with petroleum jelly to prevent corrosion recurring.

3 Battery - maintenance

1 Carry out the regular weekly maintenance described in the Routine Maintenance Section at the front of this manual.
2 Clean the top of the battery, removing all dirt and moisture.
3 As well as keeping the terminals clean and covered with petroleum jelly, the top of the battery, and especially the top of the cells, should be kept clean and dry. This helps prevent corrosion and ensures that the battery does not become partially discharged by leakage through dampness and dirt.
4 Once every three months, remove the battery and inspect the battery securing bolts, the battery clamp plate, tray and battery leads for corrosion (white fluffy deposits on the metal which are brittle to touch). If any corrosion is found, clean off the deposits with ammonia and paint over the clean metal with an anti-rust/anti-acid paint.
5 At the same time inspect the battery case for cracks. If a crack is found, clean and plug it with one of the proprietary compounds marketed for this purpose. If leakage through the crack has been excessive then it will be necessary to refill the appropriate cell with fresh electrolyte as detailed later. Cracks are frequently caused to the top of the battery cases by pouring in distilled water in the middle of winter *after* instead of *before* a run. This gives the water no chance to mix with the electrolyte and so the former freezes and splits the battery case.
6 If topping-up the battery becomes excessive and the case has been inspected for cracks that could cause leakage, but none are found, the battery is being over-charged and the voltage regulator will have to be checked and reset.
7 With the battery on the bench at the three monthly interval check, measure its specific gravity with a hydrometer to determine the state of charge and condition of the electrolyte. There should be very little variation between the different cells and if a variation in excess of 0.025 is present it will be due to either:

a) *Loss of electrolyte from the battery at some time caused by spillage or a leak, resulting in a drop in the specific gravity of the electrolyte when the deficiency was replaced with distilled water instead of fresh electrolyte.*

b) *An internal short circuit caused by buckling of the plates or a similar malady pointing to the likelihood of total battery failure in the near future.*

8 The specific gravity of the electrolyte for varying conditions of charge at a mean temperature of 68°F (120°C) are listed below:

1.260	fully charged
1.210	¾ charged
1.160	½ charged
1.110	¼ charged
1.060	fully discharged

4 Electrolyte - replenishment

1 If the battery is in a fully charged state and one of the cells maintains a specific gravity reading which is 0.025 or more lower than the others, and a check of each cell has been made with a voltage meter to check for short circuits (a four to seven second test should give a steady reading of between 1.2 to 1.8 volts), then it is likely that electrolyte has been lost from the cell with the low reading at some time.
2 Top-up the cell with a solution of 1 part sulphuric acid to 2.5 parts of water. If the cell is already fully topped-up draw some electrolyte out of it with a hydrometer.
3 When mixing the sulphuric acid and water **never add water to sulphuric acid** - always pour the acid slowly onto the water in a glass container. **If water is added to sulphuric acid it will explode.**
4 Continue to top-up the cell with the freshly made electrolyte and then recharge the battery and check the hydrometer readings.

5 Battery - charging

1 In winter time when heavy demand is placed upon the battery, such as when starting from cold, and virtually all electrical equipment is continually in use, it is a good idea to occasionally have the battery fully charged from an external source at the rate of 3.5 or 4 amps.
2 Continue to charge the battery at this rate until no further rise in specific gravity is noted over a four hour period.
3 Alternatively, a trickle charger charging at the rate of 1.5 amps can be safely used overnight.
4 Specially rapid 'boost' charges which are claimed to restore the power of the battery in 1 to 2 hours are to be avoided, they can cause serious damage to the battery plates.
5 Before charging the battery from an external source always disconnect the battery positive (+) lead to prevent damage to the alternator.

6 Alternator - general description, maintenance and precautions

The alternator generates three-phase alternating current which is rectified into direct current by three positive and three negative silicone diode rectifiers installed within the end frame of the alternator. The in-built characteristics of the unit obviate the need for a cut-out or current stabiliser.

A voltage regulator unit is incorporated in the charging circuit to control the exciting current and the current applied to the voltage coil.

Check the drivebelt tension every 5,000 miles (8,000 km) and adjust, as described in Chapter 2, by loosening the mounting bolts. Pull the alternator body away from the engine block; do not use a lever as it will distort the alternator casing.

No lubrication is required as the bearings are grease sealed for life.

Take extreme care when making circuit connections to a vehicle fitted with an alternator and observe the following.

When making connections to the alternator from a battery always match correct polarity.

Before using electric-arc welding equipment to repair any part of the vehicle, disconnect the connector from the alternator and disconnect the positive battery terminal.

Never start the car with a battery charger connected.

Always disconnect the battery (+) lead before using a mains charger.

If boosting from another battery, always connect in parallel using heavy cable.

7 Alternator - testing in vehicle

1 In the event of failure of the normal performance of the alternator, carry out the following test procedure paying particular attention to the possibility of damaging the charging and electrical system unless the notes (a) to (c) are observed.

   a) *Ensure that the alternator output 'B' terminal is connected to the battery at all times. When the ignition switch is operated, the 'F' terminal is also at battery voltage.*
   b) *Never connect the battery leads incorrectly or the rectifiers and flasher unit will be damaged.*
   c) *Never run the engine at high revs with the alternator 'B' terminal disconnected otherwise the voltage at the 'N' terminal will rise abnormally and damage to the voltage relay will result.*

2 Check the security of the alternator mountings, the terminal leads and the drivebelt tension (Chapter 2).
3 Check the flasher fuse (15 amp) and the heater fuse (20 amp) and renew them if they are blown.
4 Switch on the vehicle radio and tune into a local transmitter. Start the engine and increase its speed from idling to 2000 rev/min. If a distinct humming sound is heard from the radio speaker then this indicates that the alternator rectifier is shorted or open.
5 Connect a voltmeter and ammeter to the alternator 'B' terminal. Start the engine and gradually increase its speed to 2300 rev/min. The voltmeter should read between 13.8 and 14.8 volts and the ammeter under 10 amps. If the amperage is greater than the specified figure, the battery is either discharged or there is an internal short circuit. If the voltmeter needle fluctuates the regulator contacts may be dirty or arced, or the alternator 'F' terminal may be loose.
6 If the voltage reading is too high then, (i) the regulator contact gaps may be too wide, (ii) there is an open circuit at the regulator and voltage relay coil, (iii) 'N' and 'B' regulator terminals are open and (iv) the regulator has a defective earth connection.
7 Switch off the engine and disconnect the wiring harness connecting plug. Turn on the ignition switch and measure the voltage between the 'F' and 'E' sockets of the connecting plug. This should be 12 volts. If the reading is low or zero, check for, (i) faulty fuse connection, (ii) open circuit 'F' and 'IG' terminals, or (iii) the regulator contact points fused together.
8 Repeat the tests described in the preceding paragraphs 5 and 6 but run the engine at only 1100 rev/min with all lights and accessories switched on; the ammeter reading should be in excess of 30 amps. If the reading is less than 30 amps it is indicative of open rectifiers, open stator coil circuit or short circuited rectifiers.

8 Alternator - removal and refitting

1 Disconnect the lead from the battery negative terminal.
2 Loosen the alternator mounting bracket bolts and the adjustment link bolts and then push the alternator in towards the engine block so that the driving belt can be removed from the pulley.
3 Disconnect the electrical leads from the alternator terminals, remove the mounting bolts and lift the unit from its location.

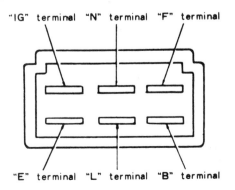

Fig. 10.1. Identification of alternator connecting plug terminals

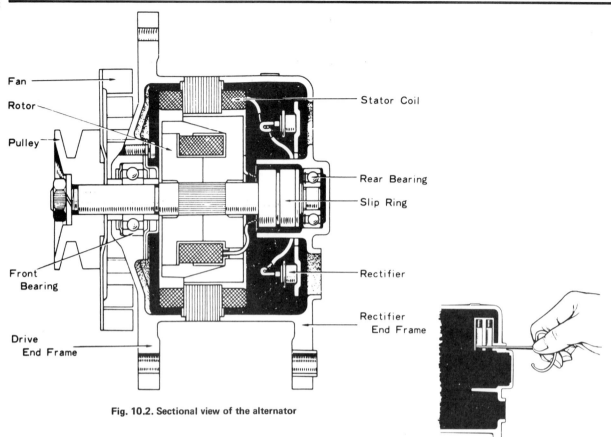

Fig. 10.2. Sectional view of the alternator

Fig. 10.4. Supporting alternator brushes during reassembly of drive end frame

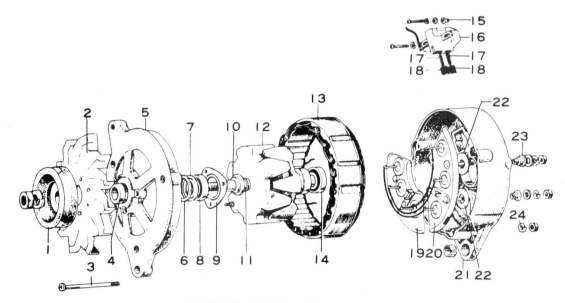

Fig. 10.3. Exploded view of the alternator

1	Driving pulley	7	Cover	13	Stator	19	Rectifier negative holder
2	Fan	8	Front bearing	14	Rear bearing	20	Rectifier positive holder
3	Tie bolt	9	Bearing retainer	15	Terminal insulator	21	Rectifier end frame
4	Spacer	10	Spacer	16	Brush holder	22	Insulating washer
5	Drive end frame	11	Circlip	17	Brush spring	23	'B' terminal insulator
6	Felt ring	12	Rotor	18	Brush	24	Insulator

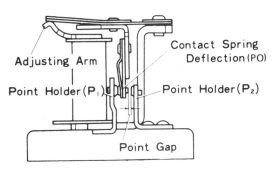

Fig. 10.5. Voltage relay

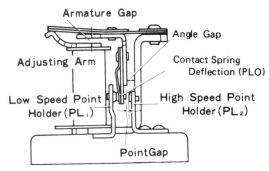

Fig. 10.6. Voltage regulator

4   Refitting is a reversal of removal, but adjust the driving belt tension, as described in Chapter 2.

9 Alternator - dismantling, servicing and reassembly

1   Remove the three tie bolts which secure the two end frames together.
2   Insert screwdrivers in the notches in the drive end frame and separate it from the stator.
3   Hold the front end of the rotor shaft still with an Allen key and remove the securing nut, pulley, fan and spacer.
4   Press the rotor shaft from the drive end frame.
5   Remove the bearing retainer, bearing, cover and felt ring from the drive end frame.
6   Remove the rectifier holder and brush holder securing screws and detach the stator from the rectifier end frame.
7   Remove the brush lead and stator coil 'N' terminals from the brush holder by prising with a small screwdriver.
8   Test the rotor coil for an open circuit by connecting a circuit tester between the two slip rings located at the rear of the rotor. The indicated resistance should be from 4.1 to 4.3 ohms, but if there is no conductance then the coil is open and the rotor must be renewed as an assembly.
9   Now connect the tester between each slip ring in turn and the rotor shaft. If the tester needle moves then the rotor must be renewed as it is earthed.
10 Inspect the rotor bearing for wear and renew if necessary by removing it from the shaft with a two legged puller.
11 Clean the slip rings and rotor surfaces with a solvent moistened cloth.
12 Test the insulation of the stator coil by connecting the tester between the stator coil and the stator core. If the tester needle moves then the coil is earthed through a breakdown in the insulation and must be renewed.
13 To test the stator coil for open circuit, the coil leads must be disconnected from the rectifier leads. Apply the soldering iron to the joint for the minimum time to prevent any heat travelling to the rectifier which is easily damaged.
14 Check the four stator coil leads for conductance. If the tester needle does not flicker than the coil has an open circuit and it must be renewed.
15 The testing of the rectifiers should be limited to measuring the resistance between their leads and holders in a similar manner to that described in paragraph 13. These tests will indicate short or open circuited diodes, but not rectifying or reverse flow characteristics which can only be checked with specialised equipment.
16 If more than one of the preceding tests proves negative then it will be economically sound to exchange the alternator complete for a factory reconditioned unit rather than renew more than one individual component.
17 Finally, examine the brushes for wear. If they are less than 0.34 in (8.5 mm) in length renew them. Remove the old brushes and insert the new ones in their holders, checking to see that they slide freely. Ensure that the brush does not project more than 0.5 in (12.5 mm) from its holder and then solder the brush lead, cutting off any surplus wire.
18 Commence reassembly of the alternator by fitting the stator coil 'N' terminal to the brush holder, then a terminal insulator followed by the brush negative lead.
19 Fit the two insulating washers between the rectifier positive

10.2 Location of voltage regulator

holder and the end frame and install the 'B' terminal and the retaining bolt insulators and secure the holder with its four retaining nuts. Secure the negative rectifier holder with its four nuts.
20 Fit the brush holder with its insulating plate and tighten the securing screws passing them through the terminal insulators. Locate the stator coil in the rectifier end frame.
21 To the drive end frame, fit the felt ring, cover (convex face to pulley) bearing (packed with multi-purpose grease) and bearing retainer (3 screws).
22 Fit the spacer ring to the rotor shaft and then press the drive end frame onto the shaft. Fit the collar, fan and pulley and tighten the securing nut to a torque of 35 lb/ft.
23 Connect the drive end frame assembly to the rectifier end frame assembly and secure with the three tie bolts. Use a piece of wire to support the brushes in the raised position during this operation. (Fig. 10.4).

10 Alternator regulator - testing and adjustment

1   Testing of the relay operating voltage and the regulator output voltage and amperage levels should be left to an auto-electrician as special equipment is needed. However, circuit testing and mechanical adjustments may be carried out in the following manner:
2   Disconnect the regulator connector plug. Remove the cover from the regulator unit and inspect the condition of the points. If they are pitted, clean with very fine emery cloth otherwise clean them with methylated spirit (photo).
3   Connect a circuit tester between the 'IG' and 'F' terminals of the connector plug when no resistance should be indicated. If a resistance is shown, then the regulator points PL1 and PL0 (Fig. 10.6) are making poor contact. Now press down the regulator armature and check the resistance which should be about 10 ohms. If it is much higher, the control resistance is defective and must be renewed.

4   Connect the circuit tester between the connection plug 'L' and 'E'
terminals when no resistance should be indicated. If a resistance is
shown then the contact points P1 and P0 (Fig. 10.5) are making
poor contact. Press down the relay armature and check the resistance
which should be about 100 ohms. If it is higher, the voltage coil has
an open circuit or if lower, the points P1, P0 are fused together or
the coil is shorted.
5   Connect the circuit tester between the 'N' and 'E' terminals when a
resistance of 23 ohms should be indicated. If the resistance is much
higher, the pressure coil has an open circuit, if lower then it is short
circuited.
6   Connect the circuit tester between the 'B' and 'L' terminals and
depress the voltage relay armature. There should be no indicated
resistance but if there is, this will show that the contact of the points
P0 and P2 is poor.
7   Connect the circuit tester between the 'B' and 'E' terminals when the
indicated resistance should be infinity. Where this is not so, the points
P0 and P2 are fused together. Depress the relay armature and check the
resistance which should be about 100 ohms. If the resistance is higher,
then the voltage coil has an open circuit and if lower, it has a short
circuit.
8   Connect the circuit tester between the 'F' and 'E' terminals when
the indicated resistance should be infinity. Where this is not the case
the points PL0 and PL2 are fused together. Depress the regulator
armature and check the resistance which should be zero. If there is a
resistance indicated on the tester then the points PL0 and PL2 are
making poor contact.
9   **With the connector plug still disconnected,** carry out the following
mechanical checks.
10 Refer to Fig. 10.5 and depress the voltage relay armature. Using a
feeler gauge check the deflection gap between the contact spring and
its supporting arm. This should be between 0.008 and 0.024 in (0.20

and 0.60 mm), if not, bend the contact point holder (P2). Release the
armature and check the point gap which should be between 0.016 and
0.047 in (0.4 to 1.2 mm), if not, bend the contact point holder (P1).
11 Check the armature gap in the voltage regulator which should be in
excess of 0.012 in (0.30 mm), otherwise bend the contact point holder
PL2 to adjust (Fig. 10.6). Check the voltage regulator point gap
which should be between 0.012 and 0.018 in (0.30 and 0.45 mm),
otherwise bend the contact point holder PL2 to adjust. Depress the
voltage regulator armature and check the deflection gap between the
contact spring and its supporting arm. This should be between 0.008
and 0.024 in (0.2 and 0.6 mm), if not, renew the regulator as an
assembly. Finally, depress the voltage regulator armature and check the
angle gap at its narrowest point. This gap should not exceed 0.008 in
(0.2 mm), otherwise renew the unit as an assembly.

11 Starter motor - general description

The starter motor is of the heavy duty type, designed to cope with
engine and gearbox drag in sub-zero temperatures. The starter operates
on the principle of pre-engagement which, through the medium of a
solenoid switch, meshes the starter drive gear with the ring gear on the
flywheel (or torque converter - automatic transmission) fractionally in
advance of the closure of the main starter motor contacts. This slight
delay in energising the starter motor does much to extend the life of
the starter drive and ring gear components. As soon as the engine fires
and its speed of rotation exceeds that of the armature shaft of the
starter motor, a built-in clutch mechanism prevents excessive rotation
of the shaft and the release of the starter switch key causes the
solenoid and drive engagement fork to return to their de-energised
positions. The armature shaft is fitted with rear and central rotational
speed retarding mechanisms to stop its rotational movement rapidly
after the starter has been de-energised.

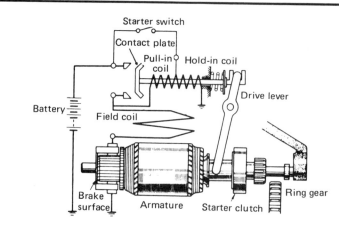

Fig. 10.7. Starter circuit (up to 1976)

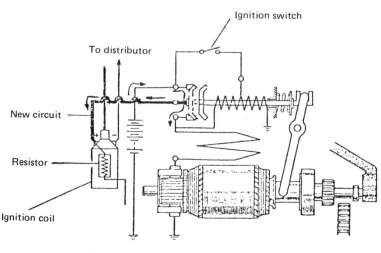

Fig. 10.8. Starter circuit (1976 onwards)

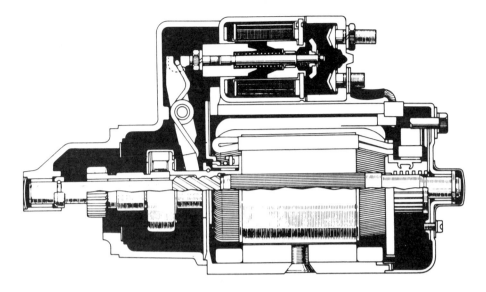

Fig. 10.9. Sectional view of standard type starter motor

On some later model vehicles built for operation in North America, a modified type of starter motor is used. In this unit, an idler gear is incorporated to provide a lower reduction gear characteristic.

As from the beginning of 1976, in order to improve cold starting, a new circuit has been integrated into the starter motor solenoid. This comprises additional wiring for by-passing the ignition coil resistor when the ignition key is turned to the start position.

12 Starter motor - testing in vehicle

1   If the starter motor fails to operate, check the state of charge of the battery by testing the specific gravity with a hydrometer or switching on the headlamps. If they glow brightly for several seconds and then gradually dim, then the battery is in an uncharged state.
2   If the tests prove the battery to be fully charged, check the security of the battery leads at the battery terminals, scraping away any deposits which are preventing a good contact between the cable clamps and the terminal posts.
3   Check the battery negative lead at its body frame terminal, scraping the mating faces clean if necessary.
4   Check the security of the cables at the starter motor and solenoid switch terminals.
5   Check the wiring with a voltmeter for breaks or short circuits.
6   Check the wiring connections at the ignition/starter switch terminals.
7   If everything is in order, remove the starter motor as described in the next Section and dismantle, test and service as described later in this Chapter.

13 Starter motor - removal and installation

1   Disconnect the lead from the battery negative terminal.
2   Disconnect the cables from the starter solenoid terminals.
3   Unscrew and remove the starter motor securing bolts and withdraw the unit from the clutch bellhousing (or torque converter housing - automatic transmission).
4   Installation is a reversal of removal.

14 Starter motor (standard type) - dismantling

1   Disconnect the field coil lead from the starter solenoid main terminal.
2   Remove the two securing screws from the solenoid and withdraw the solenoid far enough to enable it to be unhooked from the drive engagement lever fork.

3   Remove the end frame cover, the lockplate, washer, spring and seal.
4   Unscrew and remove the two tie bolts and withdraw the commutator end frame.
5   Pull out the brushes from their holders and remove the brush holder assembly.
6   Pull the yoke from the drive end frame.
7   Remove the engagement lever pivot bolt from the drive end frame and detach the rubber buffer and its backing plate. Remove the armature, complete with drive engagement lever from the drive end frame.
8   With a piece of tubing, drive the pinion stop collar up the armature shaft far enough to enable the circlip to be removed and then pull the stop collar from the shaft together with the pinion and clutch assembly.

15 Starter motor (standard type) - servicing and testing

1   Check for wear in the armature shaft bearings. The specified clearance between shaft and bearing is between 0.037 and 0.053 in (0.095 and 0.135 mm) with a maximum of 0.008 in (0.2 mm). Normally the bearings will require renewal by pressing out the old ones from the end frames and pressing in the new, but before doing this, check the diameter of the armature shaft which should be 0.492 in (12.50 mm). If this is worn then a new armature will be required and it will be more economical to exchange the starter complete for a reconditioned unit.
2   Armature shaft bearings are available in standard and undersizes as follows:

Standard: *0.4395 to 0.4945 in (12.535 to 12.560 mm) diameter*
Undersize (0.30 mm single line identification):   0.4817 to 0.4827 in
        (12.235 to 12.260 mm)
Undersize (0.50 mm double line identification):   0.4738 to
        0.4748 in (12.035 to 12.060 mm)

3   Check the armature shaft for truth or ovality and renew if evident.
4   Check the commutator segments and undercut the mica insulators if necessary, using a hacksaw blade ground to correct thickness. If the commutator is burnt or discoloured, clean it with a piece of fine glass paper (not emery or carborundum) and finally wipe it with a solvent moistened cloth.
5   To test the armature is not difficult, but a voltmeter or bulb and 12 volt battery are required. The two tests determine whether there may be a break in any circuit winding or if any wiring insulation is broken down. Fig. 10.12 shows how the battery, voltmeter and probe connectors are used to test whether, (a) any wire in the windings is broken or, (b) whether there is an insulation breakdown. In the first test the probes are placed on adjacent segments of a clean commutator.

Fig. 10.10. Exploded view of standard type starter motor

1 Solenoid
2 Engagement lever fork
3 Armature
4 Clutch assembly
5 Pinion stop collar
6 Circlip
7 Drive end frame
8 Bush
9 Plug
10 End frame cover
11 Commutator end frame
12 Insulator
13 Rubber packing
14 Backing plate
15 Lockplate
16 Washer
17 Brake spring
18 Seal
19 Brush
20 Brush spring
21 Brush holder
22 Field coil
23 Pole shoe
24 Yoke

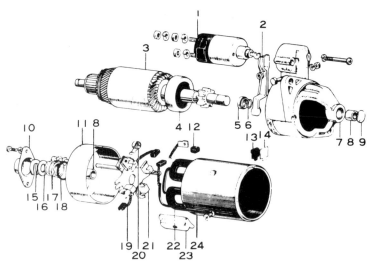

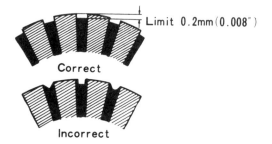

Limit 0.2mm(0.008")

Correct

Incorrect

Fig. 10.11. Mica segment undercutting diagram for starter motor commutator

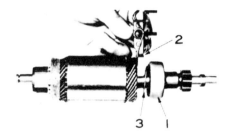

Fig. 10.13. Locating the drive engagement lever to the starter motor shaft

1 Clutch
2 Engagement lever
3 Washer

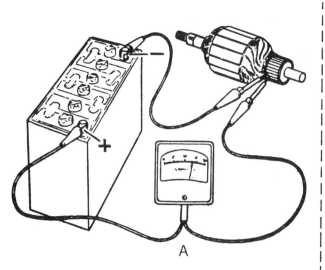
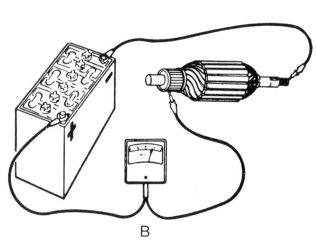

Fig. 10.12. Testing the starter motor armature for open circuit (A) and for insulation breakdown of windings (B)

All voltmeter readings should be similar. If a bulb is used instead, it will glow very dimly or not at all if there is a fault. For the second test, any reading or bulb lighting indicates a fault. Test each segment in turn with one probe and keep the other on the shaft. Should either test indicate a faulty armature the wisest action in the long run is to obtain a replacement starter. The field coils may be tested if an ohmmeter or ammeter can be obtained. With an ohmmeter the resistance (measured between the terminal and the yoke) should be 6 ohms. With an ammeter, connect it in series with a 12 volt battery, again from the field terminal to the yoke. A reading of 2 amps is normal. Zero (amps) or infinity (ohms) indicate an open circuit. More than 2 amps or less than 6 ohms indicates a breakdown of the insulation. (Fig. 10.12).

If a fault in the field coils is diagnosed then a reconditioned starter should be obtained as the coils can only be removed and refitted with special equipment.

6 Check the insulation of the brush holders and the length of the brushes. If these have worn to below 0.47 in (12 mm), renew them. Before fitting them to their holders, dress them to the correct contour by wrapping a piece of emery cloth round the commutator and rotating the commutator back and forth.

7 Check the starter clutch assembly for wear or sticky action, or chipped pinion teeth and renew the assembly, if necessary.

16 Starter motor (standard type) - reassembly

1 Fit the clutch assembly to the armature shaft followed by a new pinion stop collar and circlip. Pull the stop collar forward and stake the collar rim over the circlip. Grease all sliding surfaces.

2 Locate the drive engagement lever to the armature shaft as shown in Fig. 10.13 with the spring towards the armature and the steel washer up against the clutch.

3 Apply grease to all sliding surfaces and locate the armature assembly in the drive end frame. Insert the drive engagement lever pivot pin, well greased.

4 Fit the rubber buffer together with its backing plate and then align and offer into position the yoke to the drive end frame.

5 Fit the brush holder to the armature and then insert the brushes.

6 Grease the commutator end frame bearing and then fit the end frame into position. Insert and tighten the two tie bolts.

7 Fit the seal, washer, lockplate and end cover (half packed with multi-purpose grease). Check the armature shaft endfloat, if this exceeds 0.03 in (0.8 mm) remove the end cover and add an additional thrust washer.

8 Install the solenoid switch, making sure that its hook engages under the spring of the engagement lever fork.

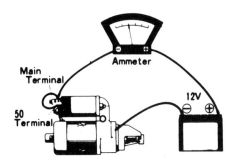

Fig. 10.14. Testing the starter motor after reassembly

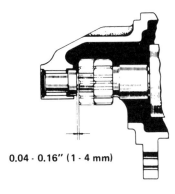

0.04 - 0.16″ (1 - 4 mm)

Fig. 10.15. Starter motor pinion to end stop clearance (standard type starter)

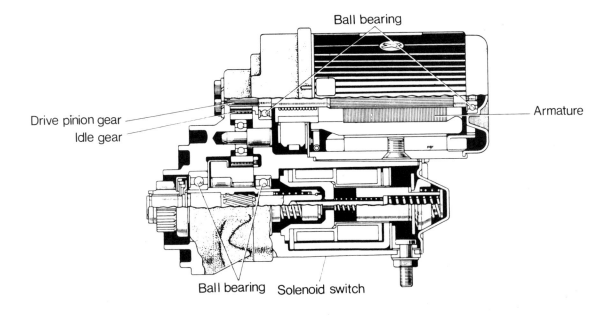

Fig. 10.16. Sectional view of reduction gear type starter motor

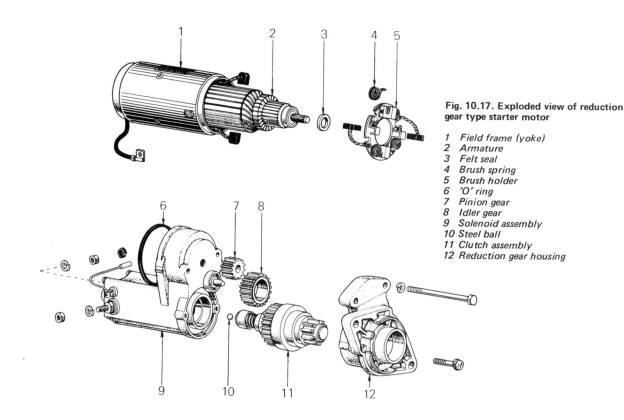

Fig. 10.17. Exploded view of reduction gear type starter motor

1 Field frame (yoke)
2 Armature
3 Felt seal
4 Brush spring
5 Brush holder
6 'O' ring
7 Pinion gear
8 Idler gear
9 Solenoid assembly
10 Steel ball
11 Clutch assembly
12 Reduction gear housing

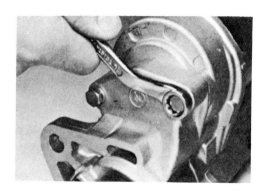

Fig. 10.18. Removing yoke securing bolts (reduction gear type starter)

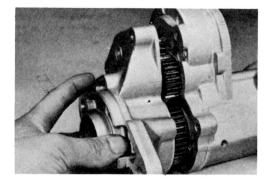

Fig. 10.19. Removing reduction gear housing from starter

9   Set up a test circuit similar to the one shown in Fig. 10.14, and check that the motor rotates smoothly at a current loading of 45 amps. With the solenoid switch energised, insert a feeler gauge between the end face of the clutch pinion and the pinion stop collar. There should be a clearance of between 0.04 and 0.16 in (1 and 4 mm). If the clearance is incorrect, remove the solenoid switch and adjust the length of the adjustable hooked stud by loosening its locknut.

17 Starter motor (reduction gear type) - overhaul

1   Disconnect the leads from the solenoid.
2   Unscrew the two securing bolts and withdraw the field frame (yoke) complete with armature.
3   Extract the 'O' ring and the felt seal.
4   Remove the two securing screws and withdraw the reduction gear housing.
5   Withdraw the clutch assembly and gears.
6   Extract the ball from the hole in the end of the clutch shaft.
7   Pull out the brushes from the brush holder, remove the brush holder and withdraw the armature from the field frame (yoke).
8   Test the armature and field coils as described in Section 15 and recondition the commutator, also described in that Section.
9   Commence reassembly by applying high melting point grease to the armature rear bearing and then insert the armature into the field frame.
10 Install the brush holder, aligning its tab with the notch in the field frame.
11 Install the brushes into their holders and make sure that their leads are not earthed.
12 Fit the felt seal to the armature shaft and the 'O' ring to the field frame. Position the field coil leads towards the solenoid and install the field frame with armature to the solenoid housing, making sure that the raised bolt anchors are in alignment with the marks on the solenoid housing.
13 Apply grease and fit the starter pinion and idler gears.
14 Place a dab of grease into the clutch shaft hole and insert the ball.
15 Fit the clutch assembly.
16 Apply grease liberally to the gears and then install the reduction gear housing.

Fig. 10.20. Withdrawing clutch and gears (reduction type starter)

Fig. 10.21. Extracting steel ball (reduction gear type starter motor)

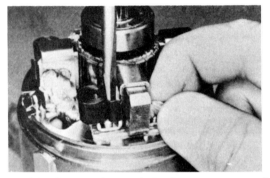

Fig. 10.22. Removing brushes (reduction gear type starter)

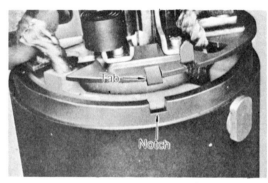

Fig. 10.23. Assembling brush holder to yoke (reduction gear type starter)

Fig. 10.24. Installing yoke to solenoid housing (reduction gear type starter)

Fig. 10.25. Fitting pinion and idler gear to reduction gear type starter

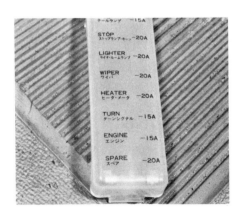

18.1a Typical fuse cover

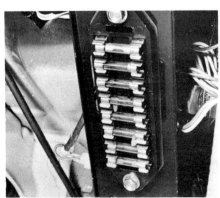

18.1b Typical fuse block

18.3 Battery positive terminal and fusible link

Fig. 10.26. Location of flasher unit (Hi-Ace)

Fig. 10.27. Location of flasher unit (Hi-Lux)

21.2 Adjusting a headlamp (Hi-Lux)

22.2 Removing a headlamp unit retaining ring (Hi-Lux)

18 Fuses and fusible link

1   The fuse block is located under the facia panel. The fuse ratings and circuits protected vary according to model and date of manufacture but the fuse block is clearly marked and the cover incorporates two spare fuses (photos).

2   In the event of a fuse blowing, always find the reason and rectify the trouble before fitting the new one. Always replace a fuse with one of the same amperage rating as the original.

3   A double protection is provided for the electrical harness by a fusible link installed in the lead running from the battery positive terminal. The fusible link must never be by-passed and should it melt, the cause of the circuit overload must be established before renewing the link with one of similar type and rating (photo).

19 Electrical relays - description and testing

1   Later Hi-Lux models are fitted with a headlight relay and on right-hand drive vehicles only, a direction indicator light relay.

2   Both these relays are located adjacent to the fuse block under the instrument panel.

3   Any fault developing in either unit can only be overcome by renewal of the relay complete.

20 Direction indicator and hazard warning flasher units

1   If the flashers fail to work properly first check that all the bulbs are serviceable and of the correct wattage. Then check that the nuts which hold the lamp bodies to the car are tight and free from corrosion. These are the means by which the circuit is completed and any resistance here could affect the proper working of the coils in the flasher unit.

2   Check the security of all leads after reference to the appropriate wiring diagram.

3   If everything is in order, then the hazard warning or flasher indicator units themselves must be faulty and as they cannot be repaired, they must be renewed. The unit is located beneath the facia panel, adjacent to the fuse block on Hi-Ace vehicles and plugged into the reverse side of the instrument panel on Hi-Lux vehicles.

21 Headlight beams - adjustment

1   It is recommended that the headlight beams are set by a service station using optical beam setting equipment.

2   In an emergency however, the adjustment screws can be screwed in or out to alter the beam in both the vertical and horizontal planes. The screws are accessible without having to remove the radiator grille (photo).

22.3 Headlamp connector plug

23.1a Removing front parking/flasher lens

23.1b Removing a rear lamp cluster lens

23.1c View of rear lamp bulb holders (Hi-Lux)

23.1d Side marker lamp (lens removed)

23.1e Interior lamp (Hi-Lux) with lens removed

23.1f Map reading lamp and lens

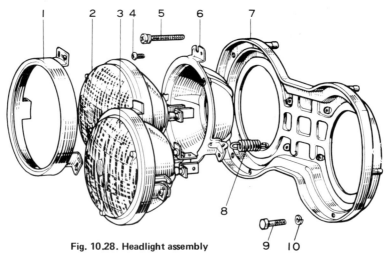

Fig. 10.28. Headlight assembly

1	Light unit retaining ring	6	Mounting ring
2	Sealed beam unit	7	Housing
3	Sealed beam unit	8	Spring
4	Retaining ring screw	9	Bolt
5	Adjusting screw	10	Lockwasher

22 Headlight sealed beam unit - renewal

1   Extract the securing screws and remove the radiator grille. Only one section of the grille need be removed (see Chapter 12).
2   On some vehicles, release, but do not remove, the sealed beam unit retaining ring screws. Turn the ring until the heads of the securing screws will pass through the keyhole slots in the ring and then withdraw the ring. On other vehicles the retaining ring screws must be completely withdrawn (photo).
3   Pull the sealed beam unit far enough forward to be able to disconnect the wiring plug (photo).
4   Connect the new lamp unit, refit the retaining ring and the radiator grille.
5   Provided the adjuster screws have not been moved, the headlight beam alignment should not have altered, but it is a wise precaution to have the beams checked by your dealer afterwards.

23 Bulbs - renewal

1   In all cases, the bulbs are accessible after removal of the lamp lens securing screws and lenses themselves (photos).
2   Renewal of the instrument panel lamp bulbs, also those for indicator/warning lamps, can be carried out after pulling the bulb holders from the rear of the instrument cluster.
3   Either reach up behind the panel or remove the instrument cluster as described in Sections 36 and 37.
4   Always renew a bulb with one of similar type and wattage.

24 Ignition switch (Hi-Ace) - removal and refitting

1   The ignition switch on early models was secured to the facia panel with a bezel nut. Unscrew this with a 'C' spanner and withdraw the switch from the rear of the panel.
2   On later models, the switch is combined with the steering column lock. To remove the cylinder lock section of the switch, turn the ignition key to 'ACC' and depress the securing plunger with a piece of wire. Withdraw the cylinder.
3   If the electrical section of the switch is to be withdrawn, first disconnect the battery and then disconnect the ignition wiring harness plug. Extract the single retaining screw and remove the switch.
4   Refitting is a reversal of removal, but align the switch components as shown in Fig. 10.31.

25 Ignition switch (Hi-Lux) - removal and refitting

1   Disconnect the battery.
2   Remove the shrouds from the upper section of the steering column.
3   Disconnect the ignition wiring harness plug.
4   Extract the single screw and withdraw the switch.
5   Refit the ignition switch by reversing the removal operations, but align the lock cylinder and switch as shown in Fig. 10.32.

26 Steering column combination switch (Hi-Ace) - removal and installation

1   On early models, remove the horn ring by depressing it and turning it in an anti-clockwise direction. Extract the spring.
2   Remove the steering wheel as described in Chapter 11.
3   Disconnect the switch wiring harness plugs.
4   Extract the three securing screws and lift the combination switch from the contact ring housing.
5   On later models, removal is similar except that the horn button assembly can be removed by extracting the two screws from the reverse face of the steering wheel spokes, and detaching the shrouds from the upper section of the steering column.
6   Installation is a reversal of removal.

27 Steering column combination switch (Hi-Lux) - removal and installation

1   Remove the steering wheel as described in Chapter 11.
2   Remove the steering colum lower shroud and disconnect the switch harness plugs.
3   Extract the three securing screws and withdraw the combination switch.
4   Installation is a reversal of removal.

28 Switches, general - removal and refitting

1   Disconnect the leads from the battery before attempting to disconnect wiring from the rear of the instrument panel.
2   Some switches have detachable knobs which must be removed (by extracting the small retaining grub screw), before the switch retaining bezel or locknut can be unscrewed. Once the switch bezel or locknut has been unscrewed, pull the switch far enough away from the mounting panel for the wiring connector to be disconnected (photo).
3   Refitting is a reversal of removal.

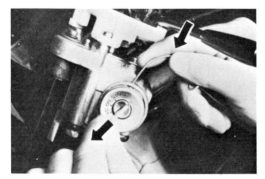

Fig. 10.29. Releasing ignition switch lock cylinder (Hi-Ace)

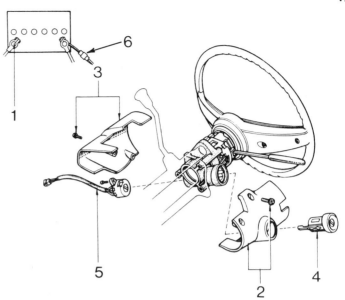

Fig. 10.30. Ignition switch and upper steering column components (Hi-Ace)

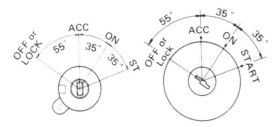

Fig. 10.32. Ignition switch and lock alignment diagram (Hi-Lux)

1 Battery negative terminal
2 Steering column shroud
3 Steering column shroud
4 Lock cylinder
5 Ignition switch
6 Fusible link

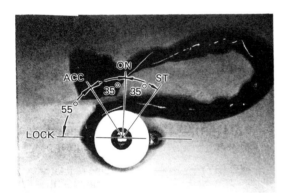

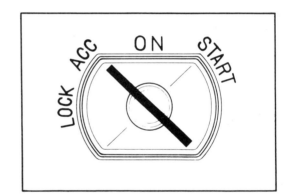

Fig. 10.31. Ignition switch and lock alignment diagram (Hi-Ace)

Fig. 10.33. Removing steering column switch (Hi-Ace)

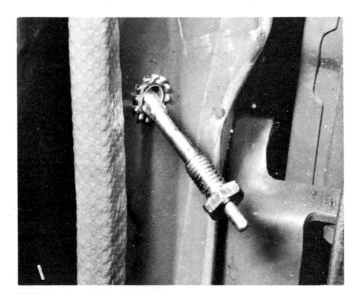

28.2 Courtesy light switch withdrawn

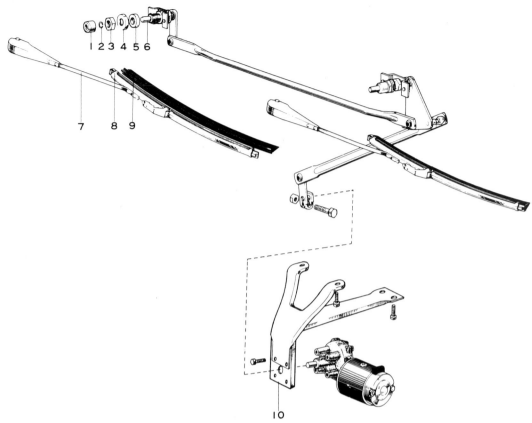

Fig. 10.34. Windscreen wiper components (Hi-Ace). Earlier type shown

1	Cap	3	Nut	5	Gasket	8	Blade
2	Circlip	4	Washer	6	Driving spindle	9	Rubber insert
				7	Wiper arm	10	Motor bracket

29 Horns - adjustment

1   According to vehicle type, the horns may be of vibrator or wind-tone (trumpet) type.
2   To adjust the horn for tone, connect an ammeter in a battery/switch circuit. Loosen the locknut which secures the smaller screw on the back of the horn, switch on the current and turn the adjuster screw in or out until the sound is acceptable with the ammeter reading as specified according to the type of horn:

| Vibrator type | 1.5 to 3.0 amps |
| Trumpet type | 2.5 to 3.5 amps |

30 Windscreen wiper blades - renewal

1   Whenever the wiper blades cease to wipe the screen clean and leave streaks, they must be renewed.
2   Rubber inserts can usually be obtained, but these are not always available and a complete blade assembly sometimes is the only alternative.
3   Lift the wiper arm away from the windscreen glass and then depress the small securing tag and pull the blade from the arm (photo).
4   Push the reconditioned or new blade assembly onto the arm until a click is heard indicating positive engagement of the arm retaining tag.
5   If adjustment of the wiper arcs is required at any time, unscrew the domed retaining nut which secures the wiper arm to the driving spindle, pull the arm from the splines and move it one spline at a time in the appropriate direction and refit and check the operation and wiper blade arc first having wetted the glass (photo).

31 Windscreen wiper motor and linkage (Hi-Ace) - removal and refitting

1   Disconnect the lead from the battery negative terminal.
2   Remove both the wiper arm/blade assemblies.
3   Release the wiper arm driving spindles by unscrewing and removing the circlips, locknuts, distance pieces and gaskets.
4   Disconnect the speedometer drive cable from the speedometer (see Section 35).
5   Disconnect the wiper harness connector.
6   Working under the instrument panel, unbolt the wiper motor mounting bracket and withdraw it complete with motor and linkage.
7   Disconnect the motor crank arm from the motor driveshaft and separate motor and linkage.
8   The motor can be unbolted from the mounting bracket and the linkage dismantled by extracting the circlips from the pivot joints.
9   Refit by reversing the removal operations, but make sure that the motor is actuated and then switched off so that it is in the parked position before installing the wiper arms. Note the setting of the driving spindle mounting plates before installation (Fig. 10.35).

32 Windscreen wiper motor and linkage (Hi-Lux) - removal and refitting

1   Disconnect the lead from the battery negative terminal.
2   The wiper motor is mounted on the rear bulkhead of the engine compartment. Disconnect the wiring harness connector plug (photo).

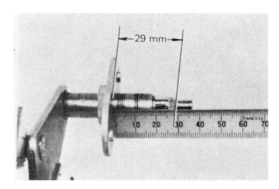

Fig. 10.35. Wiper arm driving spindle mounting plate positioning
diagram

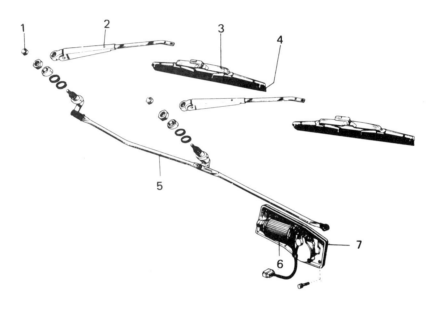

Fig. 10.36. Wiper components (Hi-Lux)

1 Dome nut   5 Linkage
2 Arm   6 Motor
3 Blade   7 Motor mounting plate
4 Rubber insert

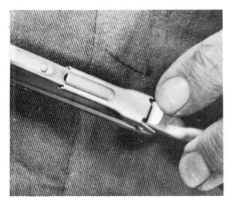

30.3 Removing a windscreen wiper blade

30.5 Removing a windscreen wiper arm

32.2 Location of windscreen wiper motor

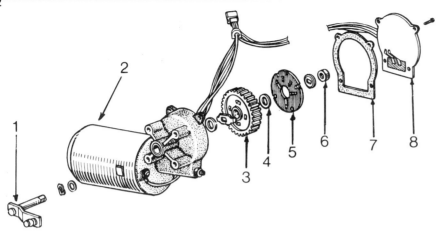

Fig. 10.37. Exploded view of windscreen wiper motor

1 Crankarm
2 Yoke
3 Gear
4 Thrust washer
5 Cam plate
6 Nut
7 Gasket
8 Cover plate
9 Steel ball
10 Armature
11 Steel ball
12 Brush holder and leads
13 Gear housing
14 Locknut
15 Adjuster screw

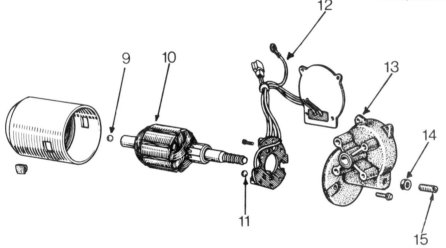

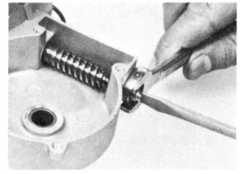

Fig. 10.38. Adjusting wiper motor armature end-float

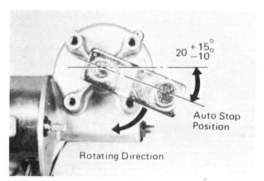

Fig. 10.39. Crankarm setting (Hi-Ace wiper motor)

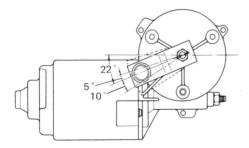

Fig. 10.40. Crankarm setting (Hi-Lux wiper motor)

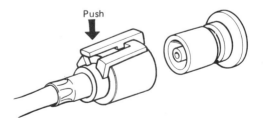

Fig. 10.41. Speedometer cable to speedometer head connection (later models)

3   Unbolt the motor mounting plate and withdraw the wiper motor far enough to be able to disconnect the motor crank arm from the linkage. Withdraw the motor and unbolt it from the mounting plate.
4   If the linkage is now to be removed, first detach the wiper arm/ blade assemblies.
5   Unscrew the driving spindle locknuts and remove them together with the distance pieces and gaskets.
6   The linkage can now be drawn out through the motor mounting plate aperture.
7   Refitting is a reversal of removal, but make sure that the motor is in the parked position before fitting the arms to the driving spindles.

33 Wiper motor - overhaul

1   Before dismantling the wiper motor, check that individual spares are available. It is very often more economical to obtain a second-hand or reconditioned unit complete.
2   There are slight differences between the wiper motors used in vehicles of different types and dates of production, but the following operations will apply.
3   Remove the gear housing cover plate.
4   Make alignment marks on the now exposed cam plate, gear and shaft end face.
5   Bend down the lockplate tab of the nut and unscrew it.
6   Extract the two securing screws and withdraw the gear housing from the stator. Take care that the brushes do not slip off the commutator during this operation and become damaged by the worm gear.
7   Pull the armature from the stator. A strong pull will be required to overcome the magnetic force.
8   Extract the steel balls from both ends of the armature shaft.
9   Clean all components and renew the brushes if they are worn below 0.26 in (6.5 mm) in length.
10 Clean the commutator and burnish it, if necessary, with very fine glass paper.
11 Check the height of the auto stop switch lever on the cover plate, the tip of the lever should be ½ in (12.7 mm) from the surface of the plate.
12 Reassembly is a reversal of removal, but observe the following points.
13 Screw in the adjuster screw on the gear housing until it just contacts the ball on the end of the armature shaft and then tighten the locknut.
14 Make sure that the marks made before dismantling on the shaft, gear and cam plate are in alignment.
15 Lock the nut in the gear housing by turning up the edge of the lockplate.
16 Temporarily reconnect the wiper motor leads and the battery and with the motor switched off in the parked position check that the crank arm is as shown according to vehicle type (Figs. 10.39 and 10.40).

34 Windscreen washer - servicing

1   The windscreen washer is of the electrically operated type having the pump mounted within the washer fluid reservoir (photo).
2   Keep the reservoir clean and the electrical connections secure, also the washer connecting pipes.
3   Never operate the washer without fluid in the reservoir nor depress the switch for periods in excess of 20 seconds.

35 Speedometer cable - removal and refitting

1   On earlier vehicles, the speedometer cable is connected to the rear of the speedometer by a knurled ring. On later vehicles the cable conduit is retained to the speedometer by a locking lever.
2   To disconnect, reach up behind the instrument panel, uncouple the cable conduit from the speedometer and then pull the cable conduit down and pull out the inner cable.
3   When installing the new cable, apply a smear of thin grease to the lower two thirds of its length only.
4   . Push the cable fully home and then twist it to make sure that its lower end engages in the speedometer driven gear pinion at the transmission.
5   Reconnect to the speedometer.

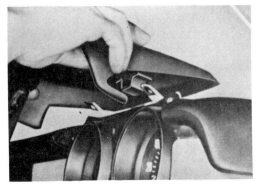

Fig. 10.42. Removing anti-glare hood (Hi-Ace)

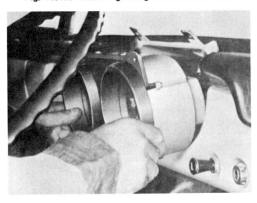

Fig. 10.43. Withdrawing instrument panel (Hi-Ace)

Fig. 10.44. Anti-glare hood securing screws (Hi-Lux)

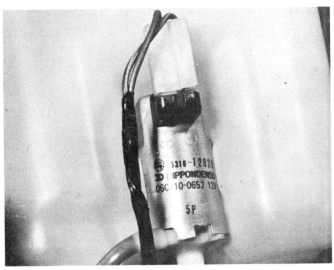

34.1 Windscreen washer reservoir and pump

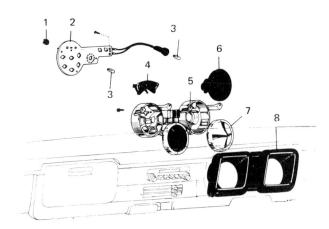

Fig. 10.45. Instrument details (Hi-Lux)

1 *Instrument bulb holder*	5 *Gauge housing*
2 *Instrument circuit board*	6 *Speedometer*
3 *Capless type bulb*	7 *Lens*
4 *Fuel gauge*	8 *Anti-glare hood*

36 Instrument panel (Hi-Ace) - removal and refitting

1 Disconnect the lead from the battery negative terminal.
2 Remove the anti-glare hood (two screws) from the top of the instrument panel.
3 Reach behind the instrument panel and disconnect the wiring harness plug and the speedometer cable.
4 Extract the instrument panel securing screws and withdraw the panel towards you.
5 The individual instruments or the indicator bulb holders may now be removed as necessary.
6 If the water temperature and fuel contents gauges have both become faulty at the same time, suspect the instrument voltage regulator which is located on the rear face of the instrument panel.
7 Refitting is a reversal of removal.

37 Instrument panel (Hi-Lux) - removal and refitting

1 Disconnect the lead from the battery negative terminal.
2 Slacken the steering column clamp bolts.
3 Extract the three screws from the instrument anti-glare hood.
4 Pull the instrument cluster towards you gently until the speedometer cable and wiring harness connector can be disconnected at the rear of the panel.
5 Remove the instrument cluster from the fascia panel.
6 Individual instruments or indicator lamp holders may now be removed as necessary.
7 Refitting is a reversal of removal.

38 Seat belt electrical interlock system

1 Vehicles produced after 1973 for operation in North America are fitted with an elaborate electrical warning and safety interlock system. Basically, if either of the two front seats are occupied, but the respective seatbelt is not fastened, the following actions occur:

(i)   A warning buzzer and lamp actuate if the ignition key is turned to the 'start' position.
(ii) The starter will not operate when the key is turned (it will operate if the driver's belt is connected and there is no weight on the front passenger seat, also the inertia belt not in use is fully retracted).

2 The engine can of course be started for repairs etc. by reaching into the vehicle interior to turn the starter switch. Although the seat belts are not fastened, there is no weight on the seats to actuate the interlock switches and so the engine can be started.
3 The system also incorporates a deceleration sensor which locks the inertia type seat belt reels in advance of impact, should a collision occur.
4 Individual components of the system are sealed units and can only be renewed as such. Maintenance should be limited to occasionally checking the security of the connecting wiring.
5 On vehicles operating in Canada, the system is similar except that there is no starter interlock circuit.

39 Fault diagnosis - electrical system

Symptom	Cause
Starter motor fails to turn engine	
No electricity at starter motor	Battery discharged.
	Battery defective internally.
	Battery terminal leads loose or earth lead not securely attached to body.
	Loose or broken connections in starter motor circuit.
	Starter motor switch or solenoid faulty.
Electricity at starter motor: faulty motor	Starter brushes badly worn, sticking or brush wires loose.
	Commutator dirty, worn or burnt.
	Starter motor armature faulty.
	Field coils earthed.
Starter motor turns engine very slowly	
Electrical defects	Battery in discharged condition.
	Starter brushes badly worn, sticking or brush wires loose.
	Loose wires in starter motor circuit.
Starter motor operates without turning engine	
Mechanical damage	Pinion or flywheel gear teeth broken or worn.
Starter motor noisy or excessively rough engagement	
Lack of attention or mechanical damage	Pinion or flywheel gear teeth broken or worn.
	Starter motor retaining bolts loose.

Symptom	Cause
Battery will not hold charge for more than a few days	
Wear or damage	Battery defective internally.
	Electrolyte level too low or electrolyte too weak due to leakage.
	Plate separators no longer fully effective.
	Battery plates severely sulphated.
Insufficient current flow to keep battery charged	Battery plates severely sulphated.
	Drive belt slipping.
	Battery terminal connections loose or corroded.
	Alternator not charging.
	Short in lighting circuit causing continual battery drain.
	Regulator unit not working correctly.
Ignition light fails to go out, battery runs flat in a few days	
Alternator not charging	Drive belt loose and slipping or broken.
	Brushes worn, sticking, broken or dirty.
	Brush springs worn or broken.
Regulator fails to work correctly	Regulator incorrectly set.
	Open circuit in wiring of regulator unit.

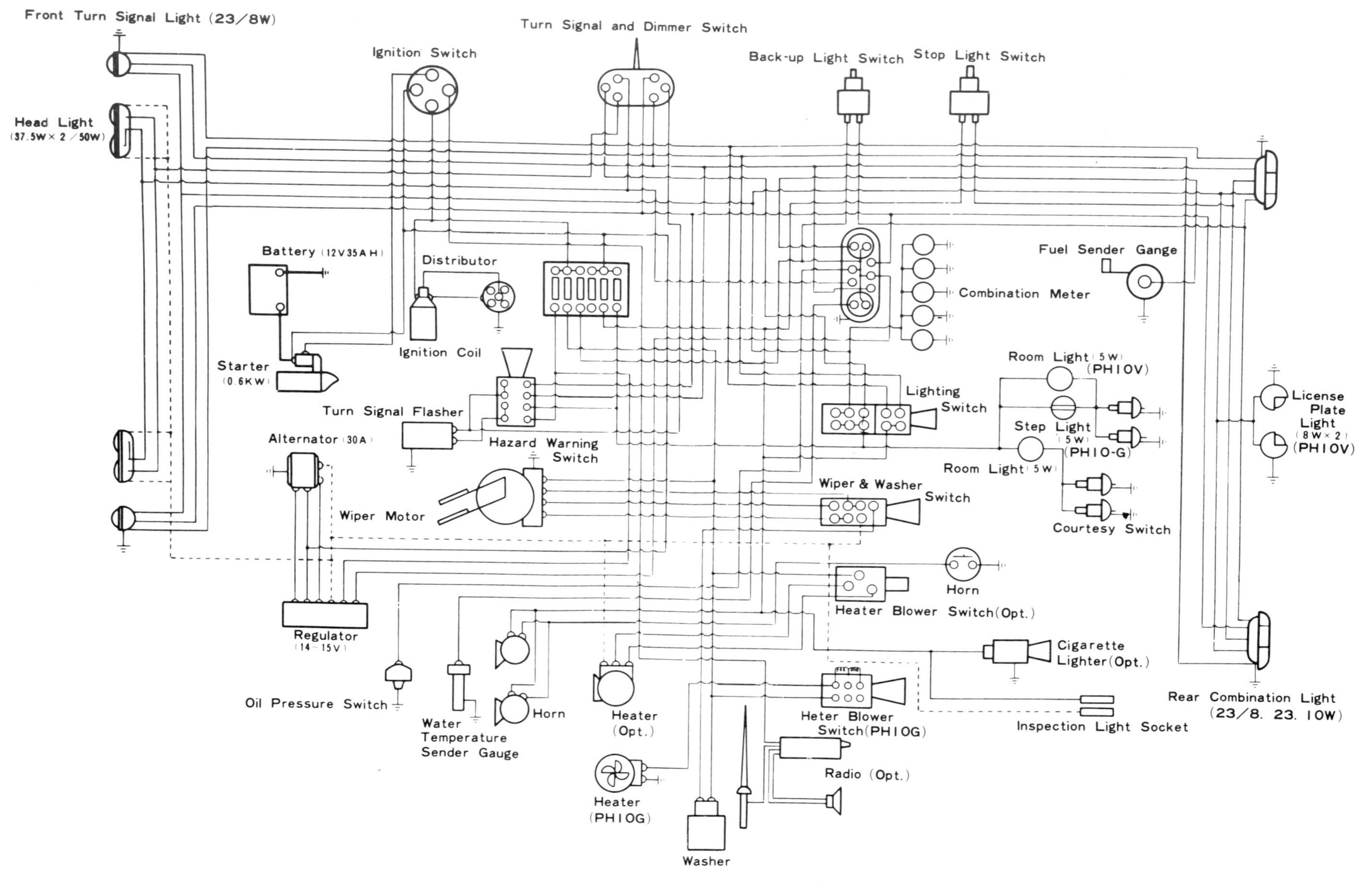

License Plate Light (8W×2) (PH10V)

Rear Combination Light (23/8. 23. 10W)

Fuel Sender Gange

Combination Meter

Room Light (5W) (PH10V)

Step Light (5W) (PH10-G)

Room Light (5W)

Courtesy Switch

Cigarette Lighter (Opt.)

Inspection Light Socket

Lighting Switch

Wiper & Washer Switch

Horn

Heater Blower Switch (Opt.)

Heter Blower Switch (PH10G)

Radio (Opt.)

Washer

Heater (Opt.)

Heater (PH10G)

Back-up Light Switch

Stop Light Switch

Turn Signal and Dimmer Switch

Hazard Warning Switch

Horn

Water Temperature Sender Gauge

Ignition Switch

Distributor

Ignition Coil

Turn Signal Flasher

Wiper Motor

Regulator (14～15V)

Oil Pressure Switch

Battery (12V35AH)

Starter (0.6KW)

Alternator (30A)

Front Turn Signal Light (23/8W)

Head Light (37.5W×2/50W)

Wiring diagram - Hi-Ace early models (RH10 series)

Wiring diagram - Hi-Ace early models (RH11 series)

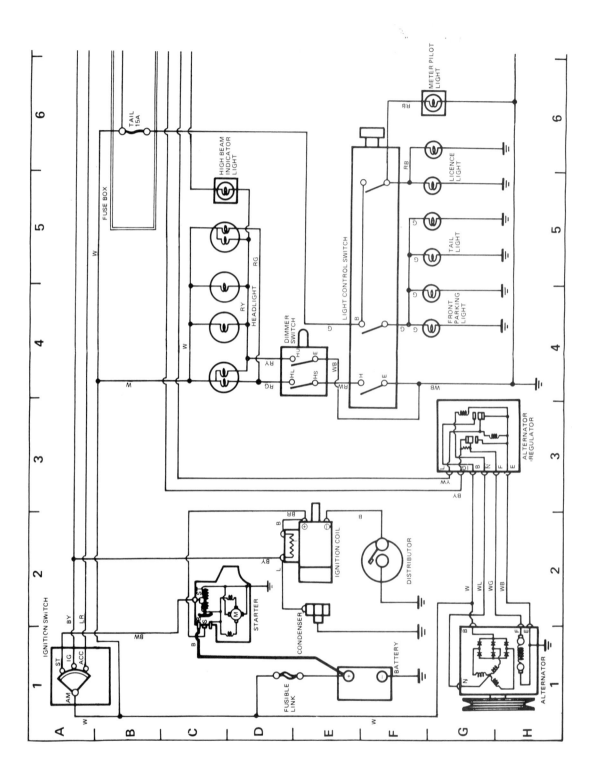

Wiring diagram - Hi-Ace later models

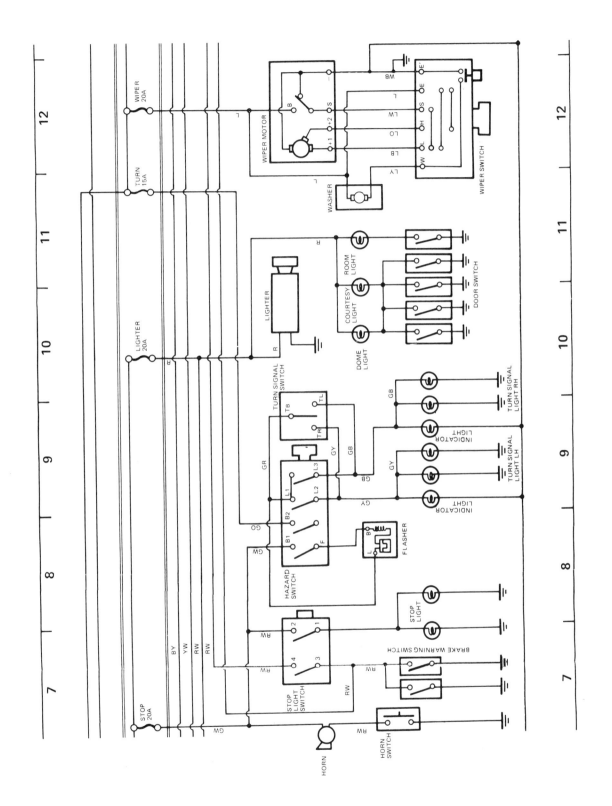

Wiring diagram - Hi-Ace later models (cont.)

Wiring diagram key - Hi-Ace later models

GRID LOCATION	COMPONENTS
H-1	ALTERNATOR
E-15	ANTENNA
F-1	BATTERY
D-10	CIGARETTE LIGHTER
F-2	DISTRIBUTOR
	EMISSION CONTROL SYSTEM:
D-16	SHIFT POINT SWITCH
C-16	VACUUM SWITCHING VALVE
D-16	WATER TEMP SWITCH
E-8	FLASHER, TURN SIGNAL & HAZARD
C-15	FUEL CUT SOLENOID
D-14	FUEL GAUGE
E-14	FUEL GAUGE SENDER
B-5	FUSE BOX
D-1	FUSIBLE LINK
E-6	HORN
E-2	IGNITION COIL
	LIGHTS:
D-15	BACK-UP
D-14	BRAKE WARNING
F-6	COMBINATION METER
D-14	CHG
F-4	FRONT PARKING
C-4	HEADLIGHT, LH, RH
C-5	HIGH BEAM INDICATOR
F-5	LICENSE PLATE
D-14	OIL PRESSURE
F-8	STOP

GRID LOCATION	COMPONENTS
F-5	TAIL, LH, RH
F-9	TURN SIGNAL, LH, FRONT & REAR
F-10	TURN SIGNAL, RH, FRONT & REAR
F-9	TURN SIGNAL INDICATOR, LH
F-10	TURN SIGNAL INDICATOR, RH
	MOTORS:
D-13	HEATER BLOWER
C-2	STARTER
E-10	WASHER
D-12	WINDSHIELD WIPER
E-16	RADIO
G-3	REGULATOR
F-16	SPEAKER
	SWITCHES:
F-15	BACK-UP LIGHT
F-7	BRAKE WARNING LIGHT
E-4	DIMMER
F-10	DOOR
D-8	HAZARD WARNING LIGHT
E-13	HEATER BLOWER MOTOR
F-7	HORN
A-1	IGNITION
F-4	LIGHT CONTROL
E-14	OIL PRESSURE
E-15	PARKING BRAKE
D-7	STOP LIGHT
D-9	TURN SIGNAL
F-12	WINDSHIELD WIPER & WASHER
D-14	WATER TEMP GAUGE
E-14	WATER TEMP SENDER

Note:

When reading the wiring diagram, following should be noted.

1. Wiring color code is shown with alphabetical letter/s.
   The first letter indicates the basic color for the wire, and the second letter indicates the spiral line color.

   B = Black
   G = Green
   L = Light Blue
   O = Orange
   R = Red
   W = White
   Y = Yellow
   Lg = Light Green

   Example: RG, is for Red and A Green line.

2. Legend in the bracket [ ] of the wiring diagram shows the grid location of mating connection.

3. Broken lines in the wiring diagram are for varied models or optional equipment.

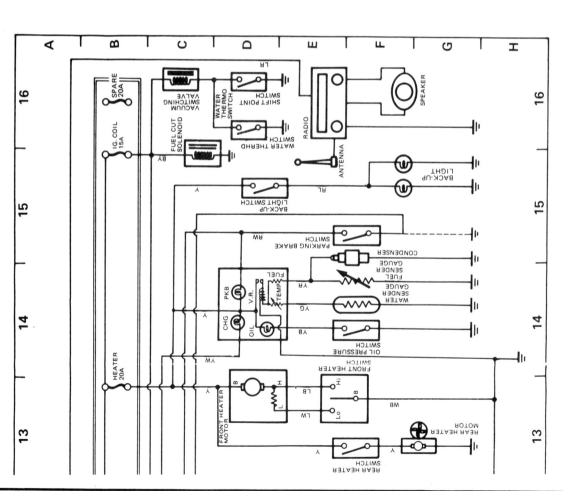

Wiring diagram - Hi-Ace later models continued

Wiring diagram - Hi-Lux early models

* : Available Equipment

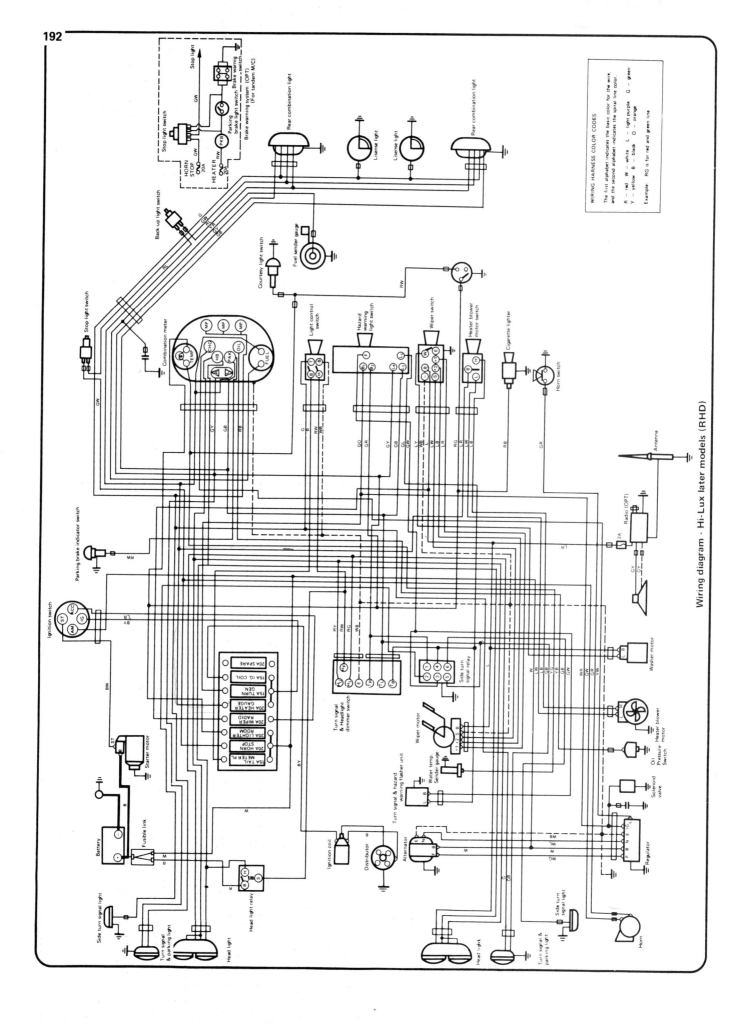

Wiring diagram - Hi-Lux later models (RHD)

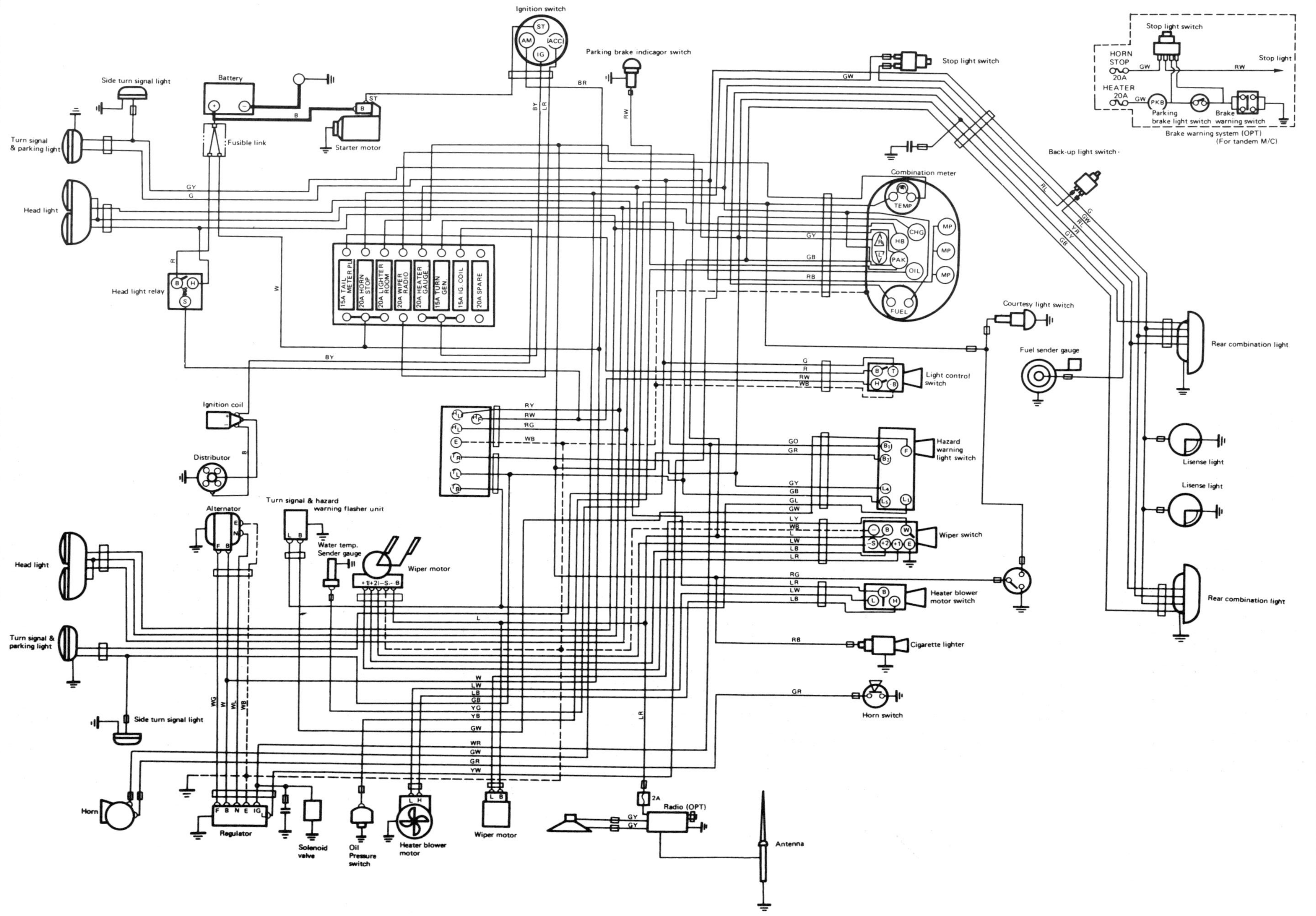

Stop light
Stop light switch
HORN STOP 20A
HEATER 20A
GW GW GW
Brake light switch warning switch (OPT)
Brake warning system (OPT) (For tandem M/C)
Parking brake switch (PKB)

RW

Back-up light switch

Rear combination light
License light
License light
Rear combination light

Courtesy light switch
Fuel sender gauge

Stop light switch

Combination meter
MP MP MP
CHG HB PAK OIL
TEMP FUEL

Light control switch
Hazard warning light switch
Wiper switch
Heater blower motor switch
Cigarette lighter
Horn switch

Parking brake indicator switch

Ignition switch
ST ACC IG AM

Antenna

Radio (OPT)
2A

20A SPARE
15A IG. COIL
15A GEN
15A TURN
20A HEATER GAUGE
20A RADIO
20A WIPER
20A LIGHTER ROOM
20A HORN STOP
15A TAIL METER P.U

Starter motor

Wiper motor
Heater blower motor
Oil Pressure switch
Solenoid valve
Regulator
B N M E IG

Turn signal & hazard warning flasher unit
Water temp. Sender gauge
Wiper motor

Battery
Fusible link

Ignition coil
Distributor
Alternator

Side turn signal light
Head light
Head light relay
Turn signal & parking light
Head light
Turn signal & parking light
Side turn signal light
Horn

Wiring diagram - Hi-Lux later models (LHD)

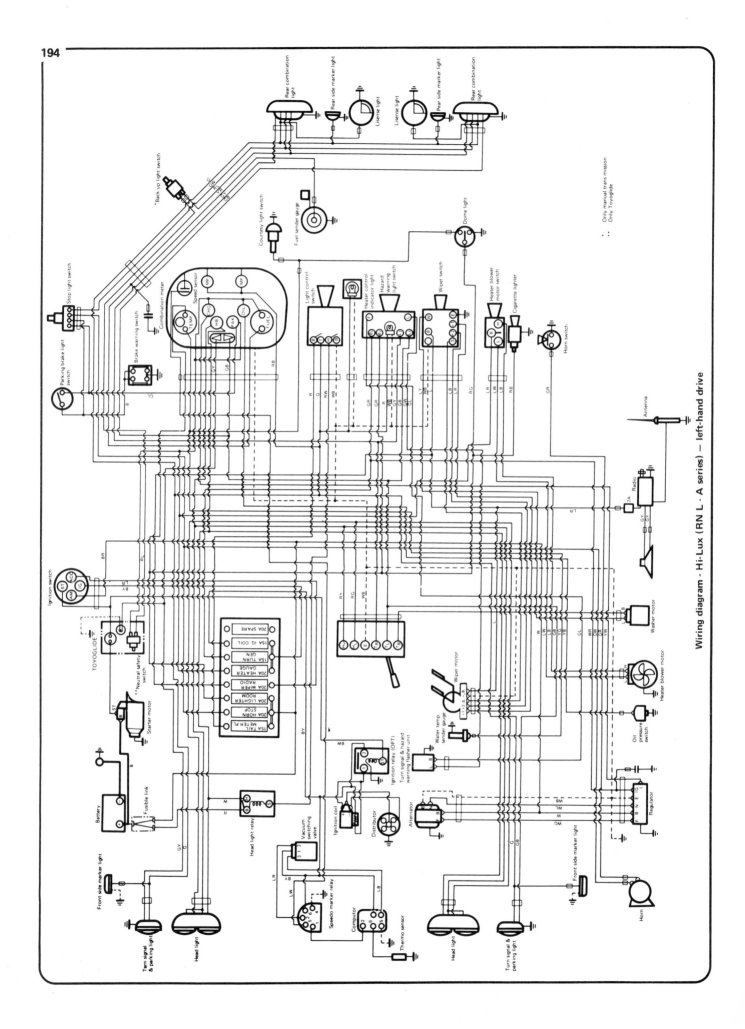

Wiring diagram - Hi-Lux (RN L - A series) - left-hand drive

Chapter 11 Suspension and steering

Contents

Specifications

Front suspension

Type ... ... Independent, upper and lower wishbones with coil springs and telescopic shock absorbers. Anti-roll bar

	* Hi-Ace (early)	** Hi-Ace (later)	* Hi-Lux (early)	** Hi-Lux (early LHD and all later models)
Camber	0° 42' pos.	0° 35' ± 30' pos.	1° 0' pos.	1° 0' ± 45' pos.
Castor	0° 24' pos.	0° 35' ± 30' pos.	0° 20' neg.	0° 30' neg. ± 45'
Steering axis inclination	7° 35' pos.	7° 40' pos.	7° 15' pos.	7° 15' pos.
Toe-in	0.173 in (4.4 mm)	0.32 to 0.40 in (8.0 to 10.0 mm) Radial tyre: 0.20 to 0.28 in (5.0 to 7.0 mm)	0.24 in (6.0 mm)	0.08 to 0.28 in (2.0 to 7.0 mm)
Front wheel turning angles				
Inner	31°	31°	39°	36 to 39°
Outer	30°	30°	31° 31'	27° 30' to 31° 30'

Early denotes steering gear of normal sector type
**Later denotes steering gear of recirculating ball type.*

Rear suspension
Type ... ... Semi-elliptic leaf springs with telescopic type shock absorbers

Steering
Type
Early Hi-Ace and Hi-Lux (right-hand drive only)	Worm and sector roller
Later Hi-Ace and Hi-Lux (including early left-hand drive)	Recirculating ball

Ratios

	Worm and sector roller	Recirculating ball
Hi-Ace	21 : 1	20.5/23.5 : 1
Hi-Lux	20 : 1	19.5/21.5 : 1

Steering wheel diameter ... ... 15.75 in (400 mm)
Turning circle
Hi-Ace: except van	33.6 ft (10.1 m)
Van	34.1 ft (10.4 m)
Hi-Lux: Standard wheelbase	34.1 ft (10.4 m)
Long wheelbase	36.8 ft (11.0 m)

Wheelbase

Hi-Ace	90.2 in (229.0 cm)
Hi-Lux: Standard wheelbase	Up to 1971 99.8 in (2535 mm)
	1972 on 101.6 in (2580 mm)
Long wheelbase	109.8 in (2790 mm)

Steering box oil capacity

Hi-Ace: worm and sector roller	0.31 Imp qt, 0.37 US qt, 0.35 litre
Hi-Ace: recirculating ball	1.0 Imp pt, 0.6 US qt, 0.7 litre
Hi-Lux: worm and sector roller	0.5 Imp pt, 0.29 US qt, 0.28 litre
Hi-Lux: recirculating ball	0.3 Imp qt, 0.3 US qt, 0.32 litre

Wheels and tyres

Wheels	Pressed steel 14 in
Tyres	Crossply, radial or bias belt
	Construction of differing size according to date of production, vehicle application and body design. Consult vehicle sticker for specification and recommended pressures

Torque wrench settings

	lb f ft	Nm
Front suspension (Hi-Ace)		
Shock absorber mounting nuts	35	48
Lower arm pivot nuts (early)	110	150
(later)	220	299
Lower arm pivot to bodyframe	65	88
Upper arm pivot nuts (early)	110	150
(later)	220	299
Upper arm pivot shaft to bodyframe	75	102
Upper swivel joint to suspension arm	20	27
Upper swivel joint to stub axle	85	116
Lower swivel joint to suspension arm	27	37
Lower swivel joint to stub axle	100	136
Front suspension (Hi-Lux)		
Upper arm pivot shaft to bodyframe	140	190
Lower arm pivot shaft to bodyframe	40	54
Upper swivel joint to stub axle carrier	80	109
Lower swivel joint to stub axle carrier	110	150
Lower swivel joint to suspension arm	26	35
Shock absorber upper mounting	20	27
Shock absorber lower mounting	15	20
Rear suspension (Hi-Ace and Hi-Lux)		
Spring 'U' bolt nuts	65	88
Spring shackle nuts	75	102
Spring hanger nuts	75	102
Wheels (Hi-Ace and Hi-Lux)		
Roadwheel nuts	75	102
Steering (Hi-Ace and Hi-Lux)		
Steering wheel nut	22	30
*Sector roller shaft nut	16	22
End cover bolts	14	19
**Wormshaft top cover bolts (Hi-Ace, later)	25	34
Drop arm nut	130	177
Steering box mounting bolts	30	41
Linkage balljoint nuts	75	102
*Centre bracket mounting bolts	40	54
*Centre bracket shaft nut	80	109
Idler bracket mounting bolts	30	41
Idler arm nut	85	116
Track rod clamps	20	27
Flexible coupling to wormshaft pinch bolt	20	27
Flexible coupling to mainshaft bolts	20	27
Steering column upper clamp bolts	10	14
**Wormshaft adjuster locknut	65	88
Sector shaft adjuster locknut	20	27

*Only with worm and sector roller steering
**Only with recirculating ball steering.

1 General description

All models have independent front suspension incorporating upper and lower wishbones, coil springs, telescopic shock absorbers and an anti-roll bar.

The rear suspension is of leaf spring type with telescopic shock absorbers. On Hi-Ace truck versions, the rear axle is mounted below the rear road spring while on all other models it is mounted above the road spring.

The steering on early models is of worm and sector type while on later vehicles, it is of the recirculating ball design.

2 Maintenance and inspection

1 Refer to the Routine Maintenance Section at the front of this manual.

2 Regularly inspect the condition of the balljoint rubber covers for splits or deterioration and renew if necessary. Also check the condition of the rear suspension spring bushes for wear and renew the rubber bushes if there is any movement.

3 Check the security of all suspension nuts and bolts, checking particularly those on the balljoints and on the rear road spring 'U' bolts. Tighten them if necessary to the torques specified.

4 Every 24,000 miles (38.000 km) clean and repack the front wheel hub bearings and adjust them as described in this Chapter. At similar mileage intervals, check the front wheel alignment (Section 23).

5 Grease the suspension arm pivots and balljoint swivels at specified intervals (see Sections 4 and 8).

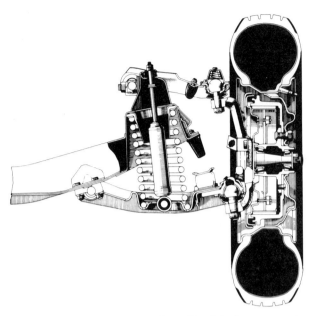

Fig. 11.1. Typical sectional view of one side of the front suspension (drum brakes)

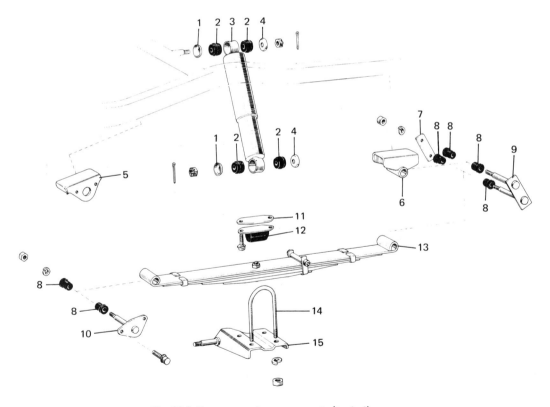

Fig. 11.2. Rear suspension components (typical)

1 Plate	9 Shackle assembly
2 Flexible bush	10 Hanger pin
3 Shock absorber	11 Spacer
4 Plate	12 Bump stop
5 Spring bracket	13 Leaf spring
6 Spring bracket	14 'U' bolt
7 Shackle plate	15 Spring seat
8 Bush	

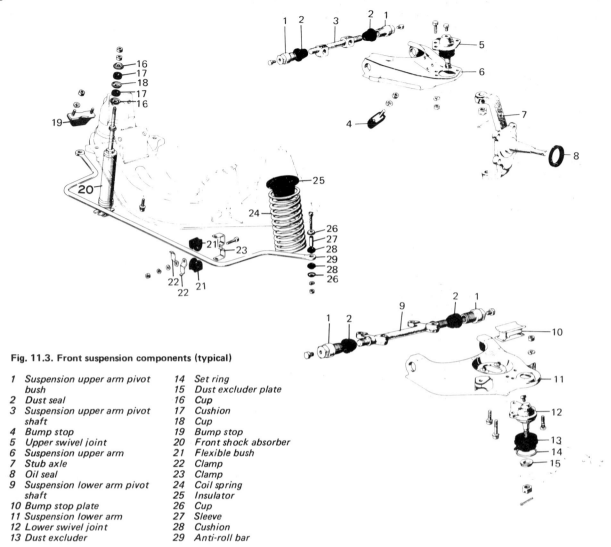

Fig. 11.3. Front suspension components (typical)

1 Suspension upper arm pivot bush
2 Dust seal
3 Suspension upper arm pivot shaft
4 Bump stop
5 Upper swivel joint
6 Suspension upper arm
7 Stub axle
8 Oil seal
9 Suspension lower arm pivot shaft
10 Bump stop plate
11 Suspension lower arm
12 Lower swivel joint
13 Dust excluder

14 Set ring
15 Dust excluder plate
16 Cup
17 Cushion
18 Cup
19 Bump stop
20 Front shock absorber
21 Flexible bush
22 Clamp
23 Clamp
24 Coil spring
25 Insulator
26 Cup
27 Sleeve
28 Cushion
29 Anti-roll bar

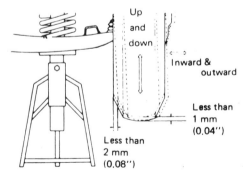

Fig. 11.4. Wear checking diagram for front suspension swivel joints

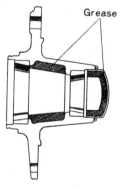

Fig. 11.5. Front hub grease packing diagram

Fig. 11.6. Tightening front hub nut with a torque wrench

3 Shock absorbers - removal, testing and refitting

1   The front shock absorber mountings comprise an eye and flexible bush at the lower end, and a threaded rod at the upper end.
2   The upper and lower mountings of the rear shock absorbers are of eye and flexible bush type (photo).
3   Removal of both types of shock absorber is simply a matter of removing the attachment nuts or bolts and withdrawing the unit. Do not renew a shock absorber with the vehicle jacked-up and the road-wheel hanging free. If working clearance is required always jack-up the car under the spring 'U' bolt plates in order to keep the springs under compression.
4   To test a shock absorber, grip the lower mounting in a vice with the unit in a vertical position. Extend and contract the shock absorber to the full extent of its travel about ten times. There should be a definite resistance in both directions, otherwise renew the unit. Any sign of oil leakage around the operating rod seal will also indicate the need for renewal as the units are not repairable.
5   Refitting is a reversal of removal but tighten the retaining nuts and bolts to the correct torque.

3.2 Rear shock absorber upper mounting

4 Upper and lower suspension arm balljoints - testing and renewal

1   To test for wear in these components, jack-up the front suspension on one side by placing a jack under the coil spring pan.
2   Grip the roadwheel and move it vertically up and down, and then in and out in a horizontal direction.
3   Assuming the wheel bearings are correctly adjusted, see Section 5, there should only be movement in any direction not exceeding the limits specified.
4   Where excessive wear is found, the balljoints must be renewed.
5   The use of a balljoint separator will now be essential as there is no room to attempt to jar them apart using the wedge or hammer method.
6   Unscrew and almost remove the lower balljoint stud nut and, using the separator tool, detach the balljoint taper stud from the stub axle carrier. Remove the balljoint from the lower wishbone by removing the three securing bolts.
7   Removal of the upper balljoint is carried out in a similar way but do not strain the brake flexible hose once it is detached by allowing the weight of the hub to hang upon it.
8   Refitting the upper and lower balljoints is a reversal of removal.
9   Tighten the balljoint taper stud nuts to the specified tightening torque.
10 Remove the grease plug from the balljoint; screw in a nipple and apply the grease gun (photo).

4.10 Removing an upper swivel joint grease plug

5 Front hubs - servicing and adjustment

1   Jack-up the front of the vehicle and remove the roadwheel. Refer to Chapter 9 for exploded drawings of front hubs.
2   *On vehicles with front drum brakes, built up to 1976,* tap off the grease cap, extract the split pin and unscrew and remove the nut, retainer and thrust washer.
3   Pull the hub/drum assembly forward an inch or two and then push it back. This will expose the hub outer bearing which can then be extracted. Now pull the hub/drum assembly straight off the stub axle. On later Hi-Lux vehicles with 12R engine, the brake drum is detachable (one screw).
4   *On vehicles with front disc brakes,* removal of the hub/disc assembly is similar to the procedure just described for hub/drum assemblies except that the caliper unit must first be unbolted and tied up out of the way. With these calipers (Girling type) the rigid brake line will have to be disconnected from the caliper — see Chapter 9.
5   Wash out all old grease from the bearings and hub interior, taking care not to damage the oil seal. Check the bearings and tracks for wear, damage or scoring.
6   If they are in good condition, repack the inside of the hub with grease.

7   If there is evidence of grease seepage onto the discs, drift out the old seal and tap in a new one using a tubular drift.

8   If either the inner or outer bearings require renewal, drift out the tracks with a brass drift and press in the new ones. Where both front hubs are being serviced at the same time, do not mix the bearing components as the race and the track are matched in production.

9   The disc or drum should not be removed from the hub assembly unless they are to be renewed or re-faced as described in Chapter 9.

10 Reassembly is a reversal of dismantling but the bearings must be adjusted in the following way.

11 *On early Hi-Ace or Hi-Lux vehicles* with finned brake drums, tighten the hub nut (while rotating the hub in the forward direction of vehicle travel) to a torque wrench setting of 36 lb ft (49 Nm). Now unscrew the nut between 1/6th and 1/3rd of a turn and insert a new split pin. Check the hub end-float which should be non-existent or only just perceptible.

12 *On later Hi-Ace or Hi-Lux vehicles* with smooth (non-finned) brake drums or discs, tighten the hub nut to a torque wrench setting of 30 lb f ft (41 Nm), at the same time turning the hub in the forward direction of vehicle travel. Loosen the nut and retighten it using only the fingers to tighten the socket on the nut. Now attach a spring balance to one of the roadwheel studs and check the starting torque. This should be between 1½ and 4 lbs. Adjust the nut if necessary to obtain this reading on the spring balance.

13 When adjustment is correct, fit the nut retainer and a new split pin.

14 Fill the grease cap 1/3rd full of grease and knock it into position.

15 On vehicles with front calipers, reconnect the hydraulic line and bleed the hydraulic system as described in Chapter 9.

16 Refit the roadwheel and lower the vehicle.

---

6   Stub axle carrier - removal and refitting

1   Jack-up the front of the vehicle supporting it securely under the main crossmember.

2   Place a second jack under the lower wishbone of the suspension and raise the jack until the rubber bump stop separates from the crossmember.

3   Remove the hub/drum or hub/disc assembly as described in the preceding Section.

4   Unbolt the shield (disc brakes) or the backplate (drum brakes). In the case of the latter, tie it up out of the way to avoid straining the hydraulic flexible hose.

5   Using a balljoint separator, disconnect the trackrod-end from the steering arm of the stub axle carrier.

6   Separate the suspension wishbone upper and lower balljoints and withdraw the stub axle carrier.

7   Refitting is a reversal of removal.

Fig. 11.8. Front suspension lower arm pivot shaft bush and dust excluder

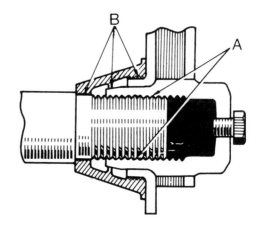

Fig. 11.9. Grease application points on front suspension lower arm pivot shaft and bush

Fig. 11.7. Checking front hub bearing pre-load

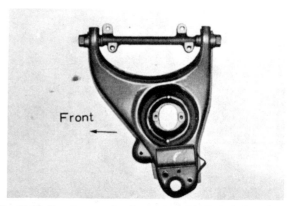

Fig. 11.10. Front suspension lower arm with pivot shaft correctly installed

7 Suspension lower arm and coil spring - removal and refitting

1 Jack-up the front of the vehicle and support it securely under the front crossmember. Remove the roadwheel.
2 Remove the shock absorber and substitute a spring compressor. This can easily be made from a length of studding, two cross plates and nuts.
3 Compress the road spring until the bottom coil is no longer in contact with the spring pan of the lower arm. Disconnect the stabiliser bar from the lower arm.
4 Disconnect the lower balljoint and lower the suspension arm.
5 Remove the coil spring after releasing the compressor.
6 Unbolt the lower suspension arm pivot from the crossmember and remove the suspension arm.
7 If the pivot bushes are worn, unscrew them and renew them.
8 Screw in the new bushes to a torque of 160 lb f ft (218 Nm), making sure that the pivot shaft is centralised by screwing in the bushes equally from both ends.
9 Commence reassembly by bolting the pivot shaft to the crossmember.
10 Install the coil spring so that it fits correctly in the upper insulator and then compress it using the spring compressor.
11 Jack-up the lower arm and connect the balljoint to the stub axle carrier.
12 Connect the stabiliser to the lower arm and do not over-tighten the nut or locknut.
13 Remove the coil spring compressor making sure that the bottom coil locates correctly in the lower arm pan.
14 Fit the shock absorber and roadwheel and lower the vehicle to the ground. Grease the bushes by removing the plugs and screwing in a grease nipple.
15 Check the front wheel alignment as described in Section 23.

8 Suspension upper arm - removal and refitting

1 Jack-up the front of the vehicle and support it securely, then place a second jack or axle stand under the suspension lower arm.
2 Disconnect the shock absorber.
3 Fit a coil spring compressor and compress the spring.
4 Extract the bolts which secure the upper balljoint to the upper suspension arm.
5 Unscrew the suspension upper arm pivot bolts and extract the steering angle adjusting shims which are located between the pivot shaft and the bodyframe. Mark and record from which side the shims are removed so that they can be refitted in their original locations.
6 Remove the suspension upper arm.
7 If the pivot bushes are worn, unscrew them and extract the dust seals.
8 Install the new pivot shaft bushes making sure that the pivot bolt holes are offset as shown in Fig. 11.13.
9 Apply grease as shown in Fig. 11.9 and tighten the bushes evenly and equally to the torque wrench setting given in the Specifications Section at the beginning of the Chapter.
10 Refitting is a reversal of removal, but make sure that the shims are returned to their original positions and all bolts are tightened to the specified torque.
11 Grease the pivot bushes by removing the plugs and screwing in nipples. Refit the plugs on completion (photo).
12 Check the front wheel alignment and steering angles as described in Section 23.

Fig. 11.12. Removing a front suspension upper arm

8.11 Removing a suspension arm grease plug

Fig. 11.11. Removing a shim from behind a front suspension upper arm mounting bolt

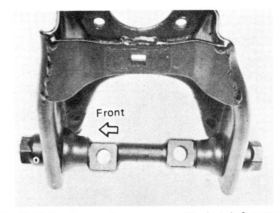

Fig. 11.13. Front suspension upper arm with pivot shaft correctly installed

Fig. 11.14. Unscrewing a rear spring 'U' bolt nut

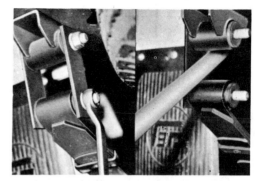

Fig. 11.15. Disconnecting rear spring shackle. Note lever used to apply tension once shackle plate is removed

Fig. 11.16. Disconnecting rear spring hanger

Fig. 11.17. Installing rear spring flexible bushes

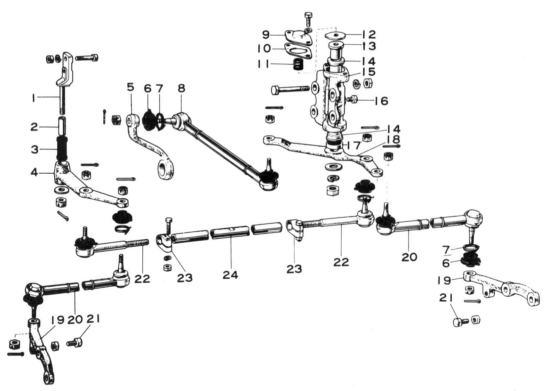

Fig. 11.18. Steering linkage (Hi-Ace, early)

1 Idler pivot	7 Retaining ring	13 Centre arm shaft	19 Steering arm (attached to stub axle carrier)
2 Sleeve	8 Drag link	14 Bush	20 Track rod
3 Flexible bush	9 Cap	15 Centre arm	21 Lock stop bolt
4 Idler arm	10 Gasket	16 Grease plug	22 Track rod end
5 Steering drop arm	11 Spring	17 Oil seal	23 Clamp
6 Dust excluder	12 Spacer	18 Centre arm	24 Relay rod

11.4 Rear spring to axle attachment (Hi-Lux)

9 Front anti-roll bar - removal and refitting

1   Disconnect the end connecting links from the suspension lower arms.
2   Unbolt and remove the clamps which hold the anti-roll bar to the bodyframe. Renew any of the flexible bushes which are perished or worn.
3   Refit by reversing the removal operations and then tighten all bolts to the specified torque.

10 Front crossmember - removal and installation

1   On all Hi-Lux and early Hi-Ace vehicles, the front crossmember can be removed complete with the suspension, if desired. This operation should not, however, be undertaken unless the necessary lifting gear and jacks are available.

Hi-Lux vehicles
2   Raise the front end of the vehicle and support it securely on axle stands placed under the chassis side frame members.
3   Remove both front roadwheels.
4   Using a balljoint separator, disconnect both track rod ends from the steering arms on the stub axle carriers.
5   Disconnect both ends of the anti-roll bar from the suspension lower arms.
6   Remove the splash shield from below the engine.
7   Disconnect the front brake flexible hoses from the rigid lines and plug them to prevent loss of fluid.
8   Disconnect the engine front mountings from the crossmember.
9   Disconnect the brake line from the clip on the crossmember.
10 Connect a hoist to the engine and raise the engine just enough to take its weight off the crossmember.
11 Place a jack, preferably of the trolley type, underneath the crossmember and then unscrew and remove the bolts which secure the crossmember to the chassis frame.
12 Lower the jack and withdraw the crossmember complete with suspension components from below and from the front of the vehicle. Take care that the transverse brake line is not damaged during this operation.
13 Installation is a reversal of removal but tighten the crossmember bolts to the specified torque before lowering the weight of the engine onto its mountings.
14 When refitting is complete, bleed the brake hydraulic system as described in Chapter 9.
15 Refit the roadwheels and lower the vehicle to the ground.

Hi-Ace vehicles
16 The operations are similar to those described in earlier paragraphs of this Section except that the cooling system should be drained and the radiator removed.
17 As it is difficult to support the weight of the engine with a hoist on this forward control type vehicle, use a second jack and wooden block under the sump instead.
18 On later Hi-Ace vehicles the front crossmember is rivetted in position and cannot be removed.

11 Rear road spring - removal, servicing and installation

1   Jack-up the rear of the vehicle and support the bodyframe on axle stands and the differential casing on a jack.
2   Remove the roadwheel and disconnect the shock absorber lower mounting.
3   On vehicles where the axle casing is secured below the roadspring, lower the jack until all tension is removed from the spring.
4   On vehicles where the axle casing is secured above the roadspring, raise the jack until the weight of the rear axle is removed from the spring (photo).
5   Disconnect the parking brake cable guides, according to type, from the side of the roadspring.
6   Unscrew and remove the nuts and spring 'U' bolts.
7   Take great care from now on not to move the rear axle excessively, otherwise the flexible brake hose or parking brake cables may be strained or in extreme cases, the front end of the propeller shaft may become displaced from the rear end of the transmission.
8   Disconnect the spring front shackle by extracting the pivot bolt.
9   Disconnect the spring rear hanger and then lift the roadspring from the vehicle.
10 Scrub the spring clean in a paraffin bath using a wire brush. Examine each leaf edge throughout its length for cracks. If a crack or broken leaf is found, do not attempt to dismantle it by removing the centre bolt or rivetted clips but, either exchange it for a new unit, or have it professionally repaired by the insertion of a new leaf.
11 The spring eye bushes are of the split rubber type and should be renewed if perished or worn; no press is required, but a little hydraulic brake fluid will assist in fitting them into the spring eyes.
12 Refitting should commence by connecting the front shackle followed by the rear hanger bolt; tighten the nuts only finger tight. Note that the shorter length of the spring (eye to centre bolt) is located to the front of the rear axle.
13 Fit the insulating pads and retainers to the spring and then raise or lower the jack under the rear axle ensuring that the spring centre bolt engages in its locating hole in the rear axle mounting plate.
14 Fit the 'U' bolts and their nuts finger tight.
15 Reconnect the handbrake cable clamps and then fit the roadwheels and remove the support stands and lower the vehicle to the ground.
16 Bounce the vehicle up and down several times to settle the suspension and then tighten the 'U' bolt nuts to the specified torque settings.

12 Steering linkage - removal and installation

1   The steering linkage on all models is similar although the design of some components differs in detail.
2   Before dismantling the steering linkage it is essential to obtain a balljoint separator. This may be of screw type or consist of a pair of wedges. It is possible to jar the balljoint taper pin free from its eye by striking opposite sides of the eye simultaneously with two club hammers, but the available space to do this is very restricted and the use of a proper extractor is recommended.
3   Unscrew and remove the nut which secures the drop arm to the shaft of the steering gear (photo).
4   Using a suitable extractor, draw the drop arm from the splined shaft.
5   Unbolt the idler arm bracket (and centre arm bracket - Hi-Ace) (photo).
6   Using a balljoint separator, disconnect the trackrod ends from the steering arms of the stub axle carriers.
7   Withdraw the complete steering linkage.
8   The individual components of the linkage may be separated using the balljoint separator and loosening the trackrod clamps.

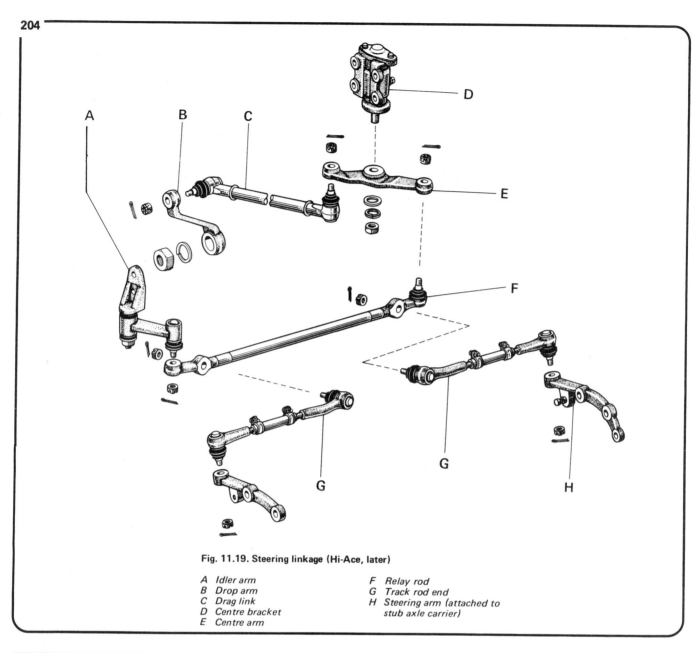

Fig. 11.19. Steering linkage (Hi-Ace, later)

A Idler arm
B Drop arm
C Drag link
D Centre bracket
E Centre arm

F Relay rod
G Track rod end
H Steering arm (attached to
   stub axle carrier)

12.3 Steering drop arm and linkage (Hi-Lux)

12.5 Steering idler arm and linkage (Hi-Lux)

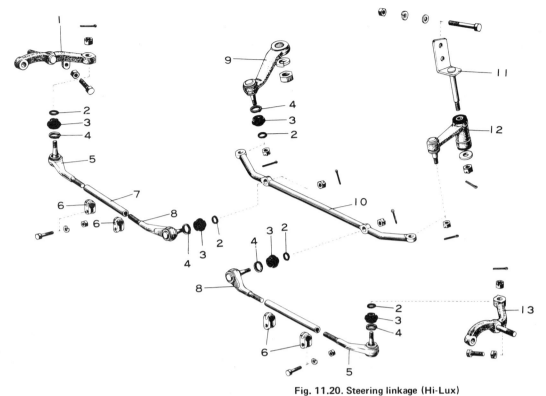

Fig. 11.20. Steering linkage (Hi-Lux)

1	Steering arm (attached to stub axle carrier)	7	Track rod
2	Retaining ring	8	Track rod end
3	Dust excluder	9	Drop arm
4	Retaining ring	10	Relay rod
5	Track rod end	11	Idler pivot
6	Clamp	12	Idler assembly
		13	**Steering arm**

Fig. 11.21. Idler arm setting angle (before tightening nut) on Hi-Ace

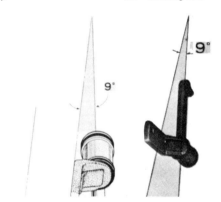

Fig. 11.22. Idler arm setting angle (before tightening nut) on Hi-Lux up to 1975. Later vehicles should be set to 7°

9 Check each balljoint for slackness or excessive stiffness, also for split or deteriorated rubber dust excluders and renew as necessary. Check the idler arm bushes.

10 When fitting a balljoint dust cover, pack the interior with multi-purpose grease.

11 Reassembly is a reversal of dismantling but observe the following points:

12 Fit the idler arm to the support so that it conforms to the specified setting angle, according to date of vehicle manufacture, before tightening the idler nut.

13 Screw the trackrod ends into their tubes by an equal amount and set the openings in the clamps in line with the slots in the tubes.

14 Refit the drop arm so that the mating marks are in alignment.

15 When refitting of the linkage is complete, check and adjust the front wheel alignment as described in Section 23.

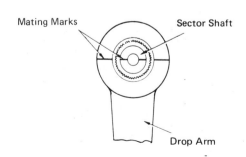

Fig. 11.23. Drop arm and sector shaft mating marks

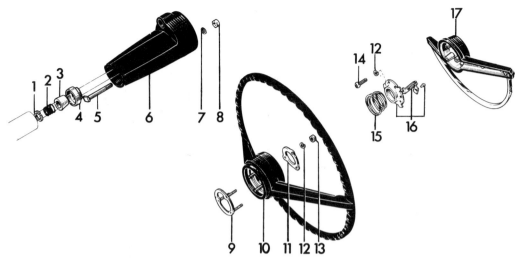

Fig. 11.24. Steering wheel and contact ring housing (Hi-Ace, early)

1 Circlip	10 Steering wheel
2 Spring	11 Horn lead spring seat
3 Thrust collar	12 Lockwasher
4 Bearing	13 Locknut
5 Retaining bolt	14 Screw
6 Contact ring housing	15 Horn ring spring
7 Lockwasher	16 Horn button stop and
8 Nut	contact plate
9 Horn button contact seat	17 Horn ring assembly

Fig. 11.26. Alignment marks made at lower end of steering column

13 Steering wheel - removal and refitting

1   Access to the steering wheel securing nut is obtained by various means according to the particular type of horn button and steering wheel design. Disconnect the battery negative lead.
2   On some early models, depress the central horn button and turn it anticlockwise.
3   With other types, disconnect the wiring harness at the connector plug under the instrument panel and then, using a screwdriver, prise off the pad in an upward direction.
4   On later models, the horn pad is secured with screws which are accessible from the rear of the steering wheel spokes.
5   Once the pad or horn button has been removed, unscrew the securing nut and then make alignment marks on the end of the shaft and the steering wheel so that the wheel can be refitted in exactly the same position. Set the roadwheels in the straight-ahead position.
6   Remove the steering wheel by tapping it gently at the rear with the palms of the hands. If it does not come off, on no account attempt to jar it off or to hammer the end of the shaft as damage to the column will result. If the wheel is stuck, use an extractor with centre screw, taking care to protect the surfaces of the steering wheel and hub.
7   Installation of the steering wheel is a reversal of removal but make sure that the mating marks made before removal, are in alignment.
8   Tighten the steering wheel securing nut to the specified torque wrench setting.

14 Steering column (Hi-Ace, early) - removal and refitting

1   With this type of steering assembly, only the contact ring housing can be removed from the upper end of the steering column, the remainder of the column is removed when the steering gear has been withdrawn from the vehicle as described in Section 18.

2   Disconnect the lead from the battery negative terminal and then disconnect the steering column wiring harness at the connectors below the instrument panel.
3   Depress the centre of the horn button and turn the horn ring in an anticlockwise direction. Remove the ring and spring.
4   Remove the steering wheel as described in Section 13.
5   Extract the securing screws and remove the direction indicator switch.
6   Extract the 'E' ring and washer from the end of the control bracket upper shaft.
7   Release the two bolts which retain the contact ring housing to the steering column and then pull the housing from the end of the column.
8   If the shaft bearing within the contact ring housing is worn, it may be driven out and a new one installed. Apply grease liberally to the bearing before refitting the contact ring housing which is a reversal of the removal operations.

15 Steering column (Hi-Ace, later) - removal and refitting

1   Disconnect the lead from the battery negative terminal and then disconnect the steering column wiring harness at the connector plugs below the instrument panel.
2   Remove the steering wheel (Section 13).
3   Remove the shrouds from the upper end of the steering column.
4   Remove the direction indicator switch and then extract the circlip just above the upper bracket assembly.
5   Remove the 'E' clip and washers, release the three bracket securing bolts and withdraw the upper bracket from the steering column.
6   Working at the lower end of the steering column, use quick drying paint to make alignment marks on the wormshaft, flexible coupling and steering shaft.
7   Disconnect the gearshift control shaft lever and control select lever then extract the clamp bolt.

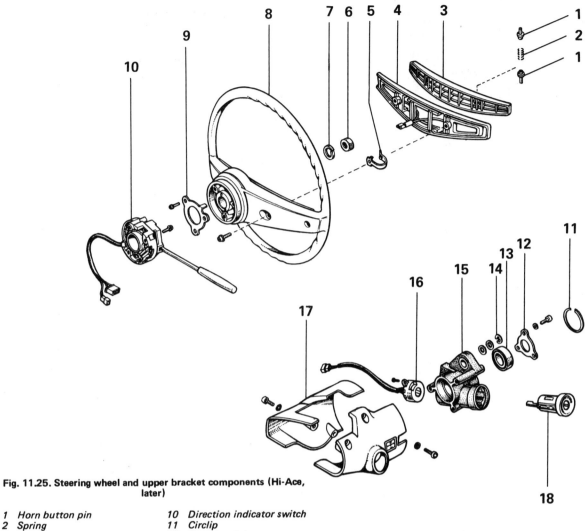

Fig. 11.25. Steering wheel and upper bracket components (Hi-Ace, later)

1 Horn button pin
2 Spring
3 Cover
4 Horn bar
5 Horn contact spring
6 Steering wheel nut
7 Spring washer
8 Steering wheel
9 Horn lead spring seat
10 Direction indicator switch
11 Circlip
12 Bearing retainer
13 Bearing
14 'E' clip
15 Upper bracket
16 Ignition switch
17 Shroud
18 Cylinder lock

8   Unscrew and remove the bolts which secure the steering column blanking plate in the floor pan.

9   Unbolt and remove the steering column upper clamp and withdraw the column and the gearshift control shaft into the vehicle interior.

10 The upper bracket can be dismantled by withdrawing the ignition switch (one screw) and depressing the lock plunger and withdrawing the lock cylinder. Remove the bearing retainer and drive out the bearing if it requires renewal.

11 The steering column can be dismantled by first removing the column with lower dust seal and then pulling out the shaft. Unbolt the flexible coupling.

12 Reassembly and refitting are reversals of removal and dismantling, but observe the following details.

13 When assembling the upper bracket, pack the upper bearing with grease and drive the bearing into position until its upper face is flush with the bracket.

14 Depress the lock tongue and set the grooves in alignment as shown in Fig. 11.33. Hold this setting and install the ignition lock cylinder with its key turned to the ACC position.

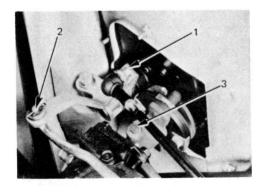

Fig. 11.27. Gearshift control rod disconnection (Hi-Ace, later)

1 Shift lever
2 Select lever
3 Coupling pinch bolt

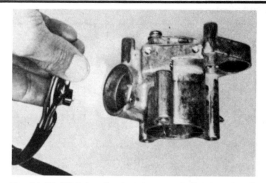

Fig. 11.28. Withdrawing ignition switch (Hi-Ace, later)

Fig. 11.29. Withdrawing ignition cylinder lock (Hi-Ace, later)

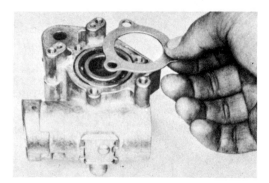

Fig. 11.30. Removing bearing retainer from upper bracket (Hi-Ace, later)

Fig. 11.31. Unbolting flexible coupling (Hi-Ace, later)

Fig. 11.32. Steering column components (Hi-Ace, later)

1 Circlip
2 Steering shaft
3 Flexible coupling
4 Column tube

5 Lower dust seal
6 Cover plate
7 Gasket

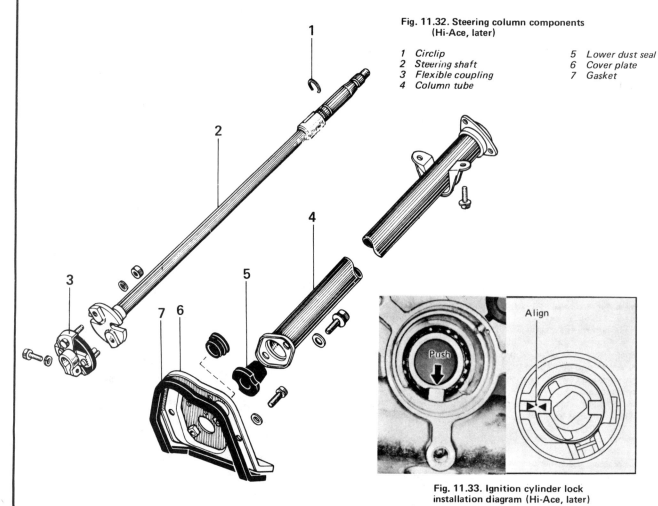

Fig. 11.33. Ignition cylinder lock installation diagram (Hi-Ace, later)

16 Steering column (Hi-Lux early) - removal and refitting

1 *On right-hand drive vehicles,* follow the operations described in Section 14.
2 *On left-hand drive vehicles,* disconnect the lead from the battery negative terminal and then disconnect the steering column wiring harness at the connector plugs.
3 Remove the steering wheel (Section 13) and the direction indicator switch.
4 Remove the lower shroud from the upper end of the steering column.
5 Remove the steering column upper clamp bracket, pull the column down slightly and remove the upper shroud.
6 If the shaft bearing is worn, extract the circlip and draw off the bearing with a puller.
7 Make alignment marks on the flexible coupling and wormshaft at the lower end of the steering column. Extract the flexible coupling pinch bolt and then unbolt the steering column cover plate from the floor pan.
8 Unbolt the steering column bracket and withdraw the assembly towards the interior of the vehicle.
9 For reassembly and refitting details on right-hand drive vehicles, refer to Section 14, paragraph 8.
10 Reassembly and refitting of the steering column on left-hand drive vehicles is also a reversal of dismantling and removal, but use a piece of tubing to drive on the new shaft bearing and apply grease to it before installing the direction indicator switch and other components.

17 Steering column (Hi-Lux, later) - removal and refitting

1 The steering column assembly (including gearshift control where fitted) and steering wheel can be removed complete. Alternatively, the steering wheel may be removed first, as described in Section 13.
2 To remove the column complete, disconnect the lead from the battery negative terminal and disconnect the steering column wiring harness at the connector plugs.
3 Using quick drying paint, make alignment marks on the flexible coupling and wormshaft at the lower end of the steering column.
4 Extract the coupling pinch bolt.
5 Disconnect the gearshift select control lever (steering column gearshift) from the shaft control lever.
6 Extract the bolts from the column cover plate on the floor pan.
7 Unbolt the steering column clamp bracket and withdraw the complete column assembly into the vehicle interior.
8 To dismantle the steering column, remove the steering wheel (Section 13) and while depressing the retaining plunger, withdraw the ignition cylinder lock (key in ACC position).
9 Remove the steering column shrouds and direction indicator switch and the bearing circlip.
10 Pull off the upper bracket and bearing. Refer to Section 15, paragraphs 12, 13 and 14 for reassembly of the upper bracket and bearing.

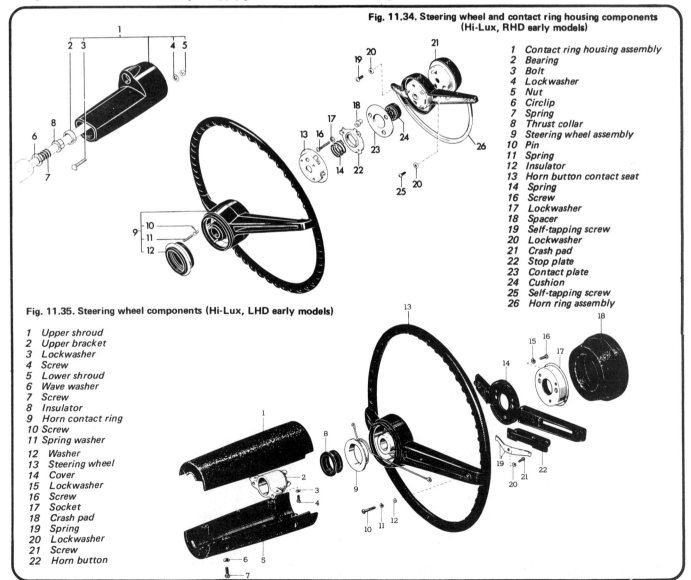

Fig. 11.34. Steering wheel and contact ring housing components (Hi-Lux, RHD early models)

1   Contact ring housing assembly
2   Bearing
3   Bolt
4   Lockwasher
5   Nut
6   Circlip
7   Spring
8   Thrust collar
9   Steering wheel assembly
10 Pin
11 Spring
12 Insulator
13 Horn button contact seat
14 Spring
16 Screw
17 Lockwasher
18 Spacer
19 Self-tapping screw
20 Lockwasher
21 Crash pad
22 Stop plate
23 Contact plate
24 Cushion
25 Self-tapping screw
26 Horn ring assembly

Fig. 11.35. Steering wheel components (Hi-Lux, LHD early models)

1   Upper shroud
2   Upper bracket
3   Lockwasher
4   Screw
5   Lower shroud
6   Wave washer
7   Screw
8   Insulator
9   Horn contact ring
10 Screw
11 Spring washer
12 Washer
13 Steering wheel
14 Cover
15 Lockwasher
16 Screw
17 Socket
18 Crash pad
19 Spring
20 Lockwasher
21 Screw
22 Horn button

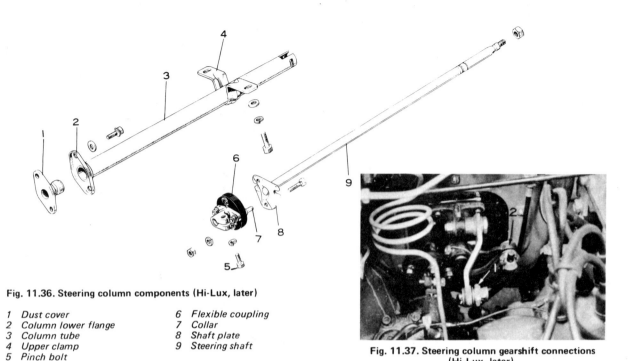

Fig. 11.36. Steering column components (Hi-Lux, later)

1 Dust cover
2 Column lower flange
3 Column tube
4 Upper clamp
5 Pinch bolt
6 Flexible coupling
7 Collar
8 Shaft plate
9 Steering shaft

Fig. 11.37. Steering column gearshift connections
(Hi-Lux, later)

1 Select lever   2 Shift lever

18 Steering gear (Hi-Ace, early) - removal, overhaul and refitting

1 Remove the steering wheel (Section 13) and the contact ring housing (Section 14).
2 Disconnect the gearshift control rods (at the bottom of the steering column) from the shift and select levers.
3 Remove the nut and washer from the steering drop arm and, using a suitable puller, remove the drop arm from the sector shaft.
4 Disconnect the steering column support bracket and stay.
5 Unbolt the column cover plate from the floor pan.
6 Unscrew and remove the steering gearbox mounting bolts and withdraw the complete assembly into the vehicle interior.
7 Clean away external dirt and then withdraw the bearing thrust collar and spring from the steering mainshaft.
8 Remove the gearshift control shaft lower bracket clamp bolt and washer and slide out the steering column tube together with the gearshift control shiftlever shaft from the steering box.
9 Drain the oil from the steering box and secure the box in the jaws of a vice.
10 Remove the sector shaft end cover and gasket.
11 Pull the sector shaft complete with adjusting plate and shims from the steering box. Lift off the end cover and gasket.
12 Withdraw the steering mainshaft and bearings from the steering box.
13 Clean all components and examine for wear or damage. Renew as necessary. If the worm bearings or sector ball bearings must be renewed, it is recommended that this work is left to your dealer as special extractors are needed and the sector roller shaft nut must be welded in position when it is refitted.
14 Obtain a new sector shaft oil seal, but do not fit it until the steering internal adjustments have been carried out.
15 Commence reassembly by installing the mainshaft and bearings into the steering box and then fit the end cover and gasket. Tighten the cover bolts to a torque of 14 lb f ft (19 Nm). Check the shaft for smooth rotation. If it is stiff, fit a thicker end cover gasket.
16 Fit the original spacer and shims onto the sector shaft and install the shaft into the steering box.
17 Exert hand pressure on the sector shaft towards the steering worm and check the backlash between the worm and sector roller. Change the adjuster shim pack, if necessary, to provide zero or imperceptible backlash.
18 Install the sector shaft end cover and gasket.
19 Temporarily install the steering wheel to the steering mainshaft and screw the adjusting screw into the end cover so that all backlash is

removed when the steering wheel is turned to the centre position (wheels straight ahead). Lock the adjuster screw.
20 Now check the sector shaft end-float. Ideally, the steering drop arm should be removed from the steering linkage and temporarily attached to the splines of the sector shaft. In any event, turn the steering mainshaft to full right lock and using a dial gauge, check and record the sector shaft end-float.
21 Now repeat the operations on full left lock. Both measurements should be the same. If they are not, adjust by removing or installing shims behind the steering worm rear bearing cup. Shims are available in three different thicknesses.
22 When the adjustment is correct, remove the sector shaft end cover and the sector shaft.
23 Assemble the steering mainshaft and steering box end cover (with gasket) onto the steering box. Tighten the bolts to 14 lb/ft (19 Nm).
24 With the steering wheel again temporarily fitted to the end of the mainshaft, attach a spring balance to one of the steering wheel spokes and check the pull required to turn the wheel. This should be between 1/3lb and 1/2 lb (0.15 and 0.25 kg) and indicates the bearing pre-load. Adjust if necessary by altering the thickness of the end cover gasket.
25 Now re-adjust the worm to sector roller backlash.
26 Assemble the sector shaft with adjusting plate (tapered end towards sector shaft flange) and shims into the steering gear. Fit the sector shaft end cover and gasket.
27 Screw in the adjuster screw into the end cover until any end-float is eliminated with the worm and roller in the central position. The backlash, measured at the rim of the steering wheel should be between 0.2 and 1.0 in (5.0 and 25.0 mm). If necessary, change the adjusting shims for ones of different thicknesses.
28 Turn the steering wheel from one lock to the other and check for smooth operation. Tighten the end cover adjuster bolt locknut.
29 With all adjustments complete, install the new sector shaft oil seal.
30 Install the steering column tube and gearshift control shaft.
31 Align the groove in the column tube with the slot in the steering box, install the washer and tighten the gearshift control shaft lower bracket clamp bolt.
32 Install the spring and bearing thrust collar onto the upper end of the steering mainshaft.
33 Refill the steering box with the correct quantity of oil.
34 Installation is a reversal of removal, but make sure that the mating marks on the end of the sector shaft and the steering drop arm are in alignment.

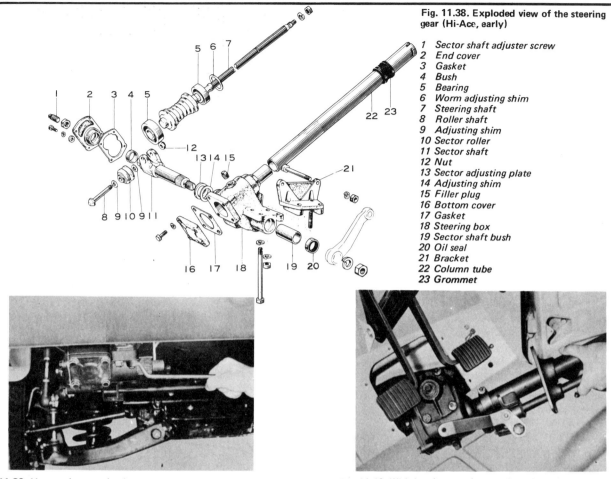

Fig. 11.38. Exploded view of the steering gear (Hi-Ace, early)

1 Sector shaft adjuster screw
2 End cover
3 Gasket
4 Bush
5 Bearing
6 Worm adjusting shim
7 Steering shaft
8 Roller shaft
9 Adjusting shim
10 Sector roller
11 Sector shaft
12 Nut
13 Sector adjusting plate
14 Adjusting shim
15 Filler plug
16 Bottom cover
17 Gasket
18 Steering box
19 Sector shaft bush
20 Oil seal
21 Bracket
22 Column tube
23 Grommet

Fig. 11.39. Unscrewing steering box mounting bolts (Hi-Ace, early)

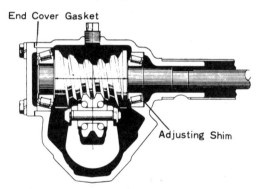

Fig. 11.40. Withdrawing steering gear into driving compartment (Hi-Ace, early)

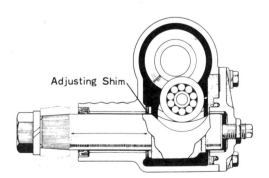

Fig. 11.41. Withdrawing sector shaft from steering box

Fig. 11.42. Steering worm and sector centred (Hi-Ace, early)

Fig. 11.43. Cut away view of worm and sector and adjusting screw (Hi-Ace, early)

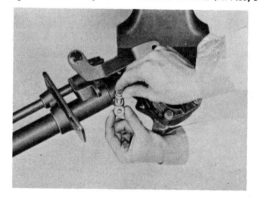

Fig. 11.44. Assembling gearshift control shaft lower bracket (Hi-Ace, early)

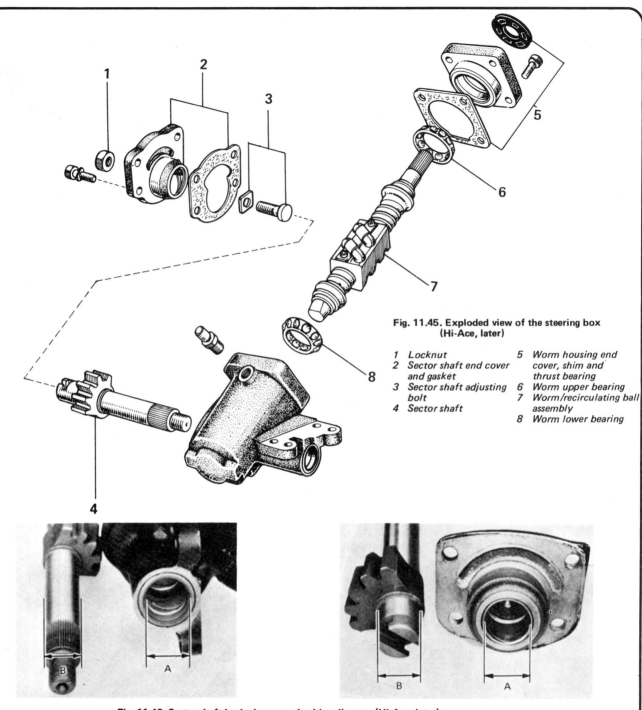

Fig. 11.45. Exploded view of the steering box
(Hi-Ace, later)

1 Locknut
2 Sector shaft end cover
   and gasket
3 Sector shaft adjusting
   bolt
4 Sector shaft
5 Worm housing end
   cover, shim and
   thrust bearing
6 Worm upper bearing
7 Worm/recirculating ball
   assembly
8 Worm lower bearing

Fig. 11.46. Sector shaft bush clearance checking diagram (Hi-Ace, later)
A less B equals running clearance (standard) 0.0004 to 0.0024 in - 0.01 to 0.06 mm.
Maximum wear limit 0.004 in (0.1 mm)

Fig. 11.47. Checking wormshaft bearing pre-load (Hi-Ace, later)

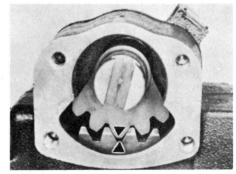

Fig. 11.48. Worm and sector centred (Hi-Ace, later)

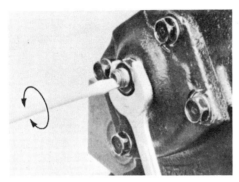

Fig. 11.49. Turning sector shaft adjuster screw (Hi-Ace, later)

19 Steering gear (Hi-Ace, later) - removal, overhaul and refitting

1 Using quick drying paint, make alignment marks on the flexible coupling and steering wormshaft.
2 Remove the nut and washer which retains the steering drop arm to the sector shaft and, using a suitable extractor, draw off the drop arm. Extract the coupling pinch bolt, unscrew and remove the steering box mounting bolts and withdraw the steering box from the vehicle. If the coupling jaws are tight on the wormshaft, expand them slightly with a wedge or screwdriver.
3 Extract the bolts from the sector shaft end cover, release the locknut and screw in the adjuster screw and remove the cover.
4 Unbolt and remove the worm end cover, retaining the shims for use at reassembly.
5 Withdraw the worm assembly and identify the bearings with a piece of masking tape so that they can be returned to their original positions.
6 If the worm assembly is worn or damaged, do not dismantle it but renew it complete.
7 Clean out all oil from the steering box interior and then carry out the following checks.
8 Measure the clearance between the sector shaft adjuster screw and the recess in the sector shaft as shown in Fig. 11.51. Change the screw thrust washer if the clearance exceeds 0.002 in (0.05 mm).
9 If the worm bearings are to be renewed, extract the outer tracks from the steering box using an extractor.
10 Renew the sector shaft oil seal, but if the sector shaft bushes are worn in the steering box, leave their renewal to your Toyota dealer as they will require honing after fitting, to provide the specified running clearance.
11 Commence reassembly by installing the wormshaft but without the sector shaft. Refit the worm housing end cover and the original shims. Tighten the cover bolts to a torque wrench setting of 25 lb f ft (34 Nm).
12 Wind a cord round the splines of the wormshaft and attach it to a spring balance. The force required to turn the wormshaft should be between 8 and 14 lbs (3.5 and 6.3 kg) shown on the spring balance. This is the correct wormshaft bearing pre-load. Adjust the thickness of the shim pack if necessary to bring the bearing pre-load within that specified.
13 Centre the worm nut and install the sector shaft.
14 Install the sector shaft end cover and gasket by unscrewing the adjuster screw through it. Fit the cover bolts.
15 Centre the worm and then wind a cord round the splines of the wormshaft again and attach it to a spring balance. The force required this time (with sector shaft installed) to just make the wormshaft start turning should be between 18 and 24 lb (8 and 10.8 kg). This is the correct wormshaft bearing pre-load (with sector shaft fitted), and, if necessary, adjust by means of the end cover adjuster screw.
16 Finally turn the wormshaft through 100° in a clockwise direction and measure the backlash; then turn it through 100° in an anticlockwise direction and again measure the backlash. Ideally, the backlash should be zero or not exceeding 0.0078 in (0.20 mm).
17 Installation of the steering gear is a reversal of removal, but make sure that the marks on the flexible coupling and shaft are in alignment when the roadwheels are in the straight-ahead position. Align the mating marks on the steering drop arm and sector shafr and finally tighten all bolts to the specified torque wrench settings.
18 Fill the steering box with oil.

20 Steering gear (Hi-Lux, early right-hand drive) - removal, overhaul and refitting

1 Remove the steering wheel (Section 13) and the contact ring housing (Section 14 as for the Hi-Ace, early).
2 Unbolt and remove the steering column cover plate from the floor pan.
3 Unbolt the column upper clamp.
4 Disconnect the gearshift control column from the select lever at the base of the column.
5 Remove the gearshift control lower bracket and connecting rod swivel.
6 Remove the gearshift control shaft and then withdraw the steering column tube.
7 Remove the nut from the steering drop arm and pull off the arm from the sector shaft using a suitable puller.
8 Unscrew and remove the steering box mounting bolts and withdraw the steering gear into the vehicle interior.
9 Clean away all external dirt and drain the oil.
10 Secure the steering box in a vice and remove the sector shaft end cover bolts. Release the adjuster screw locknut and then remove the end cover by unscrewing it off the adjuster screw.
11 Withdraw the sector shaft from the steering box.
12 Release the worm bearing adjusting screw locknut and unscrew and remove the adjusting screw. A special spanner, having two pins to engage in the cut-outs in the nut, will be required for this task.
13 Withdraw the mainshaft.
14 Clean all components and examine for wear or damage. If the worm bearings or sector shaft bushes must be renewed, it is recommended that this work is left to your Toyota dealer, as special extractors are needed and the sector roller shaft nut must be welded in position when it is refitted.
15 Commence reassembly by installing the steering mainshaft into the steering gear housing.
16 Fit the worm bearing adjuster screw and locknut.
17 Adjust the worm bearing pre-load by winding a cord round the steering mainshaft and attaching the cord to a spring balance. The force required to turn the shaft should be between 3 and 7 lbs (1.4 and 3.2 kg), as indicated on the spring balance. Turn the adjuster screw as necessary to achieve this turning torque and then lock it with the locknut.
18 Using a feeler blade, check the end-float of the sector shaft adjuster screw in its sector shaft recess. This should not exceed 0.027 in (0.07 mm), otherwise change the thrust washer for one of a different thickness.
19 Install the sector shaft end cover to the shaft by screwing it onto the adjuster screw. Fit a new gasket and then install the complete assembly into the steering box. Make sure that the adjuster screw is fully released before tightening the cover bolts.
20 Centre the sector shaft (by reference to the drop arm alignment mark) and adjust the backlash by means of the adjuster screw. This should be between 0.003 and 0.012 in (0.07 and 0.30 mm). The backlash can be checked if the steering wheel is temporarily refitted and the play then evident at the wheel rim will be between 0.2 and 1.0 in (5.0 and 25.0 mm). Lock the adjuster screw locknut.
21 Now check the sector shaft end-float adjustment. Ideally the steering drop arm should be removed from the steering linkage and temporarily attached to the splines of the sector shaft. In any event, turn the steering mainshaft to full right lock and, using a dial gauge, check the sector shaft end-float.
22 Now repeat the operations on full left lock. Both measurements should be the same. If they are not, remove or install shims which are located behind the steering worm rear bearing cup. Shims are available in different thicknesses.
23 Install the sector shaft oil seal, a new mainshaft lower 'O' ring seal and fill the steering box with oil.
24 Refitting is a reversal of removal, but make sure that the mating marks on the drop arm and sector shaft are in alignment. Tighten the mounting bolts to the specified torque.
25 Refit the contact ring housing and steering wheel by reversing the removal operations described in Sections 14 and 13 respectively.

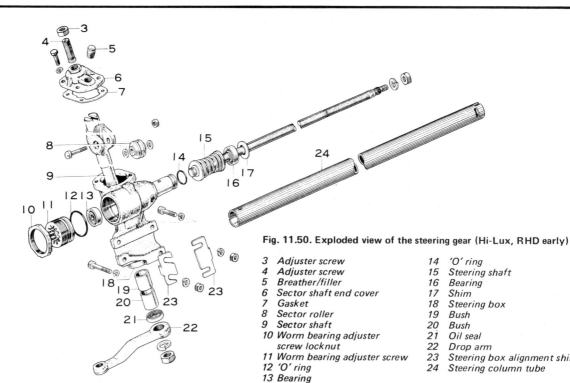

Fig. 11.50. Exploded view of the steering gear (Hi-Lux, RHD early)

3	Adjuster screw	14	'O' ring
4	Adjuster screw	15	Steering shaft
5	Breather/filler	16	Bearing
6	Sector shaft end cover	17	Shim
7	Gasket	18	Steering box
8	Sector roller	19	Bush
9	Sector shaft	20	Bush
10	Worm bearing adjuster screw locknut	21	Oil seal
		22	Drop arm
11	Worm bearing adjuster screw	23	Steering box alignment shim
12	'O' ring	24	Steering column tube
13	Bearing		

Fig. 11.51. Checking sector shaft adjuster screw end-float (Hi-Lux, early RHD)

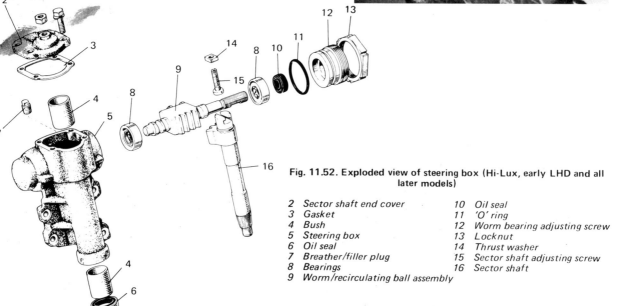

Fig. 11.52. Exploded view of steering box (Hi-Lux, early LHD and all later models)

2	Sector shaft end cover	10	Oil seal
3	Gasket	11	'O' ring
4	Bush	12	Worm bearing adjusting screw
5	Steering box	13	Locknut
6	Oil seal	14	Thrust washer
7	Breather/filler plug	15	Sector shaft adjusting screw
8	Bearings	16	Sector shaft
9	Worm/recirculating ball assembly		

Fig. 11.53. Withdrawing sector shaft from steering box (Hi-Lux, early LHD and all later models)

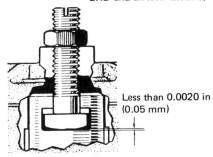

Less than 0.0020 in (0.05 mm)

Fig. 11.55. Sector shaft adjuster screw end-float diagram (Hi-Lux, early LHD and all later models)

21 Steering gear (Hi-Lux, early left-hand drive and all later models) - removal, overhaul and refitting

1 To remove this type of recirculating ball steering, first set the roadwheels in the straight-ahead position and using quick drying paint, make alignment marks on the flexible coupling and wormshaft at the lower end of the steering column.
2 Unscrew the nut from the end of the sector shaft and pull off the drop arm with a suitable extractor.
3 Extract the pinch bolt from the flexible coupling.
4 Unscrew and remove the steering box mounting bolts, taking care to retain and identify, in respect of location, any shims fitted between the steering box and the bodyframe.
5 Remove the steering box by drawing it carefully away from the flexible coupling. If the flexible coupling clamp is tight, insert a screwdriver in the clamp to expand it slightly.
6 Clean away all external dirt from the steering box.
7 Grip the steering box in a vice and release the locknut on the sector shaft adjusting screw.
8 Unscrew and remove the bolts which secure the end cover and withdraw the end cover complete with sector shaft.
9 Release the worm bearing adjusting screw locknut.
10 Unscrew and remove the worm bearing adjusting screw. A special wrench will be required for this having two pins which engage in the cut-outs in the screw.
11 Withdraw the worm assembly and bearing from the steering box.
12 Do not attempt to dismantle the ball nut from the worm. Any wear in the assembly can only be rectified by renewal of the assembly complete.
13 Always renew the wormshaft oil seal at times of major overhaul.
14 If the sector shaft end cover bush requires renewal then the complete end cover must be renewed.
15 Renewal of the other steering box bushes should be left to your Toyota dealer as a press will be required and they require reaming after installation.
16 The worm bearings should be renewed if they appear slack or noisy when turned. Extract the bearing outer tracks using a suitable extractor.
17 Commence reassembly by installing the worm and bearings into the steering box.

Fig. 11.54. Checking worm bearing pre-load (Hi-Lux, early LHD and all later models)

18 Screw in the worm bearing adjusting screw and locknut, finger tight only.
19 Adjust the worm bearing pre-load by winding a cord round the splines of the wormshaft and attaching it to a spring balance. Turn the adjusting screw until the force required to start the worm turning is as follows:
Early models   8.5 to 13.0 lb (3.9 to 5.9 kg)
Later models   6.5 to 13.0 lb (2.9 to 5.9 kg)
When the pre-load is correct, tighten the adjuster screw locknut fully.
20 Now engage the adjuster screw and thrust washer in the recess in the sector shaft and measure the end-float which should be:
Early models   0.0035 in (0.09 mm)
Later models   0.0020 in (0.05 mm)
21 Install the sector shaft onto the end cover and then fit the assembly with a new gasket into the steering box but take care, that the ball nut is at the centre of the worm and that the centre teeth of the sector shaft engage with the centre teeth of the worm nut. Make sure that the sector shaft adjusting screw is screwed fully out as the sector shaft is pushed in.
22 Screw in the sector shaft adjusting screw until, using the cord and spring balance attached to the splines of the sector shaft, the pre-load is between 15 and 24 lb (6.8 and 10.8 kg). Tighten the locknut.
23 Sector shaft adjustment is correct when, with the steering worm centralised, there is no backlash if the steering is turned 5 degrees in either direction from the centre position.
24 Install the steering box making sure that the marks on the flexible coupling and wormshaft are in alignment.
25 Install the drop arm to the sector shaft, again aligning the mating marks.
26 Fill the steering box with oil to ½ in (12.7 mm) below the combined breather/filler plug.

22 Steering idler - removal, overhaul and refitting

Hi-Ace models
1 Refer to Fig. 11.18 or 11.19 and disconnect the steering balljoints from the arms of the centre arm bracket or the idler arm.
2 Either component can be dismantled after unscrewing and removing the shaft nut.
3 The bush in the idler is of the flexible type and should be renewed if it has deteriorated.
4 If worn, the bushes and oil seal in the centre arm bracket can be removed and new ones installed.
5 When the centre arm bracket is reassembled, extract the grease plug, screw in a grease nipple and apply several strokes with the grease gun.
6 Reassemble the idler arm as shown in Fig. 11.21, tightening the nut to specified torque wrench setting.

Hi-Lux models
7 The steering linkage incorporates a flexible-bushed idler only, no centre arm bracket being installed as with Hi-Ace models.
8 Renew the flexible bush if the original one is worn or deteriorated. Tighten the idler arm castellated nut to the specified torque with the arm set as shown in Fig. 11.22 having the angle of arm to bracket at 7° or 9° according to date of vehicle production (up to 1976 9°, after 1976 7°).

23 Steering angles and front wheel alignment

1 Accurate front wheel alignment is essential for good steering and even tyre wear. Before considering the steering angles, check that the tyres are correctly inflated, that the front wheels are not buckled, the hub bearings are not worn or incorrectly adjusted and that the steering linkage is in good order, without slackness or wear at the joints.

2 Wheel alignment consists of four factors:

Camber, which is the angle at which the front wheels are set from the vertical when viewed from the front of the car. Positive camber is the amount (in degrees) that the wheels are tilted outwards at the top from the vertical.

Castor, is the angle between the steering axis and a vertical line when viewed from each side of the car. Positive castor is when the steering axis is inclined rearward.

Steering axis inclination, is the angle, when viewed from the front of the car, between the vertical and an imaginary line drawn between the upper and lower suspension swivel balljoints.

Toe-in, is the amount by which the distance between the front inside edges of the roadwheels (measured at hub height) is less than the diametrically opposite distance measured between the rear inside edges of the front roadwheels.

3 Due to the need for precision gauges to measure the small angles set in the steering and suspension layout it is preferable that adjustment of camber and castor is left to a service station having the necessary equipment.

4 *On all models,* the camber angle is varied by the inclusion of shims between the suspension upper arm pivot shaft and the bodyframe. Variation in the thickness and quantity of shims between one end of the pivot shaft and the other will also affect the castor angle.

5 Front wheel tracking (toe-in) may be checked and adjusted by carrying out the following operations.

6 Place the car on level ground with the wheels in the straight-ahead position.

7 Obtain or make a toe-in gauge. One may be easily made from tubing, cranked to clear the sump and bellhousing, having an adjustable nut and setscrew at one end.

8 With the gauge, measure the distance between the two wheel inner rims (at hub height) at the rear of the wheel.

9 Rotate the wheel through 180° (half a turn) and measure the distance between the wheel inner rims (again at hub height) at the front of the wheel. This measurement should be less by an amount which corresponds with the specified toe-in for the particular vehicle model, (see Specifications Section).

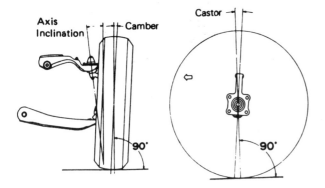

Fig. 11.56. Diagram of steering angles

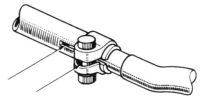

Fig. 11.57. Correct installation of trackrod clamps

Fig. 11.58. Adjusting a steering lock stop bolt

10 Where the toe-in is found to be incorrect, on late Hi-Ace and all Hi-Lux models, slaoken the four trackrod clamp bolts and rotate each trackrod equally. It is a good plan to first measure each trackrod between the balljoint centres in case they have been adjusted unevenly by a previous owner. When adjustment is correct, tighten the clamp bolts, ensuring that the clamp openings are in alignment with the slots in the trackrod tubes and that the trackrod ends are positioned in the centres of their arcs of travel (see Figs. 11.19 and 11.20). On early Hi-Ace models, release the two clamps on the centre relay rod and rotate the rod as necessary to either increase or decrease the tow-in (see Fig. 11.18).

11 Steering lock stop bolts are fitted to the rear of the stub axle carriers and are adjustable to limit the full lock travel in both directions. The inner and outer roadwheel angles on full lock should be adjusted with the stop bolts to conform with the angles given in Specifications according to vehicle model. The angle of each roadwheel (at full lock) can be marked on the ground and checked against the vehicle centre line to check the turning angles.

24 Wheels and tyres

1 Regularly check the tyre pressures including the spare.

2 Every 6000 miles (10000 km) remove the roadwheels, extract any flints which are embedded in the treads and move the position of the wheels to even out the wear of the tyres. This rotation should only be carried out if the wheels have been balanced off the vehicle. If the wheels have been balanced on the vehicle then moving the roadwheels cannot be carried out unless the wheels are re-balanced afterwards.

3 Where radial tyres are fitted any movement of the wheels should be limited to changing their position between front and rear on the same side of the vehicle, not from one side to the other.

4 When new tyres are fitted, always renew the valve at the same time.

5 Never mix radial and crossply tyres on the same axle.

6 Never attempt to mend a puncture by the insertion of a plug from the outside. The cover must be removed and a 'mushroom' type plug inserted from the inside. The wheel must be re-balanced after insertion of the plug.

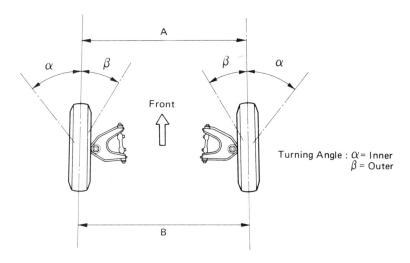

Fig.11.59. Diagram of front wheel turning angles and toe-in

Toe-in is B minus A

25 Fault diagnosis - suspension and steering

Before diagnosing faults from the following chart, check that any irregularities are not caused by:

1 Binding brakes
2 Incorrect 'mix' of radial and crossply tyres
3 Incorrect tyre pressures
4 Misalignment of the bodyframe

Symptom	Cause
Steering wheel can be moved considerably before any sign of movement of the wheels is apparent	Wear in the steering linkage, gear and column coupling.
Vehicle difficult to steer in a consistent straight line - wandering	As above. Wheel alignment incorrect (indicated by excessive or uneven tyre wear). Front wheel hub bearings loose or worn. Worn suspension unit swivel joints.
Steering stiff and heavy	Incorrect wheel alignment (indicated by excessive or uneven tyre wear). Excessive wear or seizure in one or more of the joints in the steering linkage or suspension unit balljoints. Excessive wear in the steering gear unit.
Wheel wobble and vibration	Roadwheels out of balance. Roadwheels buckled. Wheel alignment incorrect. Wear in the steering linkage, suspension unit bearings or track control arm bushes. Broken front spring.
Excessive pitching and rolling on corners and during braking	Defective shock absorbers and/or broken spring.

Chapter 12 Bodywork and chassis

Contents

Specifications

Body dimensions and weights are given in concise form in the introductory Section at the beginning of this Book.

1 General description

1 All Hi-Lux and Hi-Ace vehicles, except Hi-Ace vans or personnel carriers, are constructed on a separate channel section chassis.
2 Hi-Ace vans or personnel carriers are of unitary construction.
3 Commencing with the 1973 models, Hi-Lux vehicles have been available with a long wheelbase (LWB) option.
4 All vehicles are lavishly equipped and include heater, radio and cigar light, mud flaps and other accessories.
5 Since 1975, air conditioning has been optionally available in conjunction with the Hi-Lux 20R engine version.

2 Maintenance - bodywork and underframe

The general condition of a car's bodywork is the one thing that significantly affects its value. Maintenance is easy but needs to be regular and particular. Neglect, particularly after minor damage, can lead quickly to further deterioration and costly repair bills. It is important also to keep watch on those parts of the car not immediately visible, for instance, the underside, inside all the wheel arches and the lower part of the engine compartment.
2 The basic maintenance routine for the bodywork is washing - preferably with a lot of water, from a hose. This will remove all the loose solids which may have stuck to the car. It is important to flush these off in such a way as to prevent grit from scratching the finish. The wheel arches and underbody need washing in the same way to remove any accumulated mud which will retain moisture and tend to encourage rust. Parodoxically enough, the best time to clean the underbody and wheel arches is in wet weather when the mud is thoroughly wet and soft. In very wet weather the underbody is usually cleaned of large accumulations automatically and this is a good time for inspection.
3 Periodically it is a good idea to have the whole of the underside of the car steam cleaned, engine compartment included, so that a thorough inspection can be carried out to see what minor repairs and renovations are necessary. Steam cleaning is available at many garages and is necessary for removal of accumulation of oily grime which sometimes is allowed to cake thick in certain areas near the engine, gearbox and back axle. If steam facilities are not available, there are one or two excellent grease solvents available which can be brush applied. The dirt can then be simply hosed off.
4 After washing paintwork, wipe off with a chamois leather to give an unspotted clear finish. A coat of clear protective wax polish will give added protection against chemical pollutants in the air, If the paintwork sheen has dulled or oxidised, use a cleaner/polish combination to restore the brilliance of the shine. This requires a little more effort, but is usually caused because regular washing has been neglected. Always check that door and ventilator opening drain holes and pipes are completely clear so that water can drain out. Bright work should be treated the same way as paintwork. Windscreens and windows can be kept clear of the smeary film which often appears if a little ammonia is added to the water. If they are scratched, a good rub with a proprietary metal polish will often clear them. Never use any form of wax or other body or chromium polish on glass.

3 Maintenance - upholstery and carpets

1 Mats and carpets should be brushed or vacuum cleaned regularly to keep them free of grit. If they are badly stained remove them from the car for scrubbing or sponging and make quite sure they are dry before replacement. Seats and interior trim panels can be kept clean by a wipe over with a damp cloth. If they do become stained (which can be more apparent on light coloured upholstery) use a little liquid detergent and a soft nail brush to scour the grime out of the grain of the material. Do not forget to keep the head lining clean in the same way as the upholstery. When using liquid cleaners inside the car do not over-wet the surface being cleaned. Excessive damp could get into the seams and padded interior causing stains, offensive odours or even rot. If the inside of the car gets wet accidently it is worthwhile taking some trouble to dry it out properly, particularly where carpets are involved. **Do not leave oil or electric heaters inside the car for this purpose.**

4 Minor body damage - repair

See also photo sequences on pages 222 and 223.

Repair of minor scratches in the car's bodywork

If the scratch is very superficial, and does not penetrate to the metal of the bodywork, repair is very simple. Lightly rub the area of the scratch with a paintwork renovator, or a very fine cutting paste, to remove loose paint from the scratch and to clear the surrounding bodywork of wax polish. Rinse the area with clean water.

Apply touch-up paint to the scratch using a thin paint brush; continue to apply thin layers of paint until the surface of the paint in the scratch is level with surrounding paintwork. Allow the new paint at least two weeks to harden; then, blend it into the surrounding paintwork by rubbing the paintwork in the scratch area with a paintwork renovator, or a very fine cutting paste. Finally, apply wax polish.

Where a scratch has penetrated, right through to the metal of the bodywork, causing the metal to rust, a different repair technique is required. Remove any loose rust from the bottom of the scratch with a penknife, then apply rust inhibiting paint to prevent the formation of rust in the future. Using a rubber or nylon applicator fill the scratch with body-stopper paste. If required, this paste can be mixed with cellulose thinners to provide a very thin paste which is ideal for filling narrow scratches. Before the stopper-paste in the scratch hardens, wrap a piece of smooth cotton rag around the tip of the finger; dip the finger in cellulose thinners and then quickly sweep it across the surface of the stopper-paste in the scratch; this will ensure that the surface of the stopper-paste is slightly hollowed. The scratch can now be painted over as described earlier in this Section.

Repair of dents in the car's bodywork

When deep denting of the car's bodywork has taken place, the first task is to pull the dent out, until the affected bodywork almost attains its original shape. There is little point in trying to restore the original shape completely, as the metal in the damaged area will have stretched on impact and cannot be reshaped fully to its original contour. It is better to bring the level of the dent up to a point which is about 1/8 inch (3 mm) below the level of the surrounding bodywork. In cases where the dent is very shallow anyway, it is not worth trying to pull it out at all.

If the underside of the dent is accessible, it can be hammered out gently from behind, using a mallet with a wooden or plastic head. Whilst doing this, hold a suitable block of wood firmly against the outside of the dent. This block will absorb the impact from the hammer blows and thus prevent a large area of bodywork from being 'belled-out.'

Should the dent be in a section of the bodywork which has a double skin or some other factor making it inaccessible from behind, a different technique is called for. Drill several small holes through the metal inside the dent area - particularly in the deeper sections. Then screw long self-tapping screws into the holes just sufficiently for them to gain a good purchase in the metal. Now the dent can be pulled out by by pulling on the protruding heads of the screws with a pair of pliers.

The next stage of the repair is the removal of the paint from the damaged area, and from an inch or so of the surrounding 'sound' bodywork. This is accomplished most easily by using a wire brush or abrasive pad on a power drill, although it can be done just as effectively by hand using sheets of abrasive paper. To complete the preparations for filling, score the surface of the bore metal with a screwdriver or the tang of a file, or alternatively, drill small holes in the affected area. This will provide a really good 'key' for the filler paste.

To complete the repair see the Section on filling and respraying.

Repair of rust holes or gashes in the car's bodywork

Remove all paint from the affected area and from an inch or so of the surrounding 'sound' bodywork, using an abrasive pad or a wire brush on a power drill. If these are not available a few sheets of abrasive paper will do the job just as effectively. With the paint removed you will be able to gauge the severity of the corrosion and therefore decide whether to renew the whole panel (if this is possible) or to repair the affected area. Replacement body panels are not as expensive as most people think and it is often quicker and more satisfactory to fit a new panel than to attempt to repair large areas of corrosion.

Remove all fittings from the affected area, except those which will act as a guide to the original shape of the damaged bodywork (eg, headlamp shells etc). Then, using tin snips or a hacksaw blade, remove all loose metal and any other metal badly affected by corrosion. Hammer the edges of the hole inwards in order to create a slight depression for the filler paste.

Wire brush the affected area to remove the powdery rust from the surface of the remaining metal. Paint the affected area with rust inhibiting paint. If the back of the rusted area is accessible treat this also.

Before filling can take place, it will be necessary to block the hole in some way. This can be achieved by the use of one of the following materials: Zinc gauze, Aluminium tape or Polyurethane foam.

Zinc gauze is probably the best material to use for a large hole. Cut a piece to the approximate size and shape of the hole to be filled, then position it in the hole so that its edges are below the level of the surrounding bodywork. It can be retained in position by several blobs of filler paste around its periphery.

Aluminium tape should be used for small or very narrow holes. Pull a piece off the roll and trim it to the approximate size and shape required, then pull off the backing paper (if used) and stick the tape over the hole; it can be overlapped if the thickness of one piece is insufficient. Burnish down the edges of the tape with the handle of a screwdriver or similar, to ensure that the tape is securely attached to the metal underneath.

Polyurethane foam is best used where the holes are situated in a section of bodywork of complex shape, backed by a small box section (eg, where the sill panel meets the rear wheel arch - most cars). The usual mixing procedure for this foam is as follows: Put equal amounts of fluid from each of the two cans provided in the kit, into one container. Stir until the mixture begins to thicken, then quickly pour this mixture into the hole, and hold a piece of cardboard over the larger apertures. Almost immediately the polyurethane will begin to expand, gushing out of any small holes left unblocked. When the foam hardens it can be cut back to just below the level of the surrounding bodywork with a hacksaw blade.

Bodywork repairs - filling and re-spraying

Before using this Section, see the Sections on dent, deep scratch, rust hole, and gash repairs.

Many types of bodyfiller are available, but generally speaking those proprietary kits which contain a tin of filler paste and a tube of resin hardener are best for this type of repair. A wide, flexible plastic or nylon applicator will be found invaluable for imparting a smooth and well contoured finish to the surface of the filler.

Mix up a little filler on a clean piece of card or board - use the hardener sparingly (follow the maker's instructions on the packet), otherwise the filler will set very rapidly.

Using the applicator, apply the filler paste to the prepared area; draw the applicator across the surface of the filler to achieve the correct contour and to level the filler surface. As soon as a contour that approximates the correct one is achieved stop working the paste. If you carry on too long the paste will become sticky and begin to 'pick-up' on the applicator. Continue to add thin layers of filler paste at twenty-minute intervals until the level of the filler is just 'proud' of the surrounding bodywork.

Once the filler has hardened, excess can be removed using a Surform plane or Dreadnought file. From then on, progressively finer grades of abrasive paper should be used, starting with a 40 grade production paper and finishing with 400 grade 'wet-and-dry' paper. Always wrap the abrasive paper around a flat rubber, cork, or wooden block - otherwise the surface of the filler will not be completely flat. During the smoothing of the filler surface, the wet-and-dry paper should be periodically rinsed in water; this will ensure that a very smooth finish is imparted to the filler at the final stage.

At this stage, the 'dent' should be surrounded by a ring of bare metal, which in turn should be encircled by a finely 'feathered' edge of the good paintwork. Rinse the repair area with clean water, until all of the dust produced by the rubbing-down operation is gone.

Spray the whole repair area with a light coat of grey primer - this will show up any imperfections in the surface of the filler. Repair these imperfections with fresh filler paste or body-stopper, and once more smooth the surface with abrasive paper. If bodystopper is used, it can be mixed with cellulose thinners to form a really thin paste which is ideal for filling small holes. Repeat this spray and repair procedure until you are satisfied that the surface of the filler, and the feathered edge of the paintwork are perfect. Clean the repair area with clean water and allow to dry fully.

The repair area is now ready for spraying. Paint spraying must be carried out in a warm, dry, windless and dust free atmosphere. This condition can be created artificially if you have access to a large indoor working area, but if you are forced to work in the open, you will have to pick your day very carefully. If you are working indoors, dousing the floor in the work area with water will 'lay' the dust which would otherwise be in the atmosphere. If the repair area is confined to one body panel, mask off the surrounding panels; this will help to minimise the effect of a slight mis-match in paint colours. Bodywork fittings (eg, chrome strips, door handles etc) will also need to be masked off. Use genuine masking tape and several thicknesses of newspaper for the masking operation.

Before commencing to spray, agitate the aerosol can thoroughly, then spray a test area (an old tin, or similar) until the technique is mastered. Cover the repair area with a thick coat of primer; the thickness should be built up using several thin layers of paint rather than one thick one. Using 400 grade 'wet-and-dry' paper, rub down the surface of the primer until it is really smooth. While doing this, the work area should be thoroughly doused with water, and the 'wet-and-dry' paper periodically rinsed in water. Allow to dry before spraying on more paint.

Spray on the top coat, again building up the thickness by using several thin layers of paint. Start spraying in the centre of the repair area and then, using a circular motion, work outwards until the whole repair area and about 2 inches of the surrounding original paintwork is covered. Remove all masking material 10 to 15 minutes after spraying on the final coat of paint.

Allow the new paint at least 2 weeks to harden fully; then, using a paintwork renovator or a very fine cutting paste, blend the edges of the new paint into the existing paintwork. Finally, apply wax polish.

5 Major body damage - repair

Where serious damage has occured or large areas need renewal due to neglect, and means certainly that completely new sections or panels will need welding in, this is best left to professionals. If the damage is due to impact it will also be necessary to completely check the alignment of the bodyshell or chassis frame. The services of a Toyota dealer with specialist checking jigs are essential. If a body or chassis frame is left misaligned it is first of all dangerous, as the car will not handle properly and secondly, uneven stresses will be imposed on the steering, engine and transmission causing abnormal wear or complete failure. Tyre wear may also be excessive.

6 Maintenance - hinges and locks

1   Oil the hinges of the bonnet and doors with a drop or two of light oil periodically. A good time is after the car has been washed.
2   Oil the bonnet release catch pivot pin and the safety catch pivot pin periodically.
3   Do not over lubricate door latches and strikers. Normally a little oil on the rotary cam spindle alone is sufficient.

7 Doors - tracing rattles and their rectification

1   Check first that the door is not loose at the hinges and that the latch is holding the door firmly in position. Check also that the door lines up with the aperture in the body.
2   If the hinges are loose or the door is out of alignment, it will be necessary to reset the hinge positions, as described in Section 17 or 18.
3   If the latch is holding the door properly, it should hold the door tightly when fully latched and the door should line up with the body. If it is out of alignment, it needs adjustment or if loose, some part of the lock mechanism must be worn out and requiring renewal.
4   Other rattles from the door would be caused by wear or looseness in the window winder, the glass channels and sill strips, or the door buttons and interior latch release mechanism.

8 Bonnet (Hi-Lux) - removal and installation

1   Pull the internal bonnet lock release lever and open the bonnet to its fullest extent and support it on its strut. Disconnect the washer tube (photo).
2   Mark the position of the hinge plates on the underside of the bonnet and then unscrew the hinge bolts, while an assistant supports the lid (photo).
3   Lift the bonnet from the vehicle and store it safely to prevent scratching.
4   Installation is a reversal of removal. Any adjustment can be carried out by moving the bonnet within the limits of the hinge plate elongated bolt holes. Adjust the position of the lock assembly afterwards (photo).
5   To ensure smooth positive closure, the bonnet lock dovetail bolt can be screwed in or out as necessary after the locknut has been released.
6   The height of the rubber bonnet stops can also be adjusted if necessary (photo).

8.1 Windscreen washer tube connection on underside of bonnet (Hi-Lux)

8.2 Bonnet hinge (Hi-Lux)

8.4 Bonnet lock mechanism (Hi-Lux)

8.6 Bonnet stop (Hi-Lux)

9.1 Radiator grille centre joint (Hi-Lux)

12.2a Window regulator handle and clip (Hi-Lux)

12.2b Removing window regulator handle (Hi-Lux)

12.3 Extracting door lock remote control escutcheon plate screw (Hi-Lux)

9 Radiator grille (Hi-Lux) - removal and installation

1   The radiator grille is divided vertically at its centre.
2   Open the bonnet and support it on its strut.
3   To remove one side of the grille, extract the seven securing screws. On models which have a centrally located emblem, this must be removed before one of the grille screws, which is located behind it, is accessible.
4   Installation is a reversal of removal.

10 Radiator grille (Hi-Ace) - removal and installation

1   This is simply a matter of extracting the four securing screws and lifting the grille from the front body panel.
2   Installation is a reversal of removal.

11 Tailgate (Hi-Lux and Hi-Ace, with truck body) - removal and refitting

1   Release the tailgate latches and lower the tailgate.
2   Uncouple the two support chains.
3   Mark the location of the tailgate hinge plates on the body and then extract the hinge bolts from the body.
4   With the help of an assistant, lift the tailgate from the vehicle.
5   Refitting is a reversal of removal, but if any minor adjustment is required, the tailgate can be moved within the limits of its hinge plate elongated bolt holes. Adjust the latches, if necessary, using the same method.

12 Door lock (Hi-Lux) - removal and refitting

1   Open the door to its fullest extent.
2   Using a hooked piece of wire, slide it down behind the window regulator handle and pull out the securing clip. Remove the handle (photos).
3   Unscrew and remove the escutcheon plate (one screw) from behind the door remote control lock handle (photo).
4   Extract the accessible screw from the door pull, fold the door pull backwards, remove the second screw and take off the door pull (photo).
5   Insert the fingers under the lower edge of the door interior trim panel and give it a sharp pull to release the trim panel clip. Work round the edge of the panel until all the clips are released and the panel can be detached from the door.
6   Carefully peel off the waterproof sheeting from the apertures in the door.
7   Unbolt the lock remote control and disengage the control rod (photo).
8   Unscrew and remove the door lock plunger knob and disconnect the connecting rod from the door lock assembly.
9   Unbolt the lock assembly and withdraw it partially, so that the remaining link to the exterior handle can be disconnected, then remove the lock assembly through the door aperture.
10 The exterior handle securing nuts are accessible through one of the higher hand holes in the door.
11 If the lock mechanism is faulty, renew the complete assembly (photo).
12 Refitting is a reversal of removal.

13 Door lock (Hi-Ace) - removal and refitting

1   The operations are very similar to those described in the preceding Section, except that the interior remote control handle also serves as the locking device, no plunger type knob being fitted.

This sequence of photographs deals with the repair of the dent and scratch (above rear lamp) shown in this photo. The procedure will be similar for the repair of a hole. It should be noted that the procedures given here are simplified - more explicit instructions will be found in the text

In the case of a dent the first job - after removing surrounding trim - is to hammer out the dent where access is possible. This will minimise filling. Here, the large dent having been hammered out, the damaged area is being made slightly concave

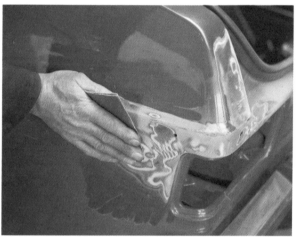

Now all paint must be removed from the damaged area, by rubbing with coarse abrasive paper. Alternatively, a wire brush or abrasive pad can be used in a power drill. Where the repair area meets good paintwork, the edge pf the paintwork should be 'feathered', using a finer grade of abrasive paper

In the case of a hole caused by rusting, all damaged sheet-metal should be cut away before proceeding to this stage. Here, the damaged area is being treated with rust remover and inhibitor before being filled

Mix the body filler according to its manufacturer's instructions. In the case of corrosion damage, it will be necessary to block off any large holes before filling - this can be done with zinc gauze or aluminium tape. Make sure the area is absolutely clean before ...

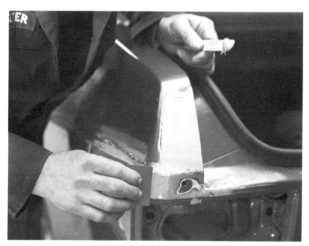

... applying the filler. Filler should be applied with a flexible applicator, as shown, for best results: the wooden spatula being used for confined areas. Apply thin layers of filler at 20-minute intervals, until the surface of the filler is slightly proud of the surrounding bodywork

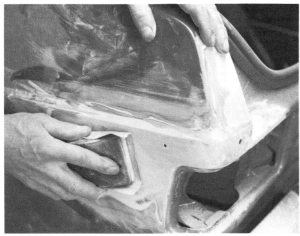

Initial shaping can be done with a Surform plane or Dreadnought file. Then, using progressively finer grades of wet-and-dry paper, wrapped around a sanding block, and copious amounts of clean water, rub-down the filler until really smooth and flat. Again, feather the edges of adjoining paintwork

The whole repair area can now be sprayed or brush-painted with primer. If spraying, ensure adjoining areas are protected from over-spray. Note that at least one-inch of the surrounding sound paintwork should be coated with primer. Primer has a 'thick' consistency, so will fill small imperfections

Again, using plenty of water, rub down the primer with a fine grade of wet-and-dry paper (400 grade is probably best) until it is really smooth and well blended into the surrounding paint-work. Any remaining imperfections can now be filled by carefully applied knifing stopper paste

When the stopper has hardened, rub-down the repair area again before applying the final coat of primer. Before rubbing-down this last coat of primer, ensure the repair area is blemish-free - use more stopper if necessary. To ensure that the surface of the primer is really smooth use some finishing compound

The top coat can now be applied. When working out of doors, pick a dry, warm and wind-free day. Ensure surrounding areas are protected from over-spray. Agitate the aerosol thoroughly, then spray the centre of the repair area, working outwards with a circular motion. Apply the paint as several thin coats.

After a period of about two-weeks, which the paint needs to harden fully, the surface of the repaired area can be 'cut' with a mild cutting compound prior to wax polishing. When carrying out bodywork repairs, remember that the quality of the finished job is proportional to the time and effort expended

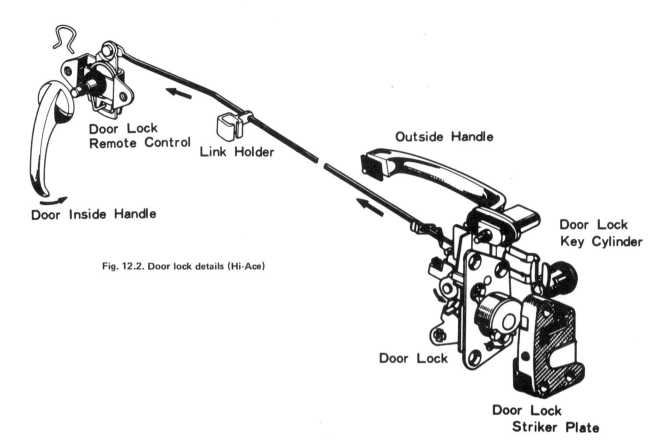

Door Lock
Remote Control

Link Holder

Outside Handle

Door Inside Handle

Door Lock
Key Cylinder

Door Lock

Door Lock
Striker Plate

Fig. 12.2. Door lock details (Hi-Ace)

12.4 Door pull (Hi-Lux)

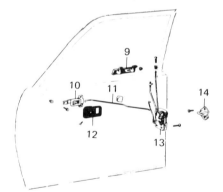

Fig. 12.1. Door lock details (Hi-Lux)

9 Door exterior handle
10 Remote control
11 Link rod
12 Remote control escutcheon
13 Door lock assembly
14 Striker plate

12.7 Door lock remote control handle
(Hi-Lux)

12.10 Door exterior handle attachment
(Hi-Lux)

12.11 Door cylinder lock (Hi-Lux)

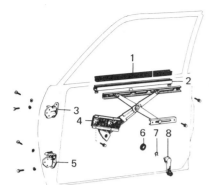

Fig. 12.3. Window regulator details (Hi-Lux)

1 *Weatherstrip*	5 *Door lower hinge*
2 *Channel*	6 *Escutcheon plate*
3 *Door upper hinge*	7 *Clip*
4 *Regulator*	8 *Regulator handle*

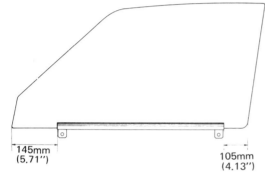

145mm
(5.71")

105mm
(4.13")

Fig. 12.4. Door glass to channel installation diagram (Hi-Lux)

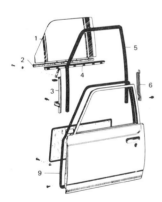

Fig. 12.5. Door components (Hi-Lux)

1 *Glass*	5 *Flexible surround*
2 *Inner weatherstrip*	6 *Guide*
3 *Guide*	9 *Weatherstrip*
4 *Outer weatherstrip*	

Fig. 12.6. Removing ventilator upper pivot (Hi-Ace)

14.3 Window channel and guide (Hi-Lux)

14 Door glass and regulator (Hi-Lux) - removal and refitting

1   Remove the door interior trim panel as described in Section 12.
2   Temporarily refit the window regulator handle and wind the glass down to its fullest extent.
3   Extract the securing screws from the regulator mechanism and move it upwards to release the lift arms from the glass channel (photo).
4   Disconnect the glass channel from the lift arm slide (two screws).
5   Remove the inner and outer weatherstrip from the glass slot at the top of the door panel, and then remove the glass upwards, turning it slightly as it is withdrawn from the door cavity.
6   If new glass is being fitted, make sure that it is positioned in the channel/weatherstrip in accordance with the diagram (Fig. 12.4).
7   Refitting is a reversal of removal, but check for smooth operation before replacing the trim panel. Any adjustment can be made by releasing the front and rear glass guide screws and moving the guides in or out as necessary.

15 Door swivel ventilator (Hi-Ace) - removal and refitting

1   Remove the ventilator upper pivot mounting screws.
2   Extract the grommet and insert a screwdriver to release the lower pivot clamp screw.
3   Pull the swivel ventilator away from the door frame in an upwards direction at an inclined angle.
4   If necessary, the rubber weatherstrip can be pulled from the door-frame and the glass extracted from the ventilator frame.
5   New glass is installed into the ventilator frame and weatherstrip using a suitable adhesive.
6   Install the ventilator assembly into position by reversing the removal operations. Tighten the lower pivot clamp screw so that the ventilator movement is reasonably stiff, otherwise if it is too slack, the ventilator will tend to close by air pressure when the vehicle is in forward motion.

16 Door glass and regulator (Hi-Ace) - removal and refitting

1   Remove the swivel ventilator assembly as described in the preceding Section.
2   Remove the door interior trim panel.

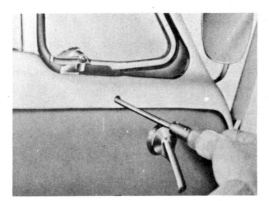

Fig. 12.7. Releasing lower pivot clamp screw (Hi-Ace)

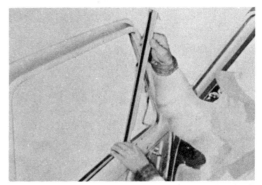

Fig. 12.8. Removing door glass dividing strut (Hi-Ace)

Fig. 12.9. Removing door glass weatherstrip (Hi-Ace)

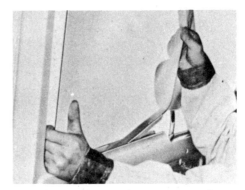

Fig. 12.10. Removing glass from door cavity (Hi-Ace)

3   Pull the ventilator frame weatherstrip from the door frame.
4   Temporarily refit the window regulator handle and wind the glass
fully down.
5   Extract the screws from the top of the glass dividing strut.
6   Remove the bolts from the lower end of the strut and then withdraw it from the door.
7   Prise off the inner and outer weatherstrips from the glass slot at the
top of the door panel.
8   Extract the window regulator securing bolts and move the assembly
to disconnect the lift arms from the glass channel.
9   Remove the glass upwards, turning it slightly as it is withdrawn.
10 The regulator assembly can be removed through one of the door
apertures.
11 If the door glass is being renewed, tap the channel onto it with a
rubber hammer, making sure that the exposed glass at either end of the
channel is of equal length.
12 Refitting is a reversal of removal.

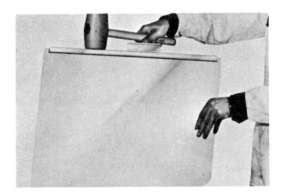

Fig. 12.11. Installing door glass channel (Hi-Ace)

17 Door (Hi-Ace, driving cab) - removal and refitting

1   Open the door fully, and support it under its lower edge on a jack
or blocks. Protect the paintwork with pads of rag.
2   Mark the position of the hinge plates on the door pillar as an aid to
installation.
3   Unbolt the hinges from the door pillar and lift the door away.
4   If the hinges are to be removed from the door, then the cover
plates must be withdrawn from the door interior panel to give access to
the bolts.
5   Refit the door by reversing the removal process, but do not tighten
the hinge bolts fully until the fit of the door in the body aperture has
been checked. The front and rear gaps of the door should be equal and
parallel and the top gap parallel. It is a good idea to remove the lock
striker plate from the door pillar during the adjustment procedure.
Finally, tighten the hinge bolts and refit and adjust the striker plate to
provide smooth positive closure.

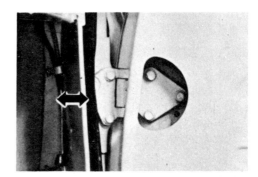

Fig. 12.12. Door hinge (Hi-Ace)

Fig. 12.13. Sliding door upper roller (Hi-Ace)

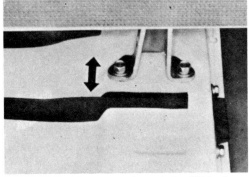

Fig. 12.14. Sliding door lower roller (Hi-Ace)

Fig. 12.15. Sliding door centre roller (Hi-Ace)

18.5 Door lock striker plate (Hi-Lux)

Fig. 12.16. Rear sliding door lock (Hi-Ace)

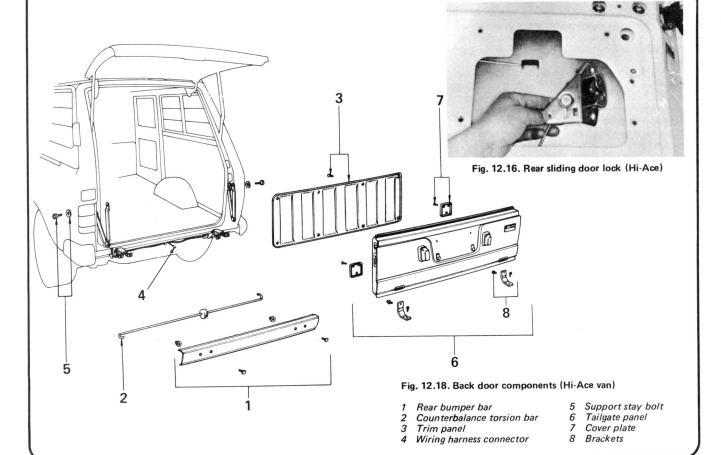

Fig. 12.18. Back door components (Hi-Ace van)

1 Rear bumper bar	5 Support stay bolt
2 Counterbalance torsion bar	6 Tailgate panel
3 Trim panel	7 Cover plate
4 Wiring harness connector	8 Brackets

18 Door (Hi-Lux) - removal and refitting

1   Open the door fully and support it under its lower edge on a jack or blocks. Protect the paintwork with pads of rag.
2   Mark the position of the hinge plates on the edge of the door frame as an aid to installation.
3   Unbolt the hinges from the door and lift the door away.
4   With the door removed, the bolts which secure the hinges to the door pillar are now accessible. Before removing them, again, mark the position of the hinge plates.
5   Refit the door by reversing the removal process, but do not tighten the hinge bolts fully until the fit of the door in the body aperture has been checked. The front and rear gaps of the door should be equal and parallel and the top gap parallel. It is a good idea to remove the lock striker plate from the door pillar during the adjustment procedure. Finally, tighten the hinge bolts and refit and adjust the striker plate (photo).

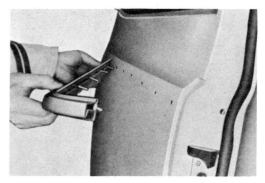

Fig. 12.17. Removing the door centre rail (Hi-Ace)

19 Rear sliding door (Hi-Ace, van body) - adjustment

1   Should the sliding door used on van and personnel carrier versions no longer close smoothly and positively, the door can be moved in one of the following ways to correct its position.
2   Release the upper roller screws and raise or lower the door.
3   Release the lower roller bolts and raise or lower the door.
4   Release the centre roller bolts and raise or lower the door.
5   In practice, a combination of adjustment of the three rollers will normally be required. If necessary, the lock latch and dovetails can be moved as necessary and shims removed or added to improve alignment of these components.

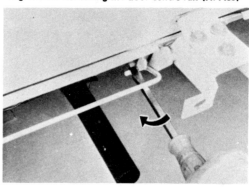

Fig. 12.19. Disconnecting tailgate counterbalance torsion bar (Hi-Ace van)

20 Rear sliding door (Hi-Ace, van body) - removal and refitting

1   Unbolt and remove the door lower roller.
2   Slide the door to the rear and lift it from the vehicle.
3   The door can be dismantled, if required, by detaching the upper and centre rollers.
4   If the door lock is to be removed, first withdraw the door interior trim panel in a similar manner to that described for the front door in Section 13.
5   Separate the control rod at the turnbuckle and withdraw the lock through one of the apertures in the door panel.
6   If the lock is worn or faulty, renew it complete.
7   The centre rail on which the door slides can be removed from the body panel once the sliding door has been removed.

Fig. 12.20. Removing rear door hinge bolts (Hi-Ace van)

21 Back door (Hi-Ace) - removal and installation

1   On some body styles, the back door comprises two opening sections split horizontally.
2   To remove the lower section of the backdoor, first unbolt and remove the centre bumper bar.
3   Using a screwdriver as a lever, release the torsion bar tension and unhook and remove it.
4   Remove the trim panel by pulling its clips from the tailgate frame.
5   Disconnect the lamp leads at the snap connections.
6   Unscrew and remove the bolts from the side arms, but support the weight of the tailgate while doing so.
7   Mark the position of the hinge plates on the tailgate, remove the hinge bolts and lift the tailgate away.
8   To remove the upper section of the backdoor, first open it to its fullest extent and mark the position of the hinge plates on the door as an aid to refitting.
9   Unbolt the support stays from the edges of the door.
10 Have an assistant take the weight of the door, then extract the hinge bolts and lift the door from the vehicle.
11 The hinges can be unbolted from the bodyshell once the roof interior cover panels have been detached.

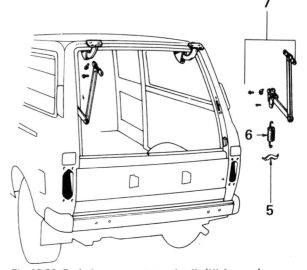

Fig. 12.21. Back door support stay details (Hi-Ace van)

5   Counterbalance spring anchor   6   Counterbalance spring
    bar   7   Support stay

Fig. 12.22. Removing a counterbalance spring anchor bar (Hi-Ace van)

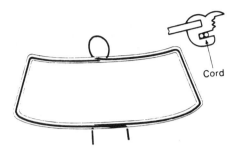

Fig. 12.23. Cord installed ready for windscreen fitting

Fig. 12.24. Removing driving cab (Hi-Ace)

Fig. 12.25. Removing rear body (Hi-Ace)

12 The spring loaded support stays can only be removed after the counterbalance spring has been disconnected from its anchorage. To do this, remove the rear lamp cluster and use a hooked rod to release the lower end of the spring from its anchor bar. Make sure that the rod used is of sufficient strength and length to accept the force required to unhook the spring.
13 Remove the anchor bar and the stay.
14 Refitting is a reversal of removal, but align both upper and lower door sections by moving them within the limits of their hinge plate elongated bolt holes. Finally, adjust the latch striker plates as necessary.

22 Windscreen glass - removal and installation

This is a job which, it is recommended, is best left to the experts, but for those who are determined to attempt it, proceed as follows:
1 Remove the wiper arms.
2 Using a small screwdriver, prise out the bright moulding from the rubber windscreen surround.
3 Remove the interior mirror and then prise the rubber surround lip (at the inside top centre) from the body frame edge. Work in both directions and exert pressure along the top part of the screen until it moves outwards.
4 Thoroughly clean the windscreen recess of the bodyframe, and examine the rubber surround. If it is cut or has perished or hardened or old pieces of sealant cannot easily be removed, then renew it.
5 Commence installation of the windscreen by locating the rubber surround to the glass. Fit a thin cord to the body seating groove of the rubber surround, so that the two ends overlap at the bottom centre.
6 Locate the windscreen accurately at the body aperture with the two ends of the pull cord hanging inside the vehicle.
7 Have an assistant press on the glass from the outside and pull the two ends of the fitting cord evenly so that the combination of pressure and cord withdrawal will engage the rubber surround lip with the body flange.
8 With the windscreen installed, inject black sealant into the space between the rubber and the glass and between the rubber and the body.

9 Install the side and top bright moulding strips by applying pressure so that its turned over edge engages with the rubber surround. A special tool is available for this job.
10 Clean off any excess sealant with a rag soaked in paraffin.

23 Driving cab (Hi-Ace, truck type) - removal and installation

1 Disconnect the lead from the battery negative terminal.
2 Remove the radiator grille.
3 Disconnect the horn leads and remove the horns.
4 Disconnect the hydraulic line which runs between the clutch master cylinder and the operating cylinder.
5 Disconnect the hydraulic line which runs between the brake master cylinder and the two-way union.
6 Disconnect all wiring harness connector plugs inside the driving cab and unclip the harness from the cab structure.
7 Using a suitable puller, extract the steering drop arm from the sector shaft.
8 Disconnect the steering column gearshift control rods from their levers at the base of the steering column.
9 Disconnect the wiring harness at the side of the steering column.
10 On vehicles without recirculating ball steering, withdraw the steering assembly as described in Chapter 11.
11 On vehicles with recirculating ball steering, disconnect the steering shaft flexible coupling and remove the column assembly.
12 Disconnect the speedometer cable from the speedometer.
13 Disconnect the parking brake cable from the intermediate lever.
14 Disconnect the HT and LT leads from the ignition coil.
15 Disconnect the choke cable and the accelerator control from the carburettor.
16 Unscrew and remove the four bolts which are used to mount the driving cab on the chassis.
17 Open the two doors and pass a substantial baulk of timber through the cab. Attach slings and a hoist to the end of the timber and raise the body, then move it forward to disengage it from the chassis and the rear body pressing.
18 Installation is a reversal of removal, but bleed the clutch and brake hydraulic circuits on completion.

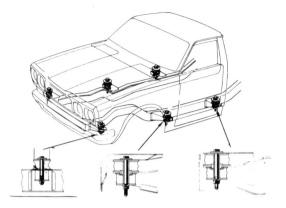

Fig. 12.26. Driving cab mounting points (Hi-Lux)

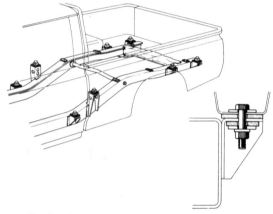

Fig. 12.28. Rear body mounting points (Hi-Lux)

Fig. 12.29. Disconnecting heater control cable (Hi-Lux, later)

Fig. 12.27. Removing driving cab (Hi-Lux)

24 Rear body (Hi-Ace, truck type) - removal and installation

1 Disconnect the lead from the battery negative terminal.
2 Disconnect the leads to the rear lamp clusters.
3 Extract the body mounting bolts and, using a suitable hoist, lift the body from the chassis frame.
4 Installation is a reversal of removal.

25 Driving cab (Hi-Lux) - removal and installation

1 Disconnect the lead from the battery negative terminal, and from the radiator bolt.
2 Disconnect the battery to starter motor cable from the starter.
3 Disconnect the hydraulic hose from the clutch operating cylinder.
4 Disconnect the hydraulic lines which run between the master cylinder and the two- and three-way unions.

5 Disconnect the headlight and rear light wiring harness at the multi-pin connectors behind the instrument panel. Also disconnect the harnesses from their securing clips.
6 On vehicles with steering column gearshift, disconnect the controls from the levers at the base of the steering column.
7 On vehicles with floor-shift, remove the gearshift hand control lever.
8 Disconnect and free the wiring which runs to the alternator.
9 Disconnect the HT and LT leads from the ignition coil.
10 On vehicles equipped with a 12R type engine, disconnect the choke and accelerator cables.
11 Drain the cooling system and disconnect the heater hoses.
12 Disconnect the speedometer cable from the speedometer and pull it from under the driving cab.
13 Disconnect the parking brake primary cable from the intermediate lever.
14 Disconnect the steering linkage from the drop arm by separating the balljoint.
15 Release the flexible coupling pinch bolt at the lower end of the steering shaft and then unbolt and remove the steering box.
16 Unbolt the front bumper by extracting the bumper bracket bolts from the chassis frame.
17 Unscrew and remove the six cab mounting bolts and then pass a baulk of timber through the cab (doors open) and lift the cab from the chassis using a suitable hoist and slings.
18 Installation is a reversal of removal, but on completion, bleed the clutch and brake hydraulic systems.

26 Rear body (Hi-Lux) - removal and installation

1 Disconnect the leads to the rear lamp clusters at the harness connectors.
2 Disconnect the rear body earth strap.
3 Unscrew and remove the eight body mounting bolts.
4 Utilise the load cover rope hooks to attach lifting slings and then hoist the body from the chassis frame.
5 Installation is a reversal of removal.

Fig. 12.30. Removing heater assembly (Hi-Ace)

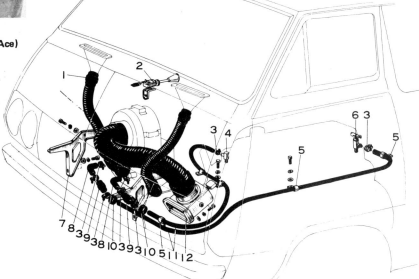

Fig. 12.31. Heater installation (Hi-Ace)

1 *Demister hose*
2 *Booster fan switch*
3 *Hose clip*
4 *Union*
5 *Support clip*
6 *Valve*
7 *Support bracket*
8 *Elbow*
9 *Connector*
10 *Grommet*
11 *Hose*
12 *Air duct*

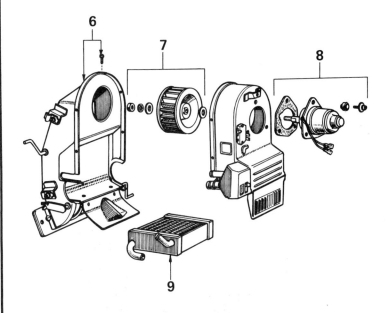

Fig. 12.32. Heater components (Hi-Ace)

6 *Front casing*   8 *Blower motor*
7 *Blower fan*   9 *Matrix*

Fig. 12.33. Removing heater matrix

27 Heater (Hi-Ace) - removal, overhaul and installation

1   Drain the cooling system.
2   Disconnect the lead from the battery negative terminal.
3   Disconnect the heater electrical leads at the wiring harness connector.
4   Disconnect the two demister hoses from the heater casing. On later models, disconnect the heater control cables.
5   Remove the ashtray from the instrument panel and then extract the heater mounting bolts.
6   Pull the heater far enough forward to give access to disconnect the two heater water hoses from the rear of the unit.
7   Remove the heater from the driving compartment, taking care not to spill any coolant which may be left in the heater matrix.
8   If the fault in the heater is due to a blockage, try reverse flushing the heater matrix with a cold water hose before dismantling.
9   If the fault in the unit is due to a leakage from the matrix or a faulty blower motor, dismantle the unit in the following way.
10 Remove the air deflector plate and separate the two halves of the heater casing.
11 Withdraw the heater matrix and renew it if it is leaking, or if it is clogged and cannot be cleared.
12 Unscrew the retaining nut and remove the blower fan.
13 Remove the blower motor from the heater casing.
14 Extract the two tie bolts and withdraw the blower motor housing.
15 If necessary, the brushes can be renewed after unsoldering the field coil wires from the brush holder.
16 Clean the commutator and if the motor armature is to be removed,

take care not to lose the thrust washers at each end of the armature shaft.
17 Reassembly and installation are reversals of removal and dismantling, but apply multi-purpose grease to the bearing surfaces of the armature shaft before reassembly. Do not overtighten the blower fan nut.

28 Heater (Hi-Lux) - removal, overhaul and installation

1   The heater assembly is very similar to the unit installed in the Hi-Ace models and is located under the instrument panel within the driving compartment.
2   All operations described in the preceding Section apply, but detailed differences should be observed from the relevant illustration.

29 Fresh air outlets - removal and refitting

1   The fresh air outlets, which are located at each side of the instrument panel, are of three section construction and are secured in position by spring clips (photos).
2   Normally, a sharp jerk will release the outlet nozzle, but, if necessary, reach up behind the instrument panel and depress the retaining clip while pulling the assembly forward.
3   Refitting is a reversal of removal, but make sure that the spring clips are correctly aligned with their notches.

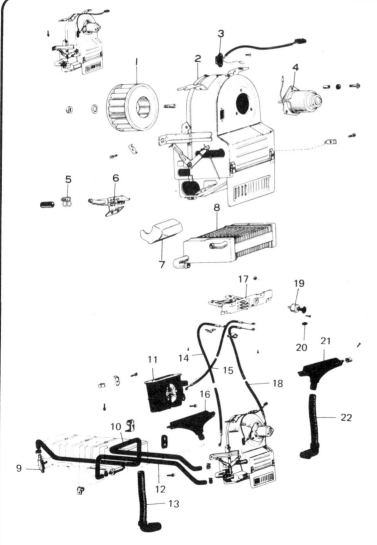

Fig. 12.34. Heater components (Hi-Lux)

1	Blower fan	12	Hose
2	Casing	13	Demister hose
3	Resistor	14	Control cable
4	Motor	15	Air inlet control cable
5	Hose clip	16	Demister nozzle
6	Water valve	17	Control lever assembly
7	Cover	18	Demister control cable
8	Matrix	19	Heater blower fan switch
9	Union	20	Control knob
10	Hose	21	Demister nozzle
11	Cowl duct	22	Demister hose

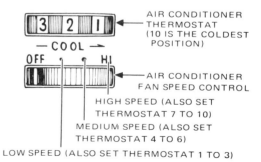

AIR CONDITIONER THERMOSTAT (10 IS THE COLDEST POSITION)

AIR CONDITIONER FAN SPEED CONTROL

HIGH SPEED (ALSO SET THERMOSTAT 7 TO 10)
MEDIUM SPEED (ALSO SET THERMOSTAT 4 TO 6)
LOW SPEED (ALSO SET THERMOSTAT 1 TO 3)

Fig. 12.35. Air conditioning system controls (Hi-Lux)

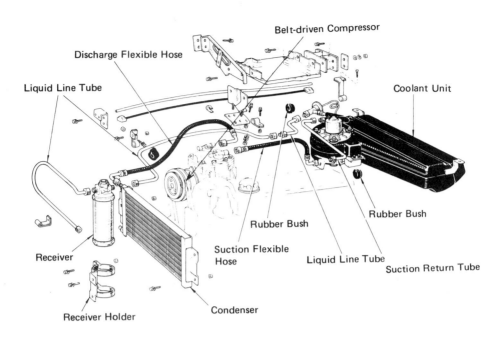

Fig. 12.36. Air conditioning system components (Hi-Lux)

29.1a Fresh air outlet (Hi-Lux)

29.1b Fresh air outlet nozzle components (Hi-Lux)

29.1c Fresh air outlet nozzle showing securing spring clips (Hi-Lux)

30 Air conditioning system (Hi-Lux option) - general description and maintenance

1   The optionally specified system comprises a cooling unit, a belt driven compressor, a condenser and a receiver together with the necessary temperature controls.
2   The oil filled compressor is driven from the crankshaft pulley and incorporates a magnetic type clutch.
3   For best results, make sure that the vehicle heater is OFF (with the temperature lever fully to the right, the blower fan switched off, and the air flow lever to RECIRC). Now switch on the air conditioner fan and move the thermostat wheel to the desired setting.
4   To maintain optimum performance of the system, the owner should limit his operations to the following:

   a) *Checking the tension of the compressor driving belt. The total deflection of this belt should be between 5/8 and ¾ in (15.8 and 19.1 mm) at the centre of its longest run. Adjust by moving the idler pulley.*
   b) *Checking the security of all hoses and unions.*
   c) *Always keeping the ignition timing correctly set.*
   d) *Checking the security of the electrical connections.*

5   Use a soft brush to remove accumulations of dust and flies from the condenser fins.
6   During the winter months, operate the air conditioning system for a few minutes each week to lubricate the interior of the compressor pump, as lack of use may cause deterioration in the moving parts.

31 Air conditioning system (Hi-Lux option) - precautions

1   Servicing of the system is outside the scope of the home mechanic as special equipment is needed to purge or recharge the system with refrigerant gas and dismantling of any part of the system must not be undertaken, in the interest of safety, without first having discharged the system pressure.
2   During engine or radiator removal, the compressor or condenser can normally be unbolted and moved aside as far as their flexible connecting hoses will allow, to provide adequate clearance. Where this is insufficient, **on no account disconnect any of the hoses or pipes of the air conditioning system** without first having the system discharged by your Toyota dealer, or a professional refrigeration engineer. Any escape of refrigerant gases can be very dangerous.

32 Fault diagnosis - air conditioning system

Symptom	Cause

Little or no cooling effect	Magnetic clutch not engaging due to:
	    blown fuse
	    defective microswitch
	    defective resistor
	    defective thermistor
	    broken electrical lead.
	Loose compressor drive belt.
	Defective compressor pump.
	Insufficient refrigerant.
	Defective expansion valve.
	Choked receiver.
	Control dampers inoperative.

Restricted air ejection	Blower fuse blown. Blower motor defective. Blower switch or resistor defective.
Noisy operation	Dry or worn blower motor bearing. Worn compressor. Compressor mountings loose. Low oil level in compressor. Magnetic clutch bearings worn. Slack drive belt. Worn idler pulley bearing.
Overheating of engine (see also Fault diagnosis, Chapter 2)	Condenser fins clogged.

Chapter 13 Supplement

Contents

1 Introduction

The contents of this Chapter update the original information contained in this manual and cover vehicles produced from late 1977, otherwise the original details given in Chapters 1 to 12 apply.

2 Routine maintenance

As a result of improvements in lubricants and materials, the service intervals have been extended for 1977 and later vehicles and the following schedule should be used for these vehicles except where operating under very arduous conditions. The original 250 mile (400 km) and 1000 mile (1600 km) (new vehicle) maintenance checks should still be observed.

Every 7500 miles (12 000 km) or at 6 monthly intervals

Engine
Renew engine oil and filter
Check exhaust pipes for corrosion
Check ignition timing and dwell angle and renew contact points if pitted

Brakes
Check pedal travel
Check disc pad wear
Inspect brake lines for corrosion

Transmission
Check transmission fluid level

Steering
Check steering gear lubricant level
Check linkage balljoints for wear or split covers
Lubricate steering and suspension points

Every 15 000 miles (24 000 km) or at 12 monthly intervals

Engine
Check and adjust valve clearances
Check and adjust drivebelt tension

Inspect coolant hoses and connections
Check and adjust slow running and fast idle
Renew spark plugs

Emission control systems
Check all connections, operation of PCV valve and charcoal canister

Brakes
Inspect rear shoe lining thickness

Transmission
Lubricate propeller shaft

Every 30 000 miles (48 000 km) or at 2 yearly intervals

Engine
Renew drivebelts
Renew engine coolant mixture
Renew fuel filter
Renew air filter

Emission control systems
Renew PCV valve
Renew fuel tank cap gasket
Service air injection system

Transmission
Renew rear axle oil
Renew automatic transmission fluid
Suspension and steering
Clean out front hub bearings and repack with grease
Lubricate steering linkage centre bracket
Check front wheel alignment and steering angles

Every 60 000 miles (96 000 km) or at 4 yearly intervals

Emission control systems
Renew charcoal canister

Brakes
Renew all hydraulic system seals and recharge with fresh fluid

3 Specifications

Engine idle speeds (20R engine 1977 on)

Initial setting of idle speed screw		
Manual transmission	870 rpm	
Automatic transmission	920 rpm	
Final adjustment of idle mixture screw (lean drop)		
Manual transmission	800 rpm	
Automatic transmission	850 rpm	

Clutch
Hi-Ace 1977 on

Pedal height from floor to centre of pad upper surface	7.44 to 7.83 in (189 to 199 mm)
Pedal free play at pad	0.02 to 0.20 in (0.5 to 5.0 mm)
Play at release arm tip	
12R engine	0.14 to 0.19 in (3.5 to 4.8 mm)
18R engine	0.08 to 0.12 in (2.0 to 3.0 mm)

Hi-Lux 1977 on

Pedal height from floor to centre of pad upper surface	6.3 in (160 mm)
Pedal free play at pad	0.02 to 0.20 in (0.5 to 5.0 mm)
Play at release arm outer end	
12R engine	0.14 to 0.20 in (3.5 to 5.0 mm)
8R or 18R engine	0.08 to 0.14 in (2.0 to 3.5 mm)

Manual gearbox
Gearbox type L40 — Hi-Ace with 18R engine

The L40 gearbox is almost identical with the L42 unit described for later Hi-Ace models in Chapter 6 except that it has a detachable clutch bellhousing

Torque wrench settings	lbf ft	Nm
Clutch bellhousing to engine	50	68
Clutch bellhousing to gearcase	50	68
Extension housing to gearcase	30	41
Front bearing retainer to gearcase	15	20

Automatic transmission

Type ... ...   A-40 three forward speeds and one reverse speed

Ratios

1st	2.450 : 1	
2nd	1.450 : 1	
3rd	1.000 : 1	
Reverse	2.220 : 1	

Fluid capacity

Fluid change ... ...   2.1 Imp. qts (2.5 US qts/2.4 litres)
Refill (dry torque converter) ... ...   5.1 Imp. qts (6.1 US qts/5.8 litres)

Torque wrench settings	lbf ft	Nm
Driveplate to crankshaft bolts	43	58
Driveplate to torque converter bolts	15	20
Torque converter housing to engine bolts	55	75
Oil pan bolts	8	11
Extension housing bolts	30	41

Braking system (Hi-Ace 1976 on)

System type ... ...   Four wheel drum or front disc rear drum

Disc minimum thickness after refinishing ... ...   0.75 in (19.0 mm)

Drum maximum internal diameter after refinishing ... ...   10.08 in (256.0 mm)

Torque wrench settings	lbf ft	Nm
Reservoir to master cylinder	30	41
Master cylinder stop bolt	11	15

Suspension and steering
Front wheel alignment angles (Hi-Lux 1977 on)

Toe-in ... ...   0.19 to 0.28 in (5 to 7 mm)
Camber ... ... $1^{\circ} \pm 30'$
Castor ... ... 1° negative to 1° positive

Turning angles (Hi-Lux)
6.00 — 14 tyres
   Inner wheel ... ... 36° to 39°
   Outer wheel ... ... 30° 30'
7.00 — 14 tyres
   Inner wheel ... ... 32° 15' to 34° 15'
   Outer wheel ... ... 28° 30'
7.50 — 14 or 185SR14 tyres
   Inner wheel ... ... 30° to 32°
   Outer wheel ... ... 27° 15'

Front wheel alignment angles (Hi-Ace)
Toe-in ... ...   2.8 to 3.5 in (7 to 9 mm)
Camber ... ...   35' ± 30' positive. Difference between sides to be less than 30'
Castor
   Truck* ... ...   35' ± 30'
   Van*
      RH20 model ... ...   50' ± 30'
      RH30 model ... ... 1° ± 30'
      RH42 model ... ... 1° 10' ± 30'
Difference between sides to be less than 30'

Turning angles (Hi-Ace)
Inner wheel ... ... 30° to 33°
Outer wheel ... ... 30°

4 Engine

1968cc engine fitted to Hi-Ace models — general

1   Certain Hi-Ace models are now offered with the 18R 1968cc engine.
Full details of this engine are included in the main Chapters of this
manual in connection with the Hi-Lux range but where the installation
of this engine in the Hi-Ace causes any variation in the original overhaul
procedures then these are given in this Supplement.

Engine service cover (Hi-Ace) — removal

2   Models built from the end of 1977 have an engine service cover which
is removable by turning a handle instead of the earlier bolt on type.

Piston ring modification

3   Commencing from January 1977, the oil control ring fitted to pistons
on 12 R type engines has been changed to a three section design and
the groove hole for the second compression ring has been deleted.

5 Fuel system

Revised float level adjustment (20R engine models)

1   Commencing with 1978 models, due to a slight modification to the
float pivot assembly, the float should be adjusted in the following way.
2   Turn the carburettor upside down and allow the float to hang by its
own weight. Measure the distance between the lowest point of the
float and the surface of the air horn (gasket removed) (Fig 13.1). The
dimension should be 0.276 in (7.0mm) otherwise bend the float hinge
at the point (A) (Fig 13.2).
3   Now raise the float gently with the finger and measure the clearance
between the fuel inlet needle valve plunger and the tab which de-
presses the plunger. This clearance should be 0.039 in (1.0 mm), otherwise bend the tab to correct (Fig 13.3).
4   When the carburettor is reassembled, check the fuel level in the
sight glass. If the fuel level is not within the tolerance indicated in the
diagram, adjust the float slightly as necessary.

6 Ignition system

Fully transistorized ignition — description and precautions

1   Commencing 1978, Hi-Lux models equipped with a 20R engine
have a transistorized ignition system instead of the previously used
conventional mechanical breaker distributor and associated components.
2   The new distributor incorporates a timing rotor, a magnet and pick-
up coil and an igniter.
3   The advantages of the transistorized system are that there is no
contact breaker to adjust or maintain, low speed performance is improv-
ed and cold starting under adverse weather conditions is less likely to
be affected.
4   Certain precautions must be observed with a transistorized ignition
system.

> *(a) Do not disconnect the battery leads when the engine is running*
> *(b) Make sure that the igniter is always well earthed*
> *(c) Keep water away from the igniter and distributor*
> *(d) If a tachometer is to be connected to the engine, always
>   connect the tachometer (+) terminal to the ignition coil (−)
>   terminal, never to the distributor.*

Fully transistorized ignition — testing

5   In the event of a fault developing in the system, the following checks
and tests can be carried out if a voltmeter and ohmmeter are available.
6   Check the air gap between the rotor and the pick-up coil projection
using a feeler blade (Fig 13.6). This should be between 0.008 and 0.016
in (0.2 and 0.4 mm) when the rotor is in the position shown (Fig. 13.7).
If necessary, release the screws which secure the signal generator baseplate and prise the generator using a screwdriver in the notch provided.
7   Carry out a spark test by pulling out the centre HT lead from the
distributor cap and while holding its end close to the cylinder block,
operate the starter motor. A strong flash should be observed from the
end of the lead. Carry out this test for the shortest possible time to
avoid damage to the ignition system components.
8   Check all connectors and wiring.
9   To check the ignition coil resistance, connect an ohmmeter between
the terminals and compare the values in the sequence shown in Fig 13.8
and in the following table.

Terminals	Resistance	Specified value
C and E	Primary coil	1.35 to 1.65 ohm
C and D	Secondary coil	12.8 to 15.2 Kilo-ohm
A and B	Resistor	1.3 to 1.7. ohm
C and F	Insulation	Infinity

10 Check the signal generator by connecting an ohmmeter to the plug
leads (Fig 13.9). The indicated resistance should be between 130 and
190 ohm.
11 To check the igniter, switch on the ignition and connect a voltmeter
between the (−) terminal of the ignition coil and the resistor terminal
(Fig 13.10). 12 volts should be indicated. Now disconnect the wiring

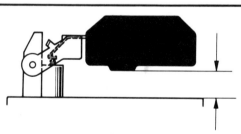

Fig. 13.1. Float level adjustment (float inverted)

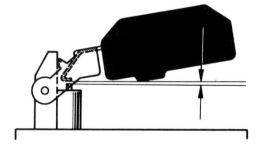

Fig. 13.3 Fuel inlet needle valve plunger clearance (float raised)

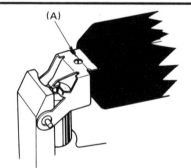

Fig. 13.2. Float hinge bonding point

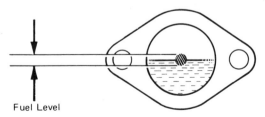

Fuel Level

Fig. 13.4. Fuel level tolerance on sight glass

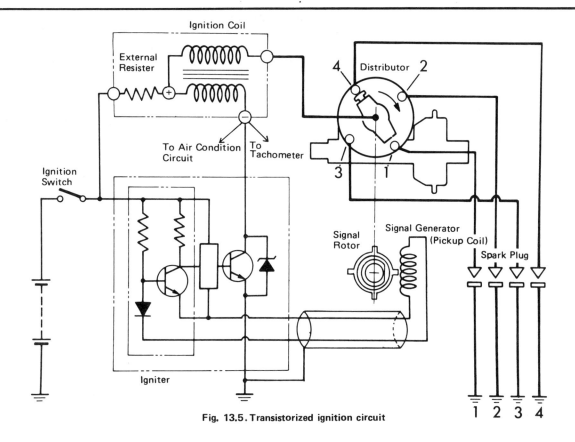

Fig. 13.5. Transistorized ignition circuit

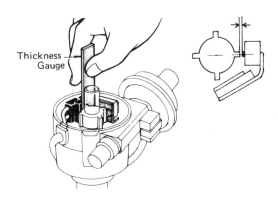

Fig. 13.6. Checking air gap (transistorized ignition)

Fig. 13.7. Removing signal generator baseplate (transistorized ignition)

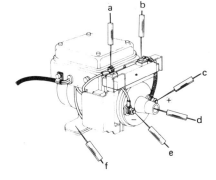

Fig. 13.8. Transistorized ignition resistance checking diagram. For terminal identification see text

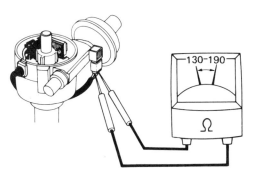

Fig. 13.9. Checking signal generator resistance

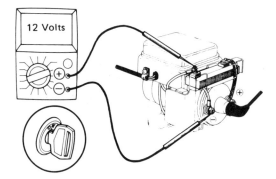

Fig. 13.10. Checking igniter voltage

connector plug from the distributor. Select the 1 ohm or 10 ohm range on the ohmmeter and then use the ohmmeter as a resistance by connecting it between the two terminals (Fig 13.11). Turn on the ignition switch and check the voltage between the (−) terminal on the ignition coil and the resistor terminal, again using the voltmeter.

12 Any failure of these tests to perform as described will mean that the component being tested must be renewed.

Distributor (transistorized type) — removal and refitting

13 Prise down the distributor cap springs and push the cap complete with leads to one side.

14 Disconnect the wiring plug on the side of the distributor body also pull off the vacuum pipe.

15 Unscrew and remove the bolt which holds the distributor clamp plate to the cylinder block.

16 Withdraw the distributor from its recess.

17 Before installing the distributor, turn the engine over until No. 1 piston is rising on its compression stroke. Continue to turn the crankshaft until the BTDC mark on the crankshaft pulley comes in line with the mark on the pointer on the timing cover.

18 Smear the distributor shaft and drive gear with engine oil and then hold the distributor ready for inserting into its recess so that the vernier adjuster (octane selector) is pointing vertically upwards with the vacuum diaphragm unit at the bottom. Set the rotor so that its contact end aligns with the cap hold-down spring at the top edge of the distributor body.

19 Push the distributor fully into position and as its drivegear meshes, the rotor will rotate through 30° in an anti-clockwise direction and

take up alignment with the No. 1 spark plug lead contact if the distributor cap is fitted.

20 Screw in the clamp plate bolt finger tight and then turn the distributor body until the projection on the reluctor is square to the one on the pick-up coil. Fully tighten the clamp plate bolt.

21 Fit the distributor dustproof cover, cap and reconnect the wiring plug and the vacuum pipe.

Distributor (transistorized type) — dismantling and reassembly

22 With the distributor removed as previously described, prise back the cap clips and remove the cap, rotor and dust excluding cover.

23 Pull the rubber seal from the rim of the distributor body.

24 Extract the screws which hold the signal generator in place and remove it.

25 Remove the connector plug assembly (one screw) and then pull out the vacuum advance unit.

26 Extract the screws and lift out the base plate.

27 If the distributor must be further dismantled, carefully grind the drivegear as shown in Fig 13.20 and then knock out the securing pin. Discard the gear.

28 Extract the two screws on the bottom face of the distributor body and then tap the shaft from the body using a plastic-faced hammer.

29 Remove the washer, spring and thrust bearing, detach the counterweight springs and prise the grease retainer out of the upper end of the shaft. Note carefully how the counterweight springs are fitted.

30 Insert a screwdriver into the recess in the upper end of the shaft and remove the screw.

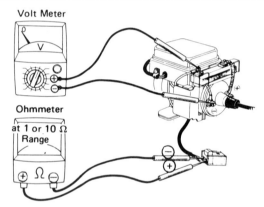

Fig. 13.11. Checking voltage between ignition coil terminal and resistor terminal on the igniter

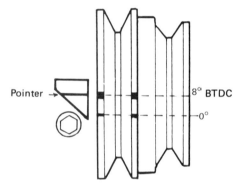

Fig. 13.12. Engine timing marks (20R engine with transistorized ignition)

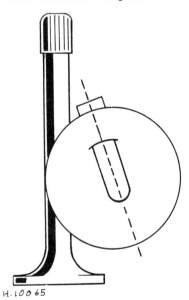

Fig. 13.13. Rotor alignment before fitting transistorized type distributor

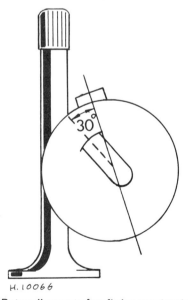

Fig. 13.14. Rotor alignment after fitting transistorized type distributor

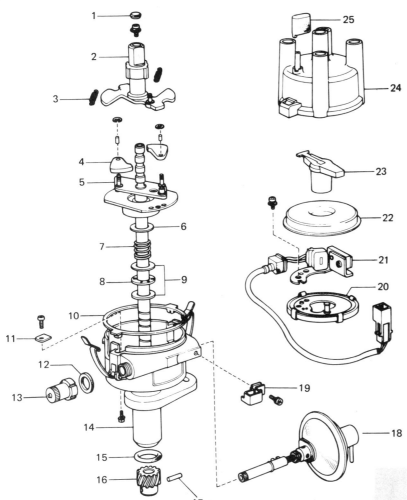

Fig. 13.15. Exploded view of transistorized type distributor

1 Lubricant seal
2 Reluctor
3 Counterweight spring
4 Counterweight
5 Shaft assembly
6 Washer
7 Spring
8 Thrust bearing
9 Washers
10 Dust seal
11 Washer
12 Sealing washer
13 Vernier adjuster (octane selector)
14 Body
15 O ring
16 Gear
17 Pin
18 Vacuum unit
19 Wire clamp
20 Baseplate
21 signal generator
22 Dustproof cover
23 Rotor
24 Distributor cap
25 Grommet

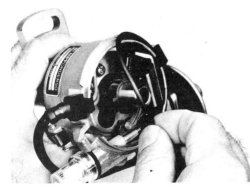

Fig. 13.16. Removing sealing ring from distributor body

Fig. 13.17. Removing vacuum advance unit screw

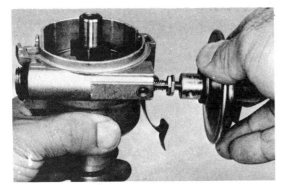

Fig. 13.18. Withdrawing vacuum advance unit

Fig. 13.19. Removing baseplate

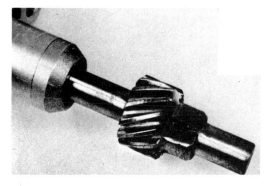

Fig. 13.20. Distributor drivegear ground away for pin removal

Fig. 13.21. Unscrewing distributor shaft bearing retainer screws

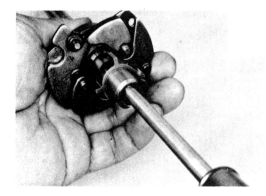

Fig. 13.22. Unscrewing distributor shaft upper screw

Fig. 13.23. Withdrawing distributor shaft reluctor

Fig. 13.24. Removing a distributor counterweight

Fig. 13.25. Distributor cam/shaft mating marks

Fig. 13.26. Refitting distributor counterweight springs

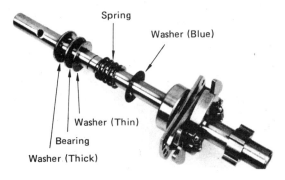

Spring

Washer (Blue)

Washer (Thin)

Bearing

Washer (Thick)

Fig. 13.27. Distributor shaft and washer identification

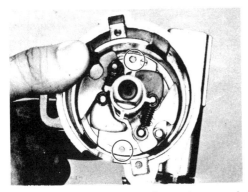

Fig. 13.28. Aligning distributor bearing retainer screw holes

Fig. 13.29. Peening distributor drivegear pin in the jaws of a vice

31 Pull off the reluctor.

32 Prise off the circlips from the counterweight pivot posts and then pull off the counterweights.

33 Inspect all components and renew any which are worn, cracked or deformed.

34 Commence reassembly by applying a little grease to the distributor shaft and inner surface of the cam. Install the cam assembly to the shaft so that the 10 mark is adjacent to the counterweight stop.

35 Fit the counterweights and their circlips, reconnect the springs, making sure that they go back in their original positions and the correct way round. Fit the reluctor.

36 Fit the screw at the top of the shaft, press in some grease and fit the grease retainer.

37 Fit the washers and bearing in their correct order as shown in Fig 13.27 and then insert the shaft into the distributor body.

38 Align the holes in the bearing retainer with those in the distributor body and fit the two screws.

39 Fit a new drivegear to the bottom of the shaft, insert the pin and peen both ends by compressing the pin in a vice.

40 Install the baseplate so that the four clips engage in the slots in the distributor body.

41 Fit the retaining screws.

42 Insert the vacuum unit so that its groove engages with the pin and then screw in the wiring connector clamp screw.

43 Fit the signal generator and adjust the air gap as described in paragraph 6 of this Section.

44 Set the vernier adjuster (octane selector) at the standard mark.

45 Refit the dust excluding seal, the dust cover, the rotor arm and distributor cap.

Mating Marks

Fig. 13.30. Hi-Ace steering shaft alignment marks

7 Manual gearbox

Gearbox — removal (Hi-Ace 1977 on)

1 On Hi-Ace vehicles fitted with the 18R (1968cc) engine, the starter motor must be removed before the gearbox can be withdrawn.

Steering column gearshift (Hi-Ace with L40 gearbox 1978 on) — removal, refitting, adjustment

2 Disconnect the two shift control rods from the levers at the base of the steering column.

3 Release the pinch bolt on the steering shaft flexible coupling.

4 Make alignment marks on the wormshaft and the coupling just below the flexible coupling. Unscrew the coupling pinch bolt.

5 Extract the bolts from the steering column upper bracket, also the bolts from the cover plate at the bottom of the steering column where it joins the floor panel.

6 Unbolt and remove the shift control rod support bracket, then withdraw the steering column into the vehicle interior (Fig. 13.33).

7 Withdraw the shift lever from the control shaft (Fig. 13.34).

8 Remove the upper shaft after prising off the circlip (Fig. 13.35).

9 To dismantle the shift lever assembly, cut the locking wire and withdraw the levers 1 and 2 (Fig. 13.36).

10 When reassembling, install the shaft lever so that its projecting boss is towards the front, screw in the locking bolt and fit new locking wire.

11 Install the shift mechanism by reversing the removal operations,

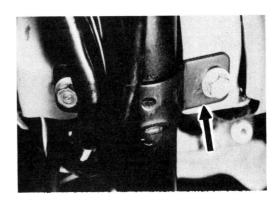

Fig. 13.31. Hi-Ace steering column upper bracket

Fig. 13.32. Hi-Ace steering column cover plate

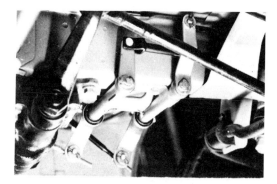

Fig. 13.33. Hi-Ace gearshift control rod support bracket

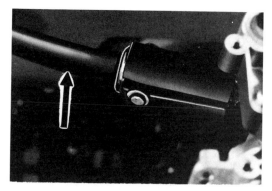

Fig. 13.34. Removing shift lever from control shaft (Hi-Ace)

Fig. 13.35. Removing gearshift control upper shaft (Hi-Ace)

Fig. 13.36. Shift lever assembly (1) select lever (2) shaft lever

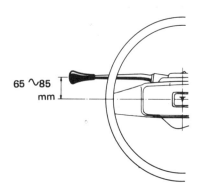

Fig. 13.37. Shift control adjustment diagram (vertical plane)

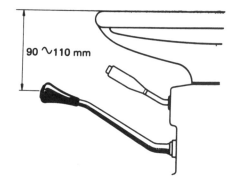

Fig. 13.38. Shift control adjustment diagram (horizontal plane)

remember to align the mating marks on the steering worm and flexible coupling.

12 Adjust the shift control rod to bring the hand control lever to the position shown in Figs 13.37 and 13.38 both in the vertical and horizontal planes.

8 Automatic transmission (A40 type)

Description

1 Commencing with 1977 models in the Hi-Lux range the later type A40 automatic transmission was offered as an option.

2 The transmission is a fully automatic three forward and one reverse speed unit.

3 The transmission is of a bandless construction and requires no periodic adjustment apart from the control cables and selector rods.

4 No rear oil pump is incorporated in the design and in the event of breakdown, the vehicle must not be towed in excess of 30 mph (48 km/h) or further than 50 miles (80 km) unless the propeller shaft is disconnected. Failure to observe this requirement may cause damage to the transmission due to lack of lubrication. Due to the complexities of dismantling and reassembly of automatic transmission units, the operations described in this Section are limited to maintenance, adjustment of the controls and removal and refitting of the unit.

Maintenance

5 If the transmission fluid is cold, withdraw the dipstick, wipe it, re-insert it and withdraw it again. The fluid level should be within the cold range. If the vehicle has travelled at least 5 miles (8 km) the fluid level should be within the hot range of the dipstick when the same checking procedure is followed. Top-up with fluid of the specified grade.

6 Keep the external surfaces of the transmission unit clean and free from mud and grease to prevent overheating. An oil cooler is fitted, make sure that the connecting pipes are secure and in good condition.

7 The automatic transmission fluid normally only requires changing

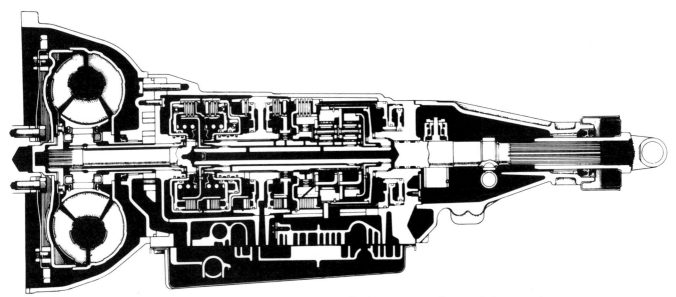

Fig. 13.39. Cutaway view of A40 type automatic transmission

at 25 000 miles (40 000 km) intervals, but if the oil on the dipstick appears burned or discolored or if particularly arduous or dusty operating conditions prevail, the fluid should be drained by removing at more frequent intervals.

8 As the torque converter will not be drained by this method, the refill quantity of fluid will be only 2.1 Imp qts (2.5 US qts/2.4 litres).

Downshift cable — adjustment
9 To adjust the downshift cable, remove the air cleaner and fully depress the accelerator pedal (use a block or piece of wood) checking that the carburettor throttle valve is fully open. Hold the pedal depressed.
10 Measure the distance between the end of the accelerator outer cable and the stop collar which should be between 2.00 and 2.17 in (51.0 and 55.0 mm) (Fig 13.41). If necessary, adjust the outer cable by slackening the two locknuts on the support bracket.

Speed selector linkage (floor shift) — adjustment
11 To adjust the speed selector linkage, slacken the swivel nut on the control rod.
12 Push the selector lever on the side of the transmission fully forward and then pull it back three notches to the 'N' position.
13 Have an assistant hold the speed selector lever in 'N' and then re-tighten the swivel nut. Check the operation of the transmission in all positions of the speed range.

Speed selector linkage (column shift) — adjustment
14 Loosen the nut on the connecting rod swivel (5) (Fig 13.43).
15 Set the lever on the side of the transmission to the 'N' position. If any difficulty is found in establishing this position, push the lever into P (Park) and count the number of 'clicks' back to neutral.
16 Now move the rod (4) (Fig 13.43) until the speed position indicator is in alignment with the 'N' mark. Without moving rod or lever, tighten the locknut at the swivel.
17 Check that the engine starts in P and N only and that the vehicle moves forward in D and reverses in R.

Neutral start safety switch — adjustment
18 If the engine will start in selector positions other than N or P and it is known that the selector linkage is correctly adjusted, adjust the neutral safety switch in the following way.
19 Loosen the bolt (1) (Fig 13.44).
20 Set the speed selector lever in 'N'.
21 Align the groove in the switch shaft with the neutral basic line (Fig 13.44).
22 Without moving the switch, tighten the bolt.

Extension housing oil seal — renewal
23 Fluid leakage from the rear end of the extension housing will indicate

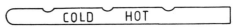

Fig. 13.40. Dipstick markings (A40 transmission)

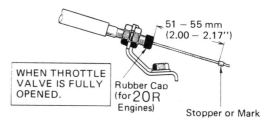

Fig. 13.41. Downshift cable adjustment diagram (A40 transmission)

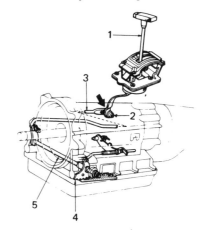

Fig. 13.42. Speed selector linkage (A40 transmission)

1 Shift lever   4 Valve lever
2 Swivel   5 Valve lever shaft
3 Control rod

the need for renewal of the oil seal.
24 Renewal of the oil seal may be carried out with the transmission unit in position in the vehicle.
25 Remove the propeller shaft as described in Chapter 7.
26 Remove the parking brake cable equalizer support and disconnect the primary cable from the intermediate lever (Fig. 13.45).

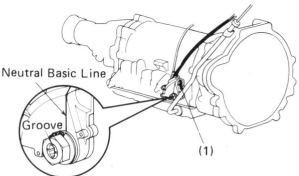

Fig. 13.44. Neutral start switch installation (A40 transmission)
1 Fixing screw

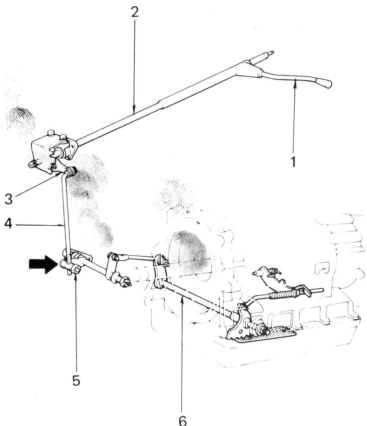

Fig. 13.43. Steering column selector linkage
(A40 transmission)

1 *Shift lever*
2 *Control shaft*
3 *Control shaft laver*
4 *Primary rod*
5 *Swivel*
6 *Valve lever shaft*

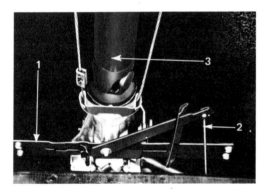

Fig. 13.45. Parking brake equalizer at rear of A40 transmission

1 *Strut*   3 *Propeller shaft*
2 *Primary cable*

27 Using a suitable two-legged puller and exerting pressure against the end of the transmission output shaft, extract the oil seal.
28 Drive in the new seal using a piece of tubing.
29 Install the propeller shaft and connect the parking brake cable and equalizer support.
30 Check the fluid level and top-up.

Automatic transmission — removal and refitting
31 It must be realised that the automatic transmission unit is of considerable weight and adequate assistance or the use of a trolley jack will be required for the following operations.
32 Disconnect the lead from the battery negative terminal.
33 Drain the cooling system and disconnect the radiator top hose.
34 Remove the air cleaner and disconnect the throttle control at the carburettor.
35 Unless the vehicle is over a pit or raised on a hoist, jack-up the front

and rear so that there is an adequate working clearance between the underside of the body floor and the ground to permit the torque converter housing to be withdrawn.
36 Drain the fluid from the transmission unit.
37 Remove the starter motor.
38 Disconnect the propeller shaft from the rear axle (see Chapter 7) and withdraw it from the transmission rear extension housing.
39 Disconnect the speed selector linkage at the transmission unit and the downshift cable at the engine end.
40 Disconnect the exhaust downpipe from the manifold and remove the support bracket from the transmission unit.
41 Disconnect the fluid cooler pipes from the transmission and plug them. Remove the pipe supports from the transmission.
42 Disconnect the speedometer drive cable from the extension housing.
43 Unbolt the two reinforcement brackets from the torque converter housing. Pull the fluid filler tube from the transmission and retain the

'O' ring seals.

44 Remove the support plate from the handbrake equalizer.

45 Extract the two rubber plugs from the lower front face of the torque converter housing.

46 Place a jack (preferably trolley type) under the transmission and unbolt the rear mounting and crossmember.

47 Using a socket inserted through one of the holes in the lower front face of the torque converter housing, unscrew the bolts which hold the driveplate and torque converter together. The bolts can be brought into view one at a time by rotating the crankshaft with a ring spanner applied to the crankshaft pulley bolt.

48 Place a jack under the engine sump (use a block of wood to protect it) and remove the bolts which secure the torque converter housing to the engine.

49 Lower both jacks progressively until the transmission unit will clear the lower edge of the engine rear bulkhead.

50 As the transmission moves away from the engine, the driveplate will remain bolted to the rear flange of the crankshaft.

51 The torque converter can now be pulled forward to remove it from the housing. The driveplate can be unbolted from the crankshaft flange if the plate has to be renewed because of worn starter ring gear.

52 Installation is a reversal of removal but tighten all bolts to the specified torque, apply grease to pilot hole in the centre of the driveplate and carry out the adjustments described earlier in this Section according to type, after first having refilled the unit with the correct grade and quantity of fluid.

Fault diagnosis — automatic transmission

Symptom	Reason/s
Oil on dipstick appears burned or discoloured	Transmission misused by towing overweight loads or by wheel spinning in mud or snow
Water on dipstick	Leak in fluid cooler tube within radiator
No vehicle movement in forward range, or reverse	Incorrectly adjusted selector linkage
Harsh engagement when any drive range selected	Incorrectly adjusted downshift cable
Screech or whine increasing with engine speed	Cracked driveplate Oil pump screen (within oil pan) clogged
Delayed upshifts or downshifts	Incorrectly adjusted downshift cable
Slip on upshifts, downshifts squawk or shudder on take off	Incorrectly adjusted speed selector linkage or downshift cable
Vehicle will not hold parked in 'P'	Incorrectly adjusted selector linkage

Before carrying out any of the foregoing checks always verify that the transmission fluid is at its correct level

9 Braking System

Modified braking system (Hi-Ace 1976 on)

1 Later Hi-Ace vehicles are equipped with a tandem master cylinder (dual hydraulic circuit) and certain models have disc front brakes.

2 Where disc front brakes are fitted, the rear drum brakes are of the self-adjusting type.

Disc pads (Hi-Ace) — inspection and renewal

3 Raise the front of the vehicle and remove the roadwheels. Look through the inspection hole in the cylinder body and inspect the thickness of the friction lining. If this has been reduced to 0.04 in (1.0mm) then the pads must be renewed in the following way.

4 Unscrew and remove the bolts from the cylinder guide plate, extract the cylinder support spring and withdraw the pad support plate.

5 Prise off the anti-rattle spring.

6 Lift the cylinder body off the disc and remove the pads. Note the different design of the two pad backing plates.

7 Depress the piston fully into the cylinder body in order to accommodate the new thicker pads. This may cause a rise in the master cylinder fluid level. Draw some fluid out of the reservoir using an old hydrometer.

8 Brush away any dust from the cylinder body taking care not to inhale it as it contains asbestos. Install the cylinder with pads onto the disc.

9 Assemble the pads, cylinder support spring, cylinder guide plate and pad support plate. Tighten the guide plate bolts to specified torque.

10 Engage the anti-rattle spring, fit the roadwheel and lower the vehicle to the ground.

11 Apply the foot brake hard several times to position the new pads against the disc.

12 Renew the pads on the opposite wheel. Always renew disc pads in axle sets (both front brakes).

Front caliper (Hi-Ace) — removal, overhaul and refitting

13 Raise the front of the vehicle and remove the roadwheel.

Fig. 13.46. Removing caliper cylinder guide plate (Hi-Ace)

1 Guide plate *3 Pad support plate*
2 Support spring

Fig. 13.47. Prising off anti-rattle spring (Hi-Ace caliper)

Fig. 13.48. Withdrawing caliper cylinder body (Hi-Ace)

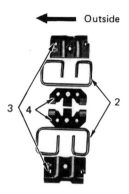

Fig. 13.49 Disc pad components (Hi-Ace caliper)

2 Support spring
3 Guide plate
4 Pad support plate

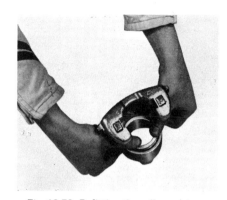

Fig. 13.50. Refitting the caliper piston

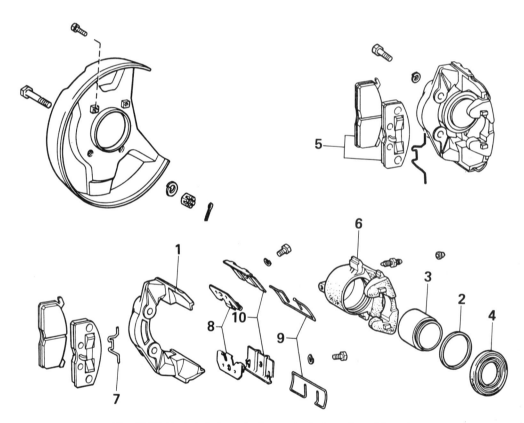

Fig. 13.51. Exploded view of a front wheel disc caliper (Hi-Ace)

1 Cylinder mounting
2 Piston seal
3 Piston
4 Dust excluding boot
5 Disc pads
6 Cylinder
7 Anti-rattle spring
8 Pad support plate
9 Support spring
10 Cylinder guide plate

14 Withdraw the cylinder body from the disc as described in paragraphs 3 to 6.

15 Tape over the vent hole in the master cylinder reservoir cap to reduce loss of fluid when the pipeline is disconnected from the caliper cylinder body.

16 Remove the pads from the cylinder body and then disconnect the flexible hose at the support bracket. Cap the open ends of the hose and the pipeline to prevent leakage of fluid and entry of dirt.

17 Clean away external dirt from the cylinder body and then pull off the dust excluding boot from the cylinder.

18 Apply a little gentle air pressure (from a hand or foot pump) to the fluid inlet hole in the cylinder body and eject the piston.

19 At this stage, examine the surfaces of the piston and the cylinder bore. If there is any evidence of scoring or if any 'bright' wear areas are visible then the complete cylinder body should be renewed.

20 If these components are in good condition extract the piston seal and discard it and then obtain a repair kit which will contain all the necessary renewable components.

21 Clean the piston and cylinder in hydraulic fluid, install the new piston seal using the fingers to manipulate it into position.

22 Dip the piston in clean hydraulic fluid and press it squarely into the cylinder. Fit the dust excluding boot.

23 Refit the caliper by reversing the removal operations, bleed the hydraulic system and fit the roadwheel and lower the vehicle.

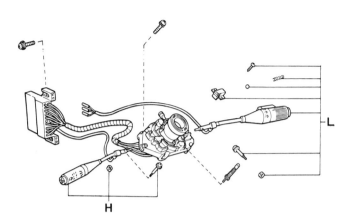

Fig. 13.52. Hi-Ace steering column switch

H Wiper Section
L Lighting switch and direction indicator switch

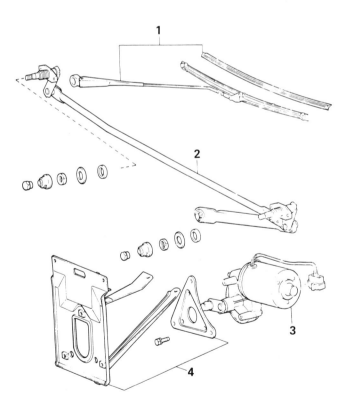

Fig. 13.53. Windscreen wiper motor and linkage (Hi-Ace)

1 Wiper arm and blade   3 Motor
2 Link   4 Mounting bracket

Rear drum brakes (Hi-Ace 1976 on) — general
24 If the vehicle is equipped with four-wheel drum brakes then the rear brake is of the type shown in Fig 9.7 of Chapter 9.
25 If the vehicle is equipped with front disc brakes then the rear brakes are of the type shown in Fig 9.8A of Chapter 9 and are automatically adjusted.
26 Refer to Chapter 9, Section 4 for full details of these drum brake systems.

10 Electrical system

Relays (Hi-Ace)
1 Later Hi-Ace models are fitted with two light control relays, one for the tail lights and the other for the headlights. These relays are mounted under the left-hand side of the facia panel.

Modified steering column combination switch (Hi-Ace)
2 On later Hi-Ace models, the steering column combination switch incorporates separate wiper and lighting switch controls.
3 The switch is accessible for removal after first withdrawing the steering wheel and column upper covers as described in Chapter 11, Sections 13 and 15.

Later type windscreen wiper (Hi-Ace)
4 A modified type of wiper motor assembly is fitted on later models.
5 To remove, take off the wiper arm and blade then disconnect the crankarm which joins the wiper motor to the linkage.
6 Disconnect the electrical leads and unscrew the wiper motor mounting bolts.
7 Refitting is a reversal of removal but before fitting the wiper arms, make sure that the motor has been switched on and then off using the wiper switch so that the crankarm is in the auto-stop (parked) position.

Rear window wiper assembly (Hi-Ace)
8 Access to the rear wiper motor is obtainable after removing the cover plate from the rear tailgate (Fig. 13.54).
9 The wiper motor assembly can be removed after first taking off the wiper arms, then extracting the cover plate screws and disconnecting the electrical leads (Fig. 13.55).
10 Refitting is a reversal of removal but refit the wiper arm when the motor has been switched on and off by means of the wiper switch and is therefore in the parked position.

Rear window washer assembly (Hi-Ace)
11 A flexible bag type reservoir is used in conjunction with the rear window washer arrangement (Fig. 13.56).
12 The washer jets can be removed from the body panel if one of the retaining locking clips is first depressed using a screwdriver (Fig. 13.57).

Radio (Hi-Ace) — removal and refitting
13 Depress the heater control knob locking tabs and pull off the knobs.
14 Pinch the top and bottom edges of the heater control indicator plate together and remove the plate (Fig. 13.59).
15 Pull off the radio control knobs and then unscrew the control bezel nuts and remove the escutcheon plate.
16 Working from under the lower edge of the facia panel, unscrew and remove the three screws which hold the heater control panel to its mounting brackets.
17 Push the radio receiver and heater control panel inward slightly and

Fig. 13.54. Tailgate cover plate removed (Hi-Ace)

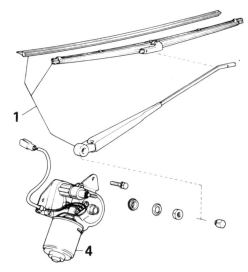

Fig. 13.55. Rear window wiper motor and linkage (Hi-Ace)

1 Wiper arm and blade 4 Motor

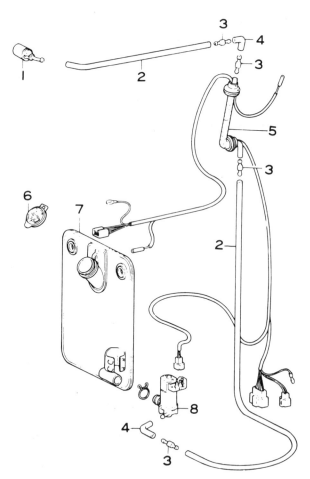

Fig. 13.56. Rear window washer components (Hi-Ace)

1 Jet   5 Wiring harness
2 Hose   6 Cap
3 Connector 7 Reservoir
4 Elbow   8 Electric pump

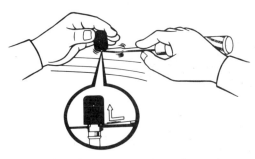

Fig. 13.57. Removing a washer jet (Hi-Ace)

Fig. 13.58. Removing a heater control knob (Hi-Ace)

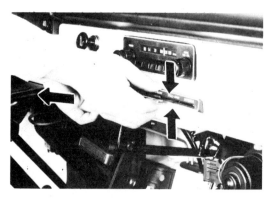

Fig. 13.59. Removing heater control indicator plate

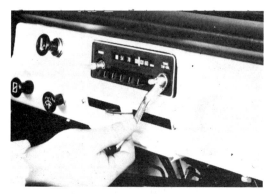

Fig. 13.60. Unscrewing radio control bezel nuts

Fig. 13.61. Withdrawing radio receiver (Hi-Ace)

withdraw the complete assembly downward from under the facia panel.
18 The radio receiver may now be unbolted from the heater control panel and the speaker, aerial and power leads disconnected.
19 An in-line fuse is incorporated in the radio power supply lead, adjacent to the rear face of the receiver casing.
20 Refitting is a reversal of removal but if a new receiver or aerial have been fitted, the trimmer screw on the receiver will have to be adjusted in accordance with the manufacturer's instructions.

Radio (Hi-Lux) removal and refitting
21 On some models, the radio is mounted on the heater control support plate and is removed in a similar way to that described for the Hi-Ace in paragraphs 13 to 20.
22 On other models, the radio is mounted independently on brackets, its mounting screws being accessible from below the facia panel.

11 Suspension and steering

Front hub adjustment (Hi-Ace with disc brakes)
1 The adjustment of the hub bearing preload on these vehicles is similar to the procedure described in Chapter 11, Section 5, paragraphs 12 to 16.

12 Bodywork

Sliding door (Hi-Ace van 1977 on) — removal, refitting and adjustment
1 Close the sliding door and from its interior surface remove the trim panel and the service hole cover plates.
2 Unscrew and remove the two securing bolts and pull out the centre roller.
3 Unbolt and slide out the upper roller.
4 Support the door and unbolt and remove the lower roller.
5 Lift the door from the vehicle.
6 The door components including the lock, handle and centre rail may be removed as necessary.
7 Bolt the lower, upper and centre rollers to the door but do not tighten the bolts fully at this stage.
8 Apply grease to the rails and rollers.
9 Offer the door into position, engaging the rollers with the rails.
10 Adjust the roller arms (after loosening the bolts slightly) in the following order (Figs. 13.67 and 13.68).

(a) Upper roller to give a clearance at top and bottom of roller
(b) Lower roller to give even contact with its rail
(c) Centre roller to provide parallel running of the roller with the rail

11 Now adjust the door lock in the half lock position so that on reference to Fig. 13.69 A is more than 0.118 in (3.0 mm), B is more than 0.039 in (1.0 mm) and C and D are more than 0.059 in (1.5 mm).

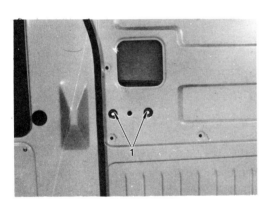

Fig. 13.62. Centre roller securing bolts (Hi-Ace sliding door)

Fig. 13.63. Removing centre roller (2) (Hi-Ace sliding door)

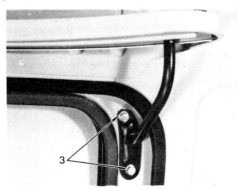

Fig. 13.64. Removing upper roller (3) (Hi-Ace sliding door)

Fig. 13.65. Lower roller securing bolts (4) (Hi-Ace sliding door)

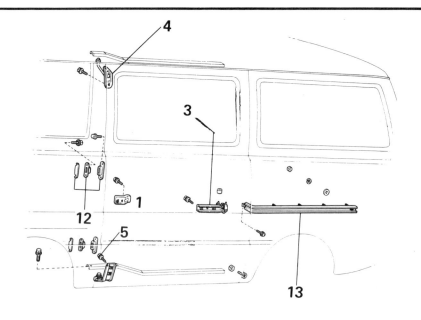

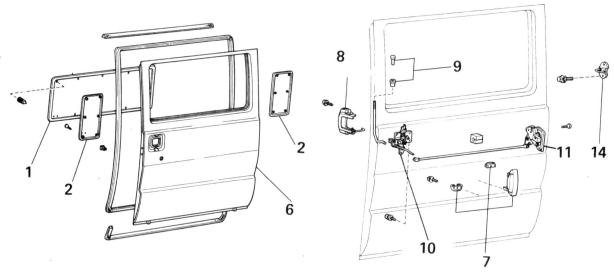

Fig. 13.66. Hi-Ace sliding door arrangement (1977 on)

1 Trim panel
2 Service hole cover plate
3 Centre roller
4 Upper roller
5 Loer roller
6 Door
7 Outside handle

8 Inside handle
9 Lock button
10 Lock remote control
11 Lock
12 Dovetail
13 Centre rail
14 Striker

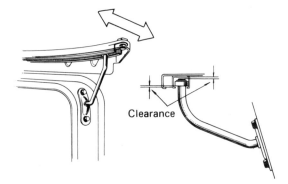

Fig. 13.67. Sliding door upper roller setting diagram

Clearance

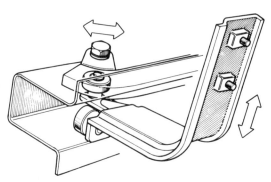

Fig. 13.68. Sliding door lower roller setting diagram

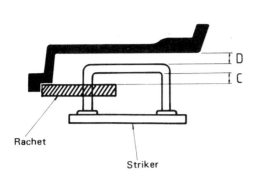

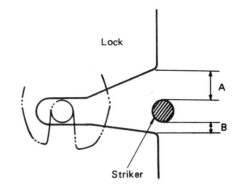

Fig. 13.69. Sliding door lock setting diagrams. For values of A, B, C, and D see text

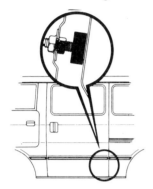

Fig. 13.70. Sliding door stop adjustment diagram

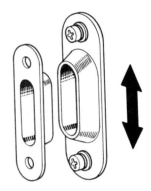

Fig. 13.71. Sliding door dovetail components

If C and D are less than specified, add shims or move the centre roller backward.

12 Now adjust the door stop so that no clearance exists between the rubber cap of the stop and the body.

13 Adjust the door closure dovetails by partially releasing the bolts on the male section, closing the door to align the components and then fully tightening them.

Rear door (Hi-Ace van 1977 on) — removal, refitting and adjustment

14 From the interior surface of the door, remove the service hole cover.

15 With the door propped open or held open by an assistant, unbolt and remove the tubular gas-filled counterbalance strut.

16 Remove the door interior trim panel.

17 Working through the aperture in the door panel, disconnect the wiring harness and draw it from the door cavity so that it will not restrict removal of the door.

18 With an assistant supporting the door, unbolt the hinges from the roof panel and then lift the door away.

19 If the counterbalance strut is to be renewed, do not puncture it or attempt to dismantle it. When fitting the new strut do not apply oil or grease to the piston rod or spray the rod with paint. The piston rod should not be rotated when it is fully extended.

20 Refitting is a reversal of the removal procedure. Do not tighten the hinge bolts until there is an even gap all round the door. The hinge bolt holes and the striker bolt holes are elongated to permit adjustment.

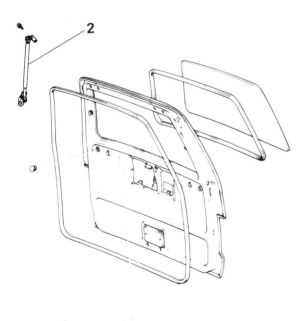

Fig. 13.72. Rear door (Hi-Ace) components

1 Service hole cover   2 Counterbalance strut

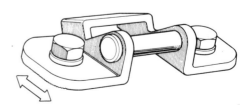

Fig. 13.73. Back door lock striker

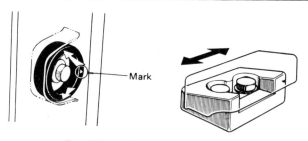

Fig. 13.74. Back door side dovetails

21 Adjust the door side dovetails to provide smooth positive closure making sure that the circular type has its mark towards the front of the vehicle.

Front interior heater (Hi-Ace 1977 on) — removal and refitting
22 Drain the cooling system.

23 Disconnect the control cables from the heater assembly.
24 Disconnect the demister hoses from the heater casing.
25 Disconnect the heater hoses from the heater matrix taking care not to let coolant run out to soak the flooring.
26 Unscrew and remove the heater mounting bolts and then pull the heater assembly towards you and remove it from the vehicle.
27 The heater matrix and blower motor can be removed for renewal if necessary after withdrawing the securing clips or screws.
28 Refitting is a reversal of removal. Refill the cooling system and check the heater hose clips for security if any slight leakage is observed.

Rear compartment heater (Hi-Ace van and personnel carrier 1977 on) — removal and refitting
29 Two different designs of rear compartment heater may be fitted depending on the type of body.
30 Removal of the heater is similar with either type; drain the cooling system, disconnect the heater hoses from the heater and then unbolt the heater mounting brackets.
31 Refitting is a reversal of removal; refill the cooling system.

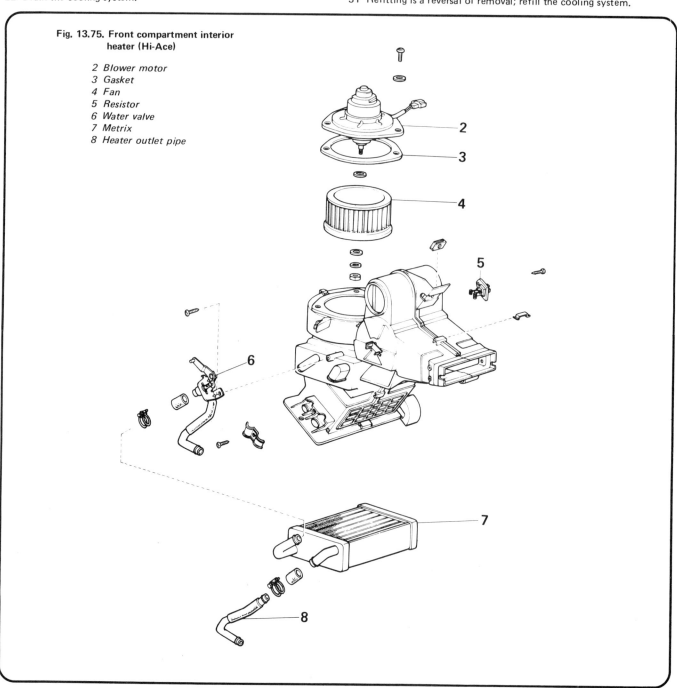

Fig. 13.75. Front compartment interior heater (Hi-Ace)

2 Blower motor
3 Gasket
4 Fan
5 Resistor
6 Water valve
7 Metrix
8 Heater outlet pipe

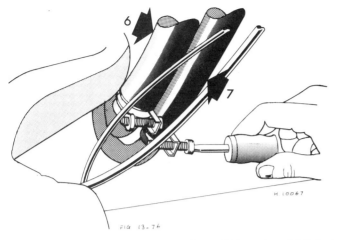

Fig. 13.76. Releasing heater hose clips (6 and 7 Heater hoses) (Hi-Ace)

Fig. 13.77. Heater cable control connections (1 and 2) and heater mounting bolt (8)

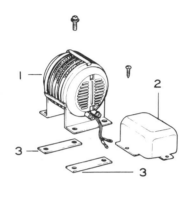
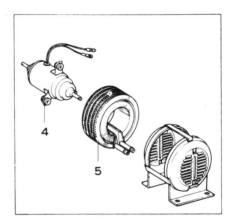

Fig. 13.78. Rear heater (Hi-Ace personnel carrier)

1 Heater   2 Protective cover   3 Reinforcement plate   4 Motor   5 Matrix

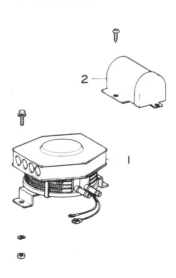
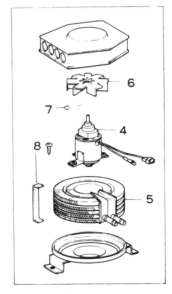

Fig. 13.79. Rear heater (Hi-Ace van)

1 Heater assembly   4 Motor   6 Fan   8 Clip
2 Protective cover   5 Matrix   7 Grub screw

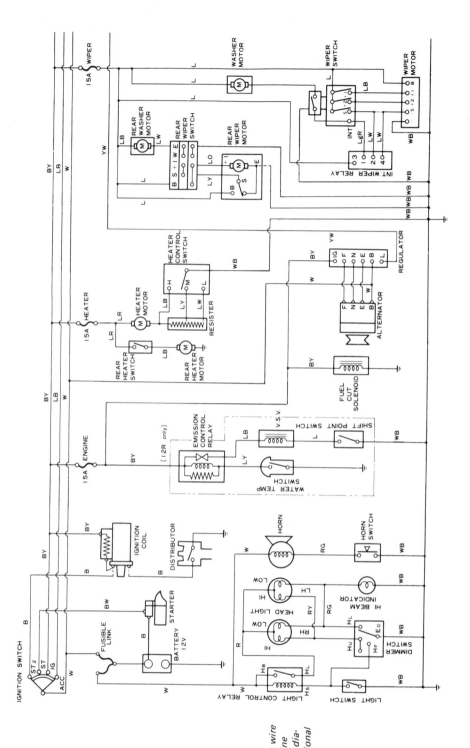

Wiring diagram Hi-Ace 1977 on

Colour code

B = Black
G = Green
L = Light blue
O = Orange
R = Red
W = White
Y = Yellow
Lg = Light green

When there are two letters on one wire the second letter gives the spiral line colour. Broken lines in the wiring diagram are for varied models or optional equipment.

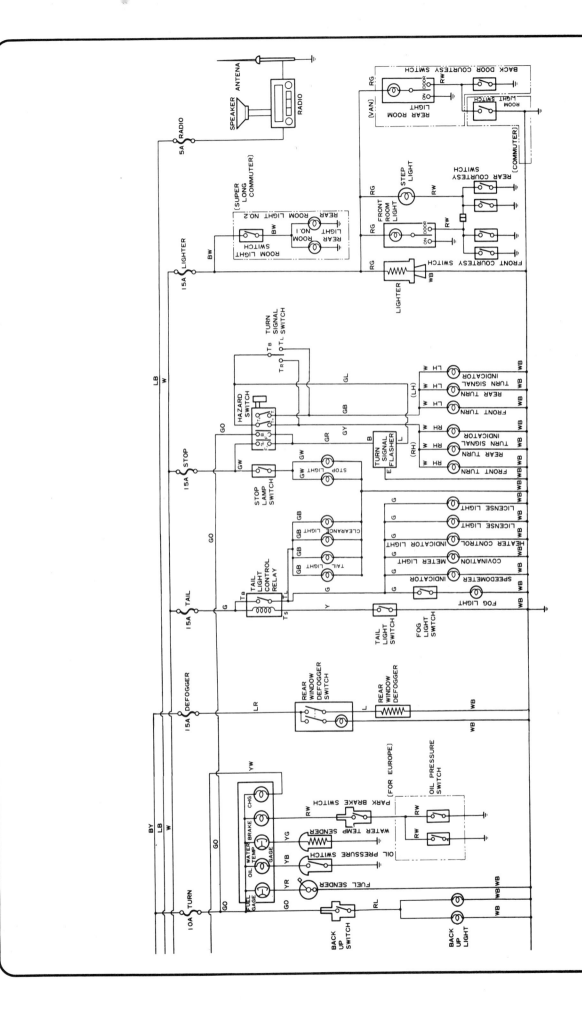

Wiring diagram Hi-Ace 1977 On (cont)

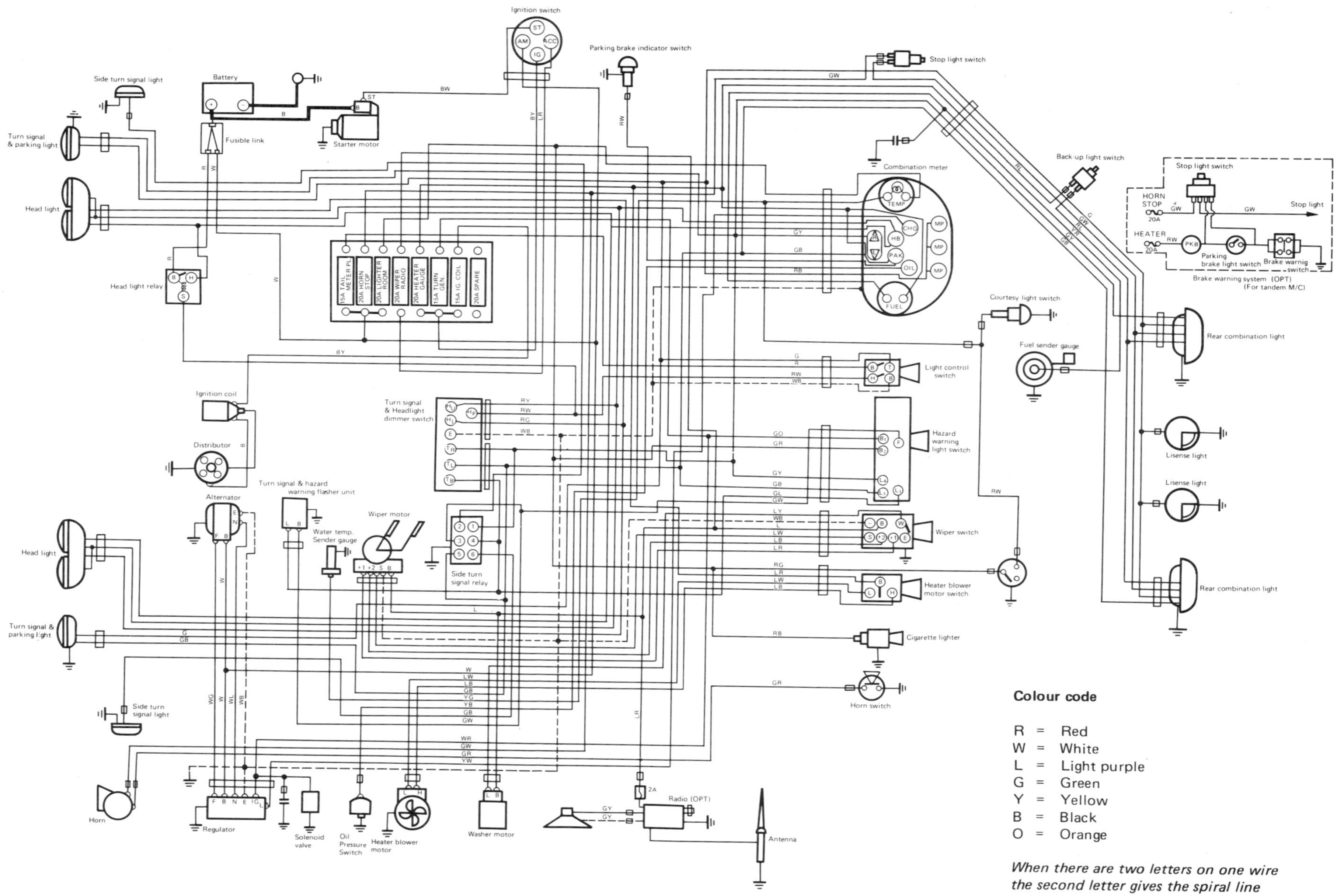

Colour code

R = Red
W = White
L = Light purple
G = Green
Y = Yellow
B = Black
O = Orange

When there are two letters on one wire the second letter gives the spiral line colour.

Wiring diagram Hi-Lux (1977 on) right-hand drive shown

Metric conversion tables

Inches	Decimals	Millimetres	Millimetres to Inches		Inches to Millimetres	
			mm	Inches	Inches	mm
1/64	0.015625	0.3969	0.01	0.00039	0.001	0.0254
1/32	0.03125	0.7937	0.02	0.00079	0.002	0.0508
3/64	0.046875	1.1906	0.03	0.00118	0.003	0.0762
1/16	0.0625	1.5875	0.04	0.00157	0.004	0.1016
5/64	0.078125	1.9844	0.05	0.00197	0.005	0.1270
3/32	0.09375	2.3812	0.06	0.00236	0.006	0.1524
7/64	0.109375	2.7781	0.07	0.00276	0.007	0.1778
1/8	0.125	3.1750	0.08	0.00315	0.008	0.2032
9/64	0.140625	3.5719	0.09	0.00354	0.009	0.2286
5/32	0.15625	3.9687	0.1	0.00394	0.01	0.254
11/64	0.171875	4.3656	0.2	0.00787	0.02	0.508
3/16	0.1875	4.7625	0.3	0.01181	0.03	0.762
13/64	0.203125	5.1594	0.4	0.01575	0.04	1.016
7/32	0.21875	5.5562	0.5	0.01969	0.05	1.270
15/64	0.234375	5.9531	0.6	0.02362	0.06	1.524
1/4	0.25	6.3500	0.7	0.02756	0.07	1.778
17/64	0.265625	6.7469	0.8	0.03150	0.08	2.032
9/32	0.28125	7.1437	0.9	0.03543	0.09	2.286
19/64	0.296875	7.5406	1	0.03937	0.1	2.54
5/16	0.3125	7.9375	2	0.07874	0.2	5.08
21/64	0.328125	8.3344	3	0.11811	0.3	7.62
11/32	0.34375	8.7312	4	0.15748	0.4	10.16
23/64	0.359375	9.1281	5	0.19685	0.5	12.70
3/8	0.375	9.5250	6	0.23622	0.6	15.24
25/64	0.390625	9.9219	7	0.27559	0.7	17.78
13/32	0.40625	10.3187	8	0.31496	0.8	20.32
27/64	0.421875	10.7156	9	0.35433	0.9	22.86
7/16	0.4375	11.1125	10	0.39370	1	25.4
29/64	0.453125	11.5094	11	0.43307	2	50.8
15/32	0.46875	11.9062	12	0.47244	3	76.2
31/64	0.48375	12.3031	13	0.51181	4	101.6
1/2	0.5	12.7000	14	0.55118	5	127.0
33/64	0.515625	13.0969	15	0.59055	6	152.4
17/32	0.53125	13.4937	16	0.62992	7	177.8
35/64	0.546875	13.8906	17	0.66929	8	203.2
9/16	0.5625	14.2875	18	0.70866	9	228.6
37/64	0.578125	14.6844	19	0.74803	10	254.0
19/32	0.59375	15.0812	20	0.78740	11	279.4
39/64	0.609375	15.4781	21	0.82677	12	304.8
5/8	0.625	15.8750	22	0.86614	13	330.2
41/64	0.640625	16.2719	23	0.90551	14	355.6
21/32	0.65625	16.6687	24	0.94488	15	381.0
43/64	0.671875	17.0656	25	0.98425	16	406.4
11/16	0.6875	17.4625	26	1.02362	17	431.8
45/64	0.703125	17.8594	27	1.06299	18	457.2
23/32	0.71875	18.2562	28.	1.10236	19	482.6
47/64	0.734375	18.6531	29	1.14173	20	508.0
3/4	0.75	19.0500	30	1.18110	21	533.4
49/64	0.765625	19.4469	31	1.22047	22	558.8
25/32	0.78125	19.8437	32	1.25984	23	584.2
51/64	0.796875	20.2406	33	1.29921	24	609.6
13/16	0.8125	20.6375	34	1.33858	25	635.0
53/64	0.828125	21.0344	35	1.37795	26	660.4
27/32	0.84375	21.4312	36	1.41732	27	685.8
55/64	0.859375	21.8281	37	1.4567	28	711.2
7/8	0.875	22.2250	38	1.4961	29	736.6
57/64	0.890625	22.6219	39	1.5354	30	762.0
29/32	0.90625	23.0187	40	1.5748	31	787.4
59/64	0.921875	23.4156	41	1.6142	32	812.8
15/16	0.9375	23.8125	42	1.6535	33	838.2
61/64	0.953125	24.2094	43	1.6929	34	863.6
31/32	0.96875	24.6062	44	1.7323	35	889.0
63/64	0.984375	25.0031	45	1.7717	36	914.4

1   Imperial gallon = 8 Imp pints = 1.20 US gallons = 277.42 cu in = 4.54 litres

1   US gallon = 4 US quarts = 0.83 Imp gallon = 231 cu in = 3.78 litres

1   Litre = 0.21 Imp gallon = 0.26 US gallon = 61.02 cu in = 1000 cc

Miles to Kilometres		Kilometres to Miles	
1	1.61	1	0.62
2	3.22	2	1.24
3	4.83	3	1.86
4	6.44	4	2.49
5	8.05	5	3.11
6	9.66	6	3.73
7	11.27	7	4.35
8	12.88	8	4.97
9	14.48	9	5.59
10	16.09	10	6.21
20	32.19	20	12.43
30	48.28	30	18.64
40	64.37	40	24.85
50	80.47	50	31.07
60	96.56	60	37.28
70	112.65	70	43.50
80	128.75	80	49.71
90	144.84	90	55.92
100	160.93	100	62.14

lbf ft to kgf m		kgf m to lbf ft		lbf/in^2 to kgf/cm^2		kgf/cm^2 to lbf/in^2	
1	0.138	1	7.233	1	0.07	1	14.22
2	0.276	2	14.466	2	0.14	2	28.50
3	0.414	3	21.699	3	0.21	3	42.67
4	0.553	4	28.932	4	0.28	4	56.89
5	0.691	5	36.165	5	0.35	5	71.12
6	0.829	6	43.398	6	0.42	6	85.34
7	0.967	7	50.631	7	0.49	7	99.56
8	1.106	8	57.864	8	0.56	8	113.79
9	1.244	9	65.097	9	0.63	9	128.00
10	1.382	10	72.330	10	0.70	10	142.23
20	2.765	20	144.660	20	1.41	20	284.47
30	4.147	30	216.990	30	2.11	30	426.70

Index

Printed by
Haynes Publishing Group
Sparkford Yeovil Somerset
England